The Provoked Wife

Susannah Cibber, by Thomas Hudson.

The
Provoked
Wife
The Life and Times
of Susannah Cibber

MARY NASH

Illustrated

Little, Brown and Company — Boston – Toronto

LIBRARY OF CONGRESS CATALOGING IN PUBLICATION DATA
Nash, Mary, 1925–
      The provoked wife.
      Bibliography: p.
      Includes index.
      1. Cibber, Susannah Maria Arne, 1714–1766. 2. Actors
—Great Britain—Biography. I. Title.
PN2598.C4N3   792′.028′0924 [B]   76–30336
ISBN 0–316–59831–3

Designed by Susan Windheim

Published simultaneously in Canada
by Little, Brown & Company (Canada) Limited

PRINTED IN THE UNITED STATES OF AMERICA

To M. N. M.

The two most fascinating subjects in the universe are sex and the eighteenth century.
— BRIGID BROPHY, *Don't Never Forget*

Acknowledgments

My thanks and gratitude to Helen Willard, former curator of the Harvard Theatre Collection, who always knew what I needed; to the late Dorothy Mason of the Folger Shakespeare Library; Jeanne T. Newlin, curator of the Harvard Theatre Collection; Martha Mahard, of the Harvard Theatre Collection, who unearthed the Folland print of Theophilus Cibber when I had despaired of finding it; Wilmarth S. Lewis, who let me visit and use his library at Farmington, Connecticut; George Nash of the Victoria and Albert Museum, who always had time to talk; Philip Highfill, Kalman Burnim, and Edward Langhans, who were always willing to share their knowledge and point out material I might not know of; Geraldine Morse, who helped with final details; my daughter, Mary Hollister Nash Mitchell, who saw me through; and to Mr. Woodhead, who pointed out the Belvidere Woods at West Woodhay and trusted me with his book.

List of Illustrations

The Provoked Wife

I

ONE April day in 1710, two of Queen Anne's gilded state coaches, splendid with armorial bearings and periwigged footmen, drew up outside a London upholstering and undertaking establishment called the Two Crowns and Cushions. Sir Charles Cotterel, Master of the Ceremonies, descended from the first coach in his robes of office and waited until four sinewy brown men emerged. They were bareheaded and wigless, their strangely cropped black hair stuck here and there with feathers. They wore black close-fitting knee breeches and capes of scarlet edged with gold, and, moving impassively through a little crowd of tradesmen, wives, and apprentices, they sprang athletically into the vehicles, two in the first, and two in the second. These men were kings. They were Tee Yee Neen Ho Ga Row, Sa Ga Yean Prah Ton, Elaw Oh Kaon, and Oh Nee Yeath Ton No Prow, Iroquois sachems who had lately come over with the West Indian Fleet to be clothed and entertained at the Queen's expense.[1] Today they were on their way to an audience at St. James's Palace.

Had they been more orthodox foreign princes, the government

The Four Indian Kings, drawn by B. Lens, Junior and engraved by B. Lens, Senior.

Tee Yee Neen Ho Ga Row, painted by J. Verelst and engraved by J. Simon.

would have put them up for the month of their London visit in apartments at a spare royal residence like Somerset House. As it was, even the middle-class opulence of their rooms at the Two Crowns and Cushions was largely wasted on men who needed hardly any wardrobe space for their attire and no furniture at all for their comfort. The Indian kings, a contemporary witness assures us, "never sit on Chairs or Benches, but on their Heels which makes their Knees when they stand upright, bag out before."² Yet to their host, the upholsterer, the richly draped and overstuffed rooms which he maintained for gentlemen lodgers were the pride of his life, and perhaps his four austere guests were not altogether unimpressed. The story went that when one of the chiefs fell ill of a surfeit of unaccustomed London voluptuizing, he was lifted from the floor where he usually slept into one of the great beds. The feverish time he spent upon that marvelously yielding yet resurgent mattress, gazing up at the underside of a canopy from which fell heavy curtains, gave this man of the forest such "a very great Veneration for him who made that Engine of Repose, so useful and so necessary in his Distress," that upon his recovery he consulted with his royal brothers and they granted their host the honorary title of "Cadaroque,"* which was the name of the most formidable fort in their part of the world.³

Whatever the Indians called their host, his English name was Thomas Arne. He was a wily, naïve man with a taste for the exotic, who may have misinterpreted the notoriety he acquired during the visit of the four savage potentates for genuine fame. For whatever their titles and dignities among their own tribes, and however ardently the Whig government was courting their military alliance against the French in North America, these solemn, painted princes were regarded by the London man on the street as curiosities rather than persons of rank — make-believe men, characters out of a play. And, in fact, the four Iroquois kings were "cloathed" for their audience with Queen Anne from the stock wardrobe of a London theater; fittted out "by the Play House Taylor, like other Kings of the Theatre."⁴

Thomas Arne was twenty-eight in 1710, and he had been mar-

* Later Fort Frontenac, on Lake Ontario.

ried for three years. That April, besides the Indian kings there was another new member of the household at the Two Crowns and Cushions. The Arnes' first child had been born in March, when the sachems were hourly expected from America, and in the flurry of their stay he was not baptized until they sailed again for Boston. In May, at St. Paul's Church, Covent Garden, just around the corner from the Two Crowns, the baby was christened Thomas, for his father and his grandfather. As soon as this third Thomas Arne was old enough to sign his name, he gave himself an Augustine in the middle, in witness of his embracing of his mother's Roman faith.

No history of the Arnes of Covent Garden survives. But the glimpses we have of various family members in several generations are consistent enough to suggest a family type. All the Arnes were upholsterers and undertakers, ambitious, political, headstrong, and ill-fated. Their names appear as high officers in guild and parish records. They earned well; they lived high; their lives were tinged with the sensational and the macabre. They gambled fiercely in business and in play, and they tended to end their days in an irreversible downdraft of bankruptcy, debtors' prison, and ignominious death. One more thing: there is no evidence of a prosperous member of the family moving to rescue or even ease the ruin of a relative — not even of a father or a brother. Possibly the Arnes were beset by familial enmities. Perhaps they were callous. Probably it was just that each Arne was steering his own financial ship so near the shoals and rocks that he had no room to maneuver on behalf of another foundering family craft. Whatever the reason, we do know that while Thomas Arne, the Indians' host, kept a rich Christmas with his wife and small son in December 1713, his father was dying of cold and hunger nearby, a debtor in the Marshalsea prison. Ten years earlier this man had been Master of the London Company of Upholsterers, highest office in his guild.

Prisoners in the eighteenth century were responsible for their own keep and only convicted felons received a free ration of bread. A warden's sole responsibility to the British government was the prevention of escape, and he ran his prison very much like an inn or tavern, with himself in the position of hostler. Inmates with money or generous friends and relatives might enjoy private accommodations, candles, beef, the use of the young prostitutes confined there, and beer and spirits, which were available day and night in the prison tap room, a sort of common room for prisoners and their visitors and the warden's most profitable operation. Should the warden or his assistants suspect that a prisoner had money (or well-to-do connections outside who were not seeing to it that their loved one was making full use of the prison's facilities and services), their methods of coercion were irresistible. A man might be starved, stripped, thrown into a dungeon, manacled, or tortured; and something of this nature seems to have been the fate of another Arne, Edward, brother of Thomas of the Two Crowns and Cushions.

In 1725, twelve years after his father's death in the Marshalsea, Edward Arne was confined to the Fleet for debt:

Whilst he was in the Tap room of the said Fleet prison during the wardership of John Huggins Esq., and behaving himself quietly, he was suddenly seized by James Barnes (agent for Huggins) and without any reason given, was forced into the Strong Room or Dungeon; which Dungeon (being then but lately built and so damp that the Drops hung on the walls) was very nauseous and unwholesome. In this Place was the unfortunate man locked up and never once permitted to go out; but by an accident on a Sunday, the door being opened, he ran into the Parlour adjoining to the Chappell, during the Time of Divine Service; he had no covering upon his Body, but the Feathers of a bed (which Bed was thrown to him by a Prisoner) into which he crept, to defend himself from the Cold, and the Feathers stuck and were clotted upon him by his own Excrements, and the dirt which covered his skin. He was immediately seized and carried back into the said Dungeon, where through Cold and the Restraint and for want of food, he lost his Senses, languished and perished.[5]

Edward Arne's body was handed over to the family, who quietly buried it in the churchyard of St. Paul's, where his father already lay. If Thomas Arne found anything unusual in the filthy and debilitated condition of his brother's body — the Arnes were undertakers, after all — he seems to have made no complaint to the authorities.

A few years later the affair was brought sensationally into the

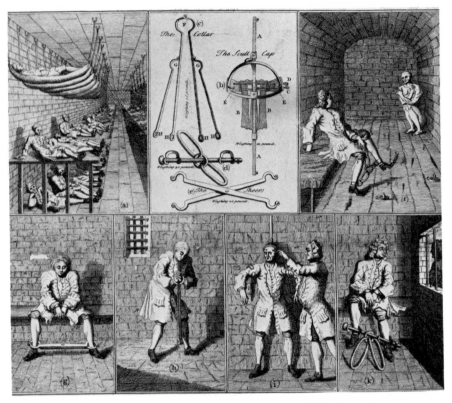

Prison cruelties were investigated by James Oglethorpe's committee of the House of Commons in 1729. The following text accompanied the upper-right engraving: "Capt. T—— M——, a merchant . . . attests . . . that on ye 25th of May, 1727, about 3 in ye Morning, a Spectre appeared to him and told him his Name was Arne, that he had been most inhumanely starved to Death in that Place, and required him to send for one Mr Gore to converse with him about ye matter, and that Justice might be done. The unhappy Gentleman says this could be no delusion because he did not at that time know that anyone had dy'd in ye Strong Room, nor did he ever hear Mr Arne's Name before then. The aforesaid Mr Gore was a Prisoner and an acquaintance of Arne's, and on the Capt's. speaking with him, did affirm that Arne dy'd in that place, and did believe his confinement there was the cause of his Death. N.B. While the Capt. was in the Strong Room, he was obliged to burn several Candles to take off the Dampness Occasioned by the Common Shore running under it."

public eye. During June 1727, the dungeon where Edward Arne succumbed was occupied by a merchant, Captain John Mackpheadris, held there because he had gone surety for a friend, since bankrupt, and was therefore liable for his friend's debts. At three o'clock in the morning of June 25, while the Captain shivered sleeplessly and rubbed his hands over the ends of candles burning near him on the floor to disperse the damp, "a Spectre appeared to him and told him his Name was Arne, that he had been most inhumanely Starved to Death in that Place." The ghost begged his terrified beholder to seek out a certain Mr. Gore "to converse with him about ye matter, that Justice might be done." The Captain afterward testified that "this could be no delusion because he did not at that time know that anyone had dy'd in ye Strong Room, nor did he ever hear Mr. Arne's Name before." Gore, who had been a prisoner of the Fleet in 1725 when Arne was languishing there, was found and "did affirm that Arne dyed in that place, and did believe his confinement there was the cause of his Death."[6]

When a committee of the House of Commons (pressed by its earnest chairman, James Oglethorpe) investigated prison atrocities in 1728 and 1729, the death of Edward Arne was one of many charges brought against John Huggins and James Barnes. Huggins was tried and acquitted, maintaining that the incident occurred during a period when he had turned over the administration of the Fleet to a deputy. James Barnes, a convicted felon who did menial work for the keepers, disappeared into the London criminal underground at the first whiff of an investigation and was never found. Everyone agreed that had he stood trial he would have hanged for murder. But perhaps the glare of public sympathy was "justice" enough to lay the unsatisfied spirit of Edward Arne, for there are no more reports of its disturbing the occupants of the Fleet's strongroom.

So much for the facts and legends that flickered about the Arnes, upholsterers and undertakers of Covent Garden, and a word or two about the family enterprises. During the Middle Ages, when domestic interiors were rough and spare, "upholderers" were a minor trade who made pillows, cushions, mattresses, and feather beds. By the seventeenth century, however, furniture had become comfortable and elaborate and specialized, and the fortunes of upholderers were on the rise. In the eighteenth century they were constructing magnificent beds and overstuffed chairs, and lining and padding the interiors of coaches and sedan chairs.

Unlike the word "upholsterer," which defined a craft, "undertaker" was a term that included anyone who outfitted funerals. An undated eighteenth-century handbill announces that "Mr. John Elphick, woolen Draper, hath a good Hearse, a Velvet Pall, Mourning Cloaks, and Black Hangings for Rooms . . . also all sorts of Mourning and Half Mourning, all sorts of Black Cypress for Scarfs, and Hatbands, Gloves and Burying Cloaths." Another handbill informs the reader that "Eleasor Malory, Joiner . . . maketh Coffins, Shrouds, letteth Palls, Cloaks, and furnisheth with all the other things necessary for Funerals at Reasonable Rates."[7]

With more and more middle-class people insisting on the sort of elaborate funeral that had formerly been reserved for aristocrats — though they merely rented the paraphernalia — the time required to make these arrangements had stretched and the problem of the preservation of the corpse became a real one. The company of barber-surgeons had received from James I a charter granting them exclusive right to all dissections, autopsies, heart burials,* and embalming. As far as the upper classes were concerned, this monopoly was undisputed. And yet, gradually, during the seventeenth century, the motley group of carpenters, tailors, and upholsterers who were setting themselves up everywhere as undertakers had quietly "undertaken," among their other services, to preserve bodies.

Not surprisingly, the barber-surgeons were outraged. In 1705, Thomas Greenhill, a surgeon, published a book called *The Art of Embalming*. "Is it not . . . a Shame," he asks, "for us, a polite Nation, to suffer a sort of men called Undertakers to monopolize the several Trades of Glovers, Milliners, Drapers, Wax Chaundlers, Coffin-Makers? . . . Art can never flourish where 'tis assumed by every ignorant Pretender. We may as well expect one who has never seen a Campaign should understand Military History . . . as that an Upholsterer, a Taylor, a Joiner or the like Undertaker should be well

---

* In the case of important people, whose bodies were to lie in state for some time, the vital organs were removed soon after death and separately interred.

skilled in the Mysterious Art of Embalming." Greenhill regarded the situation not only as a smirch on British national honor, but a threat to the future of her economic and aesthetic life. " 'Till such time as Quacks and Undertakers . . . and all such Persons as were not brought up in the Employment they profess be removed," he somberly predicts, "we can think no otherwise but that Art must sink, Trade be ruined, and every Public Office, as well at Court as in the Country be ill served."[8]

In vain Greenhill's rhetoric, in vain the petitions of his fellow barber-surgeons. The Whig government, always happy to see trade thriving, felt no need to interfere. The wealthy continued to be prepared for burial by surgeons. The poor were washed and shrouded and hurried into their graves as they had always been, and the new middle class bought the grandest funerals they could afford.

Undertaking in the eighteenth century, then, though not unlawful, was a sleazy business which had come in by the back door, was ignored by the upper classes and ridiculed by intellectuals. But Thomas Arne of the Two Crowns and Cushions was not a man to brood upon social disapproval. He was busy from morning to night with his enterprises: the funeral business, the splendid rooms to let upstairs, and his bustling upholstery shop. And by 1730, there were the careers of his two older children wherein to throw his energy.

From 1710 till 1718 the parish registers of St. Paul's, Covent Garden, record eight baptisms of the infants of Thomas Arne by Anne his wife, followed quickly in five cases by their burials. At this period when only one baby in four survived, the Arnes, who raised three children out of eight, were more fortunate than most. On February 14, 1714, a month and a half after her grandfather died at Marshalsea, Susannah Maria was born in the house on King Street. She was Anne Arne's fourth child and the second to survive.

For Susannah and for her older brother Tom, their father's aspirations were audacious and visionary. They understood that they had no more than a transient affinity with the Covent Garden tradespeople who were their neighbors and relations. Exalted lives lay in store for them, lives to be created by their father's industry, fortune, and ingenuity. Not for a moment was there any question of Tom's

Susannah Maria Arne.
Artist unknown, 1729.

learning the family business. He was to go to university and then be educated for the law; this, in conjunction with a marriage of influence, would embark him into politics, banking, mercantilism, or the bar. Susannah was to be educated as a gentlewoman for the brilliant marriage which her huge dowry would assure her. There were plenty of sons of merchant princes, and even younger sons of the gentry, who were pleased to marry wealthy tradesmen's daughters.

Thus from 1725, when Uncle Edward languished in the Fleet, until 1729, when his grisly fate was London gossip, young Tom Arne was away at Eton receiving a classical education and associating with the sons of gentlemen. And Susannah, at home in King Street and not encouraged to become too friendly with other tradesmen's daughters, was learning French and Latin and drawing and music and handwriting from fashionable masters.

There is a small ivory-on-gold miniature in the National Portrait Gallery that shows Susannah at fifteen. She is no beauty: her nose is too long, her eyes too heavy-lidded. Already she has the soft beginnings of that tense jaw and melancholy expression which characterize her later portraits. The style is too suave, too bland, to tell us much about Susannah. It is the little brooch itself, its costliness, its *ton,* which eloquently bespeaks the hopes invested in this only daughter of a man of no consequence, who has had her likeness struck in the most expensive manner possible by a society minia-turist, exactly as if she were the heiress to a duke.

While Tom's and Susannah's father did business with death, their mother Anne dealt equally practically with birth. She was a mid-wife.[9]

Well into the eighteenth century obstetrics was the exclusive province of wise women. Male physicians were willing to undertake maternity cases, but there was overwhelming popular aversion to this practice, and Queen Victoria, whose name comes down to us as synonymous with sexual prudery, was the first British queen whose lyings-in were attended by a man.

Traditionally, the gossips who assisted at births had been the same wise women who understood the management of colicky babies and brewed potions to cure barrenness or increase a mother's milk. Partly with herbs, partly with advice, partly with magic, these women had always supervised the distaff side of domestic health, standing in a complementary role to male leeches whose wound-searching, bone-setting, and bloodletting were founded on the needs of the battlefield rather than the hearth and were based on crises rather than on natural events.

By the eighteenth century a midwife — certainly a city midwife — had lost most of her earlier functions. Still her obstetrical art remained intuitive, secret, and personal. It was a mystery acquired not by university degrees or authoritative texts, but passed on by intimate apprenticeship with a practitioner.

Anne Arne was a Roman Catholic, and as such she raised her children. Though most dissenting sects enjoyed freedom in England at this time, Papists were regarded with smoldering mistrust. An English Catholic, his countrymen suspected, if put to the test, would cleave not to his race but to his creed. The truth was that for the first half of the century, until the defeat of the Young Pretender, there was a chronic threat to the Protestant Hanoverian dynasty. The Catholic Stuarts, incessantly plotting in the sympathetic capitals of Europe, had an uncomfortably convincing claim to the throne, per-sonal charm, and the pull of ancient loyalties; the Hanovers survived not because of the lukewarm affection of their English subjects but because of British determination never again to submit to continental interference.

The eighteenth-century laws against Catholics, dating from Elizabeth and added to and qualified by most of her successors, were harsh and proliferating. Had even a few of them been commonly enforced they would have driven every Catholic from the land. Legally, no Catholic could practice law or medicine or instruct the young. Nor could he hold a court office or a military commission. The estates of Catholics passed to the next Protestant heir, and estates of living Catholics could be taken over by the next Protestant heir during the lifetime of the proprietor. A double land tax was leveled against Catholics. Performing Mass was an act of high treason. There was a standing reward of £100 — a considerable sum at this time — for anyone bearing witness against a priest performing his function.

And yet most English Catholics lived unmolested and even thrived. The temper of the period was moderate, and the bristling laws on the books were rarely invoked. Astonishingly few citizens attempted to earn the £100 reward, and the few who tried found magistrates reluctant to prosecute.

Throughout most of England Catholics attended clandestine worship in public rooms like coffeehouses or taverns, but for those lucky enough to live in London there were half a dozen places where Mass and Vespers were regularly and openly performed. These were the chapels of the Catholic foreign embassies. The French, the Bavarian, the Spanish, the Neapolitan, the Sardinian, and the Portuguese embassies, all energetically supported and staffed by the Jesuit order, frankly catered to hundreds of London Catholics in chapels officially tolerated by the British government as concessions to the religious needs of the embassy personnel. In the Sardinian chapel sermons were actually given in English until the government testily pointed out that these could hardly contribute to the spiritual welfare of Sardinian officials. The Portuguese and the Sardinian chapels were the largest of the six. Each of them maintained seven resident priests, which suggests the size of their missions.

The artistic world of London had always been heavily made up

The interior of the Sardinian (or Portuguese) chapel in Susannah and Thomas Arne's youth was much more austere than this. The chapel was destroyed by fire in 1759 and rebuilt and redecorated in the Italian manner. Susannah worshiped here from early childhood until her death in 1766. From an aquatint by T. Rowlandson and Pugin from A Microcosm of London, *1808.*

of Catholics because so much of it was European. From 1720, when it opened, till 1780, when it was burned in the anti-Papist Gordon riots, the Sardinian embassy chapel, in Lincoln's Inn Fields in the heart of the theatrical and international section of London, was the center of this artistic world. Here Anne Arne brought her children, here worshiped all the singers from Handel's Italian Opera, French dancing masters, Italian sword masters like Dominico Angelo, artists like Zoffany, engravers like Bartolozzi, vocal teachers like Geminiani, chefs, scene painters, pantomimists, and acrobats. Here in 1749 David Garrick married his French dancer. And here worshiped generations of London Catholic families. The music of the Sardinian chapel was its glory. The most splendid voices, the finest instruments in Britain were heard here. Hundreds of non-Catholics attended services to listen.

For Tom and Susannah Arne, Catholicism, its intimate association with their mother, its forbiddenness and danger, the foreign glamour of the chapel and its European priests and exotic congregation — and above all its music — constituted an influence that separated them more significantly from their Covent Garden neighbors than all their father's grandiose schemes for their future. Their mother's faith alienated them from their father, too, who attended St. Paul's parish church, as the Arnes had always done. Exasperated at his wife's dangerous allegiance and his children's attachment to her, Thomas Arne was an angry force to be faced when the three of them returned from Mass, incense caught in their clothes, their ears still ringing with the sound of organ, trumpet, and choir.

"Yesterday morning," reported the *Grub Street Journal* on May 20, 1736, "about 10 o'clock, during Mass at the Sardinian Ambassadors' chapel, three or four persons . . . went into the chapel and not only ridiculed the service there performing . . . but struck several who were at their devotion and proceded up to the altar and very much abused the priest. . . . The Ambassador's porter who endeavored to put a stop to the riot was knocked down and received two cuts in the face. . . ." Violence against papistry was always close to the kindling point and readily ignited. Thomas Arne had good reason to resent what he regarded as his wife's seductive and pernicious influence over his two children. Tom could not practice law as a Catholic, and what English nobleman, however impecunious, would want to marry his son to a Romish bride?

An English Catholic survived upon sufferance: his property, his livelihood, his life dependent upon the benign mood of the populace. His lot was rarely one of overt persecution, but of unrelieved vague threat. To protect himself, the best a Catholic could do was to cultivate and ingratiate himself with powerful friends, keep his true financial position camouflaged or fluid, and avoid making enemies whose malevolence might someday betray him. The effect of their mother's Catholicism — its bond with her, its furtiveness, its theatricality, the jeopardy in which it placed them as regards the rest of their own countrymen — can be seen in the personalities of both her older children.

As a man Thomas Augustine Arne alternately acknowledged and rejected his faith, abandoning it when he felt it fueled the malice of his enemies or impeded his career, and embracing it whenever illness or the terror of death assailed him. Susannah never wavered in her devotion, which she openly confessed. But, more subtle than her brother, she made a career of charming, placating, appeasing, and ingratiating the volatile English public, who were her countrymen yet always her potential persecutors.

❧ 2 ❧

Let Arne, house of Arne rejoice, with the Jay of Bengal. God be gracious
to Arne, his wife, to Michael and Charles Burney.
— CHRISTOPHER SMART, *Jubilate Agno,* XXXI

NOBODY important noticed Tom Arne at Eton, which is a
pity since among his school fellows in 1727 and 1728
were two sharp observers, future memoirists and episto-
larians: Horace Walpole and Thomas Gray. Nor is there any record
of what sort of a scholar Arne was, though he was so wretched he
probably was a poor one. Homesick and solitary, he was away from
home as part of his father's plan to prepare him for university and the
law and to remove him from his mother's influence and the popish
world of music and theater with which he was intoxicated.

At night at school when he was too miserable to sleep, Tom
Arne consoled himself by playing snatches of Italian opera, Masses,
ballads, and the Jacobite hymns he had learned from his mother, all
upon a sour, "cracked, common flute."[1]

In the house on King Street, meanwhile, Anne Arne was practicing her profession and her religion and raising little Henry Peter,
born about 1720, her third and last child to survive. And thirteen-
year-old Susannah was earnestly perfecting the accomplishments of a

lady and faithfully accompanying her mother to the Sardinian chapel. Her religion was the one area in which, though otherwise dutiful and conciliatory, she defied her father.

As for Thomas Arne, senior: already there were forebodings of the family proclivity for financial disaster. By 1729 the situation was bad enough that Tom was called home from Eton, apprenticed clerk to a London attorney, and there was no more talk of university. There was no talk of a musical career either. Tom, at eighteen, with neither means, influence, nor practical skill, with nothing but an interrupted gentleman's education, had little choice but to live at home and accede to his father's determination to train him for the law, a profession he never for a moment intended to practice. Instead, now that he was in London again, he spent every moment he could steal away from copying deeds scratching on his own for a musical education, learning as many instruments as he could wheedle teachers to instruct him on or find privacy to practice. In the evening, when he could scrape together the price, he was at concerts or the Italian opera, dressed in servant's livery to take advantage of the cheap gallery reserved for footmen who had attended their masters to a performance. The livery Arne borrowed came from his father's funeral wardrobe, where bereaved families could rent attire for hired attendants in the procession. This appropriation of his father's property for a forbidden purpose gave the young man a special satisfaction. The defiant, contemptuous, and cynical attitude of Arne toward his father and his father's means of livelihood shows itself in the story about him and his violin teacher, Michael Festing.

The older man had come round to the Two Crowns and Cushions, knowing Arne senior was out, to give Tom a lesson. He found him in a shadowy room with new coffins and chair frames stacked along the walls. The young man was practicing his fiddle and, for convenience' sake, had set his music stand at eye level on the lid of a coffin drawn out into the middle of the room. Festing admitted that he was going to find it difficult to concentrate: his imagination would be conjuring up the notion that there was a corpse in that casket. At this, young Arne lifted away the music stand with one hand and, raising the coffin lid, showed his teacher that indeed it was not empty.[2]

To the end of his days Arne took a sardonic satisfaction in his strong stomach. He was fond of telling an episode about his early career, which, whether it is true or only Arne's dramatization of his cynical insouciance, shows the gratification he took in his ability to make fools of daintier natures.

At Cannons, the Duke of Chandos's estate, this story goes,[3] young Arne was playing his violin at a musical evening, after which there was an elaborate supper. Finding no evidence of provisions to feed the musicians, Arne wandered on his own into the vast ducal larders, where in a pantry his eye fell on a leg of mutton, garnished and ready to serve. No one being near, he took from his pocket a catgut fiddle string and minced it into fine pieces, which he sprinkled over the joint. A moment later a waiter hurried in and bore it into the dining room, where there were cries of "maggots" and "take it away!" When the flustered servant carried the leg of mutton back into the pantry, Arne stepped forth and remarked that he would be glad to eat it. The waiter remonstrated that it was wormy. "Never mind," shrugged Arne. "Fiddlers have strong stomachs," and he scraped off the bits of violin string with the back of his knife and enjoyed a hearty supper.

Over real corpses and simulated worms, over filial obligations, and, in a few years, over the tears of an ill-used wife, Arne prided himself that his strong stomach prevailed, rendering him beyond the queasiness of qualm or scruple. And yet his melodies, direct and guileless, seem true evocations of tender feeling. It is as though through song Arne maintained a passionate correspondence with the innocent years of his early childhood. He had been, until the birth of Susannah when he was four, the one surviving child of a mother who in the years before and following his birth had borne and buried one baby after another. She had loved him exclusively and perhaps a little desperately, sung to him, taught him old Jacobite hymns, and taught him her religion, which was his, too, and in some forbidden way different from his father's faith — its magic superior — putting his mother and him forever at odds with his father. In the years since those days he had lost his mother to two more living babies and to her patients, whose families called her away at any hour, sometimes to stay a day or more. But most cruel of all, she herself had relinquished him, however regretfully, to his father to be made a man of. He never forgave his mother, or any other woman, for her infidelity to that exclusive love which had characterized his first four years. Between the grown Tom Arne and his mother no warmth at all existed. He was faithful, nevertheless, to the memory of that idyllic period of which melody was the reverberant symbol.

The first thing Tom Arne did upon his recall from Eton was to acquire a clavichord. "He has told me himself," says his apprentice, Charles Burney, "that he had contrived to secrete a Spinet in the Garret of his father's house in Kingstreet in London upon which he used to practice almost all night with a handkerchief over the Strings to deaden the Sound, as he was in the greatest terror lest it be heard. For he was sure if it had it would not only have incurred the danger of being thrown out the Window when in Service, but a like Fate was to fear for himself."[4]

That Arne senior might have attacked both clavichord and player had he discovered them seems likely. He was beside himself with business worries and angry at his son's apathy toward the law. For Tom, though, the risk of discovery, the sense of outwitting his father under his very roof, like borrowing his rental livery or practicing the fiddle with the music resting on one of his father's corpses, was peculiarly gratifying.

Without the least family support or encouragement, without formal program or guidance from any musically educated adult, but by imitation and by heaven knows what obsequiousness to persuade musicians to throw a few scraps of their mystery his way, Arne succeeded in a few years, after drudging long hours at the lawyer's office, in mastering a brilliant keyboard technique (both organ and clavichord), in becoming a violin virtuoso, and in picking up a respectable amount of musical theory. Arne's legendary meanness, suspiciousness, and unscrupulousness in later life reflect the curious manner in which he had acquired his craft. He never regarded music as legitimately his. He had purloined the art. He had groveled for it, tricked it out of people, and he was indebted to neither parent nor patron; he had nothing and no one to thank but his own perseverance and his "strong stomach."

In his prime, at the height of his reputation after the successes of

Comus and *Alfred* and the Shakespeare songs, he buried his own young apprentice, Charles Burney, beneath mountains of scores to copy (as he himself had been buried as a young law clerk), and begrudged him the least instruction. He hated giving away any of the mystery that he had stolen, as if with each disclosure his own powers would be to that degree diminished. "Of a Sunday night," Burney remembers, "when Mrs Arne, Mrs Cibber, Miss Young, himself and I used to perform [the madrigals of Palestrina] in Queen Street, he was at the trouble of drawing out [copying] a tenor part for me to sing by, lest in doing it myself I should improve by examining how the several parts were constructed."[5]

Who Arne's informal "masters" were, besides Michael Festing, we do not know. Arne never gave credit to any man. "The truth is," Burney says, "that he was largely self taught, and too vain to admit himself to be the scholar of any master alive."[6]

Anthony Young,* organist at All Hallows, Barking, and a renowned keyboard teacher, may have instructed Arne, off and on. This would explain how Arne met his future wife, Cecilia (1711–1789), oldest of the three gifted Young daughters. Their father's music room on Villars Street, where scholars came for lessons, was also the location of recitals and concerts at which the Young children performed. It may well have been in Villars Street that Arne in 1730 or 1731 first heard the pure, coloratura voice of Cecilia Young, whom Burney regarded as the finest English singer of her generation.

In 1730, when Cecilia was only eighteen, Lord Perceval, later Earl of Egmont, noted in his diary:

Oct. 13 . . . went to Miss Young's . . . concert. There was much company at a crown a ticket, and all came away pleased. They agreed that her voice is better than any of the Italian women. . . . She has a clear shake above E-La-Mi, which the others have not. . . . She is . . . as yet, only a scholar and does not propose till some years hence to sing in the opera. Geminiani . . . is her master.[7]

For Cecilia herself Arne felt no affection, but he coveted her voice the moment he heard it and determined, though her father

---

* Burney gives his name as Charles, but Young's great-granddaughter Cecilia Henslowe, namesake of Mrs. Arne, firmly states in her family memoirs that it was Anthony.

detested and distrusted him, to make her his wife and to possess that voice and its income.

Michael Christian Festing (1680–1752) was certainly Arne's violin master and his crony. Festing, a German, was a member of the orchestra at the King's Theatre in the Haymarket, where Handel's opera company was entrenched. During performances, while Festing played, Tom Arne watched from the lackeys' gallery. Afterward, he and Festing went round to the Crown and Anchor or some other coffeehouse or tavern with a musical or theatrical clientele. They were apt to be accompanied by Johann Friedrich Lampe (1703–1751), bassoon player in the orchestra. They often talked of Handel's stranglehold on English music. Lampe dreamed of leasing a theater, composing his own operas, and carrying away a share of the profits.

By 1731, when Arne had been back in London two years, he had developed enough virtuosity on the violin so that he was playing in ensembles at the homes of London gentry. One afternoon Arne senior, "accidentally calling at a gentleman's house upon business, found him engaged with company; but sending in his name, he was invited upstairs, where there was a large company and a concert, in which to his great astonishment, he caught his son . . . playing the first fiddle."[8] Fortunately for Tom, his father was constrained by the decorous circumstances to control his temper and to listen and consider at length what he was witnessing. Impulsive though he was, Arne was also a hardheaded, practical, and flexible man. The longer he watched his son, the focus and admiration of every aristocratic eye (or so it seemed to Arne), the more it dawned on him that this confounding turn of events might presage the glorious and lucrative destiny to which he had always believed his son was born. To his untrained and uncritical ear Tom was a genius. And a mighty genius, too, to have picked up all that skill on the sly after a long day's clerking, when he had forbidden him to have an instrument in the house and never paid for a fiddle lesson in his life.

Thomas Arne *père* was aware that there was great profit to be made out of music. It wasn't all foreign nonsense, sponsored by the German court. At that very minute in Covent Garden, not two blocks from the Arne house in King Street, John Rich was building a new theater, the wonder of the neighborhood, solely on the profits of John Gay's *Beggar's Opera*, a work as English as roast beef and so successful that, as the town said, it had made Rich gay and Gay rich.

From the afternoon Thomas Arne heard his son perform, he was Tom's most enthusiastic—though not his wisest—ally. Old Arne's musical and aesthetic naïveté and his greed blighted young Tom's early career. He regarded his son as a finished genius, ready to astound the public and make a fortune. The further study, which this young man of twenty-one so badly needed, was never considered, and he was pushed at once into making money. Arne senior did not think of music as a science or an art, but as entertainment, like wire-dancing or sword-swallowing or any other crowd-pleasing enterprise at theaters and fair booths.

Since Thomas Arne was to be the only English composer of his day to discomfit Handel (though he never seriously rivaled him), English biographers of Handel have tended to regard Arne with ambivalence. On the one hand, they feel that it was Arne's patriotic duty to have abandoned his life of dissipation and popular songwriting, assumed the mantle of Purcell, and bested the mighty German emigré with a native "English" product. On the other hand, they revere Handel and relish the opportunity to contrast his private virtues with Arne's vices. Some of them have made Arne a sort of musical Antichrist: while Handel's motives were never tainted by monetary considerations, Arne was totally mercenary; Handel's nature was as noble as Arne's was mean, as chaste as Arne's was debauched; Handel was the better composer because he was the better man. "The life of Dr. Arne," sums up one of these Handel worshipers, "offers to the reader and to the music student an . . . instructive story, showing that natural ability, even when combined with genius, is not sufficient to ensure a triumphant and successful career. Morality and conscientious rectitude in the affairs of life are essential, and had Arne exercised these, his exceptional gifts might have enabled him to surpass his great contemporary, Handel."[9]

No man was more conscious than Arne of Handel's suffocating grip on the English musical establishment. From the King, from the Queen, and from the Princesses, perquisites and sinecures rained upon Handel's head. No man struggled more quixotically than Arne to drown what he called Handel's "heavy German Labors" beneath a flood of lyricism. The reason his enormous potential was never fulfilled was not, as the Victorians would have it, that he was immoral, but that his gifts had never been disciplined or developed. He spent his energies disguising his limitations and cursing his rivals. He could not really compete with excellence.

No sooner had Tom Arne's father discovered his firstborn's "genius" than he began erecting grandiose and proliferating structures upon it. If one of his children was this talented, why not the others? Little Henry Peter, who was only eleven, had shown no signs of musical precocity except for a piping voice with which he used to sing hymns with his mother. But Susannah was another matter. For years he had paid a fortune to teach her to sing. Coming upstairs from his workroom in the lower part of the house he had often heard her practicing. Her voice was low and sweet like her mother's. It had an odd, plaintive catch in it that suited her, wistful, trusting child that she was.

Since his financial reverses, when it became apparent that there would be no dowry for her, Susannah's fate had hung more painfully on him than any of his other burdens. What future could there be for her except to marry a tradesman and add to her husband's earnings by taking in female scholars? With the revelation about Tom's musical genius, however, a heady world opened before him. Why couldn't Susannah's dancing and singing be turned to profit? Since he could not buy her a wellborn husband, he could at least put her before the public eye, where she could ensnare a nobleman with her charms. Hadn't the Earl of Peterborough a few years back set up Anastasia Robinson, a penniless singer, in a villa, and privately married her? Hadn't the Duke of Bolton lost his heart to Lavinia Fenton the night he saw her play Polly in *The Beggar's Opera* and snatched her off the stage forever? True, there was a Duchess of Bolton standing between the lovers' legitimate union, but Lavinia and her children had been provided with an income for life, which could not be cut off, whether His Grace ever tired of her or no.

The apocalyptic hour which the upholsterer passed in the doorway of his client's music room did not affect the fate of his older son nearly so profoundly as that of his daughter. Tom, already set upon a musical career, was at a point where he could at least partially support himself, so that he cared less and less about the moment when his father discovered his secret life.

But Susannah, whose existence until now had centered upon her parents, her tutors and lessons, her daydreams of a titled husband, and her devotion to her church — Susannah's fate was to be totally changed.

⋙ 3 ⋘

AT fifteen, Susannah saw the point and purpose of her daily diligence, the focus of her daydreams collapse. At the precise time her father's fortunes were failing, the story about the death of her uncle Edward came into the glare of public gossip. Cartoons of the prison strongroom and Captain Mackpheadris starting back at the sight of Arne's naked specter could be bought in every bookstall. Something like her uncle's fate or her grandfather's might lie in store for her father and he, too, might leave his family, as they had theirs, shamed and destitute. Thomas Arne's extravagant promises, his reverses, his alternating euphoria and rage had long ago alienated her mother and made her brother contemptuous and secretive. But her father's volatility had always seemed to Susannah an elemental masculine force that, sallying forth to do daily battle with the world, now outwitting it and now returning to lick its wounds, was pledged to do wonderful things for her as long as she propitiated it.

For two bleak years, between fifteen and seventeen, living at home, helping her mother, cosseting her father, and interceding between her sullen older brother and her harassed father, Susannah clung to her hope that if she buoyed up her father with unquestioning devotion he might still make things come right. Though her tutors were gone, she continued to read and study and to sing whenever Tom could accompany her during her father's absences from home. Susannah seems to have been as serious a student at home as her brother had been derelict at Eton. "She made," says her official biography, "great proficiency in whatever was taught her, having a remarkably lively genius and a very tenacious memory."[1] There is little doubt that before her tutors left Susannah had mastered the beginnings of a respectable classical education. To the end of her days she saw that no one forgot it. Her rival queens of the eighteenth-century stage might be called "the beautiful Peg Woffington" or "pert Kitty Clive," but Susannah was "the learned Mrs. Cibber."

After the day he overheard Tom at the concert, his daughter's erudition interested old Thomas Arne no longer. Like his son's years at Eton, it was an investment that had not paid off. It was her singing voice that suddenly interested him. Though his affairs were shaky, he was not altogether without friends or properties to mortgage. He proposed to back Tom in a modest commercial musical venture, which would feature Susannah.

His father's change of heart could not have fitted more neatly into Tom's hopes. Festing's crony, Lampe, and Henry Carey, a friend of Lampe's, had been talking ever since Tom had known them about leasing a theater for their own musical dramas. They were both reputable men; all they lacked was backing. If his father put up a little money, Tom was certain they would take him in with them in a junior capacity. Such a scheme was as reasonable as most of his father's gambles. There ought to be good profit in it. The town was weary of Italian opera and crying for English music. People had flocked to *The Beggar's Opera*. If they had loved that garland of popular tunes, how much more would they love serious English music, with English voices, English words, and English plots.

The second part of his father's proposition, that he take his sister under his wing and bring her forward as a singer, was nearly as gratifying as the first. Tom was very much aware of Susannah's voice, small, low, and ardent, a sound between a chime and a sigh. But as long as his own musical endeavors had been clandestine and his father had been feeding Susannah's girlish dreams of a chimerical marriage, there had been nothing he could do about it beyond surreptitiously accompanying her on the clavichord before an audience of their mother and younger brother. Aside from the excitement of working with such an emotional voice there were practical advantages. The major expense of an opera company was its singers. Good English voices were rare and dearly come by. The English voice Tom really coveted was Cecilia Young's, but her father guarded her like a dragon, managed her public appearances, pocketed her earnings, and, it was said, was dickering with Handel for her services. To have Susannah's voice as part of his father's financial offer was a windfall, though her nature was so reticent and genteel, and she was so unlike most saucy young singers and actresses that he could not be sure what Lampe or Carey would think of her, or whether she herself would agree to sing on a public stage.

Henry Carey (1687–1743) was forty-four when the Arnes approached him — a likable, profligate Yorkshireman, illegitimate son of Lord Eland and a country girl. He had dabbled for years in the musical theater, writing farces, songs, and libretti. Something of a gentleman, something of a poet, something of a showman, he had always lacked focus, conviction of his own identity, and financial patronage. Johann Lampe was twenty-eight, a stolid, industrious Saxon of talent and probity, a better trained musician and cannier businessman than either the Arnes or Carey.

The agreements between the Arne family and Lampe and Carey were soon concluded. Arne senior gained an arrangement to polish and bring into the public eye his two golden fledglings. Lampe and Carey, though the backing of a Covent Garden undertaker did not give them the prestige of a noble patron, had, at long last, a chance to mount their own works on the stage. They were to share the profits equally with Arne *père*. Young Tom was to make himself generally useful, learning as he went, with the promise that when he finished an opera of his own it would be considered for production and his position suitably elevated. Seventeen-year-old Susannah would be paid a modest salary, which her father of course would appropriate.

From Lampe and Carey's point of view it was hard to see how they could go wrong. They had a financial backer, a gifted and energetic apprentice, and, best of all — and a total surprise — they had in old Arne's daughter an ideal Amelia, the title role in the opera they were most anxious to produce. This delicate girl with the great solemn eyes, grave movements, and low, thrilling voice embodied all they could have asked for this musical princess, selfless in love, stoic in death.

There is no record of Susannah's reaction to her father's new plan for her. Probably she started rehearsals for *Amelia* with the same dutiful acquiescence she rendered to all of his demands — except that she renounce her faith. Certainly she went on the stage for none of the reasons that attracted her contemporaries: not because, like Kitty Clive, she was a stagestruck teenager; nor because, like Peg Woffington, the grind of poverty and her extraordinary beauty pressed her into this way of earning money; but simply because she was her father's to do with as he pleased. He had, like every eighteenth-century parent, a legal right to gain profit from his minor offspring in the best way he could. But Susannah's submission was more than filial behavior. She had learned from her earliest days that where her father was concerned, neither her mother's arguments and open resistance nor her brother's sullen insubordination had ever won them anything, while she, by bending before the tempest, by obeisance, patience, and ingratiation could always avoid pain and often gain much good.

Almost directly across the street from Handel's magnificent Opera House in the Haymarket stood a small theater called the "new" or "little" or "French" theater. It had been dark a good part of the season of 1731–32, rented for a few nights at a time to shoestring theatrical operations. On March 4, 1732, the *Daily Post* briefly noted that "the new English Opera of *Amelia*" was in rehearsal there "by a set of Performers that never appeared before upon any Stage." The music was Lampe's, the libretto Carey's.

A playbill for Amelia, *1732.*

The first performance took place on Monday night, March 13, and the success of the music and the adulation for the girl who sang Amelia exceeded anything its composers or even old Arne could have foreseen. Lampe and Carey hastily composed extra songs for Miss Arne, which were interpolated into the score, and this fact was advertised to the public so that it might be induced to come again. Across the street at Handel's Opera House, a heavy-footed production of Ariosto's *Coriolanus* played to thin houses and was hurriedly replaced by a revival of Handel's *Flavio,* which did not do much better.

An anonymous pamphleteer summed up the situation in the Haymarket this way: "I left the Italian Opera, the House was so thin, and crossed over to the English one which was so full I was forced to crowd in upon the Stage and even that was thronged. Is not this odd, I say, for an English Tradesman's Daughter to spring up all of a Suddain to rival the selected Singers of Italy?"[2]

The story of *Amelia* is typical of the new sentimental drama which warmed the hearts of eighteenth-century Englishmen, still recoiling from the heartless comedy of manners of the generation past. The heroine is the bride of Prince Casimir, who has been taken captive by Osmyn, a Turkish prince. Unable to endure life without her husband, Amelia enlists the help of Casimir's best friend, Rudolpho, in a bold plan to free him. In disguise they steal into the Turkish camp, where Amelia throws herself at the feet of Osmyn and pleads for Casimir's freedom at the price of her favors. Agog at such a prospect, the gullible Turkish leader frees Casimir, who hurries home, unaware of the reason for his sudden acquittal. Back in his kingdom, finding wife and best friend unaccountably absent, Casimir leaps to the conclusion that such behavior can only signify a "lustful perfidy." Accordingly, when the weary and loyal pair return, having escaped before Amelia has had to submit to the Turk's embraces, they find themselves clapped into prison and condemned to death. Stung by her husband's lack of faith after she has risked her life and honor to effect his freedom, Amelia prepares to go to the headsman, eyes dry and lips sealed. Fortunately, Rudolpho is made of baser metal. Refusing to die for a principle, he writes a letter from his cell to Casimir, explaining his absence from court with Amelia. When Casimir reads it he rushes out to the execution block, stays the arm of the headsman over Amelia's bowed head, falls on his knees before her, and the opera ends in a gush of apologies, forgiveness, and tearful reconciliation.

If Lampe and Carey were invigorated by the success of their sentimental opera and encouraged at its ability to work some embarrassment upon Handel's fortress across the street, Arne *père* was puffed up to the point that he regarded the Handelian musical establishment as on its knees and ripe for the coup de grace. To the horror of Lampe and Carey, who refused to have anything to do with the project, he undertook for the English Opera Company's next production an unauthorized revival of Handel's *Acis and Galatea*. Susannah was to sing Galatea, Tom to direct the orchestra (since the other partners had recoiled), and the masque was to be dangled insolently in the very teeth of its composer, just across the street.

In early May the newspapers disclosed that *Acis and Galatea* was in rehearsal "with all the Grand Choruses, Scenes and other Decorations, being the first time it was ever performed in a theatrical Way." But though it was scheduled to open May 11, so ambitious and complicated were the undertaker-upholsterer-turned-impresario's "Scenes, Machines, and Decorations" that they could not be got ready in time and the first performance had to be put off until May 17.

There were only two performances of *Acis and Galatea,* on May 17 and 19. Handel, mighty in patronage and invincible in genius, routed the English Opera Company without a direct glance its way.

Across the street he was presenting *Esther,* the first English oratorio, with a galaxy of splendid Italian voices. While citizens thronged to hear it, the Arnes' elaborate and overextended *Acis and Galatea* was annihilated.

An oratorio was something new under the sun. It was not a masque nor an opera nor a religious service, but something of all three. It appealed equally to the stodgy Hanoverian court and to the middle class. Here was no effeminate, Italian fol de rol, no unfathomable, romantic plot, no castrato warbling unnaturally of love, but an elevated, biblical subject, sung in English. With its rows of decently clad singers lined up like an Anglican choir, an oratorio breathed decorum. To attend one made an onlooker feel not that he had been debauching in a theater but attending church. Now at last a prudent paterfamilias could bring his own wife and daughters to the theater with him.

Not once but four times that May the entire royal family turned out at command performances to stamp their approval on Handel's *Esther.*

But even though the brash English Opera Company had crept away defeated from the Little Theatre in the Haymarket, not every Englishman was enamored of oratorios. The same impudent pamphleteer who had poked fun at Handel's Italian opera, and praised Susannah, wrote that *Amelia*'s success

alarmed Handel, and out he brings an Oratorio or Religious Farce, for the Deuce take me if I can make out any other Construction of the Word, but he has made a very good farce of it and put near £4000 in his Pocket for which I am glad, for I love the man for his Musick's Sake. This, being a new Thing, sets the whole World a' Madding; "Haven't you been to the Oratorio?" says one. "O, if you don't see the Oratorio you see nothing," says t' other; so away goes I to see the Oratorio where I saw indeed the finest Assembly of People I ever beheld in my Life, but to my great Surprize, found the Sacred Drama a mere Concert, no Scenery, Dress or Action, so necessary to a Drama; but Handel was placed in a Pulpit (I suppose they call that their Oratory). By him sate Senesino, Strado and Turner Robinson in their own Habits . . . and Strado gave us a Hallelujah of Half an Hour Long; Senesino and Bertolli made rare work of the English Tongue you would have sworn it had been Welsh. . . .[3]

Handel's weight split the little English Opera Company at the seam of its own weakness: Lampe and Carey were irrevocably estranged from Arne after the *Acis and Galatea* debacle. Their profits from *Amelia* and the groundswell of patriotic sympathy for their underdog, native operation had been all but wiped out by his ludicrous hubris. Nothing could have been less appropriate to their declared intentions of performing English works by English composers than pilfering Handel's stockpile, and nothing could have pointed out more humiliatingly their feebleness and Handel's strength. Both Lampe and Carey had musical works of their own to produce. The last thing that could have served their purpose was to provoke a confrontation with Handel.

On the other hand Arne, Senior — until his son had an opera of his own ready — could not have cared less what music or whose music the English Opera Company used as long as it was a means to make money, attract attention, and display his daughter's voice. As far as Arne was concerned the success of *Amelia* had been due to Susannah's seductive voice and appeal, not to Lampe's insipid music. Now that her career was launched and Tom had had a year's experience in practical theatrical matters, let the devil take Lampe and Carey.

Accordingly, when the new theatrical season opened in the fall of 1732 there were not one but two English opera companies maintaining a frail hold on life since they must rival not only Handel but one another. Lampe and Carey remained at the Little Theatre in the Haymarket, while the Arnes were at Lincoln's Inn Fields, which they rented from John Rich.

Rather ominously late in November — strong companies usually began playing a month earlier — both English opera factions produced their first offerings. At the Haymarket it was Lampe's *Britannia*, with none other than Cecilia Young in the title role. Lampe's personal rectitude and professional reputation had persuaded her dragon father to allow him her services, though Young would have nothing to do with the upstart Arnes. Cecilia's performance was enormously admired, and a rapturous poem appeared in the papers calling her a reincarnation of her namesake, the patron saint of music, and prophesying the end of the reign of Italian singers in England.

On November 20 at Lincoln's Inn Fields, the Arnes brought out *Teraminta,* a work of John Christopher Smith, with Susannah as Teraminta. Despite the attractiveness of their two young female singers, neither of these rival English offerings was strong enough to draw a full house. *Britannia* survived four nights, *Teraminta* three. With the failure of *Britannia* the serious aspirations of Lampe and Carey to establish an independent English opera company were snuffed out. Both men were reabsorbed into the world of popular theater and pleasure gardens, for which they wrote farces, burlesques, afterpieces, and songs. Lampe, stable, industrious, and well liked, married Isabella Young, a singer and the younger sister of the divine Cecilia. Henry Carey, never at ease about his parentage, his place in society, or where he ought to focus his multiple talents, and subject to paralyzing attacks of depression, one morning "got out of bed from his wife in Cold Bath Fields in perfect Health," and hanged himself, leaving a destitute widow and six little children.[4]

The cocky Arne faction of English opera was by no means sufficiently humbled by the failure of *Teraminta* to bow to the inevitability of Handel's monopoly on English music. No sooner had Lampe and Carey quit the field than Tom Arne, Junior, twenty-two, a virtually self-educated musician without so much as a published song to his credit, appropriated for himself the splendid title "Proprietor of English Opera."

Starting in the beginning of 1733, the force and influence of Thomas Arne, Senior, began to wane. He did not die until three years later, but ill health seems the reason for his letting go the reins of the family's musical fortunes. The name Thomas Arne in theatrical notices more and more signified the younger, and even before his father's death Tom was no longer troubling to put "Jr." after his name to distinguish between them.

On February 22, 1733, London playgoers read that "whereas Thomas Arne Junior, Proprietor of English Opera has new set to Musick . . . the Opera of Rosamond, written by the late Mr Addison, which is now in Rehearsal . . . this is to give Notice that he . . .

hoping to receive Encouragement from the Town will (notwith-
standing his Expenses are considerably greater than any of the other
English Theatres) entertain the Town at the following Prices (viz)
Boxes 5s, Pit 3s, First Gallery 2s, Upper Gallery 1s, 6d."

The first performance took place on March 7, with Susannah as
Rosamond and young Henry Peter Arne, "who never yet appeared
in public," playing a page and "the first angel." In *Rosamond* the
Arnes had an unqualified hit, attributable in equal measure to
Tom's fresh and tuneful music and to his sister's melting appeal. At
Lincoln's Inn Theatre, even on nights when *Rosamond* was not on
the bill (the Arnes were only one of a number of minor companies
sharing Rich's facilities), Susannah was required to be at the theater
because the obstreperous audience was apt, between acts, to clamor
for her, being particularly fond of her plaintive "Was ever nymph
like Rosamond, so faithful and so fair?"

Thomas Arne's choice of Joseph Addison's old libretto was
politically and aesthetically interesting. It had been the first English
opera written as a protest against "Italian Squalling," composed
twenty years earlier, just after the introduction of Italian opera to
London. Addison's source was the ballad "Rosamond's Bower,"
which tells the fate of Fair Rosamond Clifford, mistress of Henry II
and victim of his jealous queen. It embodied a number of "anti-
Italian" qualities: based on English romance tradition, sung in
English, its setting was pastoral and its language as simple and re-
strained as its emotions were fulsome.

In 1707, the English public had eagerly awaited *Rosamond,* but
when it was presented it was a crushing flop. Though Addison's story
was admired, Thomas Clayton's music was dismissed as "an ugly
howling," and the imported Italian opera reigned unchallenged as
the chosen entertainment of the upper classes.

Joseph Addison, who knew nothing and cared less about music,
never understood how a matter as minor as Clayton's score could
have queered his *Rosamond.* One of his critical tenets was that only
the words of an opera were important: music was a rhythmic en-
hancement of about the same importance as scenery or costume. For
years after the failure of *Rosamond* the pages of his *Spectator*
crackled with fiery words against Italian opera, whose emasculatory

According to popular legend, Henry II's jealous Queen Eleanor discovered his love affair with Rosamond Clifford, sought out the girl, and gave her a choice of death by poison or dagger. In Addison's sentimental happy-ending version, the poison is only a sleeping potion, and she is borne away to a cloister. Henry is stricken with guilt at the news of her death then overcome with gratitude when told of the ruse, and vows faithfulness to his queen forever. Addison's Rosamond exemplifies the wandering husband reformed by a resourceful wife. This 1790s engraving is not of Susannah Cibber.

Handel as a Pig. This engraving dates from 1754, but the original drawing, by Joseph Goupy, was probably made twenty years earlier.

influence had traduced the natural virtue and virility of British taste. Italian opera, Addison snarled, had as its established rule that "nothing is capable of being set to music that is not nonsense."[5]

By the 1730s, Joseph Addison, in his grave since 1719, had become the patron saint of anti-Italian musical sentiment; for if the *Spectator*'s satire had been appreciated in Queen Anne's day, how much more was it now, when Italian opera, sponsored and cherished by the unpopular Hanoverian dynasty, had become a symbol to Englishmen of all that was degenerate, foreign, and tyrannical in their land.

Rosamond's history alone would have attracted public sympathy toward the little underdog English Opera Company. But its huge popular success was due to nothing so abstract, rather to its delicious melodies and to Susannah. She was the eighteenth century's ideal sentimental heroine made flesh, a slender, refined figure with a voice that was the embodiment of pathos: her songs seemed to rise from a frame too frail to support such rushes of sensibility. "She seemed, sir," reminisced an old gentleman years after her death, "to need and dispose of your tears from the delicacy of her frame."[6]

While the Arnes were enjoying the success of *Rosamond*, Handel, the favorite of George II, was beset and bedeviled in his service to his royal master. The Tory press was writing scurrilous articles against him, mostly as a displacement of their hatred toward the king and Walpole, the Prime Minister. The cartoon on page 37 is typical of this vilification. It shows Handel, a bloated and besotted swine, playing the organ, surrounded by drink and victuals. A servile monkey holds up a looking glass so that Handel may gaze rapturously at his porcine features, while in the background a donkey brays like an Italian singer, and, in place of an orchestra, a cannon fires off a volley of stench and noise.

To add to Handel's troubles, Frederick, Prince of Wales, to pique his father, was setting up with some wealthy friends a rival opera company. Taking advantage of Handel's difficulties, this new Opera of the Nobility lured away a number of Handel's finest voices.

And last, but not least, Aaron Hill, (1685–1750) dramatist, critic, and one of Handel's oldest and most loyal English friends, addressed him a public letter begging him to reform the excesses of

Italian opera and evolve a form more simple, more lyric, and more "reasonable." "Deliver us," Hill pleaded, "from our Italian Bondage. . . . I am of opinion that male and female Voices can be found in this Kingdom capable of everything that is requisite, and I am sure a Species of dramatic Opera might be invented that by reconciling Reason and Dignity with Music . . . would charm the Ear and hold fast the Heart, together."[7]

If Handel was moved by Hill's eloquence, by the treachery of the Prince of Wales, by the Arnes' runaway success with *Rosamond,* or by the venom of the press, there was no sign of it. He never attempted the slightest modification of Italian opera. Yet for some reason he did move away from opera at this time and retreat into oratorios; and significantly, among the list of principals in *Deborah,* performed that same busy spring of 1733, were the names of two young Englishwomen: Cecilia Young and Susannah Arne.

Cecilia's appearance was not surprising. If there was a singer in Britain who could rival the Italians on their own terms and was "capable," in Hill's words, "of everything requisite," it was she, born with an opulent talent into a family of musicians, disciplined by an exacting father, and trained by a brilliant Italian master.

But Susannah Arne's addition to Handel's principal voices was another matter. She was no musician. Her critics would have told you she was no singer either. Her fashionable music masters, who specialized in grooming daughters of the gentry to assume a pretty attitude and warble by a harpsichord, had never taught her to read notes, a professional skill that, in line with Susannah's image of herself as a lady and an amateur, she chose never to master. Instead, intuitive, quick to learn, she depended first on Johann Lampe, then on her brother, and now on Handel to teach her her lines.

If we need any evidence of the quality of Susannah's expressive contralto, we can gauge it from those who were affected by it. For her appeal was not merely to the beer drinkers in the pit, nor to the commercial judgment of Lampe and Carey, but to Handel himself, who had not been able to put her out of his mind since he had first heard her sing an illicit Galatea. For Susannah's role in *Deborah,* this harassed, overworked perfectionist — who expected his soloists to be note perfect by the time he worked with them and vociferously insulted them when they were not — was content to sit hour by hour in his own house with this ignorant girl, teaching her patiently, phrase by phrase.

Charles Burney, who admired Susannah to idolatry, had to admit that "her voice was a thread and her knowledge of music very inconsiderable." Yet something about that "voice and manner softened Handel's severity at her want of musicianship." And "from her intelligence of words and native feeling, she sang . . . in a more touching manner than the finest opera singer."[8]

Susannah had just turned nineteen when she won Handel's tender and lifelong admiration. She had also, though she did not yet recognize the fact, outgrown her naïve father and even her talented brother. Her life is a history of dependent relationships with creative and dominant men, relationships characterized by deference and devotion on her part, and protectiveness and gallantry on theirs. As with Handel, these were friendships more apt to be chivalrous than sexual, which may have been one of the reasons they endured so long. Each fresh direction, each advance of her career came as the result of what some man saw as her potential, and when she finally emerged as a star of the first magnitude, it had all been done for her: she had been carried to eminence by others, with no immodest straining after fame or money on her own part, and without ever losing her quality of reluctance and diffidence.

Susannah had an almost unerring sense of where power and genius lay, and she did not often ally herself to second-rate mentors. She served the men who championed her with passionate commitment. She was inclined toward loyalty, and she inspired it. Her one serious miscalculation of a strong man she could serve, and who in turn would work for her good, was her husband, Theophilus Cibber. How she came to make this mistake and how, over the course of years, she extricated herself, we shall see.

4

THOUGH for the Arnes at Lincoln's Inn Fields the most signifi-
cant theatrical event of 1733 was their runaway success
with *Rosamond,* for the average London playgoer Colley
Cibber's sale of the Drury Lane patent and the machinations that followed provided the year's most engrossing stage situation.

Drury Lane, "the old house," had until recently enjoyed a stable
and profitable two decades, secure under its royal patent, and jointly
owned and managed by three veterans of the stage, Barton Booth
(1681–1733), Robert Wilks (1665–1732), and Colley Cibber
(1671–1757). The slow and sonorous Booth generally undertook
parts requiring portentous solemnity, like Othello or Hamlet's father's ghost; roles calling for passion, ardor, or elegance, like Mirabel
or Hamlet, fell to the vehement and handsome Wilks; and Colley
Cibber dealt with fops and lively villains like Iago, with irresistibly
impudent vivacity. Over the years this triumvirate had been supported in comedy by delicious Nancy Oldfield (1683–1730), in
tragedy by majestic Mary Porter (17–?–1765).

And so things might have gone on forever, for the London public either did not mind or did not notice that their favorites were all getting long in the tooth, and protested with catcalls and splintered seats if any of these senior players took a night off and substituted a younger actor.

Alas, Nancy Oldfield died suddenly in 1730; Mary Porter was injured and permanently disabled one night in 1731, as she defended herself with her whip against a highwayman who accosted her in her smart little chaise when she was driving herself home alone from a performance; and Barton Booth, ailing and despondent, impulsively sold his share of the patent to a wealthy young gentleman, John Highmore, in July 1732.

Two months later, Wilks sank into his final illness, and though he made haste to designate Cibber to look after his theatrical interests, his widow, after his death in September, mistrusting her husband's old partner, appointed young John Ellys, a painter, her representative at Drury Lane.

Thus, as the fall season opened, Colley Cibber found himself with his four colleagues of twenty years deceased or disabled, his two business partners gone, and he himself outnumbered in every decision in the intricate management of a theater by Highmore and Ellys, two green boys. He was over sixty, and he had long before made his fortune and his reputation as a comedian and a man of letters. Best of all, he had attained a position in the most exalted London society, and in 1731 been appointed Poet Laureate. Cibber was an unabashed social climber; his life had for a long time been nourished less by his activities at Drury Lane than by his court appointment and his role as boon companion to the rich and great. Therefore, though he assures us in his autobiography that no difficulties faced him at the theater that he could not have surmounted, yet "I chose not, at my time of Day, to enter into new Contentions."[1] Instead, he signed over his interests in Drury Lane, until June 1733, to his son, Theophilus, at a rent of £442.

The young man who became his father's deputy had been born during the Great Storm of 1703. Sweeping in from the west-south-west shortly before midnight on November 26, this tempest had toppled spires, torn out ancient oaks by their roots, rolled up lead roofing sheets like paper scrolls, bearing them through the air, and killed the Bishop of Wells and Bath and his wife in their bed. It had caused over a million pounds' damage in London and the City of Westminster, the loss of countless vessels at sea, and the drowning of over fifteen hundred of Her Majesty's naval personnel.[2]

To nature's windy sympathy for his mother's pangs, Theophilus attached a numinous significance, believing that with his first breath he had drawn in a character destined for tumult. He was given, when his fits had passed, to ruminating over the storm path of emotional havoc left in their wake, with an astounded pride.

He was the only son in a large family, and his mother and many sisters lived in a state of chronic neglect on the part of Colley, their peacock paterfamilias. For several years while Theo was growing up, his parents were battling in Chancery over a legacy, which had been left to Mrs. Cibber by her childless brother, William Shore, for her personal comfort and the education of her many children. Colley, on the grounds that as a poor man and head of his burgeoning family he needed control of these funds to allocate them properly among his dependents, managed to get his hands on the principal of the Shore legacy and speedily disburse it at the gaming table and other pleasures of the town.

In 1718, only five years after the Shore estate had come into the Cibber family for the express purpose of assisting the children, the *Weekly Journal*[3] reported that one of Colley's daughters was so down at heel that his partners, Booth and Wilks, had arranged a private benefit at Drury Lane to spruce up her wardrobe. Not in the least chagrined by this publicity, her father lent himself enthusiastically to the project and, when the performance was over, serenely appropriated the proceeds.

The example of these exploited females in the Cibber household filled young Theo neither with indignation nor pity, but with a horror of weakness, a loathing for mildness of spirit, and contempt for women. Power and freedom resided not in these drabs but in his famous father — man of fashion and bon vivant — whom he rarely saw. Colley lived mostly in London, and "for her health" kept his frail, asthmatic wife and family at his country place in Hillington.

To a cheerfully ruthless hedonism, which he regarded as the

masculine principle, Theo passionately allied himself. So did the youngest daughter in the Cibber family, Charlotte, who as a very little girl took to wearing her father's and older brother's clothes and boots, to hunting, swaggering and swearing, and to strapping a brace of pistols about her small middle, shooting them off unexpectedly and terrifying her asthmatic mother out of breath. But if Charlotte Cibber undertook this bullying behavior hoping that her father would recognize her kindred manly spirit and single her out from her timid sisters for his love, Colley merely conceived for his youngest daughter a particular loathing. One morning when he was favoring his loved ones with a few days' visit in the country, Charlotte leaped astride an unbroken donkey foal and made her hell-bent course, surrounded by an admiring crowd of local children, across a field toward the house where her father sat smoking at his ease before an open window. "God demme," the great man exclaimed, turning away from the sight, "An Ass upon an Ass!"[4]

Theophilus was sent to Winchester School, but in 1720 he abruptly left it and turned up in London. At first he tried to support himself by hack writing for the *Country Correspondent* and the *Daily Gazeteer*, while tales of his cyclonic behavior in taverns and bagnios alarmed his mother and amused his father, who let him flounder and bluster for a few months before rescuing him with an offer of an apprenticeship at Drury Lane. Colley's fatherly largesse cost him little: Theo's position was menial, his pay small, and the infrequent, inconsequential character of his stage appearances in the next few years suggests that he was receiving no preferential treatment.

Theo, close at last to that mystery which was his father, threw himself with stormy energy into his new life. No sooner was he at Drury Lane than he set himself to atomize and imitate not only his father's famous stage style, his voice, his mannerisms, his gestures, but Colley's offstage personality, his vices and his eccentricities. If Colley affected foppish dress, Theo's great buckles and satin waistcoats trimmed with silver frogs[5] brought giggles to the little actresses in the green room. If Colley was an inveterate gambler, and in the presence of his noble cronies bore staggering losses with wit and sangfroid, Theophilus was presently dangerously in debt, dodging creditors, bailiffs, and prison. If Colley basked in his intimacy with such exquisite noblemen as Lord Chesterfield, Theophilus was one of the rakehells who formed the train of the notorious young Duke of Wharton on his disreputable midnight forays into the stews of London. If Colley did little to quash the rumors that he was a prodigious lover, always deep in a discreet intrigue with some highborn lady, Theophilus publicly caroused with whores.

Colley Cibber sincerely regarded himself as a benevolent father. In truth, he asked nothing from his children except that they flatter him when they chanced to meet and the rest of the year not bedevil him with demands for money or attention. After Theophilus arrived at the theater, and this obscene caricature, this scurrilous parody of himself strutted across his path a dozen times a day, the genial and fastidious Laureate began to regard his only son with shuddering aversion. Hate the sight of him though he did, Colley never recognized that it was Theophilus's debased resemblance to himself which repelled him. The more the father saw of the son, the more unbelievable it seemed to him that this creature could be any blood of his. He muttered to a sympathetic lady friend that he "would never have believed Theophilus was his son, but that he knew the mother of him was too proud to be a whore."[6] Though the elder Cibber could scarcely bear to be in the same room with the younger, there was no break between them. Colley could cut Theo, spite him, pass him over when it came to parts, but Theophilus continued to work zealously and treat his parent with fawning obsequiousness.

Old Cibber had one quality about which Theo could never wrap the envious jaws of his mimic powers, and that was what Colley himself called his "gayete du Coeur," his childlike zest for fine society and elegant conversation, a trait that made him greatly sought after by a bored nobility, whom he could always raise out of the dumps with his adoration. The Poet Laureate had a disarming habit of self-disparagement. By publicly depreciating his well-known foibles and vanities, Colley safely predetonated a good deal of censure. But Colley's merry self-belittling, which was an effective kind of social appeasement, became groveling self-loathing in Theophilus.

Neither of the Cibbers was endowed with physical beauty, but on the comic stage Colley had such élan, such exquisite timing and

Colley Cibber as Lord Foppington, painted by G. Grisoni and engraved by J. Simon.

Theophilus Cibber in the Character of Ancient Pistol.

emphasis, such a way of infecting his audience with the delight he felt in self-display, that the effect of his performances was dancelike beauty. Aaron Hill says:

> There was a peeping pertness in his eye. . . . In his face was a contracted kind of . . . sharpness, like a pig half roasted; and a voice not unlike his own might have been borrowed from the same suffering animal. . . . His attitudes were pointed and exquisite. . . . He was beautifully absorbed by the character, and demanded and monopolized attention; his very extravagances were colored with propriety; and affectation sat so easy about him that it was in danger of appearing amiable.[7]

All his father's grimaces, mannerisms, and impudences were incorporated into Theo's adulteration of the Cibber style, but what was civil, subtle, and light in Colley was thunderously overdrawn in his son. Even destructive nature, presiding deity at his birth, seemed to cooperate in Theo's debasement of his father's image, for in 1726 he broke his version of the Cibber nose while overacting Harlequin, and at some point in those early years in London, his face, so reminiscent of his parent's, became pitted and coarsened by smallpox.

Within a few years of Theo's going on the stage he had acquired a considerable following. He was applauded as Abel Drugger, the booby assistant in Jonson's *Alchemist,* and was so unforgettable as Pistol in *Henry IV* that as long as he lived the character was associated with him. "He had merit in a variety of characters," reports Thomas Davies, "but he was so apt to mix false spirit and grimace . . . that he . . . disgusted the judicious spectator. . . . Pistol was his best character; in that part he assumed a ridiculous importance . . . with turgid action, long immeasurable strides, extravagant grimaces, and the sonorous cant of the old Tragedians, so that it was impossible not to laugh."[8] *Impossible not to laugh.* Theophilus Cibber made a nightmare career of public self-abasement, drawing out of a newly genteel eighteenth-century audience, which abhorred "low" humor and admired fine feeling above all things, a reluctant, uncomfortable, and cruel laughter, an uncontrollable spasm of embarrassment and repugnance.

Cibber-baiting of both father and son was a popular pastime. An anonymous pamphlet had this to say about them:

> Of all the comedians who have appeared on the stage within my memory, no one has taken a kicking with so much humor as our present most excellent laureate, and I am informed his son does not much fall short of him in this excellence. I am very glad of it, for as I have a kindness for the young man, I hope to see him as well kicked as his father before him.[9]

Even Theo's most eager kickers, who considered him guilty of six out of the seven deadly sins, could not convict him of sloth. From the beginning of his association with Drury Lane he worked with tempestuous energy. By June 1723, before he was twenty-one, he was managing Drury Lane's summer company of young actors and had found time to adapt for them an ambitious version of Shakespeare's *Henry IV*, as well as write an afterpiece called *Apollo and Daphne* which became a standard part of the Drury Lane repertoire. At the same time, he was appearing more and more frequently, and because he was one of the quickest studies in the troupe was often called in to replace an ailing player.

In May 1725 he married Janey Johnson, a promising little singer and comedienne. From the beginning he was unfaithful, worked her shamefully hard, and appropriated her entire salary to stave off his creditors. As an eighteenth-century British husband he had every legal right to his wife's earnings, and, as his father's son, a glowing example of how to use one's wife's assets in the pursuit of personal pleasure.

Theophilus brought out a main piece of his own at Drury Lane in 1731, a comedy called *The Lover*, with leading parts for himself and Janey. With a sangfroid worthy of his parent, he wrote a preface for the opening night in which Janey confided to the audience that her husband's intemperance had made them desperately hard up, and that the success of his play would do wonders for their finances. "Give us," Janey begged in her sweet little voice and in her husband's calculatingly sentimental words, "at least an honest chance to live."

Detest him though he did, Colley took every advantage of his son's devotion, and Theophilus, as his responsibilities enlarged, began to conduct himself with the assurance of an heir apparent. Colley never discouraged his son's assumption that the Cibber share of the patent of Drury Lane was his birthright, yet when he suddenly retired from the theater in the fall of 1732 he neither gave nor sold his interest to Theo, but rented it to him until the end of the season.

Of the three young men involved in the theater's new management — Highmore, Ellys, and young Cibber — only Theophilus had the least experience. Although he was not yet thirty he had had twelve years' rigorous apprenticeship in every aspect of the theater. He assumed the role of senior partner, with an insolent condescension which cemented John Highmore's loathing. Ellys's position was never powerful. He was there only to see that the widow Wilks's interests were not abused and, finding Highmore more congenial than young Cibber, was content to go along with him and to be called "Highmore's Prime Minister" behind his back.

Despite the fact that he was outnumbered, Theo's force and know-how were enough to prevail over any protests from the other two.

Like his father, Theophilus had an acute sense of popular taste and immediately put into rehearsal several revivals. He also brought out a new play, something most eighteenth-century theatrical managers avoided as much as possible, preferring to trust a repertory of proved favorites. The new play was Charles Johnson's *Caelia*, a sentimental tragedy about an unmarried pregnant lady who, abandoned by her lover in a bawdy house, expires at last in the arms of her forgiving father. Theo selected *Caelia* as a perfect role for his Janey, who, as luck would have it, was great with child, exhausted and unwell, but hard at work in the theater, as usual. The maudlin play with its plucky little actress was an enormous success and moneymaker.

During his brief management of Drury Lane, Theo Cibber's only serious miscalculation was attempting to play serious parts like Macduff or the unfortunate apprentice, George Barnwell, in Lillo's *London Merchant*. The public accepted as an article of faith that Cibbers were born to be kicked and laughed at, never to excite sympathy. Of Theo's Macduff the *Grub Street Journal*'s correspondent fumed that "His remarkable little strut . . . put me in mind of the fly . . . who, sitting upon the spoke of a chariot wheel said . . . 'what a dust do I raise!' . . . In this light . . . all men appear who are vainly fond of showing themselves in characters to which they are unequal."[10]

Theophilus had recently endeared himself to the company by a general raise in salaries when early in December he fell ill with what the papers called "a violent cold," which prevented his leaving his bed. Janey, still playing nearly every night, holding her husband's creditors at arm's length, collapsed on December 15. For the next month both the young Cibbers were dangerously ill with what was probably a severe form of influenza. Theophilus, pale and haggard but unwilling to leave the theater any longer in the hands of Highmore and Ellys, returned to play Abel Drugger on January 19. That same day Jane Cibber, still unable to leave her bed, gave birth to her second daughter, Elizabeth.

The following Thursday King George, Queen Caroline, and the entire court went to Drury Lane for a command performance celebrating Mrs. Porter's return to the stage for the first time since her gallant encounter with the highwayman. Limping regally on her disarticulated hip, which the finest surgeons in Britain had failed to reduce, she played Queen Elizabeth in *The Unhappy Favorite* before a vast, emotional crowd. Theophilus was at the theater, while at home Janey Cibber quietly died. "She was brought to bed about a week ago," the *London Evening Post* confided next day to its readers, "and appeared very much mended; but, her fever returning, violently carried her off. . . . Her virtues in private life rendered her very amiable. Young Mister Cibber is very much indisposed."[11]

Indisposed Theophilus must have been, not yet himself recuperated, and shaken by the loss of such a popular and lucrative helpmeet; but he could not afford to languish. As soon as he had found a wet nurse for his feeble daughter, and had Janey interred in a lead coffin at St. Paul's, Covent Garden, he hurried back to the theater whence disquieting emanations rose. His father and his enemy, John Highmore, were as thick as thieves. All fall the Poet Laureate, relieved of his burdensome administrative duties at Drury

Lane, had been romping through his favorite Restoration roles at the request of his exalted friends: Foppington, "at the Desire of several Persons of Quality," Bayes, "By her Majesty's Command," and Atoll, for His Majesty himself, who came in from Richmond with the court for the occasion.

In March, while Susannah Arne was charming the town at Lincoln's Inn Fields as gentle Rosamond, the astounding news from Drury Lane was made public. Colley Cibber had sold his entire share of the "Cloaths, Scenes, and Patent" of Drury Lane to John Highmore, Esq. Owning both Booth's and now Cibber's shares — a clear controlling interest — the first thing Highmore did was to inform Theophilus that after June first, when his rental agreements with his father would be satisfied, he would have no further say in the management of Drury Lane and his services as a player would not be required. After thirteen years of passionate apprenticeship, after a brief, brilliant regency of his father's domain, Theophilus was, in a stroke, jobless, futureless, and an object of public derision. Everybody thought Colley's action in putting down this strutting son so deliciously, so heartlessly Cibberian that it was worthy of any of the cynical stage roles with which the old rascal had entertained them so long.

Neither John Highmore nor the public doubted that the force was permanently knocked out of Theophilus's gale. All he could do, if he wanted to pick up the rest of his year's salary (which he must need with those two motherless little girls and that mountain of debts), was to linger on, subdued, till the end of the season, and next year try to sell his unpleasant comic gifts to John Rich at Covent Garden or to Henry Giffard at Goodman's Fields. Theophilus technically controlled his father's interests until the first of June, but since any policies he might instigate, any plays he might put in rehearsal could all be countermanded in two months, he was, in fact, impotent.

But Theo never felt so physically well, so mentally agile, as in the teeth of a gale. The more people wished him dead, the more keenly Theophilus knew himself alive. The news of his father's passing him over was in the papers on a Saturday. That Monday Theophilus appeared as usual at the theater, dressed to kill, brash and blustering, to play the Mock Doctor in Fielding's comedy that night, and to supervise the placing of extra seats on the stage for his benefit performance on Wednesday.

All during April Highmore and Ellys watched astonished as Theophilus swaggered and strutted just as before, jostling them aside, overriding their orders, helping himself to fat parts, rehearsing the company in his new afterpiece, *The Harlot's Progress*. Every time Highmore attempted to make a stand, Theophilus dashed off a letter to the papers excoriating Highmore's ineptitude and amateurishness. These he followed with a flurry of falsely signed letters approving the perceptions of his first epistle.

There was only one reason Theophilus could carry off such behavior, and this was because a faction existed within the theater that young Highmore had never considered important enough to woo. The players at Drury Lane, serious and hardworking, were the oldest and proudest theatrical company in the kingdom. Many of them, like the Hallams and the Millses, belonged to dynasties of professional entertainers, and they refused to be assigned roles or to take stage directions from their new master, or from anyone presently involved in the management of Drury Lane except young Mr. Cibber. It was not that they liked Theophilus. Nobody would have trusted him with his wallet, his wife, or his heart's secret. Nevertheless, Theophilus knew the business from the ground up, and he was thoroughly one of them. On the other hand, every actor had contempt for Squire Highmore. Spoiled and wealthy, he had come to Drury Lane a few years before, having made a wager at White's Club that he could play Lothario in Nicholas Rowe's *The Fair Penitent* at one of the theaters royal. The wily old triumvirate at Drury Lane had given him permission to use their facilities and a splendid supporting cast for one night, knowing that with the right promotion they could fill the house with Highmore's fashionable set, who would all come, hoping to see him make a fool of himself. This is precisely what happened, but Highmore, undaunted by the laughter of the audience or the remarks in the press, and more hopelessly stagestruck than ever, had now begged to play Hotspur, and Polydore in Otway's *The Orphan*. Having counted up their profits from *The Fair Penitent,* the Drury Lane managers had graciously consented to both requests, only stipulating that the elaborate costumes which High-more had his tailor run up for each new part at enormous expense (and which everyone but Highmore knew would be worn by him only once) be turned over to the Drury Lane wardrobe afterward.

It had been during this period of Highmore's stage mania that the ailing and despondent Booth, observing this infatuated young heir who seemed bent on throwing away his patrimony in the the-ater, had asked his friend Benjamin Victor to approach Highmore about buying Booth's share of the patent.

A year later Highmore owned not only Booth's but Cibber's shares. As far as the actors at Drury Lane were concerned, Highmore might be the owner of every wig, sword, and cloak, but they had seen him perform on the stage, and not the lowliest man in the company would accept his direction. The players' insubordination annoyed Highmore, but he was sanguine about the future. After Theophilus Cibber was gone they would fall into line quickly enough. Actors were a hungry race, living from day to day, and Highmore had per-fect faith in the suasive power of his pocketbook, which so far in his short life had opened every door at which he had sought entrance.

And so the spring season advanced, with the insolent Theophi-lus at the helm, while his *Harlot's Progress,* inspired by Hogarth's drawings, brought in sellout crowds. John Highmore was biding his time until June, but the mutinous attitude of the Drury Lane actors did not lessen as the inevitability of Highmore's rule drew near. On the contrary, Theo's humiliating treatment of the patentee, and Highmore's helplessness to retaliate, only opened the actors' eyes to their potential strength. Under Wilks, Cibber, and Booth no one had ever thought of rebellion. These men, like Thomas Betterton a generation back, like Rich at Covent Garden, and like Giffard at Goodman's Fields, were gifted, experienced actors who in the course of their careers had managed to buy into management and to assume the risks, responsibilities, and profits thereof. Theatrical manage-ment was a goal to which any actor might aspire, and during the summer months when London theaters were closed many players ran theatrical booths under their own names at Southwick or Barthole-mew Fair.

Were actors rich men's toys? By what right did Highmore, who had not the least theatrical instinct or tradition, command their lives and their art? The players began to question the nature of the Royal Patent under which their company performed. What was a patent, anyway? Was it the right to impress free men of genius into providing a handsome living for a rich fool? Was it the physical theater itself: its stage, offices, green room, wardrobe, and tiring rooms? Theophilus pointed out to them that the building which housed Drury Lane belonged to the Duke of Bedford, who had rented it for years to the patentees. Suppose, asked Theophilus, the players should rent the theater directly from the duke for the coming season. What could Highmore's patent mean then? A £6000 piece of paper, sans stage or players.

In the middle of May, to the cheers of his fellows, Theophilus went to speak to one of the Duke of Bedford's financial representatives, a sober and traditional gentleman who was so scandalized at young Cibber's proposition that he hurried to Highmore to report the incident. Highmore was shaken. Was it possible that Theophilus, discredited and penniless, could seriously threaten his investment? His Royal Patent had been issued by the Lord Chamberlain himself. Provoked and frightened into action at last, Highmore moved rashly.

On May 26, when the Drury Lane players arrived to dress for the evening's performance they found the theater closed, locked, and barred. By order of Highmore, Ellys, and the widow Wilks, there were to be no more performances that season. No performances meant no salaries, and that, Highmore was certain, ought to make clear to the would-be rebels their absolute dependence upon the owner of a Royal Theatrical Patent. But six days of May remained, during which Theophilus's rental agreement with his father was still in effect and he had an unassailable right to "one third Part of the Patent, Cloaths, Scenes, etc.; and all Rights and Privileges thereunto for a Term not yet expired."[12] Highmore's action in locking him out of the theater was clearly illegal. The company was unanimous in its sense of outrage. Theophilus, with the full backing of almost every player at Drury Lane and the overwhelming sympathy of the public, stormed off to the Little Theatre in the Haymarket and, on behalf of the company of Drury Lane, rented it for the coming season.

No theatrical event in anyone's memory had so stirred public feeling or was so thoroughly hashed out in the press as the revolt of the Drury Lane players. Traditionalists were shocked by Theophilus's undercutting of Highmore's position and the sanctity of the patent, finding it reprehensible that "the son should immediately render null and worthless what the father had just received thirty-one hundred and fifty pounds for."[13] But by and large, London playgoers, while they could not overcome their personal distaste for Theophilus, admired his doughtiness, were sympathetic to the mutineers, and hoped they could outwit the theatrical establishment and make a go of it.

The illustration on page 56 is typical of the cartoons that appeared at the time. On one side stands a dejected Highmore, holding a sheet of paper that reads, "It cost £6000." Ellys and the widow Wilks cower nearby, and Mrs. Wilks's daughter is waving a banner, which proclaims, "We'll starve 'em out!" On the other side of the page stand the players, Theophilus in his famous Pistol costume, hands on his hips, backed by corpulent John Harper dressed as Falstaff. At his ease, in one corner behind a curtain, sits Colley Cibber, the Laureate, his brow crowned with bay, money bags on his lap, more money bags stacked under his chair — smiling.

The first thing Theophilus did upon inspecting his new theater in the Haymarket was insist that John Potter, his landlord, redecorate the place over the summer. The company that was coming here in the fall was no fly-by-night English Opera Company, like the year before, but the most distinguished troupe in Britain, players who attracted a fastidious and discriminating audience. Undoubtedly the royal family would grace a number of performances. Potter was delighted to comply: the place was certainly shabby. For years he had been renting it to shoestring operations for a few nights at a time, and sometimes it was vacant for weeks. For regular tenants of the caliber Cibber was bringing, he would, of course, refurbish.

There was one complication. Potter said he had already agreed with young Tom Arne to let his English Opera Company use the facilities occasionally next year, since the Prince of Wales' new opera company had taken Lincoln's Inn Fields. Potter did not think the Arnes' infrequent presence would interfere with the Drury Lane

Diminutive Theophilus Cibber, dressed as Pistol, the role which epitomized him for the public, stands, legs apart, at the head of his militant players. Harper, as Falstaff, is on his right, and the popular actress Mrs. Heron on his left, holding a banner saying, "Liberty & Property."

Opposing Theo's party are the owners of Drury Lane. Highmore, looking thin and ineffectual, holds a scroll reading, "It cost £6000." He is urged on by Ellis, wearing a painter's smock, and Mrs. Shaw, the dead patentee, Wilks's daughter, waving a banner which proclaims, "We'll starve 'em out." The Widow Wilks stands behind Highmore, weeping into a large kerchief.

In the foreground, before a large theatrical curtain, sits the Poet Laureate, Colley Cibber, a crown of bay on his head, his lap full of bags of gold from his profitable sale of Drury Lane. He is smiling serenely, and pointing a finger at Highmore's dejected back. Etching by John Laguerre, 1733.

players. Theophilus was not only amenable but enthusiastic about sharing the house with this musical company. His dramatic programs would be enriched by musical entr'actes, and the Arne family would be assured steady, rather than sporadic, employment if they would agree to provide regular musical interludes as part of the evening's bill.

Potter introduced young Cibber to young Arne, who was at that very moment rehearsing in the Little Theatre for a summer run of his new musical burlesque, *The Opera of Operas*, adapted from Fielding's *Tragedy of Tragedies*, featuring his small brother, Henry Peter, as Tom Thumb, the tiny hero. Quickly, the two rebel impresarios reached an accord about the next year.

On September 26, Theophilus Cibber and the Drury Lane mutineers opened in *Love for Love* in the Little Theatre in the Haymarket, which still smelled smartly of fresh paint. The costumes were new and elegant. So were the sets. The audience was brilliant, crowded, and enthusiastic, for laugh at him all one might, fustian little Captain Pistol seemed to be maneuvering his troops adroitly. Nearly everyone from Drury Lane had followed his banner: the Mills family; the Hallams; fat John Harper, London's most beloved Falstaff; young Mrs. Pritchard with the ringing voice; and Theo's eccentric sister Charlotte, who had come up to London to follow a manly theatrical career like her father and brother, and who played minor comic females when there was nothing better, but preferred men's parts when she could wheedle her brother to give them to her.

The only important player who stayed behind at Drury Lane was Kitty Clive (1711–1785), and this was not because she bore any particular loyalty to Highmore, but because she detested Theophilus. Back in the 1720s, when she was Kitty Raftor and Theo's future wife was still Janey Johnson, those two stagestruck girls had been best friends, following dashing Robert Wilks through the streets until one day they wheedled their idol into hearing them sing. After that he had permitted them to hang around backstage, where they studied every move of the great queens, Mrs. Porter and Mrs. Oldfield, and sometimes picked up a part with a line or two, or sang a street ballad between acts. Though both their careers had burgeoned

Catherine Clive, by J. Faber, 1734.

since then, they were still inseparable friends when Janey died. Kitty Clive was impulsive, generous, short fused, and opinionated: "a mixture of combustibles,"[14] as Tate Wilkinson put it. Buxom, florid, unreasonable, fiercely loyal to those she loved, she was as blunt of speech as she was sweet voiced singing a ballad. No matter how many Latin phrases the doctors might have trotted out to explain Janey's death, Kitty knew better. Ever since January she had been vehemently insisting that it had been years of overwork, ungentle treatment, and a heart broken by Theo's infidelities that had so undermined Janey's health that recovery was impossible.

If she had gone with the others to the Haymarket, Kitty Clive would not have been the least surprised at what she saw there: Theo hotly panting after a new woman. After all, his lechery had scarcely slackened even long enough to observe Janey's burial. One detractor stated that the very night Janey's bier was being borne into the churchyard by Theo's relatives, her goatish widower was entertaining "a Brace of Drurian Doxies"[15] at home.

Actually there was something unprecedented in Theo's latest amatory pursuit. For the first and last time in his angry life, Theophilus Cibber was in love. Despite his cynicism, despite his predatory contempt for women, he was suing, neither to despoil nor seduce, but to marry Susannah Arne, the solemn little singer from the opera company.

❦ 5 ❧

My poor friend, the Duchess of Bolton, was educated in Solitude,
with some choice Books, by a saintlike Governess. Crammed with virtue
and good Qualities, she thought it impossible not to find Gratitude, though
she failed to give Passion; and upon this plan threw away her Estate, was
despised by her Husband, and laughed at by the Public. Polly [Lavinia
Fenton, the Duke of Bolton's actress mistress], bred in an Alehouse, and
produced on the stage, has obtained Wealth and Title, and found the way
to be esteemed. So useful is early experience; without it, half of Life is
dissipated in correcting the Errors that we have been taught to receive as
indisputable Truths.
— Lady Mary Wortley Montagu to Lady Bute, December 8, 1754

IN the fall of 1733 Colley Cibber came close to becoming fond of
his son: he could not help being tickled at the way, in spite of
his own efforts the year before to thwart him, the boy was making a success of his venture in the Haymarket. Not least among
Theo's recent virtues from his father's point of view was his widow-
hood. The marriage to Janey Johnson had been a profitless business,
for though the girl had been agreeable, devoted, and industrious,
she had brought neither social standing nor real money into the
family — unlike his own model union with Katherine Shore, or
Barton Booth's to Hester Santlow, both of which marriages had
produced the capital with which the two husbands had purchased
their shares of the Drury Lane patent.

Colley now began delicately probing among his friends for a
new marriage that would settle Theo's enormous debts, insure his
future comfort, and stabilize his position in society. The little business between Theo and Miss Arne at the theater was too insignificant
to concern him. As soon as the boy had wheedled or bamboozled or

strong-armed his way into Susannah's bed — and these things took time with religious virgins who had hovering fathers — all Theo's inability to put his energies into making a sound second marriage would fade away.

So cordial were Colley's feelings toward Theophilus that he put himself to the unusual trouble of murmuring in some ears at court that a third theatrical patent, for the Little Theatre in the Haymarket, might be in order. But here the Laureate overreached himself. The Lord Chamberlain made it clear that two licenses were all the Crown had any intention of granting. The Little Theatre in the Haymarket had an unfortunate history of seditious plays, and young Cibber, its present manager, had too unsavory a reputation to justify such an act of official confidence.

Cibber never pressed the patent matter beyond the lightest hint, and this same delicacy prevented his appearing all that season on any London stage. Did he act at the Haymarket, he would seem, his pockets full of Drury Lane profits, to be supporting those bent on its destruction. If he buoyed Highmore's sinking operation he would appear to be contributing to his son's downfall, and should he perform at Covent Garden for John Rich he would be turning his back on his old house and colleagues as well as on his flesh and blood.

Any of these theatrical managers would have given much for Cibber's services but it was Highmore whom Cibber's blithe presence might have rescued from disaster. The remnant company at Drury Lane was mediocre and demoralized, playing to deserted houses and led by Roger Bridgewater, of whose hand-sawing, ranting style one wit observed:

> Hark, a noise appalls the listening Ear!
> All think it Thunder. Br-dg-wa-er appears.
> His brazen Front he thinks will do far more
> Than B--th, W-lks, M-lls, or C-bber did before.[1]

Every Saturday morning Highmore scrupulously made up his actors' salaries out of his own pocketbook. And since his weekly deficit was running to £50 or £60 a week, while his yearly income only amounted to £800, there was a desperate urgency to break the rebel players' spirits and bring them back to their legitimate home. Except for payday, Highmore spent little time among his dispirited troops — which did not matter since he had no notion of what to do in a theater. Outside Drury Lane, though, he was waging a feverish battle to save his empire: scouring the provincial theaters for talent, and haunting court levees in the hope of arousing powerful sympathy for his wrongs. In his first endeavor he did succeed in bringing to London Charles Macklin, an Irish player with a coarse, passionate, and naturalistic style. His second effort was less successful, for when he gained the ear of the Lord Chamberlain, His Grace gave Highmore no more satisfaction than he granted Colley Cibber: the Crown had no intention of recognizing the new company with a patent; neither was it inclined, so long as the Haymarket's productions continued to be as delightful and politically innocuous as they had been to date, of closing down the operation. His Grace murmured to Highmore that though he could expect no redress from the government, it might be fruitful for him to examine the law and see whether the irregular operation at the Haymarket was in violation of some obscure or forgotten statute.

A costly legal investigation seemed out of the question to Highmore with his exhausted means, when suddenly help appeared from John Rich, who offered to share the expenses. Ordinarily, Highmore's rival patentee at Covent Garden would never have been an ally, but here was a situation where the value of a Royal Patent was at stake. If the Drury Lane mutineers were allowed to survive, then any group of malcontents could defect from either of the theaters royal and set up for themselves with impunity. The two patentees and their legal experts were soon mining the law, and presently thought they had unearthed the means to bring the rebels to their knees.

At the Haymarket, meantime, Theo's "Comedians of His Majesty's Revels," as they called themselves, were offering a varied season of old favorites, new works, and plenty of music. Nearly every night between the acts Susannah Arne sang the works of Handel, Porpora, or her brother. Theophilus watched her from the wings, and her slender person, her grave, fastidious manner, and her voice, so chaste, so low, and so ardent, moved the thirty-year-old reprobate to a rev-

erent rapture unlike any sensation he had ever known. So inexperi-
enced was he with tender feelings, and so fearful of this pure girl's
rejection, that his swaggering impertinence deserted him in her presence and all he could do to relieve his lovesickness was to heap benefits upon her and her family. Tom Arne's *Opera of Operas* was
played night after night to its young composer's considerable
emolument, and a new musical, *An Impromptu Revel Masque* (in
honor of the approaching nuptials of the Princess Royal and the
Prince of Orange), was commissioned to star Susannah as Venus and
Henry Peter as Cupid. Meanwhile, Theophilus gave Susannah's father a sedentary job with the theater's accounts, which suited his
infirmity. And young Henry Peter, besides singing duets with his
sister, was groomed for dramatic roles against the day his high voice
broke.

For a time, Theo's abashment and the presence of her family
enabled Susannah to avoid a confrontation with her admirer, whose
pitted cheeks, skewed nose, cabriole legs, squints, grimaces, eye-
poppings, and sour ambience of last night's debauch all horrified her.
And she did not need Kitty Clive in the company to hear accounts of
Theo's temper, his duels, his cruelty as a husband, his obsession with
gaming, and his debts to sinister creditors. When Susannah and
Theophilus met face to face in the green room she gave him a frightened, placatory smile and hurried along.

On November 12, *Henry IV, Part I* was scheduled at the Haymarket with John Harper as Falstaff and the two Millses, father
and son, as the King and Prince Hal. That afternoon as Harper
waddled ponderously toward the theater, a pair of bailiffs seized him
under either arm and led him away to Bridewell. The charge stated
that as a player in an unlicensed theater he was "a vagabond and a
rogue."[2] Highmore and Rich had uncovered a dusty statute from
Queen Anne's time intended to deal with the mountebanks, quacks,
sleight-of-hand artists, and sleazy theatrical riffraff who drifted into
town in the summer and set up booths at fairs to cozen London
citizens. Since to arrest the entire Haymarket company would be an
unwieldy operation, the patentees had decided to make a test case of
one player.

As Highmore should have learned by now, Theophilus Cibber

was never so intrepid or so resourceful as when his back was to the wall. Although he knew that Harper was in jail, Theophilus opened the doors of his smart little theater at the usual time and allowed the audience to crowd inside and grow restive. In due time he appeared, apologized for the delay, told them where their favorite Falstaff languished and under the malevolent interference of which two jealous theatrical tyrants, and humbly offered to read the part of Falstaff so that the audience would not be too disappointed. The pit and gallery cheered their assent, and cheered him again at the end of the play, though a more improbable fat knight could scarcely be imagined than bandy-legged, scrawny Theophilus Cibber. Susannah Arne, dressed for her part as Princess Hunca Munca in the afterpiece, watched from the wings as the repulsive and sinister suitor whom she had kept at arm's length for months became the hero of the hour.

John Harper's vagrancy trial was heard at the Court of the King's Bench on November 22, and a volatile and partisan mob of his admirers saw him acquitted by Lord Hardwicke, the Chief Justice, on the grounds that no man could be called a vagabond or a vagrant who owned his own fine house in the City of Westminster. The choice of Harper as the patentees' scapegoat seems at first an odd one. There were plenty of actors in Theo's company who scarcely owned more than the clothes on their backs and were neither so personally well loved nor led such respectable lives as John Harper. Probably he was picked because his unique physical qualifications for a role like Falstaff made it seem impossible to substitute another player and prevent the canceling of the performance. Besides this, Harper was known as the most timorous actor in London, given to attacks of sweating anxiety over the least discomfiture. Highmore and Rich may have hoped that a few hours in the dank confines of Bridewell, deprived of the solace of his family and larder, would bring him to capitulate. But Harper, sustained by hampers of food and visits from his loved ones and cohorts, remained resolute. And the day his enormous bulk was borne triumphant from the courtroom on the shoulders of a cheering mob John Highmore's theatrical aspirations were extinguished. The Drury Lane patent was again for sale.

With the rout of the dragon Highmore, and the rescue from his talons of that portly maiden in distress, John Harper, Theophilus Cibber became a sort of theatrical St. George. Though his disgusting appearance and grimacing still provoked a shuddering laugh from his audience, opinion about him was suddenly tinged with respect. You could dismiss him no longer as a half-mad caricature of a famous father. Colley had run a splendid operation at Drury Lane for thirty years, and given London — whether in his capacity as impresario, playwright, or actor — more merry evenings than anyone else in the century. And his son seemed to have inherited his genius. The Little Haymarket was offering the liveliest theater in town, valiantly surviving despite the combined malice of the two theaters royal.

On January 10, 1734, the *Grub Street Journal* devoted most of its front page to the doings of the Cibbers, father and son. The leading column printed the Poet Laureate's annual, bathetic New Year's Ode, with the *Journal's* line-by-line, mock-pedantic annotations. Farther down the page a paragraph set forth the *Journal's* irreverent suggestions for "Articles of Peace between the Patentees and the Rebel Company of Comedians": first, a general amnesty should be sworn, and "The Revellers should be permitted to march out of the New Theatre in the Haymarket with their own Swords and Baggages, their own music playing before them." Further, in deference to Harper's sensibilities, "The opprobrious names of Vagrant, Rogue and Vagabond shall be erased from the Records of Drury Lane." And lastly, "for the more effective restoring . . . the Peace and Tranquillity of the Stage, the illustrious Dowager, Hester Booth* shall be given in Marriage to the most serene Infant Don Theophilus Cibber, with such . . . Portion and Dower as shall be judged necessary and proper to support their Dignity."

Two gentlemen besides the editors of the *Grub Street Journal* took an interest in the next bride of Don Theophilus. One was his father, leisurely shopping for a rich daughter-in-law. The other was Thomas Arne, Senior. In the early days of his association with young Cibber at the Haymarket, Arne had regarded this unwholesome person's carnal interest in his daughter as a threat to debauch her and cheapen her value. Now that it was clear that Theophilus doted on

---

* Barton Booth's widow, Hester Santlow Booth (1690–1773).

her and was prepared to marry her without a penny of dowry; no'
that Arne had had a few months to observe Theo's managerial verv
and to grow accustomed to his kindnesses to the whole Arne family
and especially now that he had witnessed the outcome of the Harpe
affair, from which Theo had emerged as the most powerful youn
man in London theater, old Arne had decided that Theo's physica
and moral blemishes were not nearly so disfiguring as they ha
seemed at first. He was beginning to feel impatient with Susannah
intransigent aversion to the man.

About the first of February, Highmore concluded the sale c
Drury Lane for half what he had paid Colley Cibber nine montl
before. The young amateur's stage mania had been cured. He ha
nothing more to do with theater the rest of his life, and the nam
Cibber was never mentioned in his presence.

The new owner was Charles Fleetwood, Esq., a young gentl
man with no more stage experience than Highmore, an estate i
Staffordshire, and a fortune reported to be £6000 a year. Fleetwoo
possessed not only nine times his predecessor's income, but a qualit
which the stiff-necked, upright Highmore had utterly lacked: he wa
the most ingratiating young man in London. Charles Macklin r
called that "the person, the address, the manners and solicitations c
Fleetwood [when asking for money] appeared so artless, so unpra
ticed and so delicately embarrassed as made his attacks irresistible."
And Benjamin Victor added that even when Fleetwood's fortun
health, and reputation were gone, his amiability remained, "the la
. . . quality that he kept with him to his death . . . which to the en
enabled him to deceive even persons that thought themselves arme
against him."[4] Theophilus had blown down rigid John Highmore i
nine months of bluster. Pliant Charles Fleetwood was to prove an
other matter.

One of the first things the winsome new patentee did was t
hurry over to the Haymarket and pay a call — the first of many — o
the mutineers. He disarmed John and William Mills by stammerin
that they had long been such idols of his that he was struck dumb t
approach them. He bowed over Susannah Arne's hand with th
chasteness of an older brother greeting a little sister who has take
holy orders. And he seized young Cibber's hand and blurted in h

boyish way that "he knew nothing of the art of theatrical management," and begged Theo — on any terms — to return to Drury Lane and be his "pilot."[5]

During the next few weeks, old Arne, looking up from his ledgers at the theater, observed Cibber and Fleetwood strolling arm in arm, or rubbing their hands before the green room fire, the young squire saying little and inclining his fresh countenance worshipfully toward Theo's pocked and twitching visage. It was clear that any day now, as soon as Cibber had secured the terms he wanted, the Drury Lane company would be returning to their former home. But what about the Arne family, remnants of the English Opera Company and technically outside Cibber's negotiations and concern? Fleetwood could refuse Cibber nothing. If he asked, the Arnes would go along to Drury Lane, the most venerable, prestigious theater in Britain. The brilliant fortunes Arne had dreamed of for his children, the security of his own last years were within grasp, unless Theophilus, weary of Susannah's coldness, were to leave them behind.

Arne confronted his daughter. It had been all very well to keep young Cibber at arm's length all fall and winter. Indeed, her attitude had whetted his appetite, underscored her virtue, encouraged his generosity toward her family, and forced him to offer marriage to obtain her. But the time had come when she would have to bend a little in Cibber's direction if she did not want to see her two brothers (even if she cared nothing about her own future) left behind at the Haymarket, and her old father, in uncertain health and all his money and his energies spent in launching his children's careers, cast out without employment.

Susannah, appalled at what he was asking of her, reminded her father of Theo's intemperance and his treatment of his dead wife. Arne brushed this aside. Theophilus was thirty now, a widower, the father of two, his wild youth behind him. As for the debts which people gossiped about, what high-spirited young man does not contract a few? These could all be settled when he was back at Drury Lane earning the huge salary Fleetwood was offering him. Regarding those vicious stories of young Cibber as a husband, Arne begged his daughter to remember that Theophilus had never loved Janey Johnson. The two of them had been hardly more than children when they met, and Janey had made herself too available to him. Everyone knew that Theo had already tired of her when she became pregnant with their first daughter and he had to marry her. That unfortunate situation and the present one were hardly comparable. Theophilus was dotingly in love with her. It was the wonder of the company! His fellow players who had known him from a boy had never seen Theophilus so mild and tractable, and drinking and carousing so little. If Susannah could effect such a beneficent influence over Theophilus now, how much more could she accomplish — not only for herself but for all her family — if she became his wife?

Painfully perplexed, unable to overcome her revulsion for Theophilus, Susannah still avoided any meetings alone with him. But Theophilus was apparently not discouraged, for when the Drury Lane seceders returned in triumph to their old house in early March, the Arnes went along too: Susannah as a leading singer, Tom displacing his old master, Lampe, as resident composer and musical director, Henry Peter as a singer and child actor, and Thomas, Senior, as seat numberer, a post created by Fleetwood to check up on the notorious cheating of doorkeepers and ticket gatherers.

In his negotiations with Fleetwood, Cibber had achieved far grander terms for his return to Drury Lane than even the *Grub Street Journal* had humorously projected. Most of his leading players, including Susannah Arne, won raises in salary to £200 a year. He himself received an additional £50 for his managerial efforts. And for the first time in the history of the English stage, players' rights were to be secured at the start of every season not merely by the traditional verbal agreement with the patentee, but by written articles spelling out their rights and privileges, their salaries, the financial details of their benefit nights, their allowances for stage wardrobes, and so forth.

Throughout the negotiations Fleetwood had played the naïve suppliant and Theophilus the wily besought. Actually, Cibber was as anxious to get back to Drury Lane as Fleetwood was to have him, and Fleetwood knew it. The Little Theatre in the Haymarket, even with every seat sold, was not large enough to support the splendid new scenes and costumes and the munificent salaries, which were Theo's way of doing things. Everybody on both sides was enormously re lieved to have the rebels safely reinstated — everybody with the exception of Kitty Clive (Theo's old enemy), Charles Macklin (who had hoped to be Fleetwood's new actor-manager if the negotiations with the mutineers fell through), and Johann Lampe (who lost his job to his former apprentice).

There was only one member of the Arne family who was not beholden to Theophilus Cibber, and this was Susannah's mother. Anne made no bones about her opposition to the wicked marriage her husband was promoting. Susannah's voice and her charming looks were gifts from God. They were better safeguarded by Susannah's own virtue, modesty, diligence, and faith than by a cynical marriage. As always, his wife's blunt words and simplistic piety enraged Arne. Let heiresses practice modesty, piety, and diligence! They could afford them. Was it Lavinia Fenton's modesty that had caught the Duke of Bolton's eye, when as Polly Peachum in the first performance of *The Beggar's Opera* she curtsied in her low-cut gown? And was it the Duke's appreciation of her piety that secured her a settlement of £400 a year as long as he slept with her, and £200 afterward, for life? Unless Susannah's looks secured her a good marriage or the permanent protection of a rich man she could exercise her modesty and piety and diligence till her youth was spent, and be lucky to marry some second-rate actor who made £4 a week — when he worked. This was not the destiny for which he had tirelessly labored since Susannah's birth.

Susannah listened, as she had all her life, to her parents' anger volley over her. Her mother's loathing of Theophilus echoed her own instincts. Still, she was deeply swayed by her father's arguments. Dearly as she loved and honored her mother, there was one area in her behavior that had always seemed in error to Susannah. This was her mother's understanding of the relations of the sexes. From everything Susannah had observed from her grandfather, her uncle, her father, and her brother, it seemed to her that it was the nature of men to be volatile, impulsive, and driven toward prodigal goals. Women were mercifully free of such emotions but they were too weak to thrive in the world alone. Properly allied, the two sexes could complement one another. A soothing wife could deflect her husband's destructive energy or direct it toward the good of his family. In return for her patience, tact, forgiveness, and submission she gained her husband's grateful affection and protection against the world. Ever since Susannah could remember, her mother had defied her father rather than deferring. She had never dissuaded him from a single one of his mad projects but had driven him to further excesses and deeper humiliations, forfeiting at the same time that tender solace toward herself which should have been her due.

Her mother had carved out a hard life for herself in her proud independence. Busy and harassed all day with her home, her children's concerns, and the care of her patients, at night, as often as not, she was roused out of bed to go into the fog or darkness with an anxious young husband or shivering child to the bedside of another suffering woman.

It was Susannah, not her mother, who had been the feminine lodestone toward which her father — no matter how far he strayed — had always returned; it was she who had interceded between his rage and the rest of the family, she who had averted his course many times from that dreadful vortex of debt, ruin, and sordid death into which his father and brother had already gone.

Where would her father and Tom be today if two years ago her voice had not charmed Mr. Carey, Mr. Lampe, and, above all, Mr. Handel, who had been so furious at her and Tom about *Acis and Galatea* that he meant to annihilate them and now was her most powerful friend? People said that young Mr. Cibber was a vicious brute, but were not all men brutes without a soft woman to tame them? With her he was mild, even bashful.

That Mr. Cibber's love for her had reformed his violent nature was clear. All the players told her he was a changed man. When she considered the benefits that he had heaped upon all her family, settling them here in the finest theater in the land, she felt a profound gratitude. It may even have seemed to her, seeing Theophilus alight every morning from his handsome equipage at the Drury Lane stage door, bound inside in his eccentric clothes, and bustle here and there, ordering this, tending to that, while even Mr. Fleetwood bowed, that he was not as ugly as she had found him at first.

There was one other factor in her present life that urged Susannah Arne to accept Cibber's suit. He was by no means the most disturbing of her suitors. Susannah, at nineteen, was followed — and more and more as her popularity grew and her reputation for virtue whetted appetites — by a train of London rakes and gallants, some young, some old, nearly all of them married, for whom part of the city's round of pleasures included the pursuit of actresses and singers. Dalliance with ladies of their own rank was charming, of course, but had to be carried on with a discretion that spoiled the pleasure of competing, comparing, and boasting. Women on the stage enjoyed the same social status as whores and deserved no more esteem, but they made an infinitely more delectable and challenging prey.

All unmarried actresses of this period had to come to terms with this phenomenon, which amounted as much to a class as a sexual exploitation. A few fortunate ones like Lavinia Fenton or Anastasia Robinson were taken out of the arena by arousing the serious passion of great lords. Others, like Hannah Pritchard or Hester Santlow, made sound marriages within the profession and achieved respectability and independence. Kitty Clive put off her wooers with good-natured, ribald riposte, and all her life enjoyed a reputation for virtue. But for the most part the fate of actresses and singers was a pitiful one. And it was particularly the innocent and trusting ones, the suggestible ones, the lonely, frightened ones, the sentimental ones, like George Anne Bellamy and James Boswell's tarnished little Mrs. Lewis, who were most easily blandished, who fell in love with their suitors, believed their promises, and were soon despised and abandoned.

There was nothing about Susannah Arne's earnest and melancholy character, her pious upbringing, or her curiously exalted view of her worth that prepared her to deal with these highborn and rapacious suitors. Though they might regard her as a harlot and fair game, she felt herself to be a lady by right of taste, sensibility, and education. The only defense she had against their bold overtures was her characteristic suppliant smile, a response in which her admirers only saw proof of her artfulness.

When they had nothing substantial to report, the gossip columns in eighteenth-century London dailies were padded with fictional episodes in the lives of prominent people. For some time items had appeared stating that "little Miss A—— of the Haymarket had

*Theophilus Cib-
ber, Comedian,
In the Character
of a Fine
Gentleman.*

*Susannah
Maria Arne,
by Thomas
Worlidge,
ca. 1733.*

left Lord B's chambers three nights together at a late hour in a closed chair," or that "Lady S was hastening back to London from her country seat because of rumors concerning her husband and a certain singer, Miss A——." Susannah, literal, humorless, was filled with a growing panic. And well she might be, her father gloomily agreed. Every rumor, no matter how ill founded, eroded the value of an unmarried woman. How long did Susannah suppose Mr. Cibber would wait while her fame was smirched in gentlemen's clubs, in coffeehouses, and the press?

Romance was in the air in London in March 1734. The King's favorite child, Anne, the Princess Royal, had been engaged for five long months to the ailing Prince of Orange, and it looked as if the wedding was at last going to occur. All winter the theaters had been performing special entertainments in celebration of the imminent nuptials, but the wedding had been put off so long that the original entertainments had been concluded and a second round begun. Susannah had already sung in her brother's wedding masque at the Haymarket, and now, at Drury Lane, with Henry Peter as Cupid, she sang Venus again in Tom's new *Love and Honor*.

On March 21, when the performance was over, still dressed as the goddess of love, she allowed Theophilus to declare his love for her. What she replied no one knows, but the day after they were betrothed.

The bride's father was effulgent. The groom's father was speechless with disgust. The bride's mother hurried to the Sardinian chapel to pray for her daughter's strength to preserve her spirit and her virtue in what seemed a catastrophic undertaking. Then she paid a call on her brother, Charles Wheeler, a surgeon. There were no male Arnes — certainly not her spouse or her strange, cynical elder son — whom she could trust. She wanted to see if there were not some way in which Susannah's salary and whatever she might earn in the future could be kept out of the hands of her husband and preserved for her use or the benefit of any children born of the union. Together, Susannah's mother and uncle consulted an attorney who drew up some rather extraordinary prenuptial articles, which with trepidation they showed to old Arne. To their relief he viewed the articles with approval. No matter how vociferously he might defend the coming marriage, he was aware that during Theo's previous marriage creditors had regularly appeared on every Drury Lane payday and appropriated all of Janey Cibber's salary.

According to this proposed contract, Charles Wheeler and a certain Goodwin Washbourne, wire dancer, were to be executors of a trust under which they were to draw Susannah's £200 salary (or however much more she eventually made), invest £100 of it in government securities, and turn what was left over to Susannah for her "*sole* and *separate* use." In the event that Susannah died without issue her estate was to go to her father or, if he were dead, to her mother. Should children be alive at Susannah's death, the trust was to be continued by Washbourne and Wheeler, and disbursed when the sons were twenty-one and the daughters eighteen. Only if Susannah's parents were both deceased and she left no children could her estate go to Theophilus.[6]

Perhaps the most extraordinary thing about these prenuptial articles, in an era when a wife's property was unequivocally her husband's, was that Theophilus signed them. He was in love, and he meant to have Susannah even if it meant forswearing her salary. Still it is doubtful whether Theophilus was so far gone in love that he could not see that there were advantages for him in this trust. For whereas in his first marriage his creditors had helped themselves to Janey's wages, so that practically no cash reached home, under this arrangement £100 a year of Susannah's (and more, no doubt, as he managed and developed her career) was legally hers, "sole and separate," and quite out of any creditor's grasp. And where would his docile bride choose to spend her unencumbered money if not on her husband's comforts? Theophilus was old enough to recall how easily his father had gotten his hands on the large Shore estate left to his mother in an airtight will. If it should seem advisable at a later date to question this irregular prenuptial trust, there were ways, no doubt, of doing it. But, for the moment, Theophilus was delighted to oblige the anxious Arnes, and the prenuptial articles were signed on April 20, the day before their wedding.

Their marriage took place before a priest, with all the Arnes and Theo's sisters in attendance, including the swashbuckling Charlotte, who had stayed behind at the Little Haymarket to try her hand at the art of stage management. The Poet Laureate did not grace the nuptials.

The *Grub Street Journal*, always interested in the doings of the Cibbers, produced an epithalamium "On the joyous Occasion of Mr C———r's marriage to Miss A-ne."

> How Happy, bright Cibber are all thy Inventions!
> What constant Success always crowns thy Pretentions!
> If you write, play or court; either Father or Son
> By no Soul but Yourselves can be ever outdone.
> Now all your out-doings are out-done indeed,
> Since your glorious Design on Miss A-ne did succeed!

The bride's mother watched the young couple with prayerful apprehension, her father with jubilance, and the groom's father washed his hands of them. But the London public greeted the news of their marriage as a huge joke — a union between Bottom and Titania, Vulcan and Venus — and waited complacently for the curtain to go up on the first, no doubt scandalous, act of the inevitable rift.

6

THE lavish way the young Cibbers set up housekeeping, and the effusive expressions of affection which passed between them in public, were the first things to attract comment: "One could often behold the new-married pair, in all the splendor and gaiety imaginable, their equipage continually running between their town house and country seat. Nor could they, so great was their fondness, keep it within the bounds usually practiced by other married couples. Their fond Endearments would frequently break in upon their serious Conversations, and their Entertainments at Table were often larded with the most passionate Expressions of Love."[1]

Theo's displays of bliss were quite in character. Without the corroboration of an audience's reaction he had little way of knowing what he was feeling, or even if he were feeling anything at all. Susannah's cooperation in prodigality is puzzling though. There is a hectic quality about these first years of her marriage, as if she were desperately attempting to merge her own personality and taste with her husband's.

She became pregnant almost at once, and only sang sporadically, forfeiting her £200 salary and her benefit night. From the beginning of her marriage, therefore, the trust agreement with her Uncle Charles and Mr. Washbourne was never in effect. There was no £100 to put into government bonds, and Theo, with Susannah's acquiescence, pocketed the few pounds she earned. On the whole, Theo treated her with a deference and solicitude quite unlike his behavior to Janey: she was permitted at least a partial retirement during her pregnancy, and after the baby girl was born and died in February 1735, Susannah did not appear the rest of the season.

Aside from the death of their firstborn, his marriage to Susannah was as blessed a condition as Theophilus could have dreamed of. Though her income was curtailed for the moment, she was as docile and submissive as Janey, and her refined ways, her French phrases, her beautiful voice with its genteel accent were all a great step up from Janey's street manners. Meanwhile, at the theater, Theophilus found his new employer tractable and ingenuous. Fleetwood neither begrudged Theo's requisitions for new scenes and costumes nor inquired into expenses. He allowed Theo full discretion in the choice of plays, and during the 1734–35 season, Theo undertook no less than four new works.

Backstage at Drury Lane, the atmosphere was a perpetual levee. Night and day Fleetwood played host to rakes and dandies, who hobnobbed with the players and flirted with the actresses. The new patentee not only sponsored sociability behind the scenes but gaming, and was kindness itself about extending credit to his dazzled actors, who sat down to wager with noblemen with twenty times their income. Sometimes, it was true, payday at Drury Lane came and went, and Fleetwood, blushingly referring to vague, temporary convulsions in the great financial world outside the theater, was unable to meet his players' salaries. But so many of them were in debt to him that they could not complain, and so melting was the squire's charm that it was almost a pleasure to favor him with waiting.

One might have thought that Theo Cibber would have been content at last, what with his wife's affection at home, Fleetwood's permissiveness at work, and the atmosphere of easy licentiousness at the theater. But young Cibber was soon as dissatisfied as he had been in Highmore's day. Under his nose were two formidable rivals, neither of them members of the original Drury Lane troupe, but protégés of Fleetwood. One was Charles Macklin, the Irish actor Highmore had brought to London to bolster the remnant Drury Lane company during the mutiny, and the other was James Quin.

The previous March, when the mutineers had returned to their old home and Theophilus had resumed his former roles and powers, Macklin had assumed that his chances at Drury Lane were dim and prepared to return to the provinces. But Fleetwood had cajoled him into staying and putting up with insignificant parts, holding out the promise of eventual advancement and a chance to direct. He implied that Theo's position was not inviolate, nor beyond the aspiration of others.

Macklin was proud, moody, impulsive, and unpredictable, and Fleetwood liked the challenge this black Irishman offered to his own ability to charm and soothe. Macklin quickly developed an almost slavish affection for Fleetwood. At night, when the cards were put away in the green room and the theater locked, Fleetwood liked to throw an arm across his "dear Mac's" shoulder and carry him off to White's Club for another game.

As if Macklin were not enough for Theophilus to bear — lean and hungry, petted by Fleetwood, greatly talented, and waiting an opportunity to show his skills — there was the colossal presence of James Quin to be reckoned with.

The huge and arrogant Quin (1693–1766) was, sans pareil, the most distinguished actor in London. Over the summer Fleetwood had beguiled him (with an offer of £500 a year, or twice what any other player in England was earning) to leave John Rich for whom he had been working for sixteen years. Quin had not only been Rich's leading player, but he had directed most of the serious dramas at Covent Garden. In the fall of 1734, Theophilus found that his seemingly feckless and innocent new master had placed two men in the theater who were not only more exciting actors than he, but competent to supplant him in his role of managing.

No sooner had Quin moved into the largest tiring room at Drury Lane, bringing his valet, his stage wardrobe, and his retinue of fashionable admirers, than he made it clear he would not tolerate a word of direction from Theophilus, nor even a suggestion. Theo promptly challenged him to a duel, but Quin refused to fight. To close in combat with such a base person, he had Theophilus informed by an underling, was in itself an ignominious act, "like shitting on a Toad."[2]

Theophilus Cibber was not the only person at Drury Lane to be discomfited by Quin's arrival. John and William Mills, who had succeeded to many of Booth's and Wilks's capital parts, had to give up to him such plums as Cato and Volpone. And it was a cruel wrench for John Harper to relinquish Falstaff, a role with which he strongly identified and which had made him a beloved London figure offstage as well as on. For years Harper's and Quin's rival Falstaffs had been passionately compared and defended by their supporters at the two theaters royal. Now that Quin was at Drury Lane, the highest taste decreed that Harper's Falstaff was funnier but Quin's was the "more judicious."[3] The Georgian audience, coarse by instinct but genteel by aspiration, accepted without question that a Falstaff who moved them to yawns and tears must be of a higher order than Harper's "low" interpretation. And so Harper, hero of the theatrical mutiny of 1734, was the next year stripped of his knightly title and perquisites. From this date on "this lusty fat man with a countenance expressive of much mirth and jollity"[4] began to pine and dwindle, to lose his immense appetite and with it his girth. He was reduced to smaller and thinner parts, which he performed less and less roundly, and he died in a few years, lank and destitute — this former wealthy householder and genial host — "of a fever of his spirits."[5]

If Macklin and Quin confounded Theophilus by ignoring him and treating only with Fleetwood, they had too much mutual respect to ignore each other. A state of war existed between them: for Quin the defense of his vast, theatrical territories; for Macklin, who possessed hardly an acre of this kind of property, the guerrilla harassment of Quin's borders.

Quin, an indolent monolith of a man, was, when his dresser had laced him into his tunic and secured the traditional plumes of tragedy atop his ringleted wig, inclined to do little more than pace portentously onto the stage, strike an attitude from which he verged very little in a scene, and open his mouth. From this orifice emerged the

James Quin as Coriolanus, ca. 1749.

most soronous voice of the age, whose lightest fricatives could curl
and lick around the posts of the last gallery. The accuracy of Quin's
inflection, the richness of his tone, the justness of his pauses, the
economy of his presence seem to have paralyzed opposition and put
him beyond criticism. Frederick, Prince of Wales, appointed him
elocution master to the royal children. And Handel, Quin's great
friend, scrupulously attended (and regularly slept through) every
performance of *Cato*, but would not permit a word of criticism of the
man who he maintained was the greatest actor in the world.

When Macklin, who was as molten as Quin was granitic, was
performing a minor role with him, he used to stalk and prowl and
dart about the stage behind Quin's back inventing much distracting
business and drawing titters from the audience. One night Quin,

maddened by Macklin's "damned tricks," roared off the stage in pursuit, shouting that there was "no having a chaste scene"[6] with him. Cornered in the green room, Macklin leaped at Quin's throat, forced him back into a chair, and was choking him when he was pulled off by those standing near. At this point Fleetwood came in, "all kindness, all mildness and affability"[7] as Macklin warmly recalled it years later, soothed Quin, and after the great man and his entourage had withdrawn, led Macklin away to his own house where he gave him supper and a good bottle, spoke again of Macklin's future at Drury Lane if he would only keep his temper and trust him, and finally tucked him into bed in his own guest chamber lest the two Irishmen meet again in some bagnio or tavern before a night's sleep had cooled their brains.

In May 1735 the tension at Drury Lane erupted into fatal violence. The victim was neither Quin nor Macklin, loathsome Cibber nor seductive Fleetwood, but an unlucky minor player who chanced to receive the point of Macklin's long-contained frustration.

At eight o'clock on May 10, Quin was on the stage declaiming the final act of *Cato* before a drowsy and respectful audience. In the green room backstage, the actors of the afterpiece, a farce called *Trick for Trick*, were sitting in their costumes, warming their hands before the fire. Little Henry Peter Arne was there, dressed in girl's clothes as Estifania, "a deformed little creature." Next to him on the bench sat Thomas Hallam, who was to play Guzman, wearing a black, greasy wig he had taken from the wardrobe room. It was the sort of wig suitable for misers, Jews, Spaniards, cuckolds, misanthropes, and other villainous or disgusting comic types. Old Thomas Arne, who had just finished his accounts and turned them in to his son-in-law at the property office, came in and sat down in a chair to one side of the hearth.

Suddenly, Charles Macklin, who was to play Sancho in the farce, stalked into the room and glared about. When he saw Hallam he exclaimed, "Damn you for a rogue, what business have you got with my wig?"

"I am no more a rogue than yourself," Hallam retorted. "It's a stock wig, and I have as much right to it as you have."[8]

At the urging of the other actors who knew Macklin's temper,

Hallam took off the wig and handed it sullenly to Macklin. But "the mad Irishman," as Quin liked to call him, was unplaced, and someone, sensing trouble, slipped out to find young Mr. Cibber who was in charge of the theater that night in Fleetwood's absence. The longer Macklin sat and held the wig, turning and combing it, the more the injustice of his lot at Drury Lane welled inside him. The most gifted actor there, he had had to submit all year to trivial parts, to Cibber's insolence, to Quin's condescension, and now, to-night, he could be slighted without fear of consequence by a third-rate player who had appropriated a wig that everyone knew Macklin had been wearing for several nights. "God damn you for a black-guard," he suddenly burst out. "Scrub! Rascal! How durst you have the impudence to take this wig?"

"I am no more a rascal than you," retorted Hallam, whereupon Macklin picked up a stick from near the fire and lunged. Hallam, half turning at that unlucky moment, caught the point in his left eye. Macklin pulled the stick back and threw it in the fire while Hallam, his hand clapped over his face, groaned that the stick had gone into his head and that his eye was put out.

"No," Macklin protested, pulling Hallam's hand away and put-ting his own over the lid. "I feel the ball roll under my hand."[9]

Hallam turned to Henry Peter Arne, who sat dumbstruck next to him in his girl's dress: "Whip up your cloathes, you little bitch and urine in my eye!"[10] (In the eighteenth century spittle and urine were regarded as vital fluids and sovereign remedies for wounds.) The poor boy was too terrified to be able to accommodate him, so Macklin himself obliged his victim.

At this point, Theophilus Cibber bustled in, cleared the room, called for Mr. Coldham, the surgeon, told the actors of the farce to take their places on the stage, and found somebody to read Hallam's part. And Macklin, who could still not believe he had done Hallam serious harm, put on the disputed oily wig and played Sancho. When, however, he returned backstage at the end of the performance and saw Hallam, "now in shocking condition, he thought proper to retire out of the top of the Play House, and make his escape over the London roofs," as *The Craftsman* reported.

THOMAS HALLAM,

No matter how grim the reality, the London public could find something false, absurd, and amusing in the lives (or deaths) of players. Thomas Hallam, here shown totally bald, bows to an imaginary audience beneath a bright stage chandelier, and simpering obsequiously, prepares to die in defense of a greasy wig.

Hallam died the following evening and Fleetwood, to whom Macklin had sent word of his hiding place, went to him and persuaded him to come back and stand trial for murder, promising him every help money and influence could buy. He was as good as his word. Thanks to Fleetwood's securing his bail, Macklin never spent a night in jail, and at the trial the patentee testified feelingly of Macklin's lack of malice toward Hallam before the fatal accident and of the high degree of provocation in Hallam's appropriating a part of a costume that, even though it was theatrical stock, Macklin had been wearing and needed for a part.

Thomas Arne, Senior, testified for the prosecution, and his deposition is our last glimpse of him before his death in 1736. Quin testified for Macklin's defense. He might often have wanted to kill him, but when he saw a fellow player struggling in the talons of the law, he knew where his loyalties lay. Appearing as a character witness, Quin vouched for Macklin's "peaceable disposition," an interesting opinion from a man whom Macklin had tried to choke to death with his bare hands. But Quin had elastic standards for peaceability: in his youth, before he became fat, rich, and indolent, he had killed two men in duels.

The outcome of Macklin's trial was that the charge of murder was reduced to manslaughter and Macklin was freed after a token branding on his hand with a cool iron. Eleven other defendants who stood with him that day at old Bailey were not so fortunate. All were sentenced to death: one had made off with a velvet hood, one had stolen a gelding, one man had taken a guinea.[11]

Significantly, Theophilus Cibber was not asked to be a witness at Macklin's trial, though he had been in charge of the theater the night of Hallam's injury. By the time the trial occurred, in December 1735, Theo was on the outs with Fleetwood and the patentee's friends. He was behaving just as he had under Highmore: rankling because Drury Lane was not his own, and trying to inflame the players to secede. This time he proposed setting up operations at Lincoln's Inn Fields, which had a larger seating capacity than the Little Haymarket and would support them better. Once more he sent swarms of anonymous letters to the press signed "X.Y.," or "Well Wisher," decrying the situation at Drury Lane where free men of genius must work to fatten the purse of a profligate, incompetent, amateur patentee.

Alas, the London public proved apathetic, and the players, who had regarded the rectitudinous Highmore as a tyrant (though he eked out their salaries in full from his own private pocket), thought merry Fleetwood (who owed them all money) the most agreeable master in the world.

When he failed to foment a mutiny on the grounds of Fleetwood's incompetence, Theo attacked his employer in another area. Fleetwood's finances, he whispered, were in such straits that the theater was soon to be mortgaged and all the actors thrown out of work.

But the players, who every day saw the bright form of their master, his person exuding an ambience of good wine and goodwill, refused to panic.

In the late spring, however, after a particularly convivial week, Fleetwood was confined to bed with an attack of gout. In his absence Cibber spread the word that the patentee was not ill, but lurking within doors to avoid his creditors. Fleetwood's friends, Theo added, were hurrying about London, liquidating such assets as they could, to give him cash to escape to France, leaving his estate in shambles, his theater in receivership, his actors unpaid.

There was enough truth in Theo's assertions — the players had heard rumblings from other sources — so that if Fleetwood's absence had continued they might have been prevailed upon to take some sort of impulsive action against their master. As it happened, Fleetwood's gout subsided and as soon as he appeared at the theater, rosy and benevolent as ever, he settled the dust of fear that Theo had stirred up.

Fleetwood did not fire Theophilus, though he knew all about his seditious activities. Harsh scenes and cashierings were not Fleetwood's way. Theophilus simply found that the light of his employer's countenance had been withdrawn from him. First of all, Fleetwood countermanded his earlier permission to let Theo manage a summer company, on the grounds that there were so many new productions planned for the fall that the players must attend to rehearsals.[12] This was an enormous blow to Cibber, who had already promised his creditors the extra money he would make. Fleetwood next took upon himself the reading and selecting of new plays, depriving Theophilus of the power he enjoyed over a host of would-be authors, who sued for his attention and made him many a gift. And when the fall rehearsals began, Theo discovered that no longer was he to receive £50 a year as "Bustle-Master General"[13] of the forces at Drury Lane. He was now to share directorial authority, with Quin supervising the tragedies and he the comedies, at a small bonus per play. Even this last remaining prerogative might be taken away if Macklin's murder case (still pending that fall) turned out well.

Colley Cibber was alarmed about his son's career, and particularly his finances. He made it a rule never to relieve his children's financial embarrassments even if they were in jail, as Theophilus and Charlotte sometimes were. But he had no objection to giving them advice as to ways in which they could rehabilitate themselves. And now as he scrutinized his son's situation, his gaze lingered on the delicate figure of his daughter-in-law, whom he had ignored since the marriage. Susannah had not seriously worked for more than a year, enjoying all this while as many indulgences pertaining to her pregnancy, her lying-in, and her grief over the death of her infant as if she were a vaporish princess of the blood. Clearly, the first thing to do to get Theo's affairs in order was to put Susannah back in harness. Colley had specific suggestions about her career. He did not care much for her voice. It was too small, too low, too mournful, too limited in range and variety. He much preferred the high, penetrating, sharp-sweet quality of Kitty Clive, whose every note carried over the noisy pit and who could make you split your sides one minute in a bawdy ballad, and weep the next in a lament.

Here are Colley's own recollections about his daughter-in-law:

> I thought her voice not the best, and if not best, 'tis nothing. I thought it might possibly do better for speaking. I asked her husband if he had ever heard her speak a part; he said he had, and that she did it very prettily. I tried her and was surprised to find her do it so well. . . . I believe I was the person who chiefly instructed her. I spent a great deal of time and took great delight in it, for she was very capable of receiving instruction. In forty years experience that I have known the stage, I never knew a woman so capable of the business or improve so fast.[14]

Her father-in-law's sudden interest in her, the hours of instruction at his house on Russell Street were the best tonic in the world for Susannah after her baby's death. Just as she had melted Handel's rage when he heard her sing, she was winning over her father-in-law, that most worldly, most critical of men. The pleasing of difficult, finical men was one of Susannah's most gratifying skills.

As soon as Colley was certain of the vein of gold he had tapped, and realized that in the willowy person of his daughter-in-law lay the most extraordinary aptitude for projecting emotion he had found in forty years, he set himself to considering how best to mine this ore for his son's benefit.

The uncertain road by which actresses reached preeminence, the long route of nurses, confidantes, and jealous sisters was too slow for Susannah. Theo's debts could not wait. His wife's career must be meteoric and lucrative. Her debut must be in a major part. But neither Colley nor Theophilus would have dreamed of asking Fleetwood to take any hard-won capital role from one of his established actresses. "The possession of parts," as George Anne Bellamy put it, "was considered as much the property of performers as their weekly salaries." Actors might *give* a role to another player, and public opinion sometimes pressed for a change (as in the case of Quin, Harper, and Falstaff), but no manager in his right mind would take a major part from a popular actress and give it to an untried ingenue.

The solution was for Susannah to appear in a new play, whose roles were nobody's property. But new vehicles suffered a high mortality rate. If Susannah were admired but the play failed after a night she would hardly be launched as an actress of importance. There was a new play, though, *Zara*, which had an exalted advance reputation and every chance of success.

Poor John Highmore had agreed to produce *Zara* at Drury Lane back in 1733, but in the chaos of his brief tenure it had never been put into rehearsal or even cast. It was a translation of Voltaire's *Zaire*, by Aaron Hill, Handel's friend. When Highmore had been unable to bring *Zara* out, some of Hill's admirers had hired the Great Hall on Villiers Street and put on several private performances. These had been attended by London society and bluestocking ladies, who, having already read *Zaire* aloud to one another in French, pronounced its English version chaste, elevating, and indescribably moving.

How different was this new play in which the Cibbers proposed to display Theo's second wife from *Caelia*, that gamy tragedy in which Theo had featured Janey, great with child! That was a play whose coarse, comic brothel scenes had drawn snickers from the vulgar and shudders from the fastidious. *Zara* dealt with the delicate distresses of a young noblewoman as she chooses between the conflicting loyalties of religion, family duty, and romantic love. There was not a line of bawdry in it.

No sooner had Colley Cibber let Hill hear Susannah read than Hill enthusiastically agreed she should be Zara. Her youth, her inexperience, her malleability were the qualities he especially liked about her. No bad habits had corrupted her. Hill had a passionate desire to reform the British stage. Just as he had always hoped that Handel might deliver England from the bondage of Italian opera, he had been crying out against the bombination of British tragedians. He called Bridgewater and Quin "ranters and whiners" and pleaded for a pure, English, "natural" style. In Susannah Cibber this theatrical theorist recognized (as had her brother and Handel, Lampe, Carey, and Colley Cibber) the perfect pupil, a bending reed, a tabula rasa.

When Colley Cibber saw Hill's enthusiasm he graciously withdrew from his daughter-in-law's dramatic education and turned her over to Hill. He left the public promotion of her career up to his son.

It was not easy to persuade Fleetwood to permit the production of *Zara*. Fortunately, the new patentee was uncomfortably aware that his predecessor had bespoken *Zara* for Drury Lane, and that many people felt that he, Fleetwood, had inherited an obligation toward it. For the last year Hill had been writing articles in his magazine, *The Prompter,* about the perfidy of patentees. It was certainly the pressure of this and no desire to favor Theophilus that persuaded Fleetwood to agree.

When *Zara* went into rehearsal, Theophilus assumed the supervision of the production, except that Hill was personally coaching Susannah. Hill believed that the art of acting could be "reduced into principles." He drew up a list of the ten "expressible" passions, with directions as to how, by the opening or narrowing of the eyelids, by the clenching or loosening of the jaw muscles, by the length and rapidity of strides upon the stage, and by the combination of these elements, each passion could be "correctly" rendered. "Every passion," he explained, "has its peculiar and appropriate Look, and every Look enforces . . . a particular Tone . . . and a consequent Modification of the Body. When the Heart has communicated its

Sensation to the Eye, every Muscle and dependent Nerve, catching Impulse, must concur."[15]

Hill took Susannah's working copy of *Zara* and in a shorthand of asterisks, dashes, brackets, and underlines indicated every breath, every pause, every variation in volume and pitch, every gesture and every motion. This method, which one would expect to suffocate a young actress, was utterly congenial to Susannah. In just this sort of close, exacting, devoted imitation had the happiest hours of her life been passed. Thus, as a young girl with a faultless ear, had she perfected a French accent that brought homesick tears to her tutor's eye; thus had she memorized her brother's songs and Lampe's; thus had Handel taught her, "with all the drudgery of repetition necessary to undergo in teaching persons more by ear than by the eye."[16] Susannah learned each line of *Zara* as if it were a foreign language or a phrase of music.

Theophilus was delighted with what he overheard going on between his wife and Hill. Susannah intoned her lines, sometimes in a slow, thrilling plaint, sometimes in rapidly dying and swelling peals. It was not quite like anything he had heard before, though closest to the recitatives of Italian opera; but Theo had been too many years in the sentimental Georgian theater not to recognize the inimitable quality of pathos.

There was only one alarming development. Hill insisted that the romantic male lead, Osman, be played by his nephew, a young man who had never acted in his life. Though he had been applying his dramatic methods to young Hill, the result, unlike Susannah's alchemy, was a stupefying singsong. Theo appealed to Fleetwood to insist that a strong professional play opposite Susannah — Milward was his choice. Fleetwood refused to interfere. *Zara* was Hill's and Cibber's enterprise. All he asked was to be quit of an annoying obligation and not to lose money in the process.

So young Hill remained in the cast, though the rest of it was Theo's selection: Milward was Lusignan, he himself was Nerestan, and the sturdy, clarion-voiced Mrs. Pritchard was Selina, Zara's confidante. New scenes and costumes were ordered, and Tom Arne was commissioned to write an overture, a march, and entr'acte music.

Theophilus thought it would be a good thing for Susannah,

before undertaking *Zara,* to have the experience of at least one small speaking part. Chloe, in Henry Fielding's farce *The Lottery,* seemed ideal. It was mostly a singing role, which would put Susannah at her ease. And he would be there to support her in one of his favorite parts, Chloe's scoundrel husband, Jack Stock, who sells his wife to a wealthy man in return for the settlement of his crushing debts.

Fielding had written Jack Stock for Theo and Chloe for Kitty Clive, and they had played these parts at Drury Lane since 1732. *The Lottery* was so insignificant, a mere afterpiece, that Theo did not believe its appropriation as a warm-up exercise for Susannah could give any offense to Kitty, who had more capital roles than she could handle in a season. He was mistaken. Kitty was furious. As jealous as she was generous, she might have given away this trivial part to a young actress she was fond of, but she detested Theophilus and she felt no affinity toward the genteel second wife whom he treated so differently from poor Janey and now was pushing over the heads of hardworking actresses.

Theo did not take Kitty's wrath seriously. She had no real influence, no man in the theater to champion her disputes except her brother, Jemmy Raftor, a weak player who was his sister's lackey. Colley Cibber, however, who had been keeping an eye on the fortunes of *Zara,* regarded Kitty's feelings in earnest. He had dealt adroitly with actresses for forty years and he understood how important, not for moral, but for practical reasons, was the peace of mind, the esprit, and the mutual trust of a troupe of repertory players. When Aaron Hill asked him to write the prologue and epilogue for *Zara* — no new play was considered decently launched without these — Colley wrote the caustic epilogue for Kitty Clive. Since epilogues were entrusted to the most esteemed and popular players in the company, this was an effective placating gesture. Kitty Clive accepted the honor. But her suspicions against the young Cibbers were not allayed. At the next incursion into her theatrical rights by Susannah she resolved to declare war.

Colley wrote the prologue of *Zara* for Theophilus. If Kitty Clive's epilogue was salty and irreverent — just the effervescent digestif to settle a long oily evening — Theo's prologue was the syrupy plea of a doting husband begging the audience's forbearance toward the first timid steps of his wife.

>   . . . now, the Player
> With trembling heart, proffers his humble prayer.
> Tonight the greatest venture of my life,
> Is lost, or saved, as you receive — a wife:
> If time, you think, may ripen her to merit,
> With gentle smiles, support her wavering spirit:
>   . . .
> Her unskilled tongue would simple Nature speak
> Nor dares her bounds, for false applauses, break.
> Amidst a thousand faults, her best pretense
> To please — is unpresuming innocence.
> When a chaste heart's distress your grief demands,
> One silent tear out-weighs a thousand hands.
> If she conveys the pleasing passions right,
> Guard and support her, this decisive night.
> If she mistakes, or finds her strength too small
> Let interposing pity break her fall.
> In you it rests, to save her or destroy,
> If she draws tears from you, I weep — for Joy!

Theo had strong reason to press for *Zara*'s opening in early January. Susannah was expecting another child. If *Zara* succeeded the public would want to see her in other roles and Fleetwood would be obliged to give her a benefit night. But all this lucrative activity would have to be squeezed in before her lying-in in April.

Susannah was pale, melancholy, and apprehensive. She had not had enough milk for her first baby and she would have liked to rest before this one. She would have been happy to go on with her dramatic lessons and put off *Zara* until the baby came, but she yielded to her husband's will. She was remaining very slender. Indeed, as her pregnancy advanced she seemed to be losing weight, and an audience would have no difficulty seeing her as the frail virgin, Zara. Her pallor, her tautness, her great beseeching eyes gave her every day more of the drawn and anguished look of the high-souled, sore-beset

Zara. ("Cibber, Sir, seemed to *need* your tears from the delicacy of her frame.")

Pressed by Theo, Tom Arne had his music ready by the first of January, though the dresses were not stitched nor the scenes painted. Playbills were posted, puffs sent to the papers, and after being put off once for January 9, *Zara* was definitely announced for January 12, 1736.

7

For 14 consecutive nights Susannah drowned houses in tears, and stirred the very depth of men's hearts, even her husband's, who was so affected that he claimed and obtained the doubling of her salary.
— DORAN, *Annals of the English Stage*

THE Cibbers were rarely wrong in their judgment of public taste, but they had underestimated Susannah's impact as a tragic actress.

There was only one flaw with opening night, and that was Aaron Hill's nephew. While the audience wept over Susannah, they hissed young Hill, who played her lover. His uncle's acting methods had not succeeded; in fact, the only successful pupil in Aaron Hill's life was Susannah Cibber. Moments before curtain time on the second night young Hill balked at going on stage again before a hostile audience. There was nothing for it but to have Theophilus appear before the curtain and beg permission for Osman's part to be read so that those who had bought tickets to see Mrs. Cibber would not be disappointed. Osman was read by various actors for a week until William Mills had memorized the role, and took it over on January 19.

The Osman incident was not without precedent. The chief pleasure of the Georgian playgoer lay not in witnessing a balanced and polished production, but in his connoisseurship of performers and performances. He liked to discover new talent, and compare rival interpretations. He went to the theater as he went to the opera (and as we still do), to appreciate brilliant individuals who were often, in the course of things, supported by inferiors whose flawed efforts in no way spoiled the main event.

Zara's receipts were so gratifying that Fleetwood immediately raised Susannah's salary and gave her a £50 bonus. This sum was just what Theophilus had received in former years as deputy manager, and since he took entire credit for his wife's presence at Drury Lane and her success, he appropriated the sum as his own.[1] Fleetwood also gave Theophilus his blessing to prepare Susannah in other roles, providing these did not infringe upon the territory of Mrs. Clive, Mrs. Pritchard, Mrs. Butler, and Mrs. Thurmond.

Two tender heroines were fair game: Amanda in Colley Cibber's *Love's Last Shift,* and Indiana in Richard Steele's *The Conscious Lovers.* Indiana had last been played by Mrs. Heron at Drury Lane, but this lady had recently retired in ill health, and lay on her deathbed. Amanda was one of Mrs. Porter's roles, but Mrs. Porter had defected to Covent Garden this season, forfeiting her Drury Lane parts.

There was a third role Theophilus would have liked for Susannah, one so suitable for her wistful, melting qualities that it might have been written for her. He wanted to revive *The Beggar's Opera* with Susannah as Polly Peachum and Kitty Clive as Lucy Lockit. It was such a fine idea that when he told Fleetwood about it, the manager impulsively ordered Gay's comedy into rehearsal at once.

This was the affront from Theo and Susannah that Kitty Clive had been expecting ever since they took Chloe away from her in *The Lottery.* She had played Polly at Drury Lane several years back, and felt her title to the part was clear. Lucy Lockit, to which Theophilus proposed to relegate her, was a fat and lusty part, but definitely second lead.

On January 27, Kitty placed in the *Daily Journal* the following bit of spite: "We hear that the Beggar's Opera is soon to be acted; the Part of Lucy . . . by Mrs. Clive . . . Polly by Mr. Cibber's Wife, who is to have all the first Parts, having during the Run of *Zara,* shewn her natural Genius by never any one Night varying in either Tone of Voice or Action from the Way she was taught."[2]

This catty picture of Aaron Hill's star pupil suggests how meticulously Susannah had trained, how little in this early part of her career she left to interplay with other actors, and why it was possible for her to move serenely through the first week of *Zara*, playing love scenes with a series of men who walked through the part of Osman with a book in one hand. Unfortunately, Kitty Clive's keen assessment of the limitations of Susannah's intoning style gives us no clue to her emotive power, which unfailingly brought the gentry to tears and the coarser element to open-mouthed awe.

Kitty Clive's resistance to Theo Cibber's *Beggar's Opera* project astonished Fleetwood. For the time being he called off rehearsals, assuring Theo that he would revive the idea in the fall when Mrs. Clive had cooled down. He also took Kitty aside and reminded her that she had never been a successful Polly and could not expect the part to be held sacred to her. Her articles with him, the manager reminded her, required her to play any part he demanded.

In February, after *Zara* closed, Susannah appeared in *The Conscious Lovers,* playing opposite Quin for the first time, with Hannah Pritchard and Kitty Clive in supporting roles. The Prince of Wales and some of his sisters came to see her on February 11, and on March 3 there was a command performance before Their Majesties and all the royal children.

Next came *Love's Last Shift,* whose heroine, Amanda, had special poignancy for Susannah. Amanda was a woman of means, pauperized by her rapacious, vice-loving husband, Loveless. Like Amanda, Susannah had an unfaithful husband, for Theophilus had found soon after marriage that "his constancy to Susannah began to grow troublesome to him, and not being able to confine himself to her, he frequented women of lewd fame, by which means she received an injury which not withstanding she had the temper to conceal in hopes to reclaim him by generosity."[3] Reclaim him by generosity. This indeed was the happy issue of *Love's Last Shift:* for in the final act Loveless, confounded by Amanda's inextinguishable forgiveness and devotion, falls on his knees before her and groans, "Oh, thou hast roused me from my deep lethargy of vice! . . . Thus let me kneel and pay my thanks to her whose conquering virtue has at last subdued me. Here will I fix, thus prostrate sigh my shame, and wash my crimes in never-ceasing tears of penitence."

When Susannah first played Amanda, she was very young, very patient, very perseverant, fully aware of her extraordinary powers to sway, and she had by no means given up hope of regenerating Theophilus. As a wronged wife she was in company with many of the finest ladies in the land. Some of these were the "ladies of quality" at whose "particular desire," as the play bills put it, she played Amanda over and over; a role in which she gave flesh to the sentimental dream which sustained many a lonely duchess, of someday shaming her husband into uxoriousness through guilt and gratitude.

Time was running out before Susannah's second lying-in, but Theo was able to have her ready in another major role, Andromache in *The Distrest Mother,* for his own benefit night on March 23, a wonderfully lucrative occasion at which Susannah's presence netted his creditors much more than he could have earned in any play that featured himself.

The apogee of Theo Cibber's financial season was to be Susannah's benefit on April 13, when she would again play Indiana. Unfortunately, she was delivered of a son on April 5, several weeks before Theophilus had calculated the event. It was his fourth child, and first boy. Even Colley, with his huge family of whining daughters and hungry granddaughters, was delighted, and the baby was named Caius-Gabriel after the Laureate's father, a distinguished sculptor and architect.

Susannah's confinement put an end to her appearing at her own benefit, and Theo substituted *The Alchemist* in place of *The Conscious Lovers.* Abel Drugger was one of his most popular roles. He published a notice in the *Daily Advertizer* to remind his wife's admirers that *The Alchemist* was nevertheless *her* benefit:

Yesterday, Mrs Cibber, wife of Theophilus Cibber, Comedian, was safely brought to bed of a son at her House in Great Queen Street by Lincoln's Inn Field: She is as well as can be expected; but her present Condition not permitting her to play on her Benefit Night as she proposed, She is obliged to change the Play, and Tickets given out for *The Conscious Lovers* will be taken for *The Alchemist*. And we have been desired further to inform the Town, as she is prevented paying her Duty to the Ladies of Quality, etc. in Person, as she intended, she relies entirely on their Candor and Good Nature, humbly hoping the Occasion will plead her Excuse and that she shall nevertheless be honored with their Appearance on her Benefit Night which will be next Tuesday the 13th Instant.

The style of this puff is peculiarly Cibberian, unctuous and confidential, suggesting Mrs. Cibber's personal intimacy with "ladies of quality." None of the other Drury Lane ingenues presumed such a tone in their public notices, and Theo's methods certainly contributed to Susannah's unpopularity with other actresses. The truth is, however, that even after her separation from Theophilus, Susannah's relations with them were cool. She felt sincerely that her calling was of a higher order than that of other ladies of the stage. They were entertainers, descended from a line of jugglers, dancers, and courtesans. She was something new: a priestess of sensibility.

On April 16 little Caius-Gabriel died, Susannah's second loss in fourteen months. She was too disconsolate to play again until summer, when she was persuaded to appear in two command performances before the Prince of Wales and his bride. Susannah's appeal to people of rank and fashion had convinced Theophilus that there was more profit in developing her career than in pressing his own. After sixteen years of wooing the public, Theo still was not taken seriously as a playwright or an actor. And the class of people who found Theo most contemptible made up his wife's most ardent admirers.

In August he began pressing Charles Fleetwood again about reviving *The Beggar's Opera* and found the manager more reluctant than before. Of all the women in Fleetwood's house Mrs. Clive was the greatest moneymaker. She was obdurate about giving up Polly, and if forced to do so said she would leave Drury Lane and sign with John Rich at the expiration of her articles. There were plenty of parts for Susannah, Fleetwood said: the deceased Mrs. Heron's, for instance. And Mrs. Thurmond, who was getting along in years, had just now relinquished Desdemona to Susannah of her own volition,[4] so that one of Drury Lane's first major productions this fall could be *Othello* with Quin as the Moor. Fleetwood did not believe that the young Cibbers had any complaints about Susannah's treatment, and though he too would have liked to do *The Beggar's Opera*, he had no wish to stir Clive up. Stirring people up was Theophilus Cibber's genius though, and, failing to prod Fleetwood into challenging the she-dragon, he decided to take a sword to her himself.

The one thing which would force Kitty to capitulate would be public outrage against her intransigence, and a demand to see Susannah as Polly. In order to help this unvoiced public demand materialize, Theophilus turned to his favorite activity, writing anonymous letters to the press. His first letter, signed "A. Z.," in the *Daily Advertizer* of November 12, singled out Mrs. Clive as the reason London was being deprived of its pleasure in seeing Gay's comedy. Fleetwood, A. Z. reported, had

> thought Mrs Cibber's Talents being particularly tuned for the tender and pathetic, she might properly be cast to the Part of Polly, while Mrs Clive, who being excellent for Arch, Pert and Smart, must certainly make the best Lucy his Company could produce. . . . Mrs Cibber never did desire the Part of Polly, but though it was thought proper for her by the Manager . . . she always confessed a Diffidence. Mrs Clive first appeared in this Character . . . in a Summer Season, and when there was not other Diversion to entertain the Town. . . . It had a tolerable Run at a Time when Audiences are not very critical . . . [but] it was the Opinion of the best Judges that she did not fit the Part of Polly; for from her own Turn of Nature she was rather Arch than Innocent, and a genuine Smartness which she could not conceal destroyed the Effect of the fond Simplicity for which Polly is distinguished. . . . I should reasonably conclude, as before mentioned, that her natural Fire, Vivacity and Spirit would more properly adapt her for the contrast Character of Lucy.

From early last spring until the present, A. Z. confided, Mrs. Clive had refused to surrender Polly. A. Z. commended Fleetwood's long-suffering "Candour and Tenderness" toward this lady, and praised the manager's suggestion that the rivals "play the Parts of Polly and

Lucy alternately," letting the town judge their merits. In view of Mrs. Clive's obduracy, A. Z. asked his readers, "If an Actress will hear no Reason, is a Manager to be a Slave to her Obstinacies?"

Mrs. Clive's rebuttal appeared in the *Daily Advertizer* on November 18. She made it clear she knew the identity of "A. Z." "I am extremely sorry," she began,

> to make Publick a Dispute which has happened behind the Scenes. . . . The Injuries I have received at the Play House I determined patiently to submit to, well knowing that by the Tenour of the Articles which I have unfortunately signed with Mr Fleetwood, I could not possibly receive any Redress until . . . these Articles . . . expired. . . . By my Articles it is not in my Power to refuse any Part: But that I have shewn an Unwillingness to surrender my own Part of Polly and to act the inferior Part of Lucy, I confess is true. . . . This Unwillingness did not proceed from my Jealousy of Mrs Cibber, or from any Intent of mine to obstruct the Progress of her Merit: no; the true and only Reason is this: not only the Part of Polly, but likewise other Parts . . . have been demanded of me for Mrs Cibber, which made me conclude . . . There was a design formed against me to deprive me by Degrees of every Part in which I had the Happiness to appear with any Reputation. . . .
>
> But since this idle Quarrel has made so much Noise and there has been so much said already to the Publick, I here declare that if Mr Fleetwood think fit to new cast the Beggar's Opera, to give Polly from me to Mrs Cibber and force me into that of Lucy, or make us alternately play them, I cannot without incurring the Penalty of my Articles refuse to acquiesce. . . .
>
> As to the ill Qualities of Envy, Malice, etc. with which I am charged (as I doubt not but Every one who reads that letter must conclude WHO WAS THE AUTHOR OF IT) 'tis not necessary for me at present to say anything in Justification of Myself. . . .
>
> Cath. Clive

For Theo and Kitty the state of war between them was not without its gratifications. A fight, especially a dirty one, refreshed and invigorated Theo. And Kitty was a fighter too, whose soul swelled at any call to battle. Only for Susannah was the Polly War real anguish. Patience and suasion were her tactics. She could wait to play Polly. She and Mrs. Clive might not always be at the same theater.

The public caricature of herself in this issue was less sympathetic than that of Kitty, who was regarded as an honest hussy, fighting for her rights with the street manners of her childhood. Susannah was put forward, by the Clive faction at any rate, as a hypocritical prig, as ambitious as Kitty, publicly pleading her reluctance to play Polly while in privite goading her husband to do her hatchet work.

She was well aware that her husband was the author of her humiliation, and with a passion quite unlike her habitual mildness she demanded that Theo drop the Polly matter. But Theo was too intoxicated by the storm he had raised to note the rebellion in his wife's voice. It would have made no difference if he had. By now his own letters and Kitty's constituted only a small part of the paper War of the Pollys. New poems, articles, letters, broadsides, and cartoons appeared every day. The *Daily Journal*, on December 10, remarked that "the Contention between the two rival Ladies of the Theatre" had grown to such proportions that the issue was expected "with the same Impatience as the Evacuation of Tuscany." Fashionable young men formed themselves into Cibber and Clive parties, and crowded into the green room to present their compliments to their favorites and challenge one another.

Theo found himself at the head of an army of idle young gentlemen who had elected themselves Susannah's champions. He took their attentions as "an Honour due to Him,"[5] and certainly these young rakes and dandies were far more closely associated with Theo than with Susannah. As she had treated her unwanted suitors a few years back, so she now treated these: with a mollifying smile to ward them off, and a distant civility. But to Theophilus the company of these rich young men meant supper and a bottle, and the paying off with ready silver of such creditors as might yap at his heels on the way from Drury Lane to White's Club after the evening's performance.

As general of his wife's forces, Theo emerged from anonymity in his letters to the press. The *Grub Street Journal* of December 15 carried a letter to Mrs. Clive signed by himself in which he protested that it was with reluctance he found himself forced "to enter the

Lists of a Paper War" with a woman. His duty, however, toward "one of your own Sex who in the most tender Manner ought to be dear to me" compelled him to rise in his wife's defense. Mrs. Clive's viciousness had fallen "on an innocent, inoffensive Woman who never asked for the Part of Polly, nor (without the greatest Reluctance and Terror) can ever accept it, unless Mrs Clive thought proper to make a voluntary Resignation of it in a friendly Manner." Theo went on to declare that the contest was not "between Mrs Clive and Mrs Cibber," but "between Mrs Clive's Will and the Manager's Right." He concluded by vowing that this letter was the first he had penned in the Polly contest, and that he certainly was not the notorious "A. Z."

The next day the Clive party — it may have been Kitty herself, for the tone was very like that earlier spiteful comment on Susannah's Zara — placed an item in the *Daily Journal* suggesting that Susannah forget about playing Polly, when Lucy would become her so much better: "There is, without denying Mrs Cibber to be a very agreeable Figure, a certain Narrowness between her Brows, together with a Sharpness of Face that will hit to Admiration that angry Resentment of Wrongs so strong in the Character of Lucy." The look of strain on Susannah's young face — she was only twenty-two — which Kitty and her friends liked to believe reflected her envy of roles still out of her grasp, was more probably an expression of her doubts as to whether she would ever bear a healthy child (since she had by now contracted a venereal infection because of her husband's taste for prostitutes) and of her gloomy apprehensions about her future as Theo's wife.

As winter drew on the Polly Cause showed no sign of abating. The public could not hear too many anecdotes — apocryphal or not — about Theo's effrontery, Kitty's ripostes, and Susannah's jealous sinking spells. At Drury Lane, the actors had taken sides. The green room was dangerously crowded with Clive and Cibber partisans, wearing swords and techy from wine. The only way Fleetwood could settle the tempest Theophilus Cibber had raised was to choose between Kitty and Susannah and put a definitive *Beggar's Opera* into production.

In the second week in December, the manager suddenly announced Gay's comedy for December 31, casting Mrs. Clive as Polly and Hannah Pritchard as Lucy. Mrs. Pritchard was a politic choice, for she was Mrs. Clive's dearest friend now that Janey Cibber was no more. Fleetwood had made the only decision he could, for Kitty Clive was the finest comedienne in England — a rarer commodity than any tragic actress. Besides, he hated to let the detestable toad Theophilus win a victory through his incendiary methods.

On December 31, 1736, a highly combustible audience, which Theophilus had seeded with hecklers, had filled every place in Drury Lane two hours before curtain time. The *London Evening Post* of January 1, 1737, tells the story:

> Last Night the Beggar's Opera (about the Playing of which as much Noise has been made as about several of our modern Treaties) was performed . . . to a crowded Audience, the House being full by Four. There was a prodigious Uproar, with Clapping, Hissings, Catcalls, etc. Mrs Clive, who play'd the Part of Polly, when she came forward addressed herself to the House, saying, "Gentlemen, I am very sorry it should be thought I have in any Manner been the Occasion of the least Disturbance"; and then cry'd in so moving a Manner that even Butchers wept. Then she told them she was almost ready in the Part of Lucy, and at all Times should be willing to play such Parts as the Town should direct, and desired to know if they were willing she should go on with the Part of Polly; she behaving in so humble a Manner, the House approved of her Behavior by a General Clap.[6]

Theo's minions in the audience were shamed into quiet, and the last, decisive battle in the War of the Pollys had been won by rosy, tough, resilient Kitty Clive.

Though the Polly War was over, the wounds it had inflicted upon Susannah continued to fester. The public had been so amused by the feud that it hated to let it die. Taking advantage of this, Lincoln's Inn Fields got up a burlesque called *The Beggar's Pantomime*. Two Columbines, Madam Squall (a contralto like Mrs. Cibber) and Madam Squeak (a soprano like Mrs. Clive), opened the performance caterwauling about their pretensions to the part of Polly. A character called "the stage manager" tried to settle the matter by insisting that Madam Squall play the role. "You're too pert," he rebuffed Madam Squeak and, pointing to the weeping Madam Squall, added, "She's pathetick, soft, extatick, see how tenderly she cries? Had Gay but known her, he'd have shown her, Polly was designed for her." Now an actor dressed as Pistol strutted upon the stage, bragging about his anonymous letters to the town on behalf of his wife, Madam Squall, and then belligerently denying that he had ever in his life written an anonymous letter. The din between manager, contending Columbines, and Pistol increased until the ghost of Gay appeared and ordered everyone to be quiet. The author of *The Beggar's Opera* insisted that Madam Squall play Polly, and grumpily retired to his tomb to rest. But despite the efforts of stage manager, Pistol, and Gay himself, beyond the grave, the termagant Madam Squeak refused to surrender her favorite role. The stage manager retired, exhausted, Madam Squeak flounced off the stage, and no one was left in the last scene but Pistol and his sniveling wife, whom he rallied in a concluding speech of Shakespearean humbug:

> Ha! Is this the time for sleep, this busy time
> When Pistol is at war with all the world?
> Come forth my sword, and do thy master justice.
> Ungenerous town, to serve thy Pistol thus!
> Pistol, who nightly toils on purpose to divert;
> Pistol, who studies every way to please,
> Yet always slighted, always unrewarded.
> In Tragedy majestic, Princely great;
> In Comedy a drugger, fop and fool;
> All these I am, yet Pistol is despised.
>   . . .
> Let's in, my Dove, then with mutual sorrow,
> We'll indulge our grief and mourn the loss.
> Gods! Gods! That tear has made me mad!
> My spirit, like a bladder swell'd with wind,
> At last will burst and fall to — nothing.

The Polly War was no sooner lost than Theo inaugurated a new campaign to enlarge Susannah's public image and earning power through another highly publicized feud with another actress over another disputed role. The rival now was Mrs. Butler, who Thomas Davies tells us was the illegitimate daughter of a duke,[7] a woman with an aristocratic bearing and a distinguished following. The role in question was Constance in Colley Cibber's adaptation of Shakespeare's *King John*. Ranged against the Cibbers was a coalition of Mrs. Butler's supporters and Mrs. Clive's friends, who considered that any advance for Theo Cibber's wife was a blow at Kitty.

There was yet another faction, which wanted Colley's play suppressed altogether. The law students from the Inns of Court had nothing against Susannah, but were outraged at the effrontery of her father-in-law. They regarded his presumption in mutilating Shakespeare as more than an amusing Cibberian impudence; it was an act of impiety that cried out for revenge.

Theophilus was enthusiastic about leading his wife's troops into paper battle against the combined Clive-Butler-templar forces. Fleetwood and Colley Cibber were less sanguine. No sooner was Colley's *Papal Tyranny during the Reign of King John* cast and rehearsals called than the law students announced that the night it reached performance they would riot in Drury Lane and tear the theater apart. They were quite capable of trying to do so.

One morning in March, Colley settled the fate of his "improvement" on Shakespeare by striding into the prompter's office, taking the master copy off William Chetwood's desk, and leaving the theater with it under his arm. Thus, as Pope recorded in *The Dunciad,* "King John in Modesty expired."

Colley's deed spared Susannah the mortification of another drawn out, manufactured feud with another actress, and the terror of a riot while she was on stage. But she had been saved not by her husband's loving concern but by her father-in-law's instinct for self-preservation. And there was more public humiliation in store for her.

Young Henry Fielding had taken over the management of the Little Theater in the Haymarket and with a raffish assortment of players, including Theo's sister Charlotte, he was putting on some devastating satire. *The Historical Register for the Year 1736,* performed in March 1737, was a zany review of the events of the previous year. It poked fun at the Prime Minister, Whig tax policies, society ladies and their inexplicable passion for the eunuchs of Italian opera, at the Cibbers, father and son, and at the preposterous theatrical war between "Polly Soft" and "Polly Smart." The Cibbers were old targets of Fielding, and Susannah received her share of his venom not because he disliked her but because she was inextricably enmeshed in the activities of the family she had married into.

At one point in Act II of *The Historical Register,* Pistol, "running Mad," enters with a mob and delivers himself of the following:

> Associates, Brethren, Countrymen and Friends!
> Partakers with us in this glorious Enterprize
> Which for our Consort we have undertaken
>
> . . .
>
> Thus to the Publick deign we to appeal
> Behold how Humbly the great Pistol kneels
> Say then, oh Town, is it your royal Will
> That my great Consort represent the Part
> Of Polly Peachum in the Beggars Opera?
> [Mob Hiss]
> Thanks to the Town, that Hiss speaks their Assent.
> Such was the Hiss that spoke the great Applause
> Our mighty Father met with when he brought
> His Riddle* on the Stage; such was the Hiss
> Welcom'd his Caesar† to the Egyptian Shore.
> Such was the Hiss in which Great John‡ should have expir'd.
> But wherefore do I try in vain to number
> Those glorious Hisses which from Age to Age
> Our Family has borne triumphant from the Stage.

By the spring of 1737, Susannah Cibber despaired of her relationship with Theophilus. She had endured in silence considerable personal suffering in the three years of her marriage, but until these trumped-up feuds Theo's ugly character had not publicly reflected on her. His attempts to make her into the same sort of laughable public property as himself, "Great Pistol's Consort," was an offense of a different order, against her good name and her honor.

* *Love in a Riddle,* 1729, Cibber's disastrous imitation of Gay's *Beggar's Opera.*
† *Caesar in Egypt,* 1724.
‡ Cibber's adaptation of Shakespeare's *King John.*

She had never in her twenty-three years ventured the smallest step without the strong direction and support of a man. There was no one to help her now. Her husband was her enemy. Her father was dead. She could not expect much from her brother Tom, who had become a furtive and preoccupied figure, living a double life of nighttime debauch and cynical daytime pursuit of the unattainable Cecilia Young. Susannah had neither money of her own nor powerful friends. Of course, any one of the fashionable admirers who ogled her and played up to Theo would have been glad to become her protector. But this means of escape from her marriage was as unacceptable to Susannah's sense of propriety as continuing her dependency upon her husband.

She turned finally to Fleetwood, in a move as mild and reasonable as it was naïve. She asked her employer that the prenuptial agreement signed by herself and Theo be put into effect and that her earnings be turned over to Washbourne and Wheeler. She had never to this date personally received a single one of the hundreds of pounds she had earned at Drury Lane. Even the proceeds from her benefits never came to her, for Theophilus was in the habit of turning over whole blocks of seats in advance to his creditors to sell.[8] In addition to the matter of her earnings, Susannah requested Fleetwood that she and he alone settle the question of which roles she should play, so that she would never again be embroiled in unsought differences with other actresses.

Charles Fleetwood was at ease in masculine company of any type. He was charming leaning over a paddock rail with the Duke of Bolton, watching his gelding "Fox-Hunter" lose to His Grace's entry, or bursting into a rehearsal at Drury Lane and breaking it up by inviting all the players to the boxing matches at Tottenham Court where he presided as umpire.[9] But he was out of his element with women. Aside from the discomfiture which he felt in the presence of Theo Cibber's hapless, touching, and virtuous young wife, Fleetwood was determined not to become involved in anything which touched the marital concerns of the young Cibbers, which were bound to be, given the husband's character, sordid and even dangerous.

He reminded Susannah that she, and all her family for that

matter, had come to his theater as protégés of Theophilus, who had made all financial negotiations for them with the Arnes' full consent. He begged her to remember that he had been turning her earnings over to her husband for three years without protest from her, or any knowledge of this extraordinary trust agreement of which she now spoke.* This was the course he intended to follow. And in order to wash his hands of the whole affair and make clear to Theo that there was no complicity between him and Susannah, he went straight to Cibber and told him what had happened.

At the moment Susannah chose to resist him, Theophilus was nearly maddened with debts. He had to lurk and dodge between the theater and his home to avoid the bailiff. Jail loomed. Friends advised him to flee to France. But who would support him there? Who would manage his wife's career in an aggressive way and yet be trusted to send the proceeds to him? The sudden word that his accommodating Susannah was attempting to put her earnings and even herself beyond his grasp roused him to cyclonic rage. Very drunk, he made for Susannah's dressing room — she fortunately had learned of his intentions and had time to withdraw — broke down the door, splintered the room's contents, seized her stage wardrobe and jewels, and turned them into cash.

Theo's swift and terrible retaliation crushed in Susannah any further courage to rebel. Aside from her terror of his anger, the loss of her wardrobe and jewels was devastating. The costumes of tragic actresses were often cast-off court gowns created for great ladies for an occasion like a royal birthday, worn once, then given as patronage to a favorite actress. These hooped dresses, stiff with gold thread or studded with pearls, were incalculably important to an actress's prestige and stage effect. Susannah had been reduced overnight, as if she

---

* "By marriage, the husband and wife are one person in law: that is, the very being and legal existence of the woman is suspended during the marriage . . . And therefore all deeds executed by her during her coverture are void." (Sir William Blackstone, *Commentaries on the Laws of England*, 1765.) The question was: did the fact that Susannah had for the three years of her marriage acquiesced to her husband's appropriating all her earnings, so that no trust was in fact ever established, now make the old trust agreement null and void?

Susannah and Theophilus were to battle this question for many years, and with no clearcut decision. (Public Records, Jan. 18, 1741. Susannah Arne Cibber and Anne Arne, her mother, joint complainants against Theophilus Cibber.)

were the merest bit player, to scavenging for costumes from Drury Lane's stock wardrobe, that fusty source of Hallam's and Macklin's fatal, oily wig.

When Theo saw his wife the day after his rape of her tiring room, he found her ashen and silent. He, on the contrary, was grandiloquent. He reminded Susannah of what had been her own philosophy of marriage: that a wife's happiness depended upon the goodwill which her fond obedience warmed in her husband's heart. He recalled to her the countless incidences of his tender indulgence. She had come to him dowerless and without the least hope of any future without his "care, assistance, instruction and advice." At the time of their wedding she was so poor that he had to buy her wedding costume. That she was no longer a second-rate singer, moving from one unlicensed theater to another for a few nights' work, but a rising actress at Drury Lane was the result of his doting efforts. Had she already forgotten how he had brought her "poor, unfortunate family"[10] to Drury Lane? Yet despite his exertions to advance her, exertions so prodigious that they had taken a severe toll on his own career and finances, she, "flushed with success grew more haughty and over bearing."[11] Even so, he had endured her pride and vanity, and her unnatural refusal to share his bed, until the word of her attempted treachery with Fleetwood, coming like a thunderbolt, had broken his fortitude.

He warned her that there was another intransigence on her part that he would no longer tolerate: her coldness toward those gentlemen admirers who had espoused her claim to Polly and Queen Constance. One of these, a young man named William Sloper, had for some time now, Theo told Susannah, been supporting the Cibber household. Theo owed him in the neighborhood of £400.[12] Even if she did not care if her husband were thrown into the Fleet, she would be wise, for her own sake, to be more friendly to William Sloper. The silver she ate with, the soft bed she lay in, all would have been dragged from the house by unpaid tradesmen but for Sloper's timely disbursal of funds. Yet this young man had yet to receive a smile from Susannah. The other day Sloper had asked Theo for permission to call upon Susannah at home and to teach her backgammon.[13] Theo advised his wife to receive this young man frankly and candidly into her friendship or he could not promise there would not be another lapse in his temper.

Whether it was out of fear of her husband or the prospect of losing her home and possessions (she was the daughter, niece, and granddaughter of ruined tradesmen), Susannah bowed to Theo's command to receive her admirer.

When William Sloper came to call on Susannah Cibber at her house in Wild Court he brought a backgammon board with him, and he taught her this ancient game, which was enjoying a revival in polite circles. He was a solemn young man of about thirty, and when other visitors were present in the Cibbers' gay drawing room was apt to sit apart, listening, and watching her. When he and Susannah were alone, however, he did talk, though the conversation was different from the gossip and sexual bantering she had learned to expect from gentlemen of fashion. Sloper was a country squire and did not like London, though she knew his father had a splendid house in St. James Place. He had come to town for the winter because his wife pined for the social and theatrical season. Susannah was the favorite actress of Catherine Sloper and her friends, and it was in escorting his wife to *Othello* that he had first seen and admired Susannah. Since that night he had come alone to Drury Lane every time she played. He said very little about his wife and his two small sons. But he spoke with affection of his father, and of the family estate in Berkshire. It was late spring at West Woodhay now, lambing and shearing were over, crops in the ground. He had never been away from West Woodhay in the spring since his university days at Cambridge. He would be here now if it were not for these afternoons in her company.

As spring warmed toward summer Susannah counted more and more on Sloper's quiet presence in her house. When he was there, there was food in the larder, the half-paid servants smiled, Theo was merry, and she had nothing to fear from his temper. Behind Sloper's back Theo called him "Mr Benefit."[14]

In May her husband congratulated Susannah on her enlightened attitude toward Sloper, which had just paid a remarkable dividend. All their worries about the summer were over. They could sublet their expensive house and leave the heat of London and the imprecations of creditors. Sloper had taken a villa for the three of them in Kingston, and there, safe from the prying eyes of the world, the three of them would rest or ride or ramble along the banks of the Thames, basking in each other's company like the trusted old friends they were.

Let Sloper, house of Sloper rejoice
With Gelotophye, another laughing plant.
— CHRISTOPHER SMART,
Jubilate Agno, XXVIII

THE young Cibbers moved out to Kingston in June, as soon as Drury Lane closed, and Theo had laid a false scent for his creditors by informing them that he would be out of the law's reach playing in Dublin for the summer.[1] Three months later, when he and Susannah next appeared in London — still sojourning in Kingston but coming into town for reheasals — they were noticeably irritable and on edge.

Susannah was to open Drury Lane's season in Addison's *Cato,* playing Marcia, a new role for her. But at the last moment *The Orphan,* which she had done last season, had to be substituted, because she was "not ready as Marcia."[2] What could be so preoccupying this conscientious young woman who had had all summer to learn one new part?

A week later she had a public spat with Quin "about dressing in ye Green Room."[3] Quin was always so encumbered backstage by his entourage of admirers that it was difficult for him to hold court and change costumes within the confines of his tiring room. Sometimes, with imperious disregard, Quin moved his toilet into the spacious green room. Apparently, a fastidious lady who had come backstage to compliment Susannah Cibber had been offended by the sight of Quin's vast, ungartered calf and even vaster uncinctured girth. It is not surprising that Susannah, with her reverence for propriety, should resent Quin's usurpation of the theater's public reception room for his toilet; but that this tactful and suasive woman should lash out in public rather than appeal to him in private suggests her tension.

Theophilus, no less than Susannah, was showing signs of stress. On September 13 he was too drunk in Kingston to accompany his wife to town for their evening's performance of *The Conscious Lovers*, and Macklin had to read his part.[4] Whatever Theo's flaws, missing performances was not one of them.

The long and the short of it was that Susannah and William Sloper had become lovers during the summer, and Theo's existence (out of debtors' prison) depended upon Susannah's salary and Sloper's allowance, while the lovers' continued association (without the scandal Susannah dreaded) depended upon Theo's connivance.

In view of the pains Theo had taken to promote this love affair it is at first surprising that he was so uneasy now that it was flourishing. Theo was not the sort of man to be cast down by the disaffection of a wife, especially one whose terror of him and whose horror of scandal he could count on to keep her under his thumb. The problem was Sloper, whose patient resolve, no matter how long it took, to rescue Susannah from her own husband, to love her, protect her, acknowledge her, and live with her, was an indecorum Theo had never calculated on.

When Theo had encouraged Sloper's interest in his wife he had called him "a romp and a good natured boy,"[5] taking him for one of those idle, rich young rakes of whom he knew scores, who cynically courted actresses, and whose purses were fair game to their theatrical prey. To do him justice, Theo had probably never met anyone like Sloper, this sturdy squire, this dutiful son, who ten years earlier, before he was twenty, had entered an arranged marriage with a wealthy widow, daughter of his father's friend, and now at thirty had fallen in love — a fate which henceforth he accepted as the central fact of his life, and embraced with country literalness and constancy.

In Kingston the lovers had asked Theo for a quiet separation for Susannah so that she could establish her own household in London. Theo would not hear of it. No matter what generous financial promises Susannah and William might make him now, while they squirmed to be free, once these two were out of his grasp, Sloper's purse and Susannah's career might grow harder to draw on.

In the stringent domestic regimen which Theophilus set up in Kingston he personally handed over his wife to Sloper every night at bedtime so that it remained clear to the lovers whose property Susannah was, and at whose sufferance their pleasure lay. "Mr Cibber's bed chamber and Mr Sloper's had a door opened between them," one of Theo's servants testified later. "Mrs Cibber used to undress herself in my master's room and leave her clothes there and put on a bed gown and take away one of the pillows from my master's bed and go away to Mr Sloper's room. My master used to shut the door after her and say 'good night, my dear,' and sometimes he used to knock at their door in a morning to call them up to breakfast and at other times he sent me to call them; and the pillow was always brought back again, for my master's bed was always made with the two pillows."[6]

While it lasted Theophilus was enjoying an unprecedented economic yield from a wife. Even his father had never approached such a state. In addition to Susannah's handsome rental fee from her lover, her career was flourishing. He had had no difficulty (after Fleetwood's refusal to become Susannah's ally the previous spring) in reaching an understanding with the patentee, which was incorporated into her new articles, that he, Theo, was to handle all her affairs, and should she not abide by her husband's agreements, Fleetwood was not to allow her to perform.[7]

Once they were back in London from Kingston, Theo unleashed his wife's fall theatrical offensive by attacking another stronghold of Kitty Clive's, the role of Ophelia. With her street accent, vulgar figure, and fiery complexion, Kitty had been attempting Shakespeare's fragile, tormented Danish noblewoman for several years to amazingly little public protest. She was such a popular personality that most people suffered in silence her ludicrous excursions into tragedy in consideration of the delight she gave them in comedy.

Fleetwood, however, was losing patience with her. Even with Quin as
the ghost, Milward as the prince, and Macklin as Horatio, his theater
was half empty whenever Kitty was in the cast of *Hamlet*. When
Theo suggested Ophelia as a natural part for Susannah, Fleetwood
assigned it to her despite Kitty's threat to take up arms. To his and
Theo's chagrin, Susannah nipped this new feud in the bud by refusing to study her lines, and refusing to attend *Hamlet* rehearsals. On
September 11 she incurred a fine of £5 for insubordination.[8]

Susannah's uncharacteristic defiance seems to have given Theo
food for thought. Apparently there were limits to the riches he could
extract from his golden goose. If he continued to humiliate Susannah
publicly with trumped-up feuds with other actresses she might leave
the stage altogether and elope with Sloper, depriving Theo in one
blow of her salary and her lover's extortion money. After the flareup
about Ophelia, Theo never again attempted to wrest for Susannah a
part belonging to another.

In her personal life, too, Theo seems to have recognized that he
was reining his wife too tightly. Since their return from Kingston the
Cibbers had gone back to their house in Wild Court and Sloper to
his father's town house. (His wife, Catherine, was now living separately at her own house in South Audley Street.) Though Theo
encouraged long private visits from Sloper, the course of the love
affair was far more straitened and surreptitious than it had been at
Kingston. Wild Court was an alley with a hundred interested neighbors. Susannah was a public figure. She and William could not meet
or walk or ride out in London in the easy way they had all summer.
Consequently, when on the first day of December Anne Hopson,
Susannah's maid, a woman thick as thieves with her young mistress,
suddenly informed Theo that she was that day leaving Susannah's
service and returning to the mantua-making business of her youth,[9]
he sensed that Mrs. Hopson's action might be part of a plan to facili-
tate the lovers' meetings. Sure enough, the very afternoon after her
maid's departure and nearly every day thereafter, Susannah departed
from her house or the theater in a chair and did not come home till
the wee hours. Though he did not interfere, Theo took the precau-
tion of having his wife and her maid followed, and presently found
that the trysting place he suspected was on Blue Cross Street in

Leicester Fields. Here Anne Hopson had rented two adjoining rooms for seven shillings a week from a Mrs. Hayes, who lived downstairs. Every afternoon or evening William Sloper came here from the tennis court or St. James Place. It was Anne Hopson's custom, as soon as the young people were together, to go out for some leisurely shopping, or downstairs to Mrs. Hayes's kitchen to cook supper for her young guests and chat with her landlady.

Mrs. Hayes had a husband, identified for some reason as "a foreigner," a man with no apparent employment beyond looking after his wife's property. Theophilus approached Mr. Hayes and asked him to keep as close an eye as he could on the doings of Mrs. Hopson's interesting visitors. He had no immediate use for this evidence, but it could do no harm to lay it by. Theo could not have found a more enthusiastic assistant. Mr. Hayes, whose circumstances happily combined an inquisitive nature and a great deal of free time, had, even before Theo's request, satisfied himself as to the identity of his new tenant's fashionably dressed guests. The first time he had let them in he knew he "had seen him at the tennis court, and her on the stage." But to pin things down, two nights running he had "dogged them both home in their chairs, she to Mr Cibber's house, number 12 in Little Wild Court and he to old Mr Sloper's in St James Place."[10]

On the upper floor of the house on Blue Cross Street, on the other side of the wall from Mrs. Hopson's rooms, the Hayeses had a closet. One day when everyone else in the house was out, Mr. Hayes "bored holes through the wainscot and could see very plain."[11] During the next months, squatting patiently in this closet with his eyes against these holes whenever Sloper and Susannah were alone upstairs, Mr. Hayes was able to see and hear and even to time with his pocket watch everything that passed between them.

Though the rooms at Mrs. Hayes's were an improvement over visits to Wild Court, for William Sloper the life he was leading with Susannah was stifling and unnatural. Nor did there seem, given Susannah's terror of her husband should she leave him, any hope of a better future. For more than a year Sloper had given up the country life he loved, his horses, his work with his father in their fields and model village, his county political activities. The summer in Kingston had been relatively free. Theo had quickly found the local tavern and its Hazard players and left them alone all day and every evening.[12] They had walked or driven out along the river and he had even taught Susannah to ride a gentle mare. But since their return to London, Sloper's life consisted of rattling about in his father's great empty town house, daily sets of tennis, and these stolen hours with Susannah in tawdry furnished rooms, unctuously bowed in and out by one or other of the Hayeses, for whom he felt a growing distrust.

One January afternoon when he had been waiting for Susannah for nearly two hours, pacing and muttering so loudly over her head that Mrs. Hayes took alarm, Mrs. Hopson came in from attending Susannah at the theater and was hastily sent upstairs by the landlady to soothe him. When William saw that Susannah was not with her maid he exploded, railing first at Susannah's delay and then at the Hayeses, whose motives and discretion he said he suspected. Mrs. Hopson fled downstairs to fetch Susannah, stopping on the way out to berate her landlady. "You have made a fine kettle of fish!" she told Mrs. Hayes. "You have been talking of matters and he's stark mad of it above stairs."[13]

Anne Hopson flew to Drury Lane and was back presently with Susannah, who hurried upstairs alone. Meanwhile, Mr. Hayes noiselessly climbed the back stairs and took his post in the closet. He was in time to hear Susannah, still out of breath, say she had been kept at a long rehearsal of *Comus,* her brother's new masque, along with Quin and Mills and Milward and Kitty Clive. Sloper said he did not believe her. He was certain there was something between her and Fleetwood, whose blandishing nature he had noted. Susannah protested she cared nothing at all for Fleetwood, and that if it were within her power she would leave his theater and go to Covent Garden and take her brother with her. Sloper sat down in an arm chair and drew her upon his lap. The lovers' words, their tears, their removal after a time to the bed, and the details and the duration of their embraces there were meticulously observed a few feet away.

Though Theophilus Cibber had been for some time the beneficiary of his own salary and his wife's, as well as Sloper's allowance, the sum of which exceeded £700, the money was not enough to support his appetites and his compounding debts. Fleetwood would advance him no more, and, head over heels in debt himself, began to demand repayment and withhold part of Theo's salary. In February 1738, the smart little house in Wild Court was taken from the Cibbers. Susannah went to stay with her mother in St. Giles parish, and paid her visits to Blue Cross Street from there, and Theo lurked in taverns and bagnios. By this time Sloper's aversion to the Hayeses—though he knew nothing of Mr. Hayes's spying—had reached such a point that he insisted a new meeting place be found. While new quarters were being sought, Theo, who had been told by Mr. Hayes that Mrs. Hopson was moving, informed Susannah that he knew all about the hideaway on Blue Cross Street and insisted that when new accommodations were found for her and Sloper, they be commodious enough for a home for all of them. It made him uneasy to have three such good friends rattling about London under so many separate roofs. On March 2, Susannah, Theo, Sloper, and Anne Hopson moved into lodgings in Kensington in the house of a Mr. and Mrs. Carter. But Theo was not part of the household for long. His creditors waited until both the young Cibbers' benefit nights were over and the proceeds seized — Susannah's benefit on April 12, in which she played Isabella in *Measure for Measure*, realized over £150 — and then prepared to clap Theo in jail. Warned in time, on April 17, after appearing in Mills's benefit, Theo slipped out of Drury Lane over the rooftops, as Macklin had done after wounding Hallam, made for the harbor, and took ship for France.

In Calais, Theo was half mad with frustration and inactivity. His blustering, laugh-provoking, disruptive genius was as useless to him among these foreigners as if he were a cyclone raging in a field of insensate boulders. He had no outlet for his energy but to drink all day in a quayside tavern, write interminable haranguing letters to cronies and to Susannah, and keep one eye on the harbor for the packet from England.

Even more than his concern about how vigorously his friends were working to clear his way home — especially a certain William Finch who was acting as his mediator with his creditors — what gnawed at Theo was the fear that in his absence Sloper's influence would prevail over Susannah and he would persuade her to elope, or at least to stop sending her husband money, and leave him in France to starve. As Theo had always feared, with him removed the precarious balance among the three of them had shifted: in England the other two had danced to his tune; in France he was their suppliant.

Back in London Sloper was indeed pressing Susannah to use this opportunity to effect an open break with her husband and set up her own household. Theo was wrong, though, in assuming that Sloper was trying to persuade Susannah to give up the stage. In all the years of their intimacy he never did. His original and enduring attraction to her seems to have been at least in part her romantic vocation. Sloper did not share Susannah's terror of her husband's retaliation when he returned and found the separation accomplished. As long as the two of them accepted the indefinite burden of relieving his financial needs, what would her husband gain by publicly persecuting them? Susannah was not reassured. Womanish and excessive her fears must have seemed to Sloper, but she had more intimate acquaintance than he with Theo's appetite for malevolence.

In the middle of May Susannah wrote her husband a letter which has not survived but whose gist may be gathered from Theo's long reply. She enclosed a larger than usual remittance for his living expenses, and assured him that she and Sloper were working with Finch to satisfy his creditors and speed his return to England with his personal liberty assured. This nosegay of appeasement proffered, she broke it to him that Sloper would no longer tolerate the three of them living together. She pleaded with Theo to let her go peacefully, in return for their friendship and financial tribute now and in the future. Her sufferings were great, she told him. She could not eat or sleep. Pulled one way by love for Sloper, another by fear of Theo, she was no longer mistress of herself. Her life was "a dying by inches."

Theophilus was moved to the quick by his wife's letter. The generous draft it contained and its conciliatory tone filled him with warmer feelings for her than he had known in weeks and made him regret his last few raging and threatening letters. Exhilarated by the new cash in his pocket and the realization of how greatly his wife still feared him, he replied to her as follows:

Calais, May 21st, 1738

Thou Dearest, best of Women, my Angel Tina, where, where are Words to express my Fondness! my high Opinion of You! I have wept your Letter all over: Be not uneasy, Love, they were Tears of Joy and Gratitude to my dear, sweet Preserver. If in ye Agonies of my Mind I have said one Word to give you Pain, remember, I this Instant recall 'em. The Letter I wrote last . . . I hope will not make you uneasy . . . Dear, I will be easy and you shall be easy. 'Tis my Duty to make you so, and if ever you see me have a grave Look, think, 'tis only a Reproach . . . on Myself. You shall wake me from the thought, and to entertain thee I'll laugh like a Frenchman. . . . Yes, you shall be Mistress of yourself. Your dear Heart shall feel no Pang. God forgive me for ever having given it one. But, Miss Rantipole, I'll be Master of your Conduct! You're a little, simple Child, and not to be left quite without a Leading String! And has my sweet Numps thought coolly? When she does, I'm sure she'll think right my Determination our living in a Group together. . . . May the great God I adore give me up to eternal Perdition if I think I could reconcile myself to living under a different Roof from you. . . . What! Lose the Pleasure of your Society! Then I were lost indeed! . . . No, Dear, you shall not die by Inches; I too well know ye Pain of it myself. My Dear, tis now 3 Weeks and upward since I parted from you. . . . The Melancholy of my Countenance has drawn Tears from ye Eyes of Men: I am certain I have never slept Ten Minutes at a Time and have been in one continual Fever. But you, my good Angell, were born to preserve me, and I bless you for it, Thou anguish healing Cherubin. . . .

When I read your last, how did your poor Fears alarm me! I saw in my Imagination your dear Countenance in Distress. . . . Ah, I could bear anything but to see you in Pain. If ever you see me looking Grave (I mean to your Uneasiness) you shall take me aside, reprove me with a Smile and I'll be very Good to you — you dear, saucy Pug. . . . Oh, I have a thousand things to tell you! . . . Tell Somebody* I love and honour 'em for their Caution. Yes, little Numps, I will come into any Schemes . . . for your Ease, since you still consult Mine. . . . We'll learn to laugh at what has made us

* Throughout the letter Sloper is called "Somebody," "our Friend," "a certain Friend," "Anyone."

Grave, and I'll thank God I can any way contribute to my Sweeting's Quiet.

Oh, Dear, I own you have great Power over me. Yes, Numps shall be fat and fair and saucy and I'll abuse her abundantly — I propose with this sending a letter to Fleetwood which you may carry to him, at your Leisure. . . . He's all Counterfoil, Dear. . . . Any impertinent Air he may affect I shall laugh at. . . . I'll behave like a Gentleman toward him, but, by God, I'll behave like a Man of Spirit. The Letter I send him, show to Quin and Milward. (Shew it privately to our Friend; I think he has Honour, ay, and very good Sense, and therefore should be glad of his Opinion.) . . .

Oh, my Life, my Angel, again I must repeat, if there's a Line, a Word in my Last that distresses you, I wish it recall'd. I have ever wrote undisguised — agreeable to the Truth I strictly profess to adhere to: I doubt not they are wild Letters, for God knows, my poor Brain has been in a strange Condition. . . . Pray God I may . . . never give you a Pang more. . . . Let me but live to see your little Countenance smile, and have a cheerful, friendly, social Meal with Saucy Tina and I'll think every Torture overpaid. Yes, Tina will do all she can to make him easy, who would do so much for her. . . .

I have reminded Finch (in my Letter that comes by a Vessel) not to word anything . . . that may at all tie me down to Fleetwood, for I will be free. . . . My Articles have been long made void by him in the strictest Sense of ye Law and Justice. . . . And as my Creditors seem, by Finch's Letter, to be good naturedly inclined, I will, in spite of Fleetwood's Tooth, shew myself on a Theatre, I warrant you, were it to be but a few Times sufficient to get a Morsel of Bread for myself (to vex him) and give a proper Quota to my Creditors. . . .

Prithee, Dearest, let me have some Token, too, that I may know a certain Friend thinks well of me. T'will relieve me. . . . And we'll both pray: I for being very, very naughty, and Tina for being a little, tiny bit so — a little Crime! . . . Give me all you can, at least, and then do what you will, my Child.

And so you have a great Deal to say to me when you see me? . . . Indeed, Miss, I have a great Deal to say to you and I'll dust your Jackett if you don't mind me! . . .

God love you, dear Soul, I would sooner endure Hot Needles in my Eyes than not struggle to contribute to your Satisfaction. . . . Your poor Theo . . . will do all . . . to comfort that dear Creature whom he has so often hurt, not from ill Nature, Dear, but terrible

Indiscretion. God give me Resolution to make you Amends for it.
. . . Alas, how could he, were not one Roof to contain us? Conduct
yourself with Caution, my little Numps, and seek any Relief your
poor, dear Heart would have. . . .

Well, why don't I talk a little of Business? Because, you little
Baggage, I can talk of nothing but thee! Pray let Finch get my
Papers from Captain Gilby as soon as possible. He sail'd Yesterday
in ye Morning, and indeed will be in London before this. . . . Pray,
Dear, and Finch proposes an Advertizement in the Publick Papers,*
send me the first Paper 'tis published in. And now I think on't show
my letter (which I send Fleetwood) to my Father and Sister Brown.
That I am worthy their Concern is a Consolation will help to support me with a becoming Pride.† . . . Let me but live once more to
breathe my native Air with Liberty, and to convince you how much
I love you, how highly I esteem you, how tenderly I feel for you,
and how greatly I prefer your Quiet to all Consideration, I shall
think my Follies and Crimes expiated. . . .

If that Thing, Fleetwood, gives out I owe him anything (his
damned Bond excepted) say I declare 'tis a Lie, for upon my
Honour, by Ballances, he's indebted to me, and I laugh at him!
But he will lie! Good Gods! How he will lie! The Devil never made
a greater Liar! He's in Reallity more contemptible than the lowest
Creature round his filthy Table, who daily gobble down his ill drest
Meat and strained Wine. . . . Prithee, Love, take Quin and Milward
aside and laugh at him. . . .

'Tis hardly credible how much your last Letter has relieved
me. God bless you! God love you! Yes, Dear, you have given my
Heart great Ease indeed; and I will try to purchase yours at any
Rate. . . . In ye Meantime, when I drink to Tina and all Friends,
be sure I forget not one that I hope is a very just one to you. Well,
Dear, when you and I and Anyone can drink a glass together, you'll
be convinced how I think of you and how I think of you two! May
God Almighty eternally bless and comfort you! And, believe me, my
Angel Tina, I am most cordially, most sincerely your fond, affec-
tionate Husband —

THEO. CIBBER

* Presumably for a public sale of Theo's goods or a theatrical benefit for his
creditors.

† As a matter of fact Colley and Theo's sisters (all but Charlotte) had washed
their hands of him and contributed not a penny to his relief, on this occasion or any
other, though Colley did help support Theo's daughters.

P.S. God love you, God bless you, my Sweet! Dear, dear Tina!
I will send this now, by God. . . . Yet let me say if I live to unload
the [illegible but perhaps "burden"] of my poor Mind to you and
one more, you both will still honour and pitty your unhappy Theo.
God bless you, thou worthy Angel — I may make you laugh yet![14]

Beneath the hysteria of this mad, sly letter, so groveling and so
menacing, so rambling and so calculating, one feels Theo's iron grip
on his wife's person and fate. He and she are indissolubly tied, he is
saying, bound by his passion for gaming and hers for Sloper, each
ministering to the other's lust, each at the other's mercy.

Early in June, Theo slipped back into England. He went at
once to a favorite bagnio in Goodman's Fields whence he sent word
to his wife. Susannah and Anne Hopson hurried from Kensington in
a hackney to get him. "In our return," Mrs. Hopson recalled, "we
changed our coach two or three times . . . that he might not be
discovered."[15] William Sloper was not at Kensington when Theo
returned from France, but in Buckinghamshire to sign the summer
lease for a house in Burnham for himself and Susannah. Alone with
her husband, Susannah begged Theo to find another place to stay.
She dreaded what Sloper would do when he found him. For the
moment, Theo chose not to argue with his wife. He had not a penny.
He was safe in none of his old haunts. He begged to be allowed to
stay till Sloper returned, then promised, if they gave him money, to
take lodgings elsewhere. "Within two or three days Mr Sloper came,"
Anne Hopson said, "and then Mr Cibber sent and took a lodging at
Blue Green; and after supper, about nine or ten o'clock, he went
there with a man carrying a lanthorn and candle and left Mrs Cibber
and Mr Sloper."[16]

But Theo was not bowing out of their lives. "He came back to
breakfast next morning," Mrs. Hopson recalled, "and dined and
supped."[17] And some time in the next few days there was a confrontation among the three of them in which Theo reestablished his
domination, for when the lovers moved out to Burnham a week
later, after Drury Lane closed for the summer, Theo was very much
one of the party. He strutted in a proprietary way about the spacious
country house Sloper had let, and looked over the bed chambers

"that they might contrive in what rooms to lie."[18] Theo's persuasive weapon must have been his threat to bring suit against Sloper for seducing and alienating his wife, and his disclosure that safely stored in the brain of Mr. Hayes were impressions easily translated into legal evidence that would be as electrifying to Susannah's genteel public as it would be convincing to a jury.

Though Susannah and Sloper were stunned into capitulation, there was no return this summer to the relatively cordial atmosphere of Kingston last year, none of the jolly domestic scenes Theo had looked forward to in his letter from Calais, no "cheerful, friendly meals with Saucy Tina and one other," no raising a glass and "laughing together at what has made us grave." A month after they arrived in Buckinghamshire, Sloper and Susannah sent Theophilus packing. What stiffening of her spirit could have brought Susannah, after a year of anguished mollification, to defy this dangerous and desperate man, who was armed as she now knew with the means to destroy her name and her career?

The most likely explanation was her pregnancy, a discovery she must have made at just this time, since the child was born in February. If she and Theo were living under one roof during her pregnancy and lying in, he could — and undoubtedly would — claim Sloper's child as his own, for its financial and emotional leverage over her and Sloper. And as long as the child was a minor, Theophilus would hold absolute sway over its fate. This very summer, searching for assets to turn into cash, he had suddenly remembered the existence of Betty and Jenny, aged six and seven, who had been raised since their mother's death by his older sister, Mrs. Catherine Brown. He had snatched these moppets from this worthy aunt and given them into the care of their aunt Charlotte for a course in singing, dancing, and miming so that as soon as possible they would be able to add their orphans' mite to their father's funds. It would have been hard to find a less suitable person to raise these little girls than Charlotte, who had matured into a bellicose and dissolute woman who supported herself in various unsavory theatrical enterprises, dressed in men's clothes, and strutted and brawled like a caricature of her brother, who was in turn a caricature of their father.

Whatever Susannah's aloof and mystical relationship with the hurly-burly British stage, she was determined that no child of hers would ever be associated with it. Her determination that this child be recognized as Sloper's and not a scion of the loathsome race of Cibber may well have been what enabled her to break with her husband, to commit herself to Sloper as she never had before, and to brave, though with heaven knows what apprehension, what she knew would be her husband's tornadic revenge.

❧ 9 ☙

I think her case not unlike Lady Abergavenny's, her loving spouse being
very well content with her gallantrys while he found his account in them,
but raging against those that brought him no profit.[1]
— Lady Mary Montagu to Lady Pomfret, November 4, 1742

CAST out of Burnham, Theophilus went at once to London
where he took lodgings at a Mrs. Holt's in Bow Street.
Despite his bluster to Susannah about "that thing, Fleetwood," he meekly made his peace with the patentee and began summer rehearsals. Meanwhile, his mediator, Finch, seems to have
effected a satisfactory repayment plan with Theo's creditors, for he
was able to move freely about the city.

But how on earth was Theo to live? There was no possibility of
milking Susannah's salary, even with Fleetwood's connivance, for she
did not intend to perform this year. And nothing more could be
extracted from "Mr Benefit" after the violent parting at Burnham. A
lawsuit against his wife's seducer was Theo's next, inevitable venture.
If he won he was wealthy; if he lost he was not much worse off than
now. The sum he decided to try for was £5,000 — about $200,000
today.

It was not unusual for a British husband in the eighteenth century to bring a damage suit — called an action for criminal con-

versation — against his wife's seducer, seeking financial recovery for the loss of her "services and assistance." It was an action similar to that which employers, at this same period, brought against a person who had enticed away a servant.[2]

In trials for criminal conversation the jury first heard the counsel for the plaintiff attempt to prove the adultery and alienation, and then assess the former contribution of the errant wife to the husband's household through her particular skills. Next, they heard the defendant's counsel, who might or might not deny the guilty relationship but would certainly attempt to beat down the plaintiff's estimate of his wife's value. Having heard all the facts, it was the duty of the jury to render to the husband an appropriate restitution: the more industrious or talented the wife, the higher her value.

What nearly always happened in these emotionally interesting cases was that the jury became so engrossed in the domestic dramas unfolded before them that they forgot their limited capacity as financial arbiters, and fixed the plaintiff's solatium at a figure which had little to do with the wife's "worth," but everything to do with their feelings as to the degree of sympathy deserved by her husband, and the punishment deserved by her seducer.

Theo Cibber would have no difficulty convincing a jury that William Sloper had stolen his wife and, with her, her handsome salary. But if he were also going to persuade them to give him £5,000 of Sloper's money, he could not admit having engineered the romance, having coerced his frightened young wife into admitting Sloper to her friendship, and, once the affair was begun, having profited hugely from it, sharing a household with the lovers until they themselves evicted him. He must, therefore, in the few months before the trial, construct a corrected version of these events.

Theo spent August writing four long, impassioned letters, two to Susannah, and two to her lover, giving the affair a new chronology and character. William and Susannah never received these letters, of course. Nor is it likely that Theo was naïve enough to believe he could introduce them as evidence in the trial. His purpose was to publish them as widely as possible, and to place before the London public his uncontradicted version of his wife's perfidy.

The first letter, to "my Dearest Susannah Maria," Theo predated April 16, with a note explaining that this was "the day before the husband went abroad, the wife having confessed her love for another." Broken and distracted by the revelation that Susannah has been unfaithful with a man he has regarded as an old family friend, tempted by suicide, which he only resists out of compassion for his wife's guilty suffering if he carried it out, this new and sympathetic Theo begs Susannah for the sake of her immortal soul to give up her "unjustifiable Passions and deceiving Pleasures," and return to "The Comfort and Happiness warranted and protected by the Laws of God and Man." He promises to take her back without resentment, aware both of his Christian duty to forgive and of his own shortcomings, which consist of a tendency toward liberality, and such a doting affection for her that in loading her with gifts and luxuries he has fallen into financial embarrassments. He signs the letter, "your repentant, fond, affectionate, tender, truly loving, tho' unhappy husband."

The second letter, dated August 1738, is addressed to Sloper, "a gentleman once thought a friend." Theo bitterly reminisces about the love affair which he says he now realizes began with "Masquerades and Chapell Meetings," and "a damn'd literary Correspondence." He recalls that Susannah's abrupt confession of her guilt the previous April "immediately drove me from England," omitting his own disastrous financial situation and blaming his flight to Calais on his fevered state of mind. "My humble Service to her," the letter concludes, "and I thank her and you for my Ruin, which I shall rise above."

The third letter, undated, is also addressed to Sloper. Its purpose seems to be to establish the loftiness and financial disinterestedness of Theo's position, and incidentally to inform the public of Susannah's earning capacity, a capacity he claims was developed entirely through his efforts. He informs Sloper that he is determined to get a divorce; "a thorough one, I have learned, is not so excessively expensive as some may have imagined. 'Tis all I want in lieu of a fine Lady and her Income which by my Means may yet be £400 a Year. I would beg rather than share it with her. I think Money Dirt, Sir, and scorn to pick it off Dunghills." Theo's remarks about divorce were posturing, of course, for divorce in the eighteenth century was so expensive and so drawn out, requiring both ecclesiastical and parliamentary sanction, that it was only for the very rich, the very powerful, and the very persistent.

Letter IV, dated the first of September, is addressed to Susannah. It is a long and emotional recapitulation of their courtship and marriage, with special emphasis on his magnanimity to her and to her family.

When I made you my wife I knew I wedded a beautiful, sensible young Woman . . . whose Prudence, whose Religion, whose artless Innocence, whose careful, sober Education . . . were such as nothing could tempt to any Act or even Thought that was in the least repugnant to the strictest Principles of Truth and Virtue. . . . I acted with that Nicety, that Extravagance of Honour toward you, Madam, that by my own Desire, Marriage Articles were drawn to make you Mistress of whatever Fortune might accrue to you from your own Talents. . . . You did not bring me a Shilling, and 'twas almost impossible you should ever get one without my Conduct, my Care, Assistance, Instruction and Advice. . . . What Anxiety I have endured, what Assiduity, what Diligence I have used, what uncommon Means to support you! I have hazarded Friendships, made myself a public Jest, set my own Interest at naught. . . . I am sorry I have Occasion to mention your poor unfortunate Family; but as Distress is no Crime, I shall venture to remind you, from an uncommon Regard to you, I thought of their Interest and Support, even to the Prejudice of my Own, and omitted enlarging my own Income to promote theirs . . . as I preferr'd obliging you and all that belonged to you to all Considerations upon the Face of the Earth. . . . I thought no Expense too much that supported what I must now call your Pride and Vanity. . . . Was I expensive in my Dwelling? Was my Equipage above me? My table too open to Friends? . . . Why did I not retrench all? Because my Fondness and Pride would not let me, while you were my Partner and presided as Mistress over all. . . . Love, Fondness, Tenderness! I have shewn 'em to Excess; ay, felt 'em to Excess! Nor was my Love so sickly [as] to diminish by Fruition, but rather 'Increase of Appetite did grow by what it fed on' . . . God knows, I have continued the Lover when I should have asserted the Husband; but rather chose, by Tenderness, to touch the Heart I valu'd than force myself, contrary to my Nature, to be a Tyrant or a Jailor. . . . When I went to France, you know you drove me thither. . . . I own I wished to be recall'd. Why? Because England held you. . . . My Difficulties were more owing to my distracted State of Mind on your Account than any other Impediment.

One of the things which Theo knew would be used against him by Sloper's defense was his insistence upon a ménage à trois. This outrageous charge Theo now denies in a burst of moral indignation.

I thought I knew your Sex not a little, but you, Madam, have made all that Knowledge nothing. . . . Your cunning Artifice, your strange Conduct in having private Meetings in Chapells, Masquerades and Places that shock me to think of . . . have made me start. Your presuming to lay a Plan for our living together on such audacious Terms as you proposed makes me shudder to think you could utter 'em; while I smile at your ridiculous Folly that could suppose I would go through with it. No Consideration upon Earth shall ever make me again eat a Meal with you or sleep under the same Roof.

Theo concludes his long bid for public sympathy by blaming all his financial troubles on Susannah, and asserting his right to redress.

Articles of Separation shall be drawn. . . . Those Articles, Madam, ought to leave us each as free as we were once, nor is it reasonable I should be liable to a Jail for the Indiscretions of Others. . . . You have spent me infinitely more than your own Income ever amounted to. . . . I bought your Wedding Suit, Madam! . . . My few remaining Goods I must part with, and my whole Salary must go to those good natured Creditors who have comply'd, though they [the debts] are all yours, Madam, as much as mine. Nor must my Children starve while you riot.

Theo's four letters were ludicrous, and not a bookseller in the city would touch them. He always maintained the reason for this was intimidation on the part of the Sloper family and he said as much in a note to the reader when the letters were eventually printed in January 1739: "These Letters had been offered to the Public much sooner had not some Booksellers and Printers been intimidated from publishing 'em; one in particular, by some Means, was alarmed even to the breaking of the Press, when the Whole was completely compos'd and ready to be worked off."

For once Theo may have been telling the truth. In William Sloper Theo was taking on a very different adversary from naïve and straitlaced Highmore, profligate Fleetwood, or sharp-clawed Kitty Clive. An attack on his only son and heir was an attack upon William Sloper, Senior, and this self-made man was a formidable enemy. Vigorous Whig, member of Parliament, friend of Robert Walpole, and frequent speaker on behalf of the Prime Minister's policies, one of the four original founders of the Georgia Colony,[3] trustee of nearly every charitable organization in London, tireless philanthropist, and at one time or another deputy cofferer of the Privy Purse, paymaster for His Majesty's troops in Scotland, and agent for the British Colony of New York, old William Sloper's connections and influence were far-flung and incalculable. He would have had no trouble in seeing that these letters were suppressed until the litigation was over, and he may well have done so.

Since Theo could not get his side of the story before the public in advance of the trial, it was clear he would have to think of another way to dramatize his role as a heartsick husband who, having returned from abroad, finds his beloved wife has left his house and is living with her lover. On the stage, what would such a desperate husband do? He would — by force, if necessary — go fetch her home again.

On Friday, September 8, Theophilus Cibber with a hired coach and driver and two burly toughs (a man called Fife and another called Watson) set out for Burnham, armed to the teeth. The posse arrived near Sloper's rented house about four in the afternoon, and the coach and driver were left out of sight in a field. Theo, bristling with pistols, and Fife and Watson crossed the field and burst into the unlocked house, where they found the lovers in the drawing room. Susannah, in a dressing gown, was "sitting at the tea table, and Mr Sloper [was] at the other side of it in his slippers." Sloper rose from his chair, cursed and "called Mr Cibber hard names,"[4] while Theo, brandishing his weapons, demanded his wife. The scene was melodramatic, risible, and very dangerous, as things often were with

Susannah Cibber Handing William Sloper Her Silver Watch.

Theophilus. Sloper, unarmed and alone, could not possibly have defended Susannah against three, and Susannah, who always took her husband in deadly earnest, immediately crossed the room to him and agreed to go with him to London.

The five of them left the house together, Theo leading the way across the field, Susannah following, with Fife holding one arm while she clung to Sloper with the other, Watson bringing up the rear. Before Susannah climbed into the coach she took a watch from her pocket and gave it to Sloper for safekeeping. "By God, well remembered," Fife heard the Squire say. "The rascal would have had it else!"[5] This little exchange was one of several episodes which were illustrated to accompany the pirated transcript of the Sloper-Cibber trial. The accompanying illustration shows Theo, bug-eyed with self-importance, strutting in advance of the others in his swashbuckling Pistol costume, the role which summed him up for the London public. Sloper and Susannah follow in dishabille, two fashionable, sentimental lovers, exchanging a despairing gaze, as, with a languishing gesture, she hands him her watch. Fife and Watson glower beneath their military tricornes, and the coachman looks down impassively.

The minute the coach drove off, Sloper rushed back to the house to dress and arm and presently, on horseback, to overtake it on the London road. Though he rode along beside it for miles, pounding on its side and crying out to passersby that "there was a villain in that coach,"[6] he attracted nothing but barks and stares, and, unaided, could do nothing against a closed conveyance with armed men inside.

By the time the coach had lurched and swayed as far as the town of Slough, a trip punctuated by Sloper's shouts and threats from outside, and Theo's ferocious rejoinders from the window, Susannah, who was three months pregnant, and who even in the best of health and company was a queasy traveler, had become so ill that Theo was frightened and decided to stop for the night. Leaving Fife and Watson to guard her, he went into the inn to arrange for accommodations. Inside the coach, Susannah begged her keepers to open a window and give her air. They did so and she leaned out, whereupon Sloper came up alongside. She asked him to get her something to drink, and he brought her a glass of spirits from the inn.

The entire party, Sloper and all, presently went into the inn at Slough, where Susannah, confronting the curious host, the snickering servants, and the gawking locals, "called her husband a great many villains and said that now that he had ruined her reputation she did not value it if all the world knew she was with child by Squire Sloper and that she loved him dearly."[7]

Everyone settled down for an uneasy night; Susannah in a room with a woman from the inn Theo had employed to sit with her, Fife and Watson outside her door with their pistols on their laps, Theo, downstairs in the public room, drinking, and Sloper pacing wretchedly in his own room, unwilling to abandon Susannah yet afraid to try to rescue her for fear of injury to someone. Supper was brought to Susannah, but she could not eat and had it taken away. The sight of the laden, odorous tray carried in past his nose and out again worked deeply on the mind of Fife, who reported the incident to the court when he testified, offering his opinion that the only thing which could explain Susannah's behavior was that "she was sulky."[8]

On Saturday morning, September 9, Sloper's room was discovered empty and his horse gone from the stable. Theo, afraid that he had ridden ahead to collect support and might be waiting to waylay the coach between Slough and London, did not follow the direct road to London but drove across part of the country and got to London in the evening. Nor was he foolish enough to take Susannah to his own lodging on Bow Street where a rescue party might be waiting. He took her instead to a house near Clare Market where, before his foray to Burnham, he had arranged for a room and a keeper. Susannah was placed under the care of a Mr. Stint, a candle snuffer from Drury Lane, while Theo hurried off to the theater where he was due to play Foppington in Vanbrugh's *The Relapse,* at six o'clock.

At the trial Stint testified for the plaintiff that no effort was spared by Mrs. Cibber's husband to make her comfortable. Meat was dressed and brought to her from the nearby Bull's Tavern, along with a pint of white wine and a pint of red. After her long day's drive into London, racketing over back roads and rutted lanes, Susannah was as unable to eat as she had been the night before. She only huddled in a chair and moaned that she was cold, whereupon the obliging Stint closed her window, built a fire, and withdrew, locking her door as he did. He had hardly settled himself outside to admire the brace of pistols Theo had left with him when his prisoner began to knock and call from within that her chimney was smoking. "She begged for God's Sake I would let her out or else she would be stifled,"⁹ Stint testified, and there was nothing to do but allow the lady to stand in the hall while he doused the fire and aired the room. When order was restored and Susannah secured again in her cold room, Stint settled down. But dark had not fallen over London before the unfortunate candle snuffer regretted having anything to do with the detention of Mr. Cibber's wife.

The glimpses we have had of William Sloper from the time Theo burst into his house at Burnham until he stole off from the inn at Slough at dawn suggest a young man taken off stride, and neither thinking nor behaving very effectively. At some time in those pre-dawn hours, pacing in his room at the inn, Sloper came to himself. He knew he was miscast in this burlesque drama devised by Theo, and he slipped away for London to consult the family attorneys and make sensible plans for Susannah's rescue.

On their advice he went to Susannah's family, apprised them of her situation, and turned the freeing her over to her elder brother. For a lover to attempt to wrest a wife from her husband — no matter how special the circumstances — was a criminal act. It was possible, even probable, that at the bottom of Theo's absurd abduction of Susannah was his hope of provoking Sloper into just such a rash attempt.

It did not take Tom Arne long to find his sister. Stint, after all, was employed at Drury Lane where Arne was resident composer, and nothing as sensational as Theo's seizure and imprisonment of his wife could remain a secret backstage for long.

Stint had no sooner doused Susannah's fire, slipped the bolt on her door, and settled himself outside when there was a knock on the outer door of the house. It was young Mr. Arne, whom Stint knew well, asking for the release of his sister in his care. Stint refused. Arne retired to consult with Sloper and Sloper's counsel. He returned to Stint presently, and again demanded his sister. Once again Stint refused. Once again Arne withdrew. When he came the third time it was with his younger brother, Henry Peter, and a force of men. As soon as Tom was within earshot of the house he called in a loud voice for Susannah, if she heard him, to cry out for help, so that witnesses could vouch for her being held within against her will. She immediately "cried out murder," as Stint remembered it, and as soon as she did her brothers, and the mob, which Stint reckoned at "at least a hundred," set about "to break open the house."

"I had a case of pistols and laid my back to the door," Stint assured the court, "but they were too strong for me and took my pistols out of each hand and held me fast by each arm, and beat me severely and tore all the clothes off my back, and took Mrs Cibber away with them."[10] Tom took Susannah at once to their mother's house in St. Giles. The next morning, accompanied by her mother and brothers, she appeared before a justice and swore the peace against Theophilus, after which he was forbidden to molest his wife, to interfere with her movements, or to threaten her.*

* "A husband (under the old law) might give his wife moderate correction. For, as he is to answer for her misbehaviour, the law thought it reasonable to intrust him with this power of restraining her by domestic chastizement of the same moderation that a man is allowed to correct his apprentices or children. . . . The civil law gave

Two days later, as soon as Susannah was rested, she and Sloper and Anne Hopson, who had arrived from Burnham with her mistress's clothes and effects, left London and proceeded by easy stages to Reading, the market town closest to West Woodhay, the Slopers' Berkshire estate. Reading was too far from London for Theo to be tempted — in the midst of the theatrical season — to make any overnight forays.

Theo's attempts to play the serious role of a suffering husband had rebounded against him. On the night Susannah was rescued by her brothers, word of her escape got back to Drury Lane, and Theo was loudly hissed at the final curtain.[11]

On December 1, just five days before the trial, Theo made one last public bid for sympathy. The *London Daily Post* of this day noted:

We hear a neat monument will be erected in the Church Yard of St. Paul's, Covent Garden on which will be enscribed the following epitaph:

"Juxta hoc Marmor
   Sitae sunt reliquiae
   Janie Cibberii, Histriones haud ignotae
   Illam defunctam lugent Amici.
   Potius gaudete
   Non enim moritum tantum mutatum
   Et virgo et Conjux
   Vulte venusto
   Forma egregia
   Non Intentata
   Virtutis, Fidesque tenax
   Memoriae Suavissimae

---

the husband . . . a larger control over his wife: allowing him . . . flagellis et fustibus acriter verberare uxorem. . . .

"But with us, in the politer reign of Charles the Second, this power of correction began to be doubted: and a wife may now have the security of the peace against her husband. . . . Yet the lower rank of people . . . still claim and exert their ancient privileges: and the Courts of Law will still permit a husband to restrain a wife of her liberty in case of any gross misbehaviour." Sir William Blackstone, *Commentaries on the English Laws, 1765*, in 4 vols. (Philadelphia: Rees Welsh & Co., 1897), vol. 1, pp. 444–445.

Hoc Posuit
Theophilus Cibberius
Maritus, maestus que Superstes
    Nata 1705 — Abuit 1732"[12]

For six years Janey Cibber's remains had lain in St. Paul's churchyard. Theo had never got round to ordering even a wooden marker to tell the place. Her widower's sudden recollection of his undying devotion to her and his announcement of his grand intentions cost Theo no more than some hours rummaging in his dusty Winchester classical education. The stone was never erected.

In death, as in life, gentle Janey served as a sentimental lever for her husband's enrichment; in this case, in his attempt to extract £5,000 from the lover of his second wife.

By December 1, Susannah and William were in London again to await the trial. On advice of counsel they were living separately, he at his father's town house in St. James Place, she, now seven months with child, at her mother's modest place in St. Giles.

⊰ 10 ⊱

THE Cibber-Sloper trial began at nine in the morning of December 5, 1738, at the Court of the King's Bench, before Sir William Lee, the mild and slightly dull-witted Lord Chief Justice. So unblemished was Sir William's private life, so scrupulously timid his legal decisions that he was the despair of his biographer,[1] who complained that there was nothing in his life to sink one's teeth in. Whatever Sir William's failings as a dramatic subject, he was regarded as a great man during his lifetime, and revered for his compassionate concern for the rights of women and the poor.

Representing the plaintiff was John Strange, the Solicitor General, supported by Mr. Hollings, Mr. Sergeant Agar, Mr. Marsh, Mr. Dennison, and Mr. Lawson. William Sloper's chief counsel was Mr. Sergeant Eyre, assisted by Mr. Noel, Mr. Lloyd, Mr. Barnardiston, and a junior counsel named William Murray, of whom we shall hear more. Neither of the two principals nor Susannah was in the court room.

The complaint, read out by Mr. Lawson, accused Sloper of "assaulting, ravishing and carnally knowing Susannah Maria Cibber, the Plaintiff's Wife . . . at several Periods of Time . . . and divers Days . . . whereby the Plaintiff lost the Company, Comfort, Society and Assistance of his Wife to his Damage of £5000."[2]

The first witness for the plaintiff was Colley Cibber, who was questioned about the early years of his son's marriage. Colley recalled that Theo and Susannah had been happy indeed in those days, and that Theo had supported her, not only "well and liberally" but "even to profusion." Theo's popinjay parent, though perfectly willing to corroborate Theo's counsel's hint that Theo's only flaw as a husband had been his doting prodigality, was not willing to give his son credit for having developed Susannah's astonishing dramatic talent. "Did not her husband take pains to instruct her?" asked Mr. Strange, hoping to show how professionally indebted Susannah was to her husband.

"I believe *I* was the person who chiefly instructed her," Colley corrected him, "I spent a great deal of time and took great delight in it."[3] Excused from the stand, the powdered and scented Laureate made his graceful way out of the packed courtroom and into his waiting chair.

Charles Fleetwood was called next. His testimony sounds peevish. Nine in the morning was an uncivilized hour for a gentleman to be required to be up and abroad and embroiled in the sordid domestic wranglings of a pair of players, neither of whom he liked. He had been indefatigable four years before in his efforts to help Charles Macklin evade a murder charge, but Macklin was his pet. He was asked by plaintiff's counsel for a résumé of Susannah's earnings during the three years she had been at Drury Lane. "If I had known I should be examined as to this," Fleetwood protested, "I could have been particular. As it is, I have not looked into the accounts." As best he could remember, Susannah's salary the first year had been a hundred pounds with a benefit worth about the same. The second year he had paid her two hundred pounds and her benefit had brought her a little more than a hundred. The third year her salary was two hundred pounds and her benefit "must have been worth a hundred and fifty, for she grew much in the favour of the town and 'twas a very good benefit."

Theo's counsel pressed the patentee to agree that Susannah was by now as eminent as any woman at Drury Lane and, were she under articles this season, would be receiving top salary. "I can't say that," Fleetwood snapped. "I have got more money by Mrs Clive."[4] He was excused from the stand and went off to get his breakfast, with a pint of porter to settle his head and ease the stabs of gout which by this time in his life continuously tortured him.

Now that the distinguished witnesses from the gentry had been heard — first off so as not to inconvenience them by hours of waiting — the court turned to the meaty evidence of the matter, supplied by a very different sort of witness. Mrs. Hayes from Blue Cross Street in Leicester Fields was sworn and gave her account of how Anne Hopson had rented rooms from her the previous December: "She beat them down as low as she could, for she said she was a single woman and should give but little trouble; she had nobody to come after her but a lady and a gentleman that would come to see her sometimes. She had the lodgings for seven shillings a week." Mrs. Hayes assured the court that the instant she recognized the vile nature of the visits of Mrs. Hopson's "lady" and "gentleman," she gave her lodger notice, despite the wretch's pleas.[5]

Mrs. Hayes's air of outraged respectability was somewhat spoiled by her husband, who followed her directly to the stand. His relishful account of the doings in Mrs. Hopson's rooms made it seem doubtful that his wife could have been innocent of the truth for so long as she said she was.

"When Mrs Hopson had my lodgings," Mr. Hayes explained,

Mr Sloper and Mrs Cibber came often to her, and she used to leave them together two or three hours at a time. They used to go away at one, two, or three o'clock in the morning, in coaches or chairs. I have a closet on the same floor, adjoining to the room where they used to sit. I bored holes through the wainscot and could see them very plain. He used to kiss her and take her on his lap. On the 22nd day of December I was looking through. He took her on his knees, lifted up her clothes and took down his breeches and took his privy member and put it in his hand and put it between her legs. On the 12th of January I was locked up in the closet at one o'clock in the afternoon, and he came first, and he was angry because she was not come, and he sent Mrs Hopson for her. In about two hours she came. Mrs Hopson went away and left them alone. He spoke something to her in an angry way about Mr Fleetwood. She said she would take away her brother from his house and that she did not value Mr Fleetwood. He and she grew friends again. They made it up and he took her upon his lap, took off her clothes, took down his breeches and put his privy member between her legs. I stayed there longer. Between five and six in the evening he let down the turn up bed softly, she laid herself upon it, upon her back, and pulled up her clothes. Her body was bare. He unbuttoned his clothes, hung up his bag wig upon a sconce, let down his breeches, took his privy member in his hand and lay down upon her.[6]

"Enough!" interrupted good Sir William Lee. "There is no occasion to be more particular. We are not trying a rape!" It was sufficient for the court to hear that the witness had observed with his own eyes a criminal act, or acts, between the defendant and the plaintiff's wife. The details of this act, or these acts, were beyond the scope of inquiry. And so Mr. Hayes, who was only warming to his task, whose head contained the particulars of many other occasions, stepped off the witness stand and returned to obscurity and to Mrs. Hayes.

The testimony of Mr. Carter of Kensington was an anticlimax after Mr. Hayes. Still, under cross examination by Sloper's lawyers he gave the first evidence of Cibber's complicity. "Who," asked the defendant's counsel, "bore the expense of their housekeeping" after the young Cibbers and Sloper had taken his lodgings together last March?

"Mr Sloper did," Mr. Carter answered. "Sometimes he gave my wife money to lay out. At other times my wife laid out what was necessary and made a bill of it and Mr Sloper paid it."

"Did Mr Cibber know of this?"

"Yes, Sir. It was often done before his face."

"Did he offer to pay anything?"

"No, Sir."[7]

Mrs. Carter corroborated her husband's story, though she was more vituperative. When Sloper's counsel asked her why, though she was aware of the relationship between her three tenants, she "kept such a house," she retorted, "I thought it no business of mine, if the husband consented and was satisfied." It was Mrs. Carter's opinion that "Mr Cibber was a mean spirited dog."[8]

Anne Hopson was called. She was defensive about her role in the business. "I will tell you all I know of the matter," she replied tartly to one of Theo's lawyers who suggested that she could not tell the whole truth without compromising her own reputation.

I do not fear my character. There are enough in this court who will give me a very good character. It was about March was twelve month that Mr Sloper used first to come to our house, to Mr Cibber's. The servants did not know who he was, but my master called him Mr Benefit, and used to say he was a romp and a good natured boy. Mr Cibber was then very bare of money and afraid of his creditors. I was very sorry for it, for he owed me a good deal of money and does so still. But one day he told me, "Anne," says he, "I shall have a great deal of money soon, and you shall have some." And I know he soon after had a good deal of money, and he paid me five guineas. That summer we went to lodge in Kingston, and Mr Sloper with us. My master used often to leave Mr Sloper and my mistress at home and go riding, or abroad somewhere or other.[9]

Mrs. Hopson glossed quickly over the Hayes episode, saying merely that she left the Cibbers' service after they came back to town, took lodgings of her own, and intended to return to the mantua-making business in which she had been trained as a child. She acknowledged that Mrs. Cibber and Mr. Sloper had often visited her at her rooms at the Hayeses'. When asked why she supposed they met there so often, she shrugged, "As they were acquaintances, to converse together." After she left the Hayeses' she returned to work for the Cibbers. "About last March, I lived with them again. My master took me aside and made me promise secrecy concerning something he was about to tell me. He told me he was going to France, that there was an affair between Mr Sloper and his wife; and he made me promise to live with her till he should come back."

And now the Solicitor General, John Strange, led off the plaintiff's plea to the jury. The injury inflicted upon Mr. Cibber had been, he said, the tenderest hurt possible: "to his peace of mind, his happiness, and his hopes of prosperity." No pecuniary satisfaction could ever be adequate to this injury, for money cannot restore a man's tranquillity. Nevertheless, the plaintiff rested confidently on such remedy as the law would give him.

Strange reminded the jury that the plaintiff, though a player, was a gentleman and well descended. His father was the first figure in the theatrical profession in all England, and a gentleman and an author, while the plaintiff's grandfather had been the best "statuary"* of his day. On his mother's side, young Mr. Cibber was related to William of Wickham and had received a classical education at Winchester, an institution founded by that great and pious man. Though some people were wont to regard players as not on the same footing as other of His Majesty's subjects, "as if it were more lawful to invade their properties than those of other people," Mr. Strange knew of no law that deprived actors of the same rights and comforts as other loyal citizens. As a matter of fact "the stage has long been cherished and encouraged as a school of virtue and morals."

The Solicitor General warned the jury that Sloper had gone to great lengths to spread a report about town that Mr. Cibber had consented to — even abetted — the wrong done him, so that the case had come before them with prejudice. All of this was nothing more than surmise and malicious inference, while the fact of a criminal relationship between the defendant and the plaintiff's wife was irrefutably established.[10]

Mr. Sergeant Eyre, chief of Sloper's battery of defense attorneys, rose to rebut Mr. Strange. He was surprised, he said, to learn today that the theater "was a place celebrated for virtue." He was surprised, too, to learn that the plaintiff was "descended from William of Wickham," a Romish bishop who lived long before the Reformation, and had always, he would have supposed, abided within the

---

* Caius-Gabriel Cibber (1630–1700), Colley's father.

laws of celibacy which then "prevailed among the clergy."* Mr. Eyre further "hoped that nothing criminal had passed between" his client and the plaintiff's wife, "but if it had, the plaintiff had certainly encouraged it and had no pretense to come to a jury for damages."[11]

Speaking next on Sloper's side, Mr. Lloyd also "hoped" that there had been no breach of decorum between the defendant and Mrs. Cibber, but that if certain evidence "seemed to point that way," the plaintiff was surely "privy and consenting." He reminded the jury of the old maxim of law and reason: *Volenti non fit Injuria.*[12]

Young William Murray, the junior counsel for the defense, rose last. He was the eleventh, but by no means the last child of a noble Scottish couple, the fifth Viscount Stormont and his lady, parents as fecund as they were impoverished. When young William had first come to England from Perth as a penniless King's Scholar at Westminster, his burr caused a great deal of merriment among his classmates. But so awesome was his intellect, and so able was he to defend himself with fisticuffs, that the titters quickly subsided. In maturity Murray had a fine voice and an elegant declamatory style, but he was never quite able to rid himself of his recidivous burr, so that today he addressed his senior opponent on the plaintiff's side as "Meester Soleester Gen'ral."[13]

Murray told the court he regretted he could not, like his esteemed colleagues, "hope" that nothing indecent had passed between the plaintiff's wife and the defendant. It was clear that these two — one of whom was his own client — "had gone beyond the bounds of duty." But equally clear — and how much more iniquitous! — was the evidence that the plaintiff had not only consented but "concerted" in the crime.

He begged the court's indulgence to review the circumstances: "The defendant is a young gentleman of fortune who became acquainted with a player and his wife. She, being mistress of all the alluring arts of the stage, first engaged the young gentleman's affection, then drew him in, and this with the husband's privity and assistance." Whenever young Sloper visited the Cibbers' house, "the

* To be fair, Theo's lawyer had not said that Theo was descended from, but only collaterally related to, William of Wickham (1323–1404) through the Shores.

plaintiff concealed the Defendant's true name from the knowledge of the Servants. At one place he called him 'Cousin Thompson,' at another, 'Mr Benefit'; a cant name," Mr. Murray explained to the innocent jurors, "taken from a particular night in the year when they [players] get a great deal of money." Only to Mrs. Hopson, to whom he owed wages, did Cibber confide that he would soon have a great deal of money, that Sloper was "a romp and a goodnatured boy," and, indeed, "he made a boy of him!"

To this "boy" he resigns his wife! From this "boy" he takes money to maintain his family! And then he comes to a court of justice and to a jury of gentlemen for reparation in damages! It devolves on you, gentlemen, to consider the consequences of giving damages in a case of this nature. Infinite mischiefs would ensue if it should once come to be understood in the world, that two artful people, being husband and wife, may lay a snare for the affections of an unwary young gentleman, take a sum of money from him, and then come to extort more with the assistance of twelve jurymen. I desire to be understood as by no means an advocate for the immoralities of my client; but remember, gentlemen, this is not a prosecution seeking punishment for the sake of the public; the only question here is, whether the plaintiff has been injured, and surely he cannot justly represent himself as injured if he has not only consented but received a high price for that which he does not at all value. However, gentlemen of the jury, if it be thought requisite to find a verdict for the plaintiff, we have not a denomination of coin small enough to measure the damages.[14]

The defense rested. The Solicitor General rose briefly to warn the jury of the risk to the sanctity of British homes if Sloper went unpunished. Sir William Lee summed up the evidence, and the jury withdrew. In half an hour they were back with a verdict, having found (Mr. Hayes's graphic evidence admitting no interpretation but one) that a criminal conversation had taken place, making a verdict for the plaintiff mandatory. But their contempt for Theo, and their sympathy for the young country gentleman who had fallen

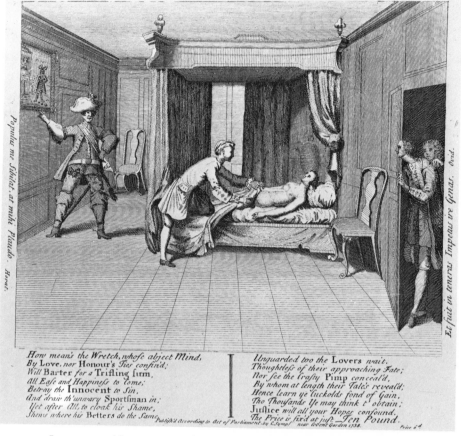

PISTOLS A CUCKOLD, OR ADULTERY IN FASHION.

Populus me Sibilat, at mihi Plaudo. Horat.

Et fuit in teneris Impetus ire Genas. Ovid.

How mean's the Wretch, whose abject Mind,
By Love, nor Honour's Ties confin'd;
Will Barter for a Trifling sum,
All Ease and Happiness to come;
Betray the Innocent to Sin,
And draw th'unwary Sportsman in;
Yet after All, to cloak his Shame,
Shews where his Betters do the Same.

Unguarded too the Lovers wait,
Thoughtless of their approaching Fate;
Nor see the Crafty Pimp conceal'd,
By whom at length their Tale's reveal'd;
Hence learn ye Cuckolds fond of Gain,
Tho Thousands Ye may think t' obtain;
Justice will all your Hopes confound.
The Price is fix'd at just Ten Pound.

Publish'd according to Act of Parliament by C.Symps near Covent Garden 1738.

Price 6ᵈ

In a magnificent, canopied bed lies Susannah, in real life a
slight woman, here a fleshy and impassive nude. William
Sloper has modestly placed a nightcap on his head and has
lowered the bedclothes. Theo Cibber, in Pistol's characteristic
stance and costume, is at the foot of the bed. He points to a
picture of Quin dressed as Cato. One of the more curious episodes in this Roman's life (not mentioned in Addison's play)
was his relinquishing his wife, Marcia, to his friend Hortensius. After Marcia had borne him several children, Hortensius
died, and Cato complacently welcomed Marcia back, garnering
in the process Hortensius's children and huge estates. Theo, in
line with his attorneys' declaration that the theater is a place
for the instruction of virtue, is showing the beholder the classical precedent for lending out one's wife for money. On the
other side of the room Mr. and Mrs. Hayes are peering at the
bed from around a closet door. Why the artist did not show
Mr. Hayes squatting in his closet with his eyes against the peepholes is hard to imagine, unless he felt that it lay beyond his
powers.

into the jaws of this theatrical fox and his lecherous vixen, was clear. Instead of the £5,000 Theo had asked, they awarded him £10; not, as Murray had suggested, the smallest coin in the realm, but at least the smallest bill in circulation.

The jury had tapped Sloper's wrist with a feather, and dashed Theo's hopes of sudden wealth. Neither of the principals was much injured or changed by the verdict: Sloper's fortune was intact, and Theo's condition no more deplorable than it had been for years. But there were two people whose lives were profoundly affected by the trial: Murray, the man whose eloquence saved Sloper, and whose fortune it made, and Susannah Cibber, who lost her good name and her livelihood.

Because of the prominence of the persons involved in the Cibber-Sloper affair, and its sensational nature, Sir William Lee had instructed that no court stenographer be present, and no record of the proceedings made. Nevertheless, somebody in the crowded courtroom (probably a poor law clerk who could use a few pounds) had taken down a shorthand account of the trial and at its conclusion hurried straight to Trott, the bookseller. A few days later a little book of thirty-odd pages, called *A Tryal of a Cause,* was offered for sale.* Within a week there was not a duchess nor an apprentice in London who did not know precisely what Mr. Hayes had seen through his closet peepholes.

The speech of the junior counsel for the defense, the speech by which he had at the last moment snatched his client's fortune from the jaws of a mountebank couple, filled London with admiration. Clients flocked to William Murray's door, including Sarah, the vastly wealthy, cantankerous, and insatiably litigious Dowager Duchess of Marlborough. Years later, when he was no longer Mr. Murray but Lord Mansfield, having succeeded John Strange as Solicitor General, risen to Attorney General, followed good Sir William Lee into the ermine of the Lord Chief Justice, and attained the peerage, he complacently dated his rise from the seamy Cibber-Sloper trial. "Hence-

* The Cibber-Sloper trial continued to be reprinted throughout Susannah Cibber's lifetime and for the next century and more. The Harvard law library has a copy published in Dublin in 1749. The little book was a favorite item for Victorian connoisseurs of naughty literature.

forth," he liked to recall, "business poured in upon me from all quarters; and from a few hundred pounds a year, I fortunately found myself in the receipt of thousands."[15]

The trial made Murray's career. It extinguished Susannah Cibber's. She had been, as no actress before her, idolized as the quintessence of chaste womanhood. Her domestic situation, married to a brute, herself undefiled, had illuminated her portrayals of imperiled virgins and suffering wives. What an Isabella, tortured by lecherous Angelo! What a Desdemona, slain by her rash husband! The revelation that she was not bearing her personal unhappiness in sweet resignation, but grasping at carnal pleasures in the embraces of a married man, was a betrayal to those gentle ladies who had been her devotees. And the possibility that she had been in league with her appalling husband to milk Sloper placed her beyond the reach of their pity.

If the trial's publicity had merely made it impossible to earn her living it would have been a grievous blow. But it was far more painful to have the most private passages of her relationship with Sloper slavered over, turned into lewd cartoons and ribald verses.

To old Thomas Arne's earnest, devout daughter, so trusting, scrupulous, and literal, becoming a lady had once meant assuming a grace which was not hers by birth, but which she meant to achieve by study, by discipline, by ingratiation, by dedicating herself to all the principles of feminine virtue and accomplishment, so that her distinction would shine out and be recognized by some highborn young suitor. After this girlish dream was broken and she began to "play" ladies, the stage became the place where she could be the self she deserved. It was a precarious identity, no more substantial than its nightly verification in her audience's response. The scandal of the trial was a nightmare come true: the exposure of her real self, her low origin, the daughter of a coarse and venal tradesman.

The vengeance Theo had promised if Susannah ever tested his authority over her body and soul had come. She was despised, ridiculed, ruined, with no more chance of a life with her lover than before the trial. Theo had won the verdict, even though the prize had been withheld. Since he still professed himself ready to take back his wife, he had set things up in such a way that if Sloper lived with

*William Murray, First Earl
of Mansfield, Lord Chief
Justice of the King's Bench,
by David Martin.*

her, visited her, or contributed to her support, he would be subject
to further suits for detaining Susannah and contributing to her continued delinquency. This jury had been willing to see Sloper as a
gulled young fool and rap his fingers lightly. A second jury would
expect him to have learned his lesson.

Despite Theo's surveillance of Mrs. Arne's house, Sloper did
manage to meet with Susannah there. Swollen of belly, white and
emaciated, she bore very little resemblance to the lovely girl he had
first seen across the foot tapers two years before, the actress with the
stainless reputation, the piteous marriage, the thrilling voice, the
slight body that seemed too frail to bear the emotions which shook it.
Now she was only a wretched, ruined woman, pitifully dependent
upon him.

And even if she did not reprove him for having made light of
her womanish fears of Theo and having urged her to defy her husband, even if she did not protest his own counsel's cruel strategy in
preserving the Sloper fortune by vilifying her (though Sloper must

have been able to convince her that he had known nothing before-
hand of the gist of Murray's speech and certainly had not known that
the trial would be published), she was that most uncomfortable of
females, a figure of dumb reproach, her suffering as encompassing as
it was unmerited, while almost no retribution had fallen on him.

Of a future together there seemed no chance whatever. That the
time had come to end this smutched affair and abandon his ruined
actress to make her peace with her husband was obvious to everybody
in London but William Sloper. This unfashionable man, with his
stubborn country ways, cherished Susannah as steadfastly as ever.
His fidelity, his staunchness, his optimism, his tenderness lit up the
next wintry months, and may well have preserved Susannah's life. It
is a period of which, thanks to Theo Cibber's unquenchable enthusiasm to injure these two people further, we have a number of
glimpses.

❧ II ❧

The calamities of an unhappy marriage are so much greater than can
befall a single person that the unmarried woman may find abundant
argument to be contented with her condition.
— MRS. CHAPONE, *On the Improvement of the Mind,* 1773

THE trial brought Theo one modest reward. His apocryphal
letters to Sloper and Susannah which book sellers had
spurned before the trial were eagerly accepted in the
hullabaloo following it. The cash they brought was welcome because
Theo had been so busy preparing his case he had not appeared on the
stage since October and Fleetwood had docked him. These preposterous missives were gobbled up as new episodes in the living legend of
Theophilus Cibber, a man so mad, so bad he was funny.

At the end of December, playbills announced that Theo would
return to the stage on January 4 as Foppington in *The Relapse.* At
once the law students, those self-appointed watchdogs over the hubris
of Cibbers, the same young men who had prevented Colley's *Papal
Tyranny* from reaching the boards the previous March, announced
that they would prevent the public appearance of this moral reprobate. Theo was exhilarated by their threats to riot in the theater, and
Fleetwood, though he had qualms about the safety of his building,
could not resist the hot demand for tickets. "I hear," wrote a young

playgoer to his father in the country, "there will be a vast riot to-night at the play, for young Cibber is to act and the Templars are resolved to hiss him off the stage."[1]

Drury Lane was packed by three o'clock in the afternoon of January 4, servants sitting in their masters' places till performance time. Ordinary citizens endured the wait until six o'clock for them-selves, while the law students placed themselves strategically, with pockets fat with rotten fruit and vegetables. Nowhere can the differ-ence in Theo's and Susannah's relation to the public be more vividly seen than in this episode; for whereas her fastidious admirers had deserted her at the first glimpse of her feet of clay, his patrons de-rived such satisfaction from loathing him that they paid good money and endured considerable discomfort to do so.

Upon the appearance of Theo the tempest broke. A hail of garbage fell upon the stage, making it difficult to walk in the slime. A thunder of foot stamping, hissing, and catcalls confused the air. But Theophilus, in his element, moved serenely through it all, smirking, grimacing, dodging, and strutting, and the play, though virtually inaudible, continued to the end. "Young Cibber was vastly hissed a Thursday," our young correspondent happily reported to his father, "but his old friend, Impudence, kept him from being either out of countenance or in the least disturbed at the noise."[2]

Having outbraved the templars and resumed his career, it seemed that Theo had brazened his way through the scandal unhurt. In truth, though, his importance in the theater declined from this time on, for he had lost the respect of his fellow players. Though there had always been something unsavory about Theo, other actors up to now had admired his energy, his stage know-how, his instinct for the public taste, his tireless political efforts to improve the play-ers' lot. As for his trick of inventing a contemptible comic personal-ity and playing this role off stage as well as on, they might wince at Theo's taste, but they recognized a device that kept him in the public eye and assured crowds whenever he played. Now, however, the hor-rific glimpse that the trial had given them into the young Cibbers' private life showed that Theo really was, in this most tender and trusting human relationship, as depraved, as rapacious, as the public role he played. Had the Drury Lane mutiny occurred in 1739 and not 1734, Theo could never have led it. British actors, like all British society at this time, after generations of civil disorder and personal cynicism, hungered after decency and decorum. They aspired to be faithfully and lovingly wed, to raise their children by gentle example, to be property holders and churchgoers. The Millses, the Crosses, the Giffards, the Pritchards were all models of domestic harmony and respectability. Actors were sensitive about their ancient reputation as rogues and pimps, their women whores. Theo Cibber, who caricatured, who corroborated the public's contemptuous view of stage people, degraded their whole profession.

As for the feelings of the Drury Laners about Susannah, they had suffered a real loss from her absence this year, and the severity of her fate appalled them. Aloof she may have kept herself from most of them, feeling as she did that hers was a higher and purer calling than most of theirs. Still she had dealt honorably with everyone in the company, and they knew her quarrels with other actresses over disputed roles had not been her doing. Thus, though her pride made a degree of humbling not ungratifying to her fellow players, not even Kitty Clive could have taken pleasure in her total annihilation.

One man at Drury Lane took Susannah's disgrace very hard. All season, James Quin had sulked through *Cato, Macbeth, Caesar, Othello,* and *Richard III,* trying out a series of substitutes for Susannah: Mrs. Giffard as Desdemona, Mrs. Mills as Lady Anne, Mrs. Roberts as Portia, and Mrs. Butler (whom he especially detested for her simpering, aristocratic airs) as Lady Macbeth. None of them had Susannah's voice, her understanding, her poetry. Not only did Quin miss Susannah on stage, he chewed on her wrongs in private. In his odd, sexless, paternal way, Quin loved Susannah more than any other woman in his long bachelor life: he all bulk, all torpor, all glutted appetite, all worldliness; she so small, so vulnerable, with no more flesh on her bones than enough to keep her nerves skinned over, all lightness, feeling, and frailty. Ever since he had joined the Drury Lane company Quin had elected himself her champion and her husband's foe. After the trial he intensified his insolence toward Theo, barging past the diminutive Cibber and crushing him against doorways, interrupting his conferences with Fleetwood, shunning rehearsals where Theo's part was uppermost.

March was approaching and with it benefit time. Quin had the first night and choice of any vehicle in the repertory. When he chose *King Lear and His Three Daughters*, Nahum Tate's adaptation of Shakespeare, Fleetwood assigned the role of Gentleman Usher to Theo. This comic-sinister part was an elaboration of Shakespeare's Oswald, Goneril's obsequious, fantastical servant, and it fit Theo like a glove. He always played it to the enormous pleasure of his audiences, who, when the actor who did Kent seized Theo by the scruff of the neck, worried him like a rat, and called him "a base, proud, beggarly, white-livered, glass-gazing, superserviceable rogue, one that would be a pimp by way of good service, and art nothing but a combination of knave, beggar, coward, pander," howled their approval, while Theo peeped out from under his tormenter's arm and gave the house a self-congratulatory smirk. That, this year, after the trial, Theo would be playing the Gentleman Usher, was enough to ensure a packed house for Quin's benefit. Suddenly, on the eve of the performance, Theo balked. He would not play for Quin. His action was unprecedented. No matter what personal animosities raged backstage, at benefit time these were suppressed in the general interest. Theo's action had exactly the effect he had intended: Quin, who had ignored his existence for five long years, was roused at last to acknowledge him.

No sooner had the final curtain of *King Lear* come down — the Gentleman Usher read by another — than Quin, hastily uncostumed and uncorseted by his dresser, surged out of the theater with his retinue of admirers, bound for the Bedford Tavern where word had it Theo was carousing and cursing him. Beneath Quin's phlegm lay a violent nature. He had killed two men in his youth, a Mr. Bowen and a Mr. Williams, stabbed in drunken brawls.* Now he burst into the Bedford Tavern, seized Cibber, and dragged him out into the street. Swords flashed and both men were nicked, Quin on the finger, Theo on his arm.[3] They were separated by their friends, led back to the tavern and their wounds dressed while they continued to vilify each other across the room. Eventually, they were escorted home, Quin to his lodgings at the Sign of the Sun, and Theo round the

---

* For these indiscretions he had received, like Macklin, suspended sentences for manslaughter.

corner to Mrs. Holt's. For the rest of the season, to the huge inconvenience of the troupe, Quin and Cibber refused to perform in the same production.

At season's end, Fleetwood sacked Theophilus. He went, predictably, to Covent Garden. Though he had to accept a loss in salary, Theo did gain permission from Rich to carry out a moneymaking scheme which Fleetwood had always denied him: a benefit for his daughters.

On August 2 Theo appeared as Foppington in a special performance of *The Relapse* for "Miss Janey and Miss Betty, two infant daughters* of the late Mrs Jane Cibber,"[4] the afterpiece consisting of a bouquet of singing and dancing by various theatrical moppets. Profitable as this sentimental event was, Theo's motherless children were not a commodity that could be tapped regularly for his support. The only spring adequate to relieve his thirst was the Sloper fortune, a source still maddeningly capped off from him until he could discover where his wife was hiding, where she and her lover were "rioting," as he put it, while he starved. Just after this summer benefit, his eight-month-long search ended.

On January 12 Susannah had been quietly spirited away from her mother's house in St. Giles to Devonshire Street and the home of a Mrs. Knightley. Her new landlady had been told she would be letting her rooms to a Mrs. Archer, "the wife of a country gentleman,"[5] who was awaiting her lying-in. Despite Anne Hopson's long service and affection, she was too familiar to Theo to run errands and answer the door in the new hideaway, and she was replaced by a Mrs. Allen.

The lodgings at Mrs. Knightley's were commodious: Susannah had the best bedroom and, adjoining it, a pleasant room to sit in. Up another flight Sloper had taken several smaller rooms for Mrs. Allen and whatever nurses might come later. Susannah was alternately despondent and agitated. She could not be persuaded once in the whole time she was at Devonshire Street to leave the house, even to ride out in a closed carriage, so terrified was she of being recognized and her whereabouts reported to Theo. She was sleepless and appre-

* They were not precisely infants, but nine and seven respectively.

hensive at night. Since good Mrs. Allen needed her rest and William himself dared not spend the nights at Devonshire Street, he hired a Mrs. Bishop to sit up with Susannah. Of all the terrors that oppressed her the most urgent was that this child she carried would share the fate of her others and starve before her eyes. She had not been able to nurse them, and how much more depleted she was now! William Sloper, man of few words but speaking deeds, came to Devonshire Street one day in the first week of February with a wet nurse whose reassuring presence now completed the little household awaiting the birth. On February 26, Susannah was delivered of a healthy baby girl.

If Mrs. Knightley had had any suspicions that little "Mrs. Archer" was something more than the wife of a country gentleman they were deepened by the munificent christening of her baby. It cost, Mrs. Knightley heard, ten guineas, and when Sloper came back from the church he distributed three guineas each to all the women in the house for their kindness.[6] The baby was christened Susannah Maria and she thrived on the breast of her nurse.

But Susannah did not revive. Her life was that of a runaway slave. Her days were spent in hiding, and not a night passed without the fear that Theo might break in upon her rest. Sloper's attorneys had been negotiating in vain with Cibber, though Sloper was willing to settle Theo's mountain of debts in return for his signing a separation from his wife. By spring Sloper was in such despair that he instructed the lawyers to investigate the possibility of a divorce for Susannah (on the grounds of Theo's flagrant and habitual immorality during the course of their marriage) even though this was a complicated and expensive course. It is a sign of Theo's tenacity that he did not accept Sloper's offer to clear his debts, for his affairs had never been so disastrous and he was shortly thrown into debtors' prison. Still his gambling spirit, to say nothing of his lust for vengeance against the woman who was the only person in his life he had ever — albeit briefly — loved, persuaded him that his long-term interest lay not in immediate relief but in keeping his hold over the lovers, subjecting Susannah to perpetual fear and harassment, Sloper to the chronic threat of litigation and ruin.

By April Sloper was so concerned about Susannah's health that he called in a physician. A removal to the suburbs was recommended, where the air would be more invigorating and she might be persuaded to walk abroad and gain strength and appetite. The doctor also prescribed a fortifying regimen of drinking asses' milk. Susannah's next hiding place was the home of a family named Smith, a charming old house across the Thames in out-of-the-way Kennington Lane, the last place where fashionable or theatrical London would think to look for her. Here, as at Mrs. Knightley's, Susannah had the best bed chamber, the family's dining room for her sitting room, and some smaller rooms upstairs for the baby, its nurse, and Mrs. Allen. The most attractive feature of the house was its large secluded garden, which had a summer house and an arbor.

Every few days Sloper went over to Kennington Lane, crossing the Thames by barge or wherry from Whitehall Stairs or Westminster Landing* and losing Theo's spies in the throngs of pleasure seekers bound for Vauxhall. In the Smiths' garden, with Susannah leaning on his arm, he brought her whatever encouraging news he could of the lawyers' progress. In May in this peaceful place, their child, whom they called Molly, sickened with smallpox. Sloper came hurrying out from the city with Mr. Blisset, the famous London apothecary. The baby did not die, thanks perhaps to Mr. Blisset's medicines, but more surely to the vigorous start her wet nurse had provided. Her face was scarred. Around the presence of this little daughter the devotion of Susannah and William dedicated itself. She was Susannah's only living child, and William's only daughter. His two sons had his name, and all that his fortune and influence could acquire for them. But his daughter had his love. In every domestic glimpse we have of Susannah and William over the years, Molly is in their midst. She was to grow, despite the awkwardness of her birth and the misfortune of her scarred face, into a happy and greatly loved woman.

At the end of June Theophilus emerged storming from prison, convinced that he had been put there by the machinations of his wife and her lover. From his point of view he was right. After Sloper's lawyers had failed to persuade Theo to trade Susannah's freedom for

---

* There was no bridge over this part of the Thames until 1750.

his own financial deliverance they had approached his creditors, apprised them of their client's desire to settle Mr. Cibber's accounts, and suggested that everyone's interest might be served just now by concerted pressure upon Mr. Cibber. Unfortunately, Theo knew very well that his creditors would not let him languish forever behind bars but would raise bail themselves rather than see the plans collapse for his benefit at Covent Garden in August and thus forfeit their entailed share. He spent, therefore, his hours of enforced idleness composing the following, which, the moment he was freed, he took round to the newspapers:

> Whereas Susannah Maria, the Wife of Mr Theophilus Cibber, has not only been, long since, convicted of Adultery, but did, on September 7th, 1738 elope from her Husband (by the Contrivance of that ungrateful bad Woman, her Mother, her villainous Brothers, and others) and still continues to abscond from him, and has also caused that scandalous Wretch, formerly his unfaithful Servant, Anne Hopson* (who has been her Convenient, or Procuress, a long time) secretly and fraudulently to convey away . . . several Effects of his, such as table linen, Sheeting, great quantities of Wearing Apparel, as Gowns, Petticoats, Riding Habits, Linen, fine Laces, and many other things of considerable Value; and as no base Endeavors have been omitted (not even Perjury) by several of the Confederates of the said Susannah Maria, unjustly, falsely, scandalously, and maliciously, to asperse and vilify her Husband's Character, distress his Circumstances and ruin his fortune; — and as the said Susannah Maria has endeavored to carry on a scandalous and malicious Prosecution in the Commons† against her Husband, to the manifest Injury of his present Circumstances, his whole Salary being assigned, and paid, to the use of his and her former Creditors; and whereas, at present, she has no visible Way of getting her Livelihood: this is to forewarn all Persons whatsoever (at their Peril) to harbour, countenance, or trust the said Susannah Maria — her Husband being resolved not to pay any Debts she shall contract, or may have contracted; and also to prosecute (with the utmost Severity of the Law) any Person who shall give her Harbour or Assistance, she having declared she will endeavor to ruin her Husband by Law,

* Theo must have thought that Anne Hopson was still working for Susannah.
† The divorce proceedings, which were dropped.

who is too well convinced she must be privately supported by One whose real Name need not be mentioned, and is omitted only in Respect to his Relations. And whereas a base Lie was artfully spread Abroad and villainously asserted that her Husband had received a Sum of Money for a Consideration too infamous to mention: Now this is to certify, the said Theophilus Cibber was, on June the 27th, 1739, arrested for a Debt due on his Bond, to which Action he gave Bail, merely because he would not sign such an Article of Separation to his Wife as would have left her at Liberty to have pursued her infamous Practices with her vain, insolent Paramour with Impunity.

THEOPHILUS CIBBER[7]

Despite its ferocious legal jargon, the notice was Cibberian humbug. Though it masqueraded as a legal proclamation, it was no more than a paid advertisement. But Theo had not undergone the expense of such a long notice merely to vent his spleen. His purpose was to strike terror into the heart of whoever was lodging Susannah, suggesting that "harbouring or assisting" Susannah was itself a crime, and persuading her landlord or lady to reveal her whereabouts.

The unworldly, suburban Smiths either did not read the London papers, or did not recognize their gentle Mrs. Archer in Theo's picture. They had grown very fond of Susannah and her baby, and also of Sloper, whom they knew as "Mr. Wheeler" — though they debated a good deal between themselves as to whether he *was* her brother — who visited her so faithfully, walked with her so solicitously in the garden, sat with her so chastely in the dining room (the door always open), and never, no matter how late the hour or how foul the night, could be persuaded to sleep over.

But no matter how uninquisitive and affectionate the Smiths, how discreet the servants, how cunning Sloper in shaking Theo's spies, it was only a matter of time till her husband smoked Susannah out. Late in July Mrs. Smith had a professional visit from a London surgeon, Mr. Shaw. Looking out the long window of his patient's room at the garden, Mr. Shaw observed a pale young woman seated there. That, said Mrs. Smith, was little Mrs. Archer, their lady lodger, with the loveliest voice and manners, who had recently lain in and was here to breathe the good air and drink asses' milk. The surgeon laughed. The woman sitting in her garden was no lady, but the notorious actress, Mrs. Cibber, who after the most sensational adultery trial in memory — even Mrs. Smith here in the suburbs must have read of it — had mysteriously dropped from sight. Mr. Shaw, swelled with news, returned to London.

A few mornings later, Theo, accompanied by several henchmen, including the same Watson who had followed him on his raid to Burnham last year, was pounding on the Smiths' door. They demanded the way to Susannah's room and tramped up the stairs unannounced. Susannah was in bed when they burst in and, to Theo's chagrin, alone as an anchoress. She was to come, Theo said, with him to London. She agreed, only begged him to leave her while she dressed.

But a few minutes later when Theo and his troops crowded back into her room where she waited, dressed and trembling, he suddenly changed his mind about taking her with them. Was it possible he was moved by her haggard appearance? She had changed woefully in the ten months since he had seen her, the day he seized her from Sloper in the country. Or was it only that he remembered that he was still under a recognizance not to threaten or molest her? Whatever his reason, he now only demanded that she meet him later that same day, in London, at two o'clock, at the Rummer Tavern where he was to dine. She promised to obey. While she stood there Theo stripped her room, piling the arms of his men with her gowns, her mantuas, boots, gloves, even the linen from her bed. Whatever Susannah owned, according to English law, belonged to him. Her purse was lying nearby. Theo turned it upside down. There was nothing inside but eighteen pence and her silver watch. It was the one which last year she had narrowly saved by passing it to Sloper. Theo threw back the purse and the change, and pocketed the watch.

Susannah did not meet Theo at the Rummer Tavern. As soon as he left she had word sent to Sloper and waited the whole day till he came by carriage, having lumbered the long way round to Kennington Lane across London Bridge, to take her, little Molly, the nurse, and Mrs. Allen to a new retreat.

Here we lose them, and so did Theo. But he did not need to persecute Susannah further. Now that he knew where she had been these past months he had all the witnesses he needed, however reluctant the Smiths were to testify that Sloper was the young man they had known as Mr. Wheeler, that he had been a regular visitor to "Mrs. Archer," and had paid all her lodging bills.

On September 4, at the court of the King's Bench, mild Sir William Lee presided again over an action brought by Theophilus Cibber against William Sloper, Esq. The charge this time was not for adultery — that, God knows, had been proved explicitly — but for "detaining" his wife. In the nine months between litigations the plaintiff had doubled his estimate of his injuries, which he now set at £10,000. Much of the cast of characters in this new court drama was familiar. Besides Sir William, most of Sloper's attorneys, including the chillingly effective Murray, were the same. Theo had a nearly new slate of lawyers, having either neglected to pay his previous team, been dissatisfied with their performance, or both. And, as the previous December, there was a furtive scribe in the jammed courtroom ready to take down new episodes in this tale of a lust so obdurate and insatiable that it defied all warnings and sanctions.

Alas for this scribe and the booksellers who waited, the tone of this trial was very different from the first. Mrs. Knightley spoke of "Mrs. Archer's" quiet stay, of her lying-in, and of the elegant christening. The Smith family — father, mother, grown son, and grown daughter Sukey — spoke fondly about "Mrs. Archer's" convalescence with them, of her baby's illness, and of "Mr. Wheeler's" visits, visits so chaste that when the couple walked in the garden they took care to stay "within the view of ten or twelve windows of the house" and, when they talked indoors, either "sat with us,"[8] or with the door open between themselves and the rest of the house.

Young Mr. Smith recalled "a night of terrible thunder and lightening last summer. He [Sloper] happened to be there that night. He went away in the midst of that weather, though we pressed him to stay and offered to get ready a bed for him. But he went away and I lent him my great coat."[9] Mr. Smith, Junior, also told the court that the clerk of one of Mr. Cibber's lawyers had come out to Kennington Lane before the trial and, falsely representing himself as one of Mr. Sloper's lawyers, begged them to speak frankly to him about the behavior of Sloper and Mrs. Cibber.

So pained was Sir William to hear this last that he interrupted the trial, termed this "a foul piece of practice," and called Theo's lawyer forward to explain himself. This gentleman declared he knew nothing of such an incident and had never sent a clerk of his to do anything of the sort. The trial resumed.

All the precautions, the continence, the propriety observed by William and Susannah for the past months were no impediment to Theo's case. He was not obliged, as he had been before, to prove sexual intimacy between the pair, only that Sloper was continuing to see Susannah after the verdict against him, and that by supporting her was, since Susannah had at this time no source of livelihood, enabling her to stay away from her husband. The most damning evidence of this trial was a far cry from Mr. Hayes's testimony: it was nothing more than an account book in Sloper's hand (regretfully verified by his banker, Mr. Campbell) that read, "Account at Mrs Smith's, April 19th; Allen having 20 guineas in hand, left in Allen's hand 50 guineas. Brought forward."[10]

Mr. Strange, the Solicitor General, summed up the plaintiff's case. There had been, he reminded the jury, a trial in this same court on this same matter some months before with a verdict in favor of the plaintiff. After this it might have been expected that the defendant would have discontinued his connection with the plaintiff's wife. On the contrary, he had "secreted her from her husband in an obscure part of the world, Kennington Lane," and there visited her. The present trial lacked evidence of the kind which before had "offered so much mirth and entertainment to the bystanders," yet he left it to the jurors to decide whether Sloper kept "an actress . . . merely to look on." Had this woman not been thus abetted and encouraged, but "left to the influence and proper expostulations of her long-suffering husband, who had always been ready to forgive and cherish her, she might have been reclaimed." But since the defendant had not been deterred by the previous verdict, but flaunted the dignity of this very court, "there appeared no remedy against this conduct except another verdict," this time, "with such damages as may be sufficient warning to him." Mr. Strange concluded on a very ominous note: if Sloper "did not learn his lesson on this occasion, he might have to continue this commerce at the expense of submitting to small damages and costs yearly."[11]

The defense was curiously perfunctory. Sloper may well have tied his lawyers' hands by forbidding them to excite sympathy for him by calumniating Susannah. One of them rose (the record does not indicate whether it was Murray or someone else) to ask testily how it was that the plaintiff, who maintained his only motive in bringing this suit was to interdict the criminal intimacy between his wife and Sloper and rehabilitate her, had not, when he found her last summer, removed her from her life of sin, but merely stripped her of everything she had with her?

The jury retired. They were back shortly with a verdict for the plaintiff. Sloper's peers were out of patience with him. It was one thing for a young gentleman of fortune to fall into the amorous cantrip of an actress, "mistress of all the alluring arts." It was another, after that trap was sprung and a merciful jury had extricated him with hardly a scratch, to continue his folly. Of course, £10,000 was a preposterous sum to pay a rogue husband for the favors of this common woman, but Sloper needed a rap sharp enough to recall him to his senses. They awarded Theo £500.

It was a far cry from £10,000, but more than twice what Theo earned a year. How right he had been not to sign articles of separation from Susannah! As long as the lovers stayed together there would be these periodic financial bloodlettings and, between them, for ready cash he could raid Susannah's dwelling and take her clothes, jewels, plate, linen, money, all of which, for the rest of her life, was his.

What Theo did not realize as he celebrated with his creditors was that, today in court, he had fatally overtaxed the ovigenous potential of his golden goose. The bird was, in fact, quite dead, and not another nugget would ever be squeezed out of it. Sloper, Susannah, and their child had disappeared from London. Their reason for staying, the hope of a legal resolution, was gone. Theo lost sight of them for two years, and so do we. They may have gone into the country to Wiltshire or Hampshire where William's father had farms and property. They may have gone, as star-crossed English lovers often did, to

Italy. William's only sister, Mrs. Smart Lethieullier,[12] was there at this time, lively, musical Margaret, patroness of amateur theatricals in the British expatriate colony, devoted to her brother, and defender of his alliance with Susannah.

Wherever they were, the secret was safe with their families, William's banker, and Susannah's friends, among the most staunch of whom were Quin and Handel, who had never despaired of seeing her restored to the stage and of working with her again. When we find Susannah Cibber again, in November 1741, she is far from Theo's long reach and under the protection of these two portly chevaliers.

❧ 12 ❧

Woman, for this all thy sins be forgiven thee!
— DR. PATRICK DELANY, at the first performance of *Messiah* in Dublin, 1742

I N 1739 George Frederick Handel and James Quin each reigned
uneasily over his branch of London entertainment. Both were
favored by the Crown, constantly honored by command performances, and Handel was the Princesses' music master, just as Quin
had been the young Prince's elocution master.

But George II's devotion was no guarantee of public enthusiasm. Handel was as often hurt as helped by being identified as the
official German composer for an unpopular "foreign" court. And
Quin's lazy self-complacency was fed, to the deterioration of his talent, by being petted by the mighty. Handel's operas were so poorly
attended that he was in financial difficulty and filled with discourage-
ment. Meanwhile people were flocking to English operas like Arne's
lovely and accessible *Comus*, and Lampe's and Carey's *The Dragon
of Wantley*. As for Quin, every year his audience grew less reverent
and more restive as, from a prominent place on the stage, he sawed
the air rhythmically with his right hand in accompaniment to the
famous voice which alternately trumpeted and dropped to a stage

whisper, though whether by way of dramatic emphasis or to keep his nodding audience on edge no man could tell.

In August 1740, the Prince of Wales sponsored a fête in his gardens at Clivedon to celebrate the birthday of his daughter, Augusta, and the anniversary of the accession of the house of Hanover. Two new masques of Arne's were featured, *The Judgment of Paris* and a patriotic pastoral, *The Masque of Alfred,* which electrified its aristocratic audience with its dashing ode and chorus, "Rule, Britannia." Handel could no longer ignore this half-trained, surly young Englishman, and the following winter, after his newest Italian opera, *Deidamia,* failed, he brought out an expanded version of *L'Allegro, il Penseroso, ed il Moderato,* based, like Arne's *Comus,* on Milton's English words.

This same season his friend Quin was openly challenged by a rival from his own company, Charles Macklin, whom Quin had for years dismissed as a murderous Irish churl with a natural affinity for such "low" parts as paid assassins and drunken louts. It happened thus:

In the 1740–41 season Fleetwood revived three Shakespeare comedies, long unperformed at Drury Lane: *As You Like It, Twelfth Night,* and *The Merchant of Venice.* To ornament these he commissioned Arne to set some of the songs to new music. So delicious were Arne's melodies that in January, while Handel's *Deidamia* was expiring at Lincoln's Inn Fields, audiences were coming back over and over to Drury Lane, not only to slake their thirst for Shakespeare but to hear again "Where the Bee Sucks," "When Daisies Pied," "Under the Greenwood Tree," "Come Away, Death," and "Blow, Blow, Thou Winter Wind." When *The Merchant of Venice* was put into rehearsals in January, Quin, whose articles gave him first choice of roles in any new production, selected the title part, Antonio, as the character most befitting his dignity. Fleetwood then assigned the "low" part of Shylock to his wild Irishman, Macklin. It attracted no comment among his fellow players that Macklin simply walked through his part in rehearsal. Shylock was a role everyone understood. Its "correct" tradition came straight out of the seventeenth century by way of Richard Burbage and Thomas Doggett. The comic stage Jew always wore a kinky red wig, baggy pantaloons, and a false nose hooking down over a false chin, so that in his rapacious frenzies the two clicked together like a huge nutcracker.[1] No one thought it strange that Macklin should not exert himself in rehearsal upon a character whose effect depended upon its elaborate makeup and familiar costume, and the audience's shrieks of laughter at Shylock's ferocious feints with his long knife and paroxysms of foiled revenge.

Just before the performance on the night of February 14, Macklin stalked into the green room wearing a severe black robe of rich material, a blood-red tricorne reminiscent of a Venetian doge, and neither false nose nor false chin to distract from his own malevolent, dark features. With Shylock's first words, "Three thousand ducats; well," licked over, speculatively, like a whetted blade, a shudder went through the house. It was too late for Quin or the others to protest, and Macklin played Shylock as a majestic, remorseless villain, and in a night metamorphosed the role and the play. His shaken audience emerged from Drury Lane to spread the word. The play was repeated and repeated. The King attended and went home to a sleepless night. Every time the royal eyes were closed Macklin's visage and Macklin's knife filled His Majesty's mind. *The Merchant of Venice* was the sensation of the season, but it was not Quin in the title role the public came to see.

As for Handel, on April 4 an anonymous letter appeared in the London *Daily Post* upbraiding the public for neglecting him and showing such ingratitude for the "noble and elevated" pleasure he had lavished all these years upon his adopted country. The writer hoped the citizens of London would take it as a moral and patriotic duty to fill Lincoln's Inn Fields on Wednesday next for *L'Allegro*, the master's last performance of the season, a performance which might otherwise be his last in England, for the writer had heard that Handel was so disheartened by neglect he was considering quitting these shores forever.[2]

Handel was indeed considering removing himself from Britain, and so was Quin, though hardly forever. Both of them thought the time ripe to absent themselves a season so as to let the dry well of public interest fill again. A splendid possibility had presented itself to them. In March the Duke of Devonshire, Lord Lieutenant of

Ireland, had returned for his annual report to His Majesty, and his visits to his English estates. Patron of music and the stage, and friend of both Handel and Quin, His Grace had urged them to come to Dublin for the following season. Irish society was starved for music and theater and he promised them his patronage. At this moment, His Grace reported, an elegant new music room was being erected on Fishamble Street. What an honor to Dublin if Handel's music seasoned this hall its first year!

In the spring of 1741, in her retreat, Susannah received letters from her two devoted elders, Quin and Handel, inviting her to join them in Ireland next fall and lend her talents to their ventures there. The Lord Lieutenant himself would be their patron, and hers. Dublin, a city with a rich theatrical heritage, was sure to appreciate her, and Ireland was far from her husband's reach. Quin wrote that the proprietors of the theater royal on Aungier Street would pay her £300. Of Handel's offer we know nothing.

Susannah accepted. What can explain the willingness of this timid woman to leave her haven with William Sloper and little Molly and return to that capricious, disreputable profession which had brought her so much suffering and, almost literally, not a penny for her own use? Was it the prospect of making money? It is true that Susannah craved financial security, which is not surprising considering her childhood and her marriage. But she never showed an appetite for gaining riches as a goal in itself, and Sloper supported her elegantly. Could it have been that her love affair had soured and she felt she must reestablish her independence? Not the least of the stresses that she and William had undergone since they fell in love must have been these last two years of exile, cut off from normal activities, old friendships, and family relationships, and dependent upon each other for almost every gratification. Amazingly, their affection had not waned. The reason Susannah returned to the stage seems to have been that she needed to perform, that when she was idle for long she experienced a profound unease. Though she herself would never have chosen to be an actress and had been throughout her brief career the instrument of ambitious men, her gift for moving an audience's sympathy had become an exercise of power and a reassurance she now could not live without. Acting was an extension of that capacity for propitiation and persuasion that she had developed as a child as peacemaker in her family. All the terrors of the pious, scrupulous, studious little girl in the warring household on King Street were laid to rest each time that, dressed in the robes and dignity of a tragic queen, she brought from hundreds of hard dry eyes a reconciling gush of tears. When Handel and Quin offered her this chance to perform again, safe from Theo and under their protection, she seized it.

On June 5, the packet *The Pearl Galley* put into Dublin and James Quin came ashore, corseted and periwigged, followed by his valet and trunks of theatrical paraphernalia. There was another prominent theatrical personality aboard *The Pearl Galley*. Quin had brought Catherine Clive with him to play comedy until the fall when Susannah Cibber had promised to join him. Kitty had reasons of her own for leaving England. If Quin had been bedeviled by Macklin, and Handel by Arne, Kitty's position as London's first comedienne had been badly jolted last season by the first London appearance of the greatest rival she was ever to know. Peg Woffington (1717–1760) was beautiful, stylish, and enormously talented. She loved competing with other women and she totally lacked Susannah Cibber's respect for the precedents of other actresses. She could play all of Kitty's hoydens, minxes, and gamines — she had grown up in the streets of Dublin — and she could do what was beyond Kitty: play "high" comedy, aristocratic, diamond-witted ladies like Millamant and Rosalind. Her Venetian Portia was as suave as Kitty's was ludicrous. She loved "breeches parts" (a youth, or a lovely girl disguised as a youth) because these costumes showed off her elegant legs. This was an audacity out of the question for Kitty, who needed all the help a corset and swirl of petticoats could give.

Quin and Clive settled down at the theater royal in Aungier Street for a gratifyingly profitable summer season. There was not much love lost between these two veterans, which may have been the reason they displayed such energy in scenes of male versus female conniving, false dealing, and roughhouse. When September came Kitty returned to England, her pockets full, her spirits restored by the honest sound of Irish laughter, ready to defend her prerogatives

This crude drawing from 1746 does not do justice to Peg Woffington's beauty, but it does show her slim figure in a "breeches part." In the background, tossed on a stool, are her stays and bonnet. Her shift hangs carelessly on the wall behind.

and capital parts at Drury Lane, where Woffington had just signed articles for the season.

On November 18 Handel arrived in Dublin with the scores of eight old works and one new one, a sacred oratorio he called *Messiah*. Susannah joined him and Quin a week later. She was in excellent health and spirits. She went at once to a house on Aungier Street -which had been taken for her. There is no record that William Sloper or little Molly traveled with her. It is even possible that she crossed the Irish Sea alone and lived apart from them for nearly a year, but it seems more likely that her loved ones were in Dublin with her. Sloper and Susannah never forgot the publicity of the trials, and after Susannah returned to the stage Sloper became more and more painstakingly elusive. Susannah's arrival on the Chester packet had been widely expected and was noted in the Dublin press,[3] and there is no mention of anyone else in her party. But if Sloper arrived with child and nurse on another day his name would probably never have attracted the attention of a newsman.

Susannah's first appearance in Dublin was on December 12. She and Quin played Bevil Jr. and Indiana in *The Conscious Lovers*.

The theater was all but empty and the managers of Aungier Street who had guaranteed Susannah £300 for the season did not take in £10.[4] Provincial Dublin society, though dying to have a look at this notorious actress, were not sure they ought to patronize a woman who could not show her face before decent people in her own country. Fortunately, the Lord Lieutenant had not forgotten his promise to support the enterprises of Quin and Handel. The day after the disastrous first performance of *The Conscious Lovers,* Faulkner's *Journal* announced that "By their Graces', the Duke and Duchess of Devonshire's special Command, on Thursday next at the Theatre Royal in Aungier Street will be acted *Venice Preserved* . . . Pierre by Mr Quin, Belvidera by Mrs Cibber, being the second time of her Performance in the Kingdom." Reassured by this ducal sanction, Dublin's gentry turned out to see the exile and from then on Aungier Street played to capacity crowds.

During her Irish visit Susannah undertook some fifteen roles, more than two a month, many of them new to her, including the leading female characters in *Love's Last Shift, Comus, The Old Bachelor, Measure for Measure, The Spanish Friar, The Fair Penitent, The Betrayer of His Country, The Orphan, The Double Gallant, The Siege of Damascus, The Man of Mode, Othello,* and *The Distrest Mother.*

And this was only part of her activity, for as soon as she arrived she began rehearsing with Handel. His season was to begin at the end of December with a series of six subscription concerts, followed, if these were well received, by a second series. The season would culminate and conclude in Holy Week with the premiere of *Messiah,* a performance for the benefit of three prominent Dublin charities: The Prisoners of the several Jails, Mercer's Hospital, and the Infirmary on Inn's Quay.

Handel's rehearsals with Susannah in his house on Abbey Street were, as years before in England, painstaking, personal, unorthodox occasions, with Handel going over each phrase on the keyboard till she got it by heart. Just how atypical was Handel's patience with Susannah's limitations is suggested by his treatment of another singer only a few weeks before. In early November, on his way to Ireland, Handel had had to lay over in Chester because of adverse winds. Using the time to "prove" some of the hastily transcribed score of *Messiah,* he hired some Chester musicians, including a highly recommended bass named Janson, to run through various choruses. When Janson stumbled in the fugue "And with his stripes we are healed," Handel "let loose his great bear upon him," swore "in four or five languages," called him a "shcountrel," and demanded whether he had not represented himself as capable of reading at sight. "Yes," replied Janson, "but not at *first* sight."[5] He was fired.

Susannah Cibber's critics complained that she sang when she spoke tragedy and spoke tragedy when she sang, and Burney bears this out when he describes her effectiveness in recitative. Colley Cibber and Aaron Hill had taught her to "place" and "tone" her voice, that is, to use its rise and fall in a way very close to chanting. When she *did* sing, it was not her limited range and mediocre musicianship that moved people but her emotional projection of the words. She seems to have been as much an actress on the concert stage as she was a musician in the theater.

Handel's two subscription series included *L'Allegro, Acis and Galatea, Ode for St. Cecilia's Day, Esther, Alexander's Feast,* and *Hymen.* It is impossible to reconstruct Susannah's precise share in these, and though she was the most interesting of Handel's soloists, she was by no means the only one. He had brought two sopranos with him, Signora Avoglio and a Mrs. Maclaine. His male soloists were all vicars choral from the two Dublin Anglican cathedral choirs, St. Patrick's and Christ Church. True to his promise, the Duke of Devonshire endorsed Handel's presence to the utmost of his influence. Every performance of the first subscription series was announced in the papers with the flourish: "By their Graces' the Duke and Duchess special Command." Handel wrote to Charles Jennens (who had compiled the sacred texts that were the libretto for *Messiah*) that "My Lord Duc" attended every performance and that the audience was composed "beside the flower of Ladys of Distinction and other people of the greatest quality, of . . . Bishops, Deans, Heads of the Colledge [and] the most eminents people in the Law, [such] as the Chancellor, Auditor General, etc."[6]

Though the twelve concerts were an unqualified social and

financial success, they were not without behind-the-scenes crises. In order to use voices from St. Patrick's choir Handel had had to gain permission from Dean Jonathan Swift, permission that had been granted in December, though not with much enthusiasm. The Dean could not abide music himself and saw no reason for promoting it.[7] Soon after the turn of the year Swift went stark mad, and on January 28 sent round the following bewildering notice to his Sub-Dean, Chancellor, and Prebendaries:

> Whereas it hath been reported that I gave a licence to certain vicars to assist at a club of fiddlers in Fishamble Street, I do hereby declare that I remember no such licence . . . and that if ever such pretended licence should be produced I do hereby annul and vacate the said licence; intreating my said Sub-Dean and Chapter to punish such vicars as shall ever appear there as songsters, fiddlers, pipers, trumpeters, drummers, drum-majors, or in any sonal quality, according to the flagitious aggravations of their respective disobedience, rebellion, perfidy and ingratitude.[8]

This embarrassing matter was resolved when Swift was confined to his rooms and all the administration of the cathedral taken over by the second and third in command, Dr. John Wynne, the Sub-Dean, and Dr. Patrick Delany, the Chancellor.

More nerve-wracking to Handel than Swift's raving was Susannah Cibber's illness, which necessitated substitutions and postponements during March, and delayed the final concert of the series until April 7, only two days before the public dress rehearsal of *Messiah*. *Faulkner's Journal* told the long, frustrating story: "March 6th, The new Serenata called *Hymen* that was to have been performed on Wednesday next, the 10th, at Mr Handel's musical entertainments at the New Musick Hall in Fishamble Street is by the sudden illness of Mrs Cibber put off to the Wednesday following, and . . . it is humbly hoped the subscribers will accept of the *Allegro and il Penseroso* for the next night's performance." "March 9th, Mrs Cibber being in a fair way of recovery, the new Serenata called *Hymen* will be certainly performed on March 17th." "March 16, Mrs Cibber continues so ill that the new Serenata called *Hymen* cannot be performed." We

have no idea of the nature of Susannah's disorder, though its relaps-
ing quality suggests that it may have been an early episode of the
stomach trouble that plagued her for years. At any rate she was well
enough to rehearse *Messiah* and to sing in Handel's last concert,
Esther.

When Handel wrote *Messiah* in September 1741, Susannah had
promised him her presence in Dublin and he composed "He Was
Despised" with her voice in mind. It is, as Larsen[9] says, an air based
on declamation rather than cantabile (as it would have been for a
trained Italian voice) and depends more than any other part of the
oratorio upon the singer's expressiveness rather than vocal skill.
After Handel began rehearsing with Susannah in Dublin — he had
not heard her sing for four years — he reset several other arias, originally for soprano, for her. "If God Be for Us," originally in G Minor,
was dropped to C Minor,[10] and "He Shall Feed His Flock," written
in B-flat Major, was transposed "una quarta bassa," to F Major.[11] It
was not, apparently, that Signora Avoglio and Mrs. Maclaine were
unsatisfactory (Avoglio, at least, was performing to acclaim in the
concert series), but rather that, hearing Susannah's voice once again,
he could not resist letting it be the instrument for his tenderest
music.

There was a public rehearsal of *Messiah* at Fishamble Hall on
Friday morning, April 9, the musicians consisting of a small orchestra under the direction of Matthew Dubourg, Handel at the organ,
men and boys from the cathedral choirs, and the three imported
female singers. The *Dublin News Letter* declared next day that "Mr
Handel's new sacred Oratorio . . . surpasses anything of that nature
which has been performed in this or any other kingdom." *Faulkner's*
did not hesitate to pronounce it "the finest composition of Musick
that ever was heard."

For the charity performance itself, the stewards of the Charitable Music Society hoped that the hall, designed to accommodate six
hundred, would actually squeeze in one hundred more, "to increase
the charity." With this in mind they placed a notice in the paper
requesting "the favour of the ladies not to come with hoops this day
. . . the gentlemen . . . without their swords."[12] Seven hundred diminished citizens crammed good-naturedly into Fishamble Hall as soon

as its doors opened at 11:00 A.M., April 13. His Grace, the Lord Lieutenant, who had been so instrumental in Handel's visit and such an enthusiastic patron, could not attend: he had prorogued the Irish parliament and returned to England for his annual report to His Majesty on the state of the realm. The Lord Justices were therefore the highest officers in the kingdom and they attended *Messiah* to a man.

In the nineteenth century it was popularly believed that the composing of *Messiah* was a variety of divine revelation, Handel having transcribed it in a sustained religious transport, weeping and praying and refusing sustenance as he copied at breakneck speed the heavenly chords that filled his brain, while his servants and visitors huddled in awe outside his study door. Twentieth-century critics look coolly at this charming tradition (whose only basis in fact seems to be that Handel did compose *Messiah* in a burst of creative energy in twenty-four days), but the Dubliners who made up *Messiah*'s first audience did not trouble themselves at all to define its "sacredness." If coming to listen to Handel's stately treatment of the promise of Christian redemption was not a "churchly" act, they were satisfied it was one of those "naturally" religious occasions of which the eighteenth century was so fond, in which all that is good and holy in human nature spontaneously wells up and overflows. The premiere of *Messiah* took place in Holy Week when decent folk denied themselves playgoing and public entertainment, and business was so bad that theaters usually closed. Here at Fishamble Hall, on the last dull Tuesday in Lent, was an opportunity to mingle in the finest company and to enjoy oneself blamelessly while engaged in Christian charity toward one's unfortunate brothers. Handel and all the principals in the company had waived remuneration for this performance, "satisfied with the deserved applause of the publick, and the conscious pleasure of promoting such useful and extensive charity."[13] With sweet good humor, the ladies of Dublin stepped down from their chairs and coaches and lifted their limp, suddenly-too-long skirts out of the spring mud in Fishamble Street. The gentlemen, bereft of their clanking dress swords, were sober, almost clerical in their mien. Four hundred pounds was taken in, of which £127 went, after expenses, to each of the three charities.

If attending *Messiah* had not been an act of piety as well as propriety, Dr. Patrick Delany, Chancellor of St. Patrick's Cathedral, would never have been in the audience. His wife, Margaret, had died only a few months before,[14] and he was still in first mourning. And this week, Passion Week, his skinned-over sorrow was laid open again, for stone masons had just arrived at the cemetery to raise the inscribed tablet over her remains.[15] Another personal sorrow contributed to Dr. Delany's highly emotional state as he listened to *Messiah*, for he had not only lost his beloved wife, but, in Swift's recent lapse into madness, his best friend and benefactor. Delany, convivial, self-indulgent, and tenderhearted, had always lived beyond his means, constantly entertaining his friends and giving large sums impulsively to charity. For years, Swift, his superior, had scolded him for his incontinence and rescued him with a new benefice, curacy, or preferment to add to the list of sinecures whose incomes he already enjoyed. It was in the nature of Swift's madness that he had turned viciously upon his oldest, most devoted friends. And Delany had never needed his fatherly chastisement and support more than now, when debts pressed, and word had just come from England that rapacious relatives of his Margaret's first husband, a wealthy Mr. Tennison, were preparing to dispute in Chancery his right to the large income which Tennison had left to his widow, and which Delany had counted on for the rest of his life.

Packed into Fishamble Hall, Delany was sitting with the son of old family friends: young Thomas Sheridan was twenty-three, Swift's godson, a student at Trinity, stagestruck, and a passionate admirer of Susannah Cibber. Until today Delany had not seen Susannah perform (her arrival in Ireland occurring just when Margaret died), but he had heard young Sheridan extol her public gifts and private graces, and like everyone in Dublin he knew her deplorable history. His first appraisal of her then was when she came forward on the stage to sing "He Shall Feed His Flock," a slight figure with large eyes, and a mouth which, when she was not singing, she kept tightly, even painfully, compressed.

In the second, "suffering" section of the oratorio, she sang the air which Handel had written expressly for her, "He Was Despised," an anguished dialogue between human voice and the strings of the small orchestra, which seemed to shudder at each of the singer's phrases, as if sentient nature were wincing at Christ's scourges. "He was despised . . . rejected . . . acquainted with grief . . . a Man of Sorrows . . . He gave His back to the smiters . . . despised . . . rejected . . . acquainted with grief." The small voice, warm, wounded, and personal, ceased; but it had been too much for Patrick Delany. Brimming with pity for his Savior's stripes, full of his own tribulations and of compassion for this frail, lost sinner on the stage, he suddenly rose to his feet, extended his hands toward the stage, and tearfully exclaimed, "Woman, for this all thy sins be forgiven thee!"[16]

Dr. Delany's ejaculation overstepped decorum, but he was such a dear, good man, such a pet of genteel Dublin, a man whose worst fault was his generous impetuosity, that no one took offense. Besides, though his action was extravagant, the feelings he expressed about Susannah Cibber were shared by everyone in the hall. *Messiah* is not a dramatic oratorio. There is no plot. The soloists are not given identities, but everyone in Fishamble knew who Mrs. Cibber "was." She was Mary Magdalene, and they marveled at the daring and magnanimous genius of Handel who had put the account of Christ's degradation and physical suffering into the mouth of a fallen woman.

Word of Susannah's success at Aungier Street had already reached London. Her extraordinary effect in *Messiah* followed. For four years there had not been a single voice raised to restore her to her native stage. Now her countrymen could not wait to prove they could outdo provincial Dublin in the expression of Christian forgiveness. Fleetwood and Rich opened negotiations across the Irish Sea, and Theophilus Cibber stepped forward to use his good offices to bring his wife home.

It had been a lean three years since Susannah and Sloper abandoned him. His elder daughter, Jenny, had at last reached an age to be put to work full time (she was eleven), but her salary at Drury Lane was not enough to relieve him. He had been in and out of jail, back and forth from Drury Lane to Covent Garden and Drury Lane again as he enraged both managers. He realized that his grand strategy of intimidating and bleeding the lovers had been too stringent and had backfired. Better, now that Susannah had so triumphantly surfaced again, to help her return to the London stage. He was still her husband, still had indissoluble claims to her and hers as long as she lived. The affair with Sloper was five years old. Who could tell what disillusions and recriminations might have set in? Sloper might be tired of her, and if he were to withdraw his strong protection, Susannah, whom Theo knew to be the most easily cowed of women, might find it hard to resist a reconciliation. The public would love that. It was the plot of *Love's Last Shift* in reverse: a debauched wife raised, contrite, out of the mire of her lust and gathered to the bosom of her Christian husband. There was no question but that under his aggressive management and with her enlarged and colorful reputation Susannah could soon be earning £500 a year.

In Dublin she was guardedly enthusiastic about returning to her native land. Her mother was there, and lonely for her return. Henry Peter had died, and Anne Arne was not on close terms with her older son. Sloper's boys and his failing father needed William's presence. Her terror of Theo had lessened. Her mother and Tom wrote that he was a public laughingstock these days, and such a recognized trouble-maker it was doubtful if either Rich or Fleetwood would take him on for the next season. On one matter Susannah was adamant: her husband was to take no part in the negotiations of her articles, nor would she play at any house where he was engaged. She was not, it seemed, as much Theo's chattel as she had once believed. There was that prenuptial trust, signed by them both on the eve of their wedding in 1734, granting her the right to all her stage earnings. In April, her London lawyers had hailed Theo into Chancery to explain what had happened to the hundreds of pounds he was supposed to have handed over to her trustees to invest for her between 1734 and 1738.[17] Not that they expected to recover a shilling from Theo. Raising the matter of the old trust simply served notice on Theo that he would not find his wife the broken creature of a few years back, but, in the event of attack by him, armed with weapons of her own.

Susannah did not work out her London theatrical arrangements herself, but characteristically turned the bargaining over to a man who loved her. When Quin left Dublin in the spring of 1742 he took Susannah's empowerment to settle matters with Rich at Covent Garden for the following season.

She was in no hurry to leave Ireland. The circumstances of her life there, both public and private, were those on which she thrived. To her house on Aungier Street Handel and Quin had brought their Irish admirers who quickly became hers: Lord Tyrawley, Lord Orrery, Lord Mountjoy (later Earl of Blesington), Dr. Edward Barry (Dublin's first physician), Benjamin Victor, and young Thomas Sheridan and his friends from Trinity. The men who met her now in Ireland remained her courtiers and friends into their old age. Years after her Dublin visit Orrery was writing a friend in England to ask wistfully after his "sweet syren."[18] Thomas Sheridan always recalled her performance in *Messiah* as the most affecting moment in his life, words and music miraculously fused.[19] Dr. Barry corresponded with her solicitously after she returned to England, advising her about her health; and in 1759, seventeen years after she returned to England, took it upon himself to act as her defender when she wrote him of what she regarded as unjust treatment on David Garrick's part.[20]

There was something inconsolable, something irremediably melancholy about Susannah Cibber. She accepted the visits and attentions of her admirers with gratitude, as if she drew sustenance from their strong presence ("Cibber, Sir, seemed to *need* your tears"). She did not attract all men, but those she did were held for life. It is safe to say that anyone who enjoyed the society of Peg Woffington would rarely seek that of Susannah Cibber, which was as restful as Peg's was exhilarating. Thomas Sheridan, who felt ennobled in the company of Susannah, was troubled by Peg's sexual challenge, her wit, her self-sufficiency.

To adore Susannah Cibber was the easiest yoke in the world; it threatened nothing, demanded nothing. There was no sexual sparring among Susannah's admirers, no question of supplanting Sloper. Thomas Sheridan, a faithfully married man, became a close friend of Sloper's, and long after Susannah's death the two old gentlemen met to share memories of her. The anecdotes which survive of the fascinating Woffington are examples of her lacerating wit, of her putting down the pomposities of one man to the delight of other aspirants for her favor. Stories about Susannah suggest no wittiness at all, but her affection for her admirers, and her skill at drawing wit out of them. Once when Handel had just finished entertaining a group at her house with the overture from *Siroe* on the harpsichord, she turned to Quin and asked if he did not like Handel's dexterous hand. "Hand, Madam?" exclaimed fat Quin, who loved the opportunity to insult his equally corpulent friend. "You mistake! 'Tis a foot."[21]

Besides her social success in Dublin, Susannah was happier than ever before in her relationship to the theater public. In London her husband's stratagems had suggested that she was clawing her way to eminence over the legitimate claims of other actresses, and that her life backstage was characterized by hair-pulling and caterwauling. Here in Dublin she was regarded as a heavenly visitant, protégée of two men of genius who had brought her to be their instrument. There were no prominent native singers for her to threaten, and Irish actresses such as Mrs. Furnival and Mrs. Elmy seem to have wisely maintained their dignity by deferring to her genius and joining the ranks of her admirers.

Before she returned to England there was a role Susannah wanted to try. Ever since 1737 when she had suffered so much humiliation in the Polly War she had had it in her mind to do *The Beggar's Opera*. She was not a vindictive woman, but an extremely tenacious one. On May 17 she played Polly to a packed house, and *Faulkner's* reported that she "excelled everything that had been seen in the part."

One female type remained which Susannah had never attempted, the virago or "heavy." Lady Macbeth was such a part, and Cleopatra, Roxana, Jane Shore, and Queen Elizabeth — women made reckless by some monomania such as political ambition, sexual passion, jealousy, or desire for revenge. In their active drive toward gratification these characters were very different from the soft, yielding ladies whose suffering Susannah projected so well. On May 31 it was announced that Mrs. Cibber would attempt Cleopatra in Dryden's *All for Love*.* At the last minute Susannah recoiled and the play was canceled. Try as she had in rehearsal, Susannah could not understand the Egyptian queen who roistered into the night in what,

---

* Shakespeare's *Antony and Cleopatra*, from which Dryden's tragedy is derived, though conceded to be full of beauties, was regarded as too gross and rank for public presentation, and was not revived until 1759 by Garrick and Mrs. Yates.

it could only be conceded, were orgies, and publicly boasted of her lust for Antony. Susannah never again attempted Cleopatra.

As if Dublin had not already known the most exciting theatrical and musical season in its history, the summer of 1742 brought five more London luminaries. After Quin returned to England, Dennis Delane arrived to play opposite Susannah at Aungier Street. And, urged by letters from Susannah about Dubliners' enthusiasm for music, Arne and his wife, the former Cecilia Young, came over in June to stay with Susannah in her house and present a series of concerts.

The Arnes and Delane were the least of the English entertainers in Dublin that summer. During the season just past, Dublin's second theater royal, Smock Alley, had been overshadowed by the brilliant doings at Aungier Street. But its proprietor, Lewis Duval, had been angling for London theatrical fish of his own, and in June he landed the greatest catch ever hauled into Dublin, David Garrick and his exquisite mistress, Peg Woffington. This incandescent pair at Smock Alley quickly extinguished Susannah and Delane at Aungier Street. Peg's presence was not in itself threatening to Susannah, since her specialty was dashing ladies of fashion and intrigue, and Susannah's was sad queens and threatened virgins. But Delane was no match for the young Garrick, whose fire and intelligence made every rival seem stale, bombastic, an advocate of an exhausted declamatory tradition.

Without Quin, Susannah performed faintly and uncertainly. Her genius was receptivity and response. Delane and Susannah had scarcely known each other in England and had never played together. Delane had not come to Ireland prepared to court Susannah, to draw emotion out of her, or to tune his own voice with hers in a mutual chord, but to engage in a desperate, manly duel with David Garrick.

Richard III had made Garrick's reputation in London last October, and now he played it at Smock Alley on June 18. On June 22 Delane assayed it at Aungier Street before a thin and hostile house. His delivery was strenuous and hollow. Next morning Garrick wrote home to his brother, Peter: "Delane has played against me, but . . . has quitted ye field."[22] Delane returned to England. To shine

alone was not Susannah's way. She did not attempt to carry on at
Aungier Street supported only by the resident Irish company. However, she stayed on in Dublin another month singing at Fishamble
under her brother's direction, in joint concerts with her sister-in-
law.

On August 23 the packet *Lovely Jane* left Dublin for Parkgate.[23] Aboard were Susannah Cibber with her brother, and David
Garrick, traveling with his aristocratic admirer, James O'Hara, Lord
Tyrawley. (Sloper had apparently returned to England in June
when the Arnes came to share Susannah's house. Peg Woffington was
staying on in Ireland to visit her mother and sister.) Garrick himself
might have left Dublin earlier — his last performance was August
19 — but he had waited over so as to travel with Tyrawley, as he took
pains to let his brother know: "My affairs are quite finished here and
with great success . . . I have an invitation from Lord Tyrawley to
come with him and I believe I shall stay for ye honour of his Lordship's company."[24] The honor of a lord's company was a confirma-
tion of his own value which Garrick was never able to do without
till the end of his days, but now, at the start of his career, it was
especially necessary to him, for he was trying to reassure his bourgeois family (who were aghast at his quitting a decent trade and
going on the stage) that his new vocation had enhanced, not jeopar-
dized, his social position.

Since Tyrawley and Garrick were traveling companions and
Tyrawley knew and admired Susannah, she and Garrick must have
exchanged civilities aboard the *Lovely Jane*. But he did not now, or
for some time, attempt to cultivate her. As a woman she did not
interest him. He liked vivacious ladies, and she was quiet and perpetually triste. Also, she was three years older than he — a great
difference to a young man of twenty-five. In any case he was absorbed
by his passion for Peg, of whose faith and serious commitment he
lived in perpetual doubt. For all his merry, convivial nature, Garrick
was the least promiscuous, most conventional of men. Though Peg's
waywardness fascinated him, he wanted to marry her and make a
decent matron of her. He was shocked by Susannah Cibber, tainted
as she was by her connection with the disreputable Cibber tribe,
openly living with a married man whose child she had borne, and

sister and confidante to that notorious lecher and bad husband, the fiddler Tom Arne. Professionally there was nothing about her to attract him. Garrick did not like music, so it is doubtful he had attended Susannah's summer concerts. And though he had seen her play when he went to appraise Delane at Aungier Street he had discerned nothing in her dispirited performance to interest him.

On the other hand, Susannah Cibber was not unmoved by Garrick: she had, like all of Dublin, seen him play, and been stunned by his intensity. She herself had not, she knew, played well since Quin had gone. She recognized in Garrick the energizing, virile impulse she had missed all summer, as well as a shining seriousness she had found in no association — with Hill, the Cibbers, even Quin — except with Handel. Even before their chance voyage home together, Susannah had probably set her course, infinitely flexible and patient, toward a point of impact with Garrick. When come together they did — reluctantly on Garrick's part — their effect upon each other was so reciprocally enhancing that they seemed "formed by nature for the illustration of each other's talents."[25]

But their theatrical marriage was still two years away, and unthought of by David Garrick as he and Susannah exchanged perfunctory pleasantries on the windy deck of the English packet. Both these young people were leaving the scene of personal triumphs and returning home to even greater expectations. Garrick had signed articles at Drury Lane for six hundred guineas, the largest salary ever paid an actor to that date. Susannah was engaged at Covent Garden to undertake all the capital female roles with James Quin, returning to the forgiving arms of the native city from which she had fled three years ago in secrecy and shame.

❦ 13 ❧

THE Drury Lane company which Garrick joined in the 1742–
43 season included a chastened Dennis Delane (playing
second leads and turning his energies to the bottle), Charles
Macklin, Kitty Clive, Peg Woffington, and Hannah Pritchard. At
Covent Garden, James Quin and Susannah Cibber led a mediocre
company. Among the other actresses were Mrs. Horton, who specialized in heavies, simpering Mrs. Vincent for ingenues, and Mrs.
Porter who made an annual, regal, command appearance. To all
practical purposes, the feminine half of the Covent Garden stage
was Susannah's.

A huge, emotional audience crowded the redecorated theater on
September 22 to celebrate her restoration to the stage as Desdemona
to Quin's Othello. What they found was no longer a fragile girl with
a heartbreaking voice but a woman who played with new concentra-
tion and fire. In the final scene where Desdemona threw herself before her husband and begged for her life in words like echoes of
Susannah's own history, "[My sins] are loves . . . oh, banish me, but

kill me not . . . let me live tonight," the audience was so startled by her power that they burst into cheers.[1]

On October 13 both theaters offered *Richard III,* the vehicle which had catapulted Garrick to fame a year before. Susannah played Lady Anne at Covent Garden; Mrs. Mills played the role at Drury Lane. This first duel between Quin and Garrick was inconclusive but wonderful for business at both houses.[2] Noting *Richard's* crowd-catching effect, another candidate for fame in this role pressed his claim, a man not in the least abashed by Quin's grandeur or Garrick's vitality. It was Theophilus Cibber. Having failed to find employment with either Rich or Fleetwood, Theo had joined Henry Giffard's troupe of irregulars who were struggling to put on a season at Lincoln's Inn Fields without a license from the Lord Chamberlain. To no one's surprise, Theo's Richard was a critical disaster, but Lincoln's Inn Fields Theatre, which had been nearly empty all season, was filled with people come to laugh.

On January 14, old William Sloper died in his great house in St. James Place.[3] His remains were carried to West Woodhay and buried in the church he had built there. His will in its entirety reads: "I, William Sloper of West Woodhay, give and devise all that I shall be possessed of at the time of my decease to my son, William Sloper, and I appoint William Sloper my sole executor."[4] With less fuss than an old lady dividing her trinkets did he divest himself of stocks and securities in the City, of West Indian and North American interests, and of thousands of acres in Berkshire, Hampshire, and Wiltshire, with their rents, livings, liens, and manors. His laconic testament suggests the excellent order of his estate and the confidence between father and son. If there were bequests to old servants, or understandings with tenants, the younger William already knew them and could be trusted to implement them without encumbering codicil or clause. Young William was old William's immortality: he so thoroughly assumed his father's identity — moving to live at West Woodhay, serving on the same charitable committees, winning the same seat in Parliament (Whitchurch, Wiltshire) — that, reading rolls and records and seeing the signature "Wm. Sloper, Esq." bridge the year 1743 and continue on, it is as if there had been no death.

The tone in which people spoke of Susannah Cibber's liaison lost some of its lickerishness after old Sloper's death. It was not that she had advanced a hairsbreadth in respectability, but that her paramour was no longer the same person. When William had been an idle young man of fashion living on the generosity of an indulgent father, his affair with an actress was regarded as a scrape, an escapade. Now that he was a gentleman of wealth and political power, his second, irregular household, presided over by a famous actress, was an ornament to his position.

Handel had returned from Ireland to England about the same time as Garrick and Susannah. His first test of whether London's affection had rekindled in his absence was a new oratorio, *Samson*, adapted from Milton's *Samson Agonistes*. First performed in February at Covent Garden, *Samson* delighted people. The soloists were popular singers: John Beard was Samson; Susannah Cibber, Micah; Kitty Clive, Dalila; Thomas Reinhold, Harapha. The only Italian voice was Signora Avoglio, who leavened the earnest tone of the oratorio with ornamental arias, sometimes as a Philistine, sometimes as an "Israelitish" woman.

Kitty Clive made a slightly shrill, slightly vulgar, altogether human Dalila. She had a high, sugary soprano, and a way with a love song that even her enemies conceded was irresistible. Some of Handel's biographers, knowing Susannah Cibber's racy history, have assumed it was she who played Samson's seductress, and have pointed out this bit of casting as an example of Handel's dramatic acumen.* No character, of course, could have been less congenial to Susannah's nature than Dalila, nothing less suited to her limited contralto than the high, coquettish warbles and trills with which Handel delineated the Philistine temptress. Handel composed Micah expressly for Susannah. There is no such character either in the Bible or in Milton. Yet Handel regarded Micah as so important that he developed him into the second longest role in the oratorio, just shorter than Samson. Micah is Samson's sexless, devout confidant, who laments the lost glory of the Israelites, pities the blind hero's humiliation,

* See P. H. Lang, *Handel* (New York: W. W. Norton 1966), p. 406.

comforts Samson's old father, urges Samson to assay his strength once more for the sake of his oppressed people, and rises, in the passionate supplication "Return, O God of Hosts," to the most emotional moment of the work. If the character irritates us today, unused as we are to loquacious characters outside the action, who only comment upon it, Micah was regarded by sentimental eighteenth-century audiences as the heart and soul of *Samson*, and perfectly interpreted by Susannah Cibber. When *Samson* was revived in 1745 and Micah sung by the Italian Francesina, there were vehement complaints that without Mrs. Cibber the oratorio had lost all its "lustre."[5] And when Charles Burney wrote about *Samson* fifty years after Susannah's performance he recalled that "the songs which Handel expressly composed for Mrs Cibber's limited powers were never half so touching when sung by Monticelli, Guarducci or Guardagni, great singers as they were, as by our country woman, though comparatively ignorant of music and possessing but a thread of a voice. However, from the excellence of her understanding . . . and natural pathos of her tone . . . she never failed to penetrate . . . the soul of every hearer."[6]

Horace Walpole took no pleasure in *Samson;* it was against his aesthetic principles to agree with middle-class taste, and anyway he had a financial interest in the rival Italian opera company which was foundering at King's Theatre while Handel made money at Covent Garden. "Handel has set up an Oratorio against the Operas and succeeds," he wrote his friend, Horace Mann, in Florence. "He has hired all the Goddesses from the Farces, and the Singers of *Roast Beef* from between the Acts . . . with a Man with one Note in his Voice and a Girl with never a One; and so they sing and make brave Hallelujahs."[7] Kitty and Susannah were the Goddesses; Beard, the man with one note; Susannah, the girl with none. Walpole's reference to hallelujahs is odd and prophetic, for there is not one in *Samson;* however, within a month of his letter, Handel brought out *Messiah* and London heard for the first time what shortly became the most celebrated hallelujahs in the world.* Susannah and Signora

---

* The reputation of *Messiah* had preceded it, of course. And Walpole may even have heard parts of it at private musicales. See page 268 for Susannah's little preview of *The Oracle* for Lady Caroline Petersham.

Avoglio sang their Dublin parts and John Beard and Thomas Reinhold those of the Irish vicar chorals.

London did not embrace *Messiah* as unequivocally as had
warmhearted, provincial Dublin, where even Dr. Delany, a man of
the cloth in profoundest mourning, had felt no qualms about attending.[8] On the eve of *Messiah*'s first performance a letter signed
"Philalethes" appeared in the *Universal Spectator* asking the public

> to consider the Impropriety of Oratorios as they are now performed.
> . . . An Oratorio either is an Act of Religion or it is not; if it is, I
> ask if the Play House is a fit Temple to perform it in, or a Company
> of Players fit Ministers of God's Word. . . . If it is not performed as
> an Act of Religion but for Diversion and Amusement only . . . what
> a Profanation of God's Name and Word is this, to make such light
> use of them! . . . It seems the Old Testament is not to be profaned
> alone . . . but the New must be joined with it, and God, by the most
> sacred and merciful Name of Messiah. For I'm informed that an
> Oratorio by that Name has already been performed in Ireland and
> is soon to be performed here . . . I must ask again if the Place and
> the Performers are fit.[9]

Society was divided into those who agreed with "Philalethes"
that playhouses and players desecrated sacred subjects, and those who
thought Handel's "Hallowed Lays"[10] sanctified both place and performer, even as a spoiled priest becomes miraculously pure while he
celebrates the Mass.

The question of the fitness of a public theater and common
players for a treatment of Christ's life was officially silenced if not
resolved when Handel's most prestigious patron attended a performance. At the opening chords of the Hallelujah Chorus His Majesty
rose solemnly to his feet in the royal box. His gesture was hastily
followed by every person in the hall whether they shared King
George's feelings or not.

At the end of the theatrical season, in early June, Susannah
joined Sloper at West Woodhay. Her presence in their neighborhood
touched off considerable talk among the Berkshire gentry. Ever since
he had moved into his father's old-fashioned manor house, Sloper
had been renovating it. When Susannah arrived the rumor flew that,

to welcome her, he had done up the quaint mansion entirely in white satin, as one huge boudoir.[11] Since no decent lady could call upon her, it was difficult to verify this story, which does not sound like anything else we know of Sloper's taste.

Susannah had not signed articles for the coming year, because there were delicate negotiations in progress between Quin and Garrick to play together, at what theater was not certain, and she did not want to commit herself prematurely to Covent Garden. Characteristically, she had removed herself from the arena and left the bargaining up to Quin.

For Theo Cibber, the season had been disappointing. He had discerned no way to siphon off the profits of his estranged wife. The irregulars at Lincoln's Inn Fields had disbanded. On April 26 Theo sailed for Dublin, engaged for the summer at Smock Alley. He went there under the sponsorship of young Thomas Sheridan who had that winter, after earning his M.A. from Trinity, renounced the respectable academic or clerical life for which his family had intended him and gone on the stage. It is puzzling why Sheridan should have invited Susannah's monstrous husband to Dublin, idolizing her as he did. Probably his reasons were precisely the straightforward ones he expressed in his letter to Theo in March:[12] that he had heard Theo wanted to visit Ireland, that he recognized Theo's drawing power, that he believed that Dublin, unlike London, was not large enough to supply two audiences, that if they played together they would reinforce each other, while if Theo went to Aungier Street they would draw away from each other.

Sheridan was not afraid of Theo's malodorous reputation. Probity was his armor. He intended to deal distantly and honorably with Cibber. He could not conceive of any situation in which they could be brought into personal conflict. In Sheridan's rectitude and naïveté, his humorlessness, his gentle background, his stagestruck boyhood, his impulsive plunge into the shifty theater world, he was not unlike John Highmore, Theo's early victim.

The summer season at Smock Alley began mildly: Theo was obsequious to his patrician young benefactor. The only unpleasantness was that the theater was in a bad way financially, and its manager, Phillips, bedeviled by creditors. On July 10, Sheridan arrived to dress for the title role in *Cato,* in which Theo was to play Syphax. The theater was confusion: Phillips had fled, the musicians refused to play unless they were paid, trunks and closets yawned where bill collectors that afternoon had ransacked the scene room and wardrobe for anything of value. To Sheridan's horror, the voluminous robe he always wore as Cato was missing. He panicked. He was twenty-four years old, awkward and stringy. His appeal as Cato lay in the ringing intelligence of his delivery, for there was nothing in his meager person to suggest a portly, mature Roman patriarch, and he absolutely depended upon his encompassing robe to convey a sense of substance and grandeur. In his shirt and kneebreeches he rushed to the green room where the rest of the cast was waiting and told them that his robe was gone and that he could not play without it.

While some of the others went to see if a substitute cloak or cape might not be found, Theo snarled to Sheridan that play he could and must, dressed just as he was if nothing better could be found, or show himself a vain, cowardly, and irresponsible amateur. Theo himself rather gloried in his scrawny body and bandy legs. Far from taking pains with his costumes to disguise it, he displayed his form as prominently as possible. But Sheridan had not an ounce of humor about himself and none of Theo's exhibitionistic self-loathing, and the prospect of presenting himself as a grave Roman stoic in his present garb was intolerable.

Beyond the curtain the whistles, stamps, and catcalls of the impatient public grew loud, and impulsively Sheridan rushed out before the curtain to apologize and to put off the performance to another time. One step behind him came Theophilus Cibber — not for nothing was one of his London nicknames "Bustle Master General" — and, interrupting Sheridan's awkward explanation, he gallantly offered, so that no one would be utterly disappointed, to play his own part, Syphax, and at the same time read Cato. The audience cheered, and when Sheridan tried to stammer a remonstrance they howled so viciously at him that he fled the theater, calling over his shoulder that he would never again set foot on a stage.

Next day he wrote a long, abject letter to the town, acknowledging that, robe or no robe, he should have played for the honest

Thomas Sheridan as Cato. Here the "meagre" form which so humiliated him on the stage is flattered by a voluminous robe.

citizens who had paid for their tickets and waited for him. He asked their indulgence for his excessive sensitivity regarding the "defects"[13] of his figure, took full responsibility for the incident, and never mentioned Theo's name. As far as Dubliners were concerned the affair was ended. They had no stomach further to humiliate this earnest young gentleman who in a few months had added such luster to his native stage and now so humbly acknowledged last night's error.

But Thomas Sheridan's anguish was only beginning, for Theo now unsheathed his pen and composed a long letter of his own to the press. It was his duty, he assured the public, to reveal that Sheridan's action on the night of July 10 had been even more despicable than the audience imagined. "Master Tommy" had never been asked to play Cato in his britches. It was true that the robe he customarily wore was missing, but another one, equally fine and new this year, which had just been worn, as some of them might remember, by Mr. Husband in *Julius Caesar,* had been found and offered to Sheridan. He had scorned to wear it. The real reason for Sheridan's refusal to play was not the lack of his "gew-gaw tinsel train," but that, peeking through the curtain after he arrived at the theater and finding the house very thin, this "sweet, meagre sir" did not deem it worthy of his genius to play for so few.

When Sheridan read this, his resolve never to stoop to Theo's level (never, as Quin had put it years before, to shit on this toad) was forgotten. He dashed off a public letter charging Theo with lies, meddling, and ingratitude toward a man who had gone out of his way to make it possible for Theo, broke and of evil repute, to play in Dublin, personally interceding with the manager and even using his influence with Irish booksellers to prevent, during Theo's visit, the publication of the shameful law trials between Theo and his wife's lover.[14]

Theo's next letter was an exquisite change of pace, haughty, wronged, and manly. How contemptible of Sheridan, he wrote, "infamous villain, notorious poltroon,"[15] to threaten him with the public exposure of these unhappy private matters, and how useless to try to terrify him with them! Let the trials be published! What could they show except that he had been "an unfortunate man, a hurt lover, an injured husband and a friend, betrayed."[16]

Cibber was as much in his element in this phantasmal world of trumped-up wrongs, false feeling, and hysterical posturing as Sheridan was out of his. Sheridan was a genteel player of the new sort, like Garrick and Susannah Cibber. He regarded the stage as a cultural institution, actors as debators of moral issues, and himself as a reformer. Theo came from an earlier tradition. Emotions were his bag of tricks, and he was ready to weep, to lie, to laugh, to fight, to do anything as long as his behavior advertised himself and attracted crowds. Indeed, the audiences at Smock Alley had swollen since the paper war began. People read the latest exchange and hurried to the theater hoping to discern the tension between Cibber and Sheridan, or even to witness physical violence between them. For Theo there was nothing incongruous about sharing a stage with Sheridan at night, no matter what he had called him in the paper earlier that day. Poor young Sheridan, on the other hand, quite literally could not bear the sight of Cibber. In August he precipitately left the Smock Alley company and finished the summer at Aungier Street, leaving his English protégé victor in the field.

In the fall Theo returned to London, trumpeting his arrival

with a puff that he placed in the *Daily Advertizer* on October 4. It was a gleeful account of "General Theophilus Cibber's" summer campaign in Dublin, "where he maintained the field with great reputation against the illustrious Count Sheridan."

Theo's boast that he had been reengaged by Fleetwood (who a few months ago had sworn he would never have him in his company again) seems a piece of Cibberian effrontery. Actually, it was true: Fleetwood had been wooing him anxiously by letter in Dublin. Both the fortune and health of Drury Lane's patentee had deteriorated to the point where their true states could no longer be glozed with charm. He was dying, excruciatingly, of a generalized gout, confined to his house for fear of arrest, and in arrears to all his players. The Drury Lane company had borne for years with Fleetwood, but when, that summer, he asked them to sign new articles for the coming year without having paid them for the last they rebelled and seceded en masse under the leadership of Garrick and Macklin. In order to open, Fleetwood had to recruit actors from the provinces. By default, therefore, Theo Cibber, who had not been able to get a job in either theater royal last year, was back as Drury Lane's leading player and Fleetwood's right-hand man. With his usual energy and sense of what the public really liked, he plunged into a season of the risqué Restoration comedies so frowned upon by the new audiences of sensibility, playing Foppington in Vanbrugh's *The Relapse*, Captain Brazen in Farquhar's *The Recruiting Officer*, and Brisk and Fondlewife in Congreve's *The Double Dealer* and *The Old Bachelor*.

Susannah was not at either theater this fall. The negotiations between Garrick and Quin had fallen through, and she remained at West Woodhay for the fall and then went to Bath.

The new Drury Lane mutineers under Garrick and Macklin were determined, just as Theophilus Cibber and his followers had been ten years before, to set up an independent company at the Little Theatre in the Haymarket. The stability of their enterprise depended upon a royal patent from the Lord Chamberlain, and this third license had thus far been denied to every applicant. Theo Cibber had failed to win it despite his father's connections at court. Henry Giffard had failed despite his blameless political beliefs and ability as a manager and director. And now Garrick and Macklin failed despite their reputations and their friends in high places. As soon as the Lord Chamberlain's decision was clear, many of the Drury Laners stampeded to Covent Garden where Rich turned them away. He and Fleetwood were in complete accord in their policy toward malcontents: in the long run, it was in the interest of both patentees not to hire each other's defectors, but to see that they were starved into submission to their old masters.

Garrick and Macklin had earned more money than the others and had some laid by. They both had standing offers from Ireland. But things were desperate for the lesser players. They had not been paid last year. This year they had not even worked. They had no other place to go to earn a living. William Mills, a distinguished and respectable man, was seized in the street and hustled off to jail for £500 debt, and genteel Mrs. Butler (Susannah's old rival for the part of Lady Constance in *King John*) had been barricaded in her rooms all fall, depending on friends for provisions, so great was her terror of the bailiffs.[17]

In November, on the pleadings of his fellow players, Garrick approached Fleetwood to talk about capitulation. The manager was candid and cordial. He acknowledged that he owed his players. Alas, if he had any money would he not have paid them long ago and avoided all this pain for everyone? Of course they could all come back: Garrick, Havard, Berry, Blakes, the Mills family, the Pritchards. He could not promise what he could pay them: a half, in some cases, of their former salaries. But at least they would not starve as they were doing now. There was only one stipulation: never again was Charles Macklin to set foot in Fleetwood's theater. He could not forgive him. Years ago when Macklin had killed Hallam and run away over the London roofs it had been Fleetwood who had searched out his hiding place, fed him, kept up his courage, and bought his life and freedom. It was Fleetwood who had humored his ambition to play Shylock in a new way, defended him against Quin's jealous rage, made him famous and rich. For ten years Macklin had been his "dear Mac," his boon companion when they caroused. When Macklin had been drunk and in his murdering mood, it had been Fleetwood who led him away from the fracas and tucked him in bed in his own home till he had slept off the fumes. Yet now, when Fleetwood was sick and poor, Macklin had not only abandoned him but had instigated and led the desertion of his mates.

Garrick carried back Fleetwood's word to the rest. In September when they rebelled, the company had vowed to act as a unit, making no individual treaties with the manager. Macklin now bitterly reminded them of their covenant. His position was unassailable. In capitulating to Fleetwood the others were betraying their word and sacrificing him. Garrick returned to Fleetwood and offered in vain to take a £100 cut in salary if Macklin could be reinstated. Meanwhile, he begged Macklin to consider the pitiable condition of the lesser members of the troupe and go to Ireland for the rest of the season and let his friends work for his cause. Macklin was unappeasable. Garrick stood, as he himself put it, "between the players' pressing, real necessities, and Macklin's intractable, unreasonable obstinacy."[18] The easiest course for Garrick at this point would have been to accept the Smock Alley offer, leave the mutineers and Fleetwood to make their peace the best way they could, and only return to England when the dust had settled. Instead, he led the others back to Drury Lane, negotiated a job for Mrs. Macklin at Covent Garden so the family would have some income, and promised Macklin a part of his own salary until Fleetwood could be brought around. Macklin would have none of Garrick's charity. He threw himself into writing savage pamphlets against Garrick and instigating riots at Drury Lane to prevent Garrick's appearing there. As Fleetwood could forgive all the mutineers but Macklin, so Macklin forgave everyone (including the feckless manager) but Garrick. Like Shylock, Macklin clung, remorseless and implacable, to the terms of the compact and demanded that his bond be honored, no matter how excessive the suffering, how innocent its victims.

It had been clear for two years that Garrick's genius as an actor was of an order by itself. After the Drury Lane secession and capitulation it was apparent that he also possessed extraordinary qualities of leadership. It had been to Garrick — a twenty-six-year-old bachelor, the newest member of the company, rich, lionized, without chick or child to support — that the others turned for compassion, not to Macklin, their old mate, a married man, a father, but, alas, all his life a cantankerous loner. Garrick's childhood had been characterized by a large family of brothers and sisters, by the constant absence of his father and older brother, and by his frail mother's chronic despondency. He had been her solace, her cheer, her favorite, her right arm: an animated, mischievous, affectionate boy. Garrick all his life played the favorite son. The darling of his age, he regarded the players around him with no small measure of condescension. At the same time he felt a profound family affection for them. They were his lesser siblings, and his privileged position committed him to responsibility for their well-being.

At West Woodhay and later at Bath Susannah was keeping in touch with the on-and-off negotiations between Garrick and Quin. Her gratitude toward Quin was profound, and her position with him secure, but without promise. She did not want to return to London another year as his exclusive partner and protégée. Her gifts were only as great as the genius of the man who drew them forth. As Handel towered over every other English musician, Garrick towered over every player. If he and Quin could reach terms and play at the same theater, she could enlarge her own capacities, playing certain roles with one, certain with the other. At Bath, to her despair, she heard that Garrick had again signed articles at Drury Lane, and Quin would be at Covent Garden.

In June Handel wrote his librettist, Jennens, about his plans for the coming year: "I have hopes that Mrs Cibber will sing for me. She sent word from Bath where she is now that she would perform for me next winter with great pleasure if it did not interfere with her playing, but I think I can obtain Mr Rich's permission, where she is now engaged."[19] Handel assumed she would be with Quin at Covent Garden. Quin assumed the same thing. They were wrong. When the 1744–45 season began she had signed at Drury Lane. She had left her faithful dragon. She had waited in the background for two years for Quin to come to an agreement with Garrick, and when he proved incapable of doing so, she acted alone. Quin felt she had betrayed him, but she saw her action as a means to bring Garrick and Quin together. Once she was with Garrick she was certain she could influence him to ask Quin to join them.

At Covent Garden Quin was incredulous, angry, bereft.[20] There was not a lady in that theater to take Susannah's place in his heart or on the stage. Both Mrs. Clive and Mrs. Pritchard were at Covent Garden this year. But bathycolpian Mrs. Pritchard was too robust to appeal to Quin's chivalry or to contrast poetically with his own monumental person, and Mrs. Clive had always been too shrill, too red in the face for his taste. In October his gloomy eye fell upon a new member of the troupe, a dewy, fourteen-year-old girl named George Anne Bellamy. She was the illegitimate daughter of Garrick's Irish admirer, Lord Tyrawley, meltingly pretty, trustful, vain, and with no more sense of her mortal danger from the pack of green room wolves who had already scented her than a kitten licking itself in a patch of sun. Quin followed her solicitously with his eyes for weeks, a fact of which George Anne was thrillingly aware. She was not surprised one day to be summoned to the imperial dressing room. The great man took her childish hand in his elephantine fist: "My dear girl, you are vastly followed, I hear. Do not let the love of finery or any other inducement prevail upon you to commit an indiscretion. Men in general are rascals. . . . If you want anything in my power which money can purchase, come to me and say, 'James Quin, give me such and such a thing,' and my purse shall always be at your service."[21] The pleasure of granting her free use of his purse was the only favor James Quin ever asked of George Anne. His sexuality never involved the women he loved.* Quin took George Anne under his wing, pushed her forward over the senior actresses into the roles he used to play with Susannah, snarled at her amorous pursuers and kept them at bay. He lectured her, made sure she had a good supper after performances, and saw her safely home. Whatever the superficial resemblances of their slight bodies and air of wistful vulnerability, Susannah Cibber and George Anne Bellamy, the two beneficiaries of Quin's passionate protection, could not have been more different. Susannah Cibber was a serious, melancholy woman; George

* The following anecdote may shed light on Quin's tastes. The Duchess of Queensberry, observing that he rarely played lovers, asked him, "Pray, Mr Quin, do you ever make love?" "No, Madam," he replied, "I always buy it ready made." *Letters of Lady Mary Coke*, vol. I, p. LXXIII.

George Anne Bellamy as the Comic Muse, painted by F. Cotes and J. H. Ramberg and engraved by F. Bartolozzi.

Charles Fleetwood gazes nonchalantly toward France, while an unsympathetic creditor apprehends him from behind with a bill in his hand.

Anne a reckless girl, greedy for experience. Susannah had responded to Quin's devotion with filial gratitude; George Anne treated him like the duenna in a comedy whose dramatic function is to be gulled, got round, and eluded. Poor, eager George Anne: her later years, destitute, diseased, and despised, read like a cautionary tale for young girls on the perils of trusting men who offer undying love, caskets of jewels, but never a marriage license.

Meanwhile at Drury Lane the season was advancing and Susannah and Garrick, in the same company at last, had not once played together. The situation was odd enough to be remarked in the press,[22] though what the impediment was is not clear. It may have been Peg Woffington's reluctance to surrender her romantic leads with her lover to another actress. It may have been that Garrick himself was resisting a closer association with Susannah. Certainly, there was something about proximity to her that made Garrick skittish.

November saw the final collapse of the master of Drury Lane, the "strange, profligate, unprincipled, swindling, gay, winning, fascinating Charles Fleetwood."[23] In a last effort to stave off bankruptcy he raised the price of tickets. The result was two riots, an aborted one on November 17, while Susannah and Delane were doing *The Conscious Lovers,* and a fierce one two nights later when the benches were ripped up from the floor and broken over the heads of Fleetwood's hired bruisers and all the candle sconces torn off the walls and hurled on the stage. After it was over the theater was closed, the glass and splinters swept up, carpenters and plasterers called in, and the patent put up for sale. Two bankers, Green and Amber, purchased it, and wisely turned the management over to James Lacy (1698–1774), an Irish businessman who had served as Rich's assistant for years. Fleetwood, who had come into an inheritance of £5,000 to £6,000 a year, was glad to accept a £600 annuity for the purchase of Drury Lane and to sail to France, where he soon died, out of the reach of his legions of unsatisfied creditors. Just before he left England he persuaded his old friend, the poet Paul Whitehead, to co-sign a note for £3,000. When this was unpaid after Fleetwood's flight, Whitehead was hauled away to jail, there to languish for several years, a martyr to friendship.[24] Fleetwood's sweet plausibility "was the last and only remaining quality which he kept with him to his death, and no doubt that would have vanished with the rest if he had not found it of constant use to him."[25]

London in the late winter of 1745 was full of rumors of a Catholic invasion. The Young Pretender, Charles Edward Stuart, was poised in France with seven thousand troops and a convoy of sail under Admiral Roguefeuil. It was an excellent time for both theaters to revive Shakespeare's *History of King John,* written when the Catholic Armada was lurking off the British coast and the future of Protestantism uncertain. The play bristles with timely patriotic exhortations:

> This England never did, nor never shall
> Lie at the proud foot of a Conqueror (Act V, scene vii)

and anti-Papist spleen:

> Thou canst not, Cardinal, devise a name
> So slight, unworthy and ridiculous as the Pope.
> Tell him this tale; and from the mouth of England
> Add this much more, that no Italian priest
> Shall tithe or toll in our Dominion. (Act III, scene i).

At Covent Garden Rich was using Colley Cibber's version, the very play, *Papal Tyranny in the Reign of King John,* which the anti-Cibber templars had suppressed eight years earlier, but which in the country's current mood they found acceptable. At Drury Lane, Lacy and Garrick were dusting off Shakespeare. Garrick would play John; Delane, Faulconbridge; and Macklin (reinstated the moment Fleetwood was gone), the papal emissary, Pandulph. But who would play Lady Constance, mother of little Prince Arthur, the rightful heir to the British throne? There was pressure from Susannah Cibber's admirers to let her try it, but Garrick had qualms. He was willing to concede her effectiveness in suffering and clinging roles. But Lady Constance was a tiger of a mother, driven by a ferocious will to see her son on the English throne and to destroy all who imperiled his birthright. The part was typical virago and Garrick knew how inadequate Susannah was in "heavy" roles.

One day in January Garrick ran into Quin at the Bedford Coffee House and they fell to discussing the forthcoming rival *King Johns*. At Covent Garden, Quin reported, the tragedy would feature three generations of Cibbers. Quin himself, of course, would be John, and Mrs. Pritchard, Constance. Old Cibber, the play's author, was coming out of retirement to do Pandulph, Theo would be the Dauphin, and young Jenny Cibber would play the ill-fated Arthur. Garrick said that at Drury Lane they had no Constance yet. Many people were pressing him to let Mrs. Cibber try it, but "he doubted her being able to do justice to so vigorous and trying a part." Quin was still smarting from Susannah's desertion, but he would not hear a word against her. " 'Don't tell *me*, Mr Garrick!' he roared. 'That woman has a heart, and can do anything where passion is required!' "[26]

Quin's vehemence impressed Garrick. This was the man who knew Susannah's capabilities better than anyone alive and who had much reason just now to disparage her. Susannah was given the part of Constance. During the first performance her "piercing notes of wild, maternal agony"[27] where Constance learns of the capture of her son by his wicked uncle John so unnerved the other players that they could not pick up their lines but stood amazed and had to be prompted. All during *King John*'s run, people who had already seen it slipped in for the third act, merely to watch Susannah flutter like a veil to the ground and say in an ecstasy of grief: "I will instruct my sorrows to be proud. To me and to the state of my great grief let Kings assemble . . . Here I and sorrows sit. Here is my throne, bid Kings come bow to it."

Quin had been right in understanding the difference between Constance's character and that of most stage viragos. It was what he meant by "heart." Susannah was incapable of playing women who committed crimes, broke laws, or even exceeded the rules of politeness in pursuit of their own gratification. But where mother love was concerned, violent excess could be noble and sacrificial. Her performance in *King John*, in which people agreed she outshone Garrick, marked the end of his resistance to her. For his benefit night he chose *Othello,* a character he had never attempted, and insisted that Susannah play Desdemona. Macklin, still eaten up with hatred for Garrick, made a wonderfully malevolent Iago.

At the end of March Garrick and Susannah appeared together in a new tragedy, James Thomson's *Tancred and Sigismunda,* which was not much liked in itself, though the performances of Garrick and Cibber ravished the heart of every beholder. Fiery Garrick, melting Susannah: as Tancred and Sigismunda, "They seemed formed by nature for the illustration of each other's talents. In their persons they were both somewhat below the middle size. He was, though short, well made; she . . . by the elegance of her manner and symmetry of her features . . . very attractive. From similarity of complexion, size and countenance they could have been easily supposed to be brother and sister; but in the powerful expression of the passions they . . . approached a nearer resemblance."[28]

Though London was intoxicated by the new team of Garrick and Cibber, one man was still able to observe them with a cold eye. "I mean not to depreciate them," wrote Theo Cibber, "when I say they are not equal in all parts or that their attempts in comedy are much inferior to their tragic performances . . . and I beg to be excused by their great flatterers and enthusiastic admirers if I can't allow all acting was nothing till they appeared. Let it suffice they have their peculiar talents." Though Theo, cynical comedian of the old school, distrusted their fashionable sentimental style ("certain proof of their feeling themselves is manifest in the tears they draw from their spectators," he sneered), he himself was not above squeezing a few sentimental drops of pity out of the memory of his first wife, who seemed to grow dearer to him the longer she lay in her unmarked grave.

> I cannot forbear [her widower went on] remembering another uncommon genius who quitted the stage and the world not a long time before Mr G. and Mrs C. commenced players; This was Miss Jenny Johnston whom I early married. . . . She had a strong, natural genius, a sweet voice . . . and an elegant and pleasing form, though she came on the stage at a less advantageous juncture than the first two mentioned. Mrs Oldfield, Mrs Porter, Mrs Younger, Mrs

Booth, Mrs Horton, Mrs Thurmond, Mrs Heron (all in their prime) left not that opening for Mrs Jane Cibber as the death of performers of both sexes luckily afforded Mr G. and the present Mrs C.[29]

By the spring of 1745 Susannah had persuaded the public (easily) and Garrick (with difficulty) that she was his ultimate partner, his twin, his female counterpart. And she had achieved this, not by backstage maneuvering, hair-pulling, or overriding the claims of other actresses, but by a patient application of her art, by constant proof of her superior gifts, and by public acclamation.

The question of James Quin remained very much on her conscience. However perfidious Quin might think her, her own love for him and sense of obligation remained unchanged. She had gone to Drury Lane determined to smooth a path for him there. The obstacle which had always stood between Quin and Garrick was the division of capital parts. Susannah did not believe the problem was insuperable. Quin was aging and obese, and preposterous as hero or lover. On the other hand his glorious voice and majestic appearance made him much more convincing than little Garrick as tyrant or king. There were roles like the ghost in *Hamlet,* like Cato, Coriolanus, Falstaff, and Sir John Brute, where no one would dispute his superiority to Garrick.*

Behind her immediate goal of a rapprochement between Quin and Garrick lay a further dream, whose scope would have astonished her visionary father. The old speculator Thomas Arne had never aspired to own a theatrical patent, but this was what was in Susannah's mind. She and Quin and Garrick together had the money and the experience to buy Drury Lane. From Shakespeare's day until recently the theaters royal had always been owned and operated by actor-managers: Burbage, Betterton, Doggett, Booth, Wilks, and Cibber. There had even been two actress patentees, Mrs. Barry and Mrs. Bracegirdle, who had owned shares at Lincoln's Inn Fields Theatre with Congreve and Betterton.[30] Men like Fleetwood and Lacy, who were not themselves players, cared nothing for the dignity

---

* "In Brute he shone unequalled — all agree / Garrick's not half so great a Brute as he." C. Churchill, *The Rosciad.*

of the stage but thought only of how it might make them money. Basically they despised their players and the art itself.

The time was ripe for the purchase of Drury Lane. Fear of the Catholic invasion had depressed business everywhere. Green and Amber, the bankers, were foundering. Lacy was struggling to keep Drury Lane open. The patent could certainly be had, and cheaply. Susannah Cibber's tactics were those with which she had waged every campaign since her childhood: diplomacy, perseverance, and ingratiation. The obstacles she faced were the passivity of Quin, who had all the fame and money he desired and really did not want the responsibility of managership, and the deep distrust of Garrick toward the idea of a woman as a partner. What happened we shall see.

⊰ *14* ⊱

My Mother taught me when I was very young that the farthest way about
was the nearest way home, and you see the force of Education.
— Susannah Cibber to David Garrick, January 1746

Be a little upon your guard. Remember he is an ACTOR!
— Horace Walpole to Horace Mann in Florence, September 1, 1763,
on the subject of Garrick's intended visit to Italy

A⊥ the beginning of April of their first season together, Garrick fell violently ill and did not perform for the rest of the
year. While he was convalescing in his rooms over the
great Piazza in Covent Garden, he received an invitation to dinner
at Susannah Cibber's before one of her Sunday evening musicales:
"Sir — I am very glad to hear you are better, and if you dare venture
out shall be glad of your company at dinner. As you are an invalide
[*sic*] pray send me word what you can eat and at what hour you will
dine. I shall send to Tom [Arne] to meet you, and am, Sir David,
your most humble friend and servant to command till Death — Margery Pinchwife."[1] Tom always supervised the musical part of his
sister's "Sundays." But who is Margery Pinchwife, whose naughty
name Susannah has appropriated? She is the heroine of Wycherley's
bawdy *The Country Wife*, bride of a jealous squire who has kept her
locked away from the temptations of the city. The play concerns her
first season in London, her discovery that her lusty and cunning
nature gives her a wonderful affinity for the amorous jungle of Res-

toration society. She signs her note inviting the lecherous bachelor Horner to an assignation, "Your most humble friend and servant to command till death — Margery Pinchwife." It is tempting to pounce upon Susannah's invitation to Garrick and her other coquettish letters to him as evidence of an affair between them. But that is too heavy-footed: their relationship was much more tenuous, an uneasy and unresolved erotic tension, playful, calculating, disingenuous, and useful to them both.

Susannah's conscious purpose when she signed her invitation to Garrick was to make the low-spirited invalid laugh at the comparison between the two of them and Wycherley's characters. Margery Pinchwife was randy, bold, and apple-cheeked; Susannah was pale, prudent, and brimming with scruples. Garrick was an honorable young man, doggedly faithful to Peg Woffington; Horner was a cynical womanizer. Margery's invitation was to a sexual tumble, Susannah's to a quiet supper with her brother and other close friends before one of her decorous Sunday evenings where Handel and Quin (except during the few years of his estrangement) were fixtures, where Sloper's political friends met, where Lord Lyttelton, William Pitt, their protégé, the poet James Thomson, and Christopher Smart liked to come, and where the entertainment might be Handel at the harpsichord, Arne and a string ensemble, or Italian madrigals sung by Susannah, Cecilia Arne, Thomas Lowe (the tenor), Arne, and nineteen-year-old Charles Burney, Arne's apprentice.[2]

During their long friendship, Susannah and Garrick were committed to others. But the tone of their correspondence, the stage characters in whose personae they presented themselves to one another in letters, and the intensity that informed their performances together always carried the pressure of something more. In 1757 when they had been acting together for fourteen years, the *Morning Chronicle* still marveled at how "they seemed to warm and animate each other to such a degree that they were both carried beyond themselves."[3]

The very survival of Susannah's letters to Garrick is proof of the chasteness of their friendship. After his retirement Garrick catalogued and annotated and weeded his vast correspondence. He saved nothing that compromised him with women, and, alas, very few letters to or from other players. He was much more interested in preserving his social correspondence with the nobility and the literati of England and France. Had he imagined that his letters from Susannah Cibber would be interpreted as anything but the flattering wit of his most important stage partner, they would have gone into his hearth fire as did all Peg Woffington's letters and heaven knows what other youthful outpourings. Only half of the Garrick-Cibber correspondence survives. After her death Sloper destroyed some of Susannah's papers, and what was left was destroyed after Sloper's death by his widow Catherine. Fortunately, during the period of their intensest exchange, Garrick was also writing his friend and confidant Somerset Draper letters full of frank references to Susannah, which reveal Garrick's feelings much more honestly than his epistolary gallantries to her.

Soon after Susannah's supper and musicale in May, she joined

Sloper at West Woodhay for the summer, and Garrick went with Peg to complete his convalescence in the village of Teddington. He was as fascinated as ever by Woffington, but her extravagance, her exhibitionism, and her insistence upon her right to enjoy as many other lovers as she chose had lately given him misgivings about marrying her. As he ceased to press Peg to set their wedding date, and even evaded the subject, she, who for three years had laughed at the notion, began to warm to it. No one but Garrick and Peg was present at their break, but Charles Macklin claimed she told him how it happened. One morning at Teddington as they rose together Peg teasingly asked Garrick if it had been apprehension at the prospect of marrying her that had made him toss and groan all night beside her. " 'As you love frankness,' [he replied,] 'it was; and I have worn the shirt of Dejinira for these last eight hours.' 'Then, Sir, . . . arise and throw it off,' [she said,] 'for I would not after this . . . become your wife. From this moment I separate myself from you.' "[4] Whether or not Macklin's version of it was accurate, there was a break between these two proud spirits in June 1745, and it was sudden, final, and cruelly felt by them both.

Garrick's reaction was to fling himself into a summerlong round of visits to friends and watering places, while he distracted himself with conquests of the hearts of provincial maidens. In August he wrote his brother Peter in Lichfield (where he was expected next):

[T]he company here [at the spa at Buxton] . . . was very glad to see me . . . viz., three young ladies with whom I was very merry and happy last night. . . . Pray my best affections to Miss Polly Fletcher and desire her not to believe her sister if she tells her I am fallen in love with Miss Vernon . . . and I must desire you to ward off any blow Miss Molly may design me. . . . I hope your ball goes swimmingly and that you intend to procure an Haut Bouy to enliven the dancing. . . . I beg you to give my best compliments to Miss Levett and let her know I shall come on purpose to have ye pleasure of dancing with her.[5]

Not a word of Peg, just a slightly hectic determination to be heart-free, irresponsible, nonsensical.

One of Garrick's most active correspondences this rootless summer was with Susannah Cibber, who was pressing him to visit them in Berkshire. He was moving so restlessly from spa to spa and ball to assembly that her letters did not easily reach him. "I want to know if you don't deserve to be huffed for not telling one where to direct to you," she chided him in July. Though he was evasive about visiting her, he was encouraging her letters: "When you say I have wit or something better," she went on, "I suspect you are trying flattery, but if you are content with my follies you are welcome to my letters."[6] Airy and flirtatious as was her tone, her letters were not really feckless, never without design. No matter how convoluted, each one wound inexorably to the same point: how soon could she see him so that they could talk stage business together? "Joking apart," she wrote, "I long to see you that we may consult together."[7] As the summer advanced it grew clearer to her that Garrick was being deliberately vague about the fall. She was being pressed by both Rich and Lacy, but she was determined to play only where Garrick did. "I must tell you," she wrote him in an attempt to pique him into giving away his intentions, "that I hear we are both to be turned out of Drury Lane Playhouse to breathe our faithful souls out where we please. But as Mr Lacy suspects you are so great a favorite with the ladies that they will resent it, he has enlisted two swinging Irishmen of six feet high to silence that battery."[8] The swinging Irishmen were Thomas Sheridan and Spranger Barry, with whom Lacy, as uneasy as Susannah about Garrick's plans, was negotiating. Sheridan was not, as we know, a prepossessing figure, but Barry (1719–1777) was the handsomest man on the stage, six feet tall (a great height at that time), with Attic features and a melodious voice. Susannah was well aware how sensitive Garrick was about his appearance, for he was a small man and not classically handsome.

The last thing Lacy wanted to do, of course, was to "turn out" his two greatest drawing cards, Susannah Cibber and David Garrick. But he was fighting for his life at Drury Lane and had asked them both to take a salary cut. In their country retreats neither Susannah nor Garrick seemed to have much awareness of Lacy's plight or the tension in London. The Young Pretender had landed in Scotland and was marching south almost unopposed. The London financial

Spranger Barry, by Joshua Reynolds. Barry, best dressed of his contemporary players, is wearing a bag-wig (the hair behind is caught in a silk bag), a stock collar (buckling in the back of the neck), and a matching coat and waistcoat of studied understatement.

world trembled. There were runs on the Bank of England. The modest banking firm of Green and Amber which held the patent of Drury Lane was at the point of breaking. Yet Garrick wrote haughtily to Lacy that he would not treat with him about next year's articles until the £250 that Fleetwood had left still owing him was paid by the present manager; otherwise he was going to Ireland for the season. At this news, Lacy struck a threatening tone, calling Garrick avaricious, arrogant, and dishonest to the terms of his old articles which required that he give the manager of Drury Lane preference over any other offer. This attack upon his honor enraged Garrick. The truth was he did not want to return to London: he was still restless, wounded, and depressed, and dared not see Woffington yet. But like many scrupulous people he felt compelled to justify any action that smacked of weakness with some unassailable moral principle. In his old home in Lichfield where he had come to rest after his giddy summer and where he was surrounded and petted by his brothers and sisters, he brooded on Lacy's rascality. He could not in honor return to Drury Lane after the things Lacy had said. He wrote and rewrote drafts of an interminable letter to Lacy refuting each point of his attack and protesting that there was "no reason why I should suffer from the schemes of managers."[9] He wrote Susannah of Lacy's villainy (though significantly he never mentioned to her his half-formed plan to go to Ireland) and she, all sympathy, replied that she agreed with him and would not sign at Drury Lane either, protesting that it was not "in the power of Mr Lacy, with all his eloquence to enlist me in his ragged regiment."[10]

There was real doubt whether there would be any theatrical season in London in 1745–46. The *Daily Gazeteer* reported on September 5 that all the minor players were scurrying like rats between the two theaters royal, unwilling to sign articles until they saw where the big names would settle. But these mighty ones were lying low, or out of town: "Temperate Jack is swilling Hogsheads of Claret in Boeotia [Quin was abroad], Poor Pistol is in Durance Vile [Theo Cibber was confined again to the Fleet], and penitent Calista [Susannah Cibber, after her popular role in *The Fair Penitent*] is solacing at her villa and sliding down the Slope of Pleasure." (Eight years after the scandal there was still a snicker to be drawn from any allusion to Susannah's liaison with Sloper).

About the middle of September, still with no idea of Garrick's plans, Susannah returned to London. Unwilling to play opposite such pallid partners as Delane, Mills, Ryan, or Bridgewater, she attached herself to neither theater and continued to write beseechingly to Garrick. She did make one public appearance to further a project of her brother's and show her loyalty to the Protestant regime. Lacy had asked Arne to come up with a rousing patriotic song that could be sung before the curtain to invigorate the scant, cold audiences that came trickling into Drury Lane this ominous fall. The night of September 28, just after London had learned of Sir John Cope's humiliating defeat by the Highlanders at Prestonpans, three oratorio singers, Susannah Cibber, Beard, and Reinhold, stepped solemnly before the Drury Lane curtain and sang Arne's new anthem, described in the playbill as "God Save our Noble King." The sturdy air and resolute words were greeted with tears, huzzahs, and demands for encores. A few days later a delegation of players from Covent Garden approached young Burney to copy out an arrangement for their theater.[11] As the popularity of "God Save the King" swelled, the grandeur of its theatrical presentation grew. A trio of oratorio singers would no longer do. By October 10, Benjamin Victor was writing the self-exiled Garrick: "The stage at both houses is the most pious as well as the most loyal place in the three kingdoms. 20 men appear at the end of every play, and one, stepping forward from the rest with uplifted hands and eyes, begins singing to an old anthem tune."[12] Arne had first heard the tune as a child attending Mass with his mother in one of the Catholic embassy chapels, those pockets of Jacobite feeling. It tickled Arne's saturnine humor, wavering Catholic that he was, to know that while the entire British nation was tunefully pouring out its Protestant devotion to George, few but himself knew that the song had been written as a rallying cry for the Papist grandfather of the young Stuart prince marching ever closer to London, and that its original words had been, "God Save Great James, our King."

In Lichfield, Garrick still could not decide what to do that fall. "My thoughts bend toward Ireland,"[13] he wrote Draper. Yet it seemed ignoble to leave his country now: "If this rebellion had been demolished I would have returned to Ireland directly."[14] In October he wrote his friend William Zuylestein, fourth Earl of Rochford, to volunteer for the regiment he had heard Rochford was raising. His Lordship replied that he was honored Garrick desired to place his life under his command, but there were, "thank God, old regiments enow . . . to quell those rash traitors without raising new." The British stage, Rochford continued, was Garrick's proper battlefield and it lay in disorder and confusion. He urged Garrick to hurry back, slay his enemies, and "take command yourself."[15] But returning to London was precisely what Garrick would not do, despite Rochford's tactful call to arms, Lacy's shaken fist, and Susannah Cibber's siren song.

All fall Garrick put her off, never closing the possibility that he could be persuaded back to London to perform with her, nor mentioning his negotiations with Smock Alley. Meanwhile, her letters, harping on her need to see him for the discussion of secret matters, had reached such a pitch that Garrick began to wonder if there were something personal and passionate in her intentions. "Mrs Cibber still presses me to *visit her* that we may settle something," he wrote Draper, "but my mind runs on the *Buck Basket,* and no more intrigues for me."[16] Having spent the summer healing his heart with a series of gallantries, and temporizing and flirting by letter with Susannah, Garrick was full of dark fears about the machinations of the opposite sex. To Draper he also commented, "Woffington, I hear, shews my letters about; pray have you heard anything of the kind? What she does now . . . little affects me . . . excepting her shewing my . . . love and nonsense to make me ridiculous."[17] Garrick, like Susannah, often enfleshed emotions he did not care to acknowledge in dramatic personae. The Buck Basket refers to the humiliation of Sir John Falstaff, who, in *The Merry Wives of Windsor,* embarked upon an amorous adventure with two lusty matrons who turned out not to be the accommodating rustic simpletons he had taken them for. To teach him a lesson, they maneuvered him into a large laundry basket in which he was tossed and nearly suffocated in dirty clothes and laughed to scorn by the whole town. Garrick, by no means comfortable about his recent behavior toward women, saw Susannah and Peg, like those cruelly merry wives, as somehow contriving to "make him ridiculous" before the world, a fate to which, like Falstaff himself, he was aware that he had laid himself open.

Though she had been waiting for months to reveal her scheme about the Drury Lane patent to him in person, when Garrick had not returned by October 24, Susannah wrote him of her plan to take over the empty King's Opera House this year and do, gratis, a series of benefit performances to raise money for the recruitment of guards.

> There will be no operas this year, so if you, Mr Quin and I agree to play without salary and pick up some of the best actors and actresses that are disengaged at what salary you both think proper, I make no doubt we shall get a license to play there for fifty, sixty or any number of nights you agree upon. Mr Heidegger shall pay scenes, etc. and pay those that receive wages, and deliver the overplus to some proper person to enlist men to serve in any of the regiments of the guards, at five pounds per man. . . . If we succeed, which I have very little doubt of, I desire nothing better than we three playing at the head of any company of actors we can get together.
>
> I did not know of Mr Quin's being in England till since I came to town. I hear he is in the country and refuses to engage yet awhile.

I have not seen him, and shall say nothing of this affair to him . . .
till I have your answer, which I desire you will send by the return of
the post, and let it be positive, one way or the other: if you agree to
it, I beg you will come to town directly. I must beseech you not to
think of not making Mr Quin the offer; the friendship I have received from him makes it impossible for me to act in such a manner,
and though I apprehend his esteem for me is greatly lessened, yet
as I am conscious I have never done anything he ought to take ill,
I shall always behave with the same friendship towards him that I
ever did.

It may, perhaps, have been unnecessary to have said what I
have done about Mr Quin, but I was not sure but you might
imagine there would be some difficulties about parts. . . . I think
that . . . may be easily settled when we meet.

Her letter was long and serious: no fancy, no coquetry. Reading it
over she must have felt its tone needed leavening, for she ended with
one of her little flourishes of nonsensical stage consanguinity: "I have
wrote so much of this thing that I have no time to say any more, but
that your wife is well and in town, and sends her love to you. I am,
your most affectionate mother, S. Cibber."[18]

If her plan for the recruitment fund succeeded it would advance, in the most judicious way, every one of her goals: it would
help her country, underscore her patriotism, put the lie to Lacy's
accusations of her and Garrick's avarice, reconcile herself and Quin,
bring Quin and Garrick together, and serve as a testing ground for
their managerial triumvirate without any long-term commitment.
Her letter so agitated Garrick, who had all but concluded his arrangements with Smock Alley, that he sent off a letter at once to
Somerset Draper, though he had written him only three days earlier:
"I should not have troubled you so soon again," he wrote, "was it not
to tell you I have received a letter from Mrs Cibber who proposes a
scheme for our acting with Mr Quin, gratis, at the Haymarket, in
order to raise a sum of money to enlist men for his majesty's service.
Now, although I imagine this proposal merely chimerical and
womanish, yet, as I would not give my opinion too hastily upon such
an affair, I must desire you to wait upon her."[19] Draper at once did
so, but even while he probed Susannah's "womanish" plan in order

to report to his friend, Garrick concluded his bargaining with Ireland and prepared to ride directly from Lichfield to Chester to embark.

When Susannah learned this on October 30, she wrote:

I am sorry to hear you propose going to Ireland without calling at London. I should think it would be right to see your friends here first. You don't know what events may happen in your absence, as I have no notion the theatre can go on long in the way it now is. I should have been very glad to have had two or three hours conversation with you before your journey; but if I have not that pleasure I heartily wish you your health. I won't say a word of success because cela va sans dire. I am, your most sincere friend and humble servant, S. Cibber.[20]

Her letter was so civil, so reasonable, her reproof so mild, so full of solicitude, and at the same time her tone was so cool that it put Garrick into a flutter of reparation, and his first letter to her from safe across the Irish Sea must have been full of gallantry for it drew forth from her this exquisite reply:

Sir, I had a thousand pretty things to say to you, but you go to Ireland without seeing me, and to stop my mouth from complaining you artfully tell me I am one of the number you don't care to take leave of. And I tell you I am not to be flammed in that manner. You assure me also you want sadly to make love to me; and I assure you, very seriously, I will never engage upon the same theatre again without you make more love to me than you did last year. I am ashamed that the audience should see me break the least rule of decency (even upon the stage) for the wretched lovers I had last winter.* I desire you always to be my lover upon the stage and my friend off of it.[21]

Garrick's anxious effusions had shifted the balance of their relationship. Up to now, Susannah had been the pursuer; now he was courting her, and she had an opportunity to define the limits of the relationship she wanted with him: her lover on stage, her chaste

* Sheridan, Delane, et al.

admirer off it. There were no buck baskets to fear, no sexual demands, no confrontation with Sloper. But the kind of tender friendship that existed between Susannah and Quin and Handel, so natural
to all three of their natures and so fruitful to their talents, was a good
deal more awkward to establish with young Garrick. Her friendship
with him was never so stable or tranquil as with those two confirmed
bachelors her father's age. But she had, for the moment at least,
reassured him, and his relief was apparent in his next letter to
Draper: "Mrs Cibber is a most sensible and I believe sincerely, a well-
meaning woman; pray go and see her."[22]

Though she refused to play a regular season this year without
Garrick, she was restless and anxious to work. Her mind was still full
of the plan that Garrick had dismissed as female foolishness. On
December 7 she published a notice in the *Daily Advertizer* offering
to play Polly in *The Beggar's Opera* to benefit the Veteran's Scheme.
Her offer took Lacy by surprise and enraged Kitty Clive, who regarded the proposal as a renewed attack upon her sovereignty over
that role under guise of patriotism. On the night Susannah's proposal
was published, Susannah wrote to Garrick that "the Green Room
was in uproar. I was cursed with all the elegance of phrase that reigns
behind the scenes and Mrs Clive swore she would not play the part of
Lucy."[23] While Lacy was trying to placate Kitty, John Rich sent
Susannah a handsome offer from Covent Garden: she could have his
theater and as many of his company as she required for her *Beggar's
Opera,* and he would assume the house charges so the benefit would
be "clear." Since Theo was under articles at Covent Garden this year,
Rich guaranteed that Susannah's husband would not be in the the-
ater during performances or rehearsals of *The Beggar's Opera.*
Susannah accepted.

Doing *The Beggar's Opera* at Covent Garden did not pacify
Kitty Clive and her friends, who placed an anonymous letter in the
General Advertizer of December 9 calling Susannah's proposal "a
Jesuitical Stroke of a Papist Actress in Pursuit of Protestant Popular-
ity" and reminding its readers that "her whole family are, in the
strict sense, Roman Catholick." That same day the *Daily Advertizer*
carried a letter from "A. B." volunteering, since he was a devout
Catholic, to play Macheath for Mrs. Cibber. If anyone questioned

"A. B.'s" qualifications for the role, he pointed out that Macheath was a brigand, murderer, and scoundrel, a character instinctively congenial to any Catholic.

The noisy malice of Kitty did Susannah infinite good, for it gave her an opportunity to define publicly her position as an English Catholic. She was indeed, she wrote in a letter to the *General Advertizer* on the following day, of the Romish persuasion. But her faith was a private matter, she was unswervingly loyal to the present royal family and its line, and she prayed her humble efforts as Polly would be accepted as evidence of this.

The Beggar's Opera was performed at Covent Garden on December 14, 16, and 17. Beard was Macheath and the obliging Hannah Pritchard undertook, as she had in the past, the despised Lucy. Susannah was "to the eye, the ear and the heart, the best Polly that ever there was."[24] After a decade of patience, she emerged as the final victor of the Polly War, not through the renewal of hostilities but by an altruistic gesture. She wrote Garrick on December 19:

> I promised you an account . . . of the success of *The Beggar's Opera*. . . . I played it Saturday, Monday and Tuesday last to the fullest houses that were ever seen. . . . Mr Rich has pressed me, of all things, to engage there next year, but as there is no Tancred I am resolved they shall have no Sigismunda. . . . P.S. Mr Rich has just brought me the account of the three nights which amounts to upwards of £600.

The money-raising scheme, for which she had asked Garrick's cooperation and which he had rejected, she had carried out alone and with acclaim. Having made sure he understood that, she reverted, as she did in every letter, to the Drury Lane patent:

> I know you reckon yourself a very politic prince with your journey to Ireland; and I think the great Garrick never acted so simply* since I had the honor of knowing him. You are out of the way at the very time that the fate of the stage is depending, nor would you let me see you before you went. . . . I wish you would tell me . . .

* In the sense of foolishly naïve.

how far you would care to go if it [the patent] was now to be sold and we should join in the purchase.

Then she added, "I must know your real sentiments."[25]

His "real sentiments" were precisely what Garrick could not reveal. For all the while he was showering her with letters and urging Draper to pay court to her and keep an eye on her activities lest she pull off the purchase of the patent, he had other nets in London's theatrical waters and other business partners he preferred. The day Garrick received her account of *The Beggar's Opera* he wrote Draper:

I was most heartily rejoiced at her success, and though it is intimated to me [by other correspondents] that she was not so excellent in the character, yet I cannot think but three crammed houses are certain proofs of the contrary. . . . As to the patent, what can I say to her? Mure,* you know, is the person I have hopes of joining with, and yet, if she can procure it . . . why should not I — upon a good agreement and easy terms — be concerned with her? We ought always to play together and I could wish we were both settled at the same house . . . visit Mrs Cibber.[26]

Visit her Draper continued to do, and Garrick meanwhile wrote her a letter of such extravagant congratulations upon her Polly that she chaffed him: "I suppose if you were sober enough to read it over you imagined the wine made you write like an angel." Then she returned to the patent:

Mr Draper called upon me a day or two before I had your letter and told me you proposed Mr Quin should be one of the triumvirate; that you were studying parts in a different cast and that you were willing to make everything easy to him. This has given me great pleasure. . . . I did not know whether you would give up any of your parts and if it was likely you could live in friendship playing them alternately. He is an honest, worthy man, and besides

* Hutchison Mure [Meure], 1709–1794, a wealthy upholsterer who held a £7,000 mortgage on the "Cloaths and Scenes" at Drury Lane, which he had acquired in Fleetwood's time.

being a great actor he is a very useful one and will make the under actors mind their business. I have not set eyes on him since he came to England, and was I to see him I should not mention this affair to him. . . . I desire it may come from you; it may be a means of friendship between you.

She finished her letter, as she always did after a serious passage, with one of her stage jokes: "Your wife sends her duty: she is the greatest coquet in England and has half a dozen husbands in bank,* in case of your death."[27]

After Draper's January visit and Garrick's effusions from Ireland, Susannah believed that Garrick's intentions regarding the patent were clear and that their joint purchase only waited Garrick's return, an event she expected from week to week. Actually Garrick was writing:

My dear Draper, look about a little, and *if you can conveniently wriggle your little friend into the patent upon good terms you make me forever!* [Garrick's italics] If Mure gets it, I shall be with him. . . . I shall be glad of your visiting Mrs Cibber. She certainly has had proposals made to her; but how can she be a joint patentee? Her husband will interfere or somebody must act for her which would be equally disagreeable.[28]

Unless death freed her, her iniquitous husband would always have the power to challenge Susannah's property and her earnings. It was conceivable that the financial operation of Drury Lane might be chronically hamstrung by litigation with Theo who, even if he were to lose every claim, could be a debilitating nuisance. Even if Susannah Cibber had no husband, it was an awkward matter in the eighteenth century to have a woman as a business partner. Her interests must be represented by a close male relative or someone appointed for her. Garrick would have to deal not with Susannah, whose deference toward men and malleability might make her the most gracious of associates, but with a delegate over whose identity he would have

---

* Delane, Sheridan, et al.

no control. It might be Tom Arne, her lecherous, litigious, fiddling brother, whom Garrick loathed as much as Theo. It might be some officious stranger put forward by Sloper. Garrick's misgivings about Susannah Cibber as a partner were as realistic and as self-protective as his doubts about Peg Woffington as a wife.

In February, when Garrick had not yet returned to England, Susannah wrote that she was longing to go to West Woodhay. "Come as soon as you can, I beseech you," she said, "for I grudge the time I lose in London."[29] Garrick, who was not only making a great deal of money in Dublin but was delightfully engrossed in a new love affair,[30] was in no hurry to return to England and countered her urgings with an invitation to join him in Ireland. All her old friends were longing to see her, he wrote, and her theatrical welcome was assured. She replied, "My love of Ireland is as great as yours and I always think with respect and gratitude of the favors I received there," but "between friends, I cannot muster up courage even to think of crossing the sea."[31]

While she was waiting confidently for Garrick she agreed to do another benefit, this time at Drury Lane for the Arnes. "My brother is to thank you for my playing for him," she chided Garrick in April, "for had you come to England according to your first design, I had been in the country before this."[32] The Arnes' benefit (*The Orphan*) was scheduled for April 12, two days after Theophilus Cibber's benefit, *The Lady's Last Stake,* on April 10. Theo had left Covent Garden in March in what he himself conceded had been "a foolish pet." Now both he and his creditors were counting the days till his night at Drury Lane. However, it was Susannah's adamant condition that her husband be nowhere on the premises of any theater where she was rehearsing or performing. And so, for the second time in months, Theo was ordered to stay away from the theater where he was engaged. It had been humiliating enough at Covent Garden while Susannah rehearsed *The Beggar's Opera.* It was intolerable now when he was preparing *The Lady's Last Stake,* a revival totally unfamiliar to the other actors and therefore requiring extra rehearsals. This time Theo resisted expulsion so belligerently that Arne, alarmed for his sister's safety, told Lacy he would have to take his benefit to Covent Garden unless the Drury Lane manager could guarantee the leashing and muzzling of Theophilus. Lacy warned Cibber that he would be out of both benefit night and job if he did not comply, whereupon Theo took his rehearsals to the large public rooms of various taverns, and vented his indignation in another public letter.

It is with reluctance I trouble the town [he confided to the *General Advertizer* on April 8], especially with a subject on which I have long chose to be silent . . . but . . . a report has been invidiously spread . . . that I removed to Drury Lane only to impede Mrs Cibber in her performance there. . . . I never had, nor have I, any such intention. Were I . . . to exert the authority I have an undoubted right to over her, I have had many opportunities. . . . She has sought every occasion to disturb my peace of mind, to stab my reputation. . . . I should undoubtedly be justified . . . in any act of severe justice toward her that would not debase my manhood or shock my humanity. But, low as she has reduced my fortune, my mind has never sunk low enough to seek a mean revenge, even against the most faithless, artful and ungrateful woman that ever disturbed the heart of a weak man. My greatest fault toward her has been too much lenity.

It is now about eight years since her elopement from me. . . . My profusion (chiefly bestowed on her) had loaded me with debts. I found myself involved in law suits and . . . pestered by her with suits in the Commons and Chancery. . . . In hopes of a quiet life — though I despaired of a happy one — at Mrs Cibber's request I consented she should engage at any theatre she pleased and be mistress of her income on condition she did nothing to prejudice me. Yet the first use she made of this indulgence was her privately agreeing that whatever managers she played with should by no means receive me in the same company. Consequently, last year, I was, for half the season excluded both theatres. . . . No wonder that last summer I was again a prisoner of the Fleet and close confined upward of six months. Some friends of mine (without my knowledge or desire) gave Mrs Cibber a hint [after her performance in *The Beggar's Opera*] it would . . . further ingratiate herself with the world to make a proffer of playing a night for my benefit; which . . . she absolutely refused. . . . I have dwelt too long on an irksome topic . . . yet, stories propagated of my intentions to disturb her . . .

are injurious, false, and without foundation. Whether my provoka-
tions are not unparalleled, let the world judge. . . .

Theo could see no reason why the wife he harassed should not graciously rescue him from his creditors with a benefit night, and he
continued alternately to threaten her and Sloper with more lawsuits
and plead for her loving mercy. Susannah Cibber was, by all accounts, both tenderhearted and generous. After his birth in 1740 she
assumed the rearing and education of her brother's illegitimate son
Michael; she subsidized her sister-in-law, Cecilia, when Arne abandoned her. More than once through the years she rescued from
prison or starvation Theo's mad and self-destructive sister, Charlotte,
who acknowledged that she would have perished without Susannah's
assistance after her father had left her to her fate.[33] But where Theo
was concerned, Susannah's attitude remained one of frozen horror.
She would not speak his name, nor occupy the same room or even
the same building with him.

After the Arnes' benefit, Susannah joined Sloper in West
Woodhay. She missed Garrick by only a few weeks. He returned to
London in early May, his heart cured of Peg Woffington, his pockets
full, and just in time to help the city celebrate the crushing of the
Jacobite uprising. The Thames mouth was clogged with prison ships,
so crowded with rebels that many of them died before they could be
transported. In Southwark Gaol the proud lairds Kilmarnock,
Cromartie, and Balmerino awaited public execution. The fat Prince
of Hesse, whose mercenaries had rescued the British regulars from
their retreat before the advancing Scots, lingered in London to receive the grateful adulation of the English populace. Both theaters
royal were staying open to take advantage of the festive crowds in
town. Garrick, still unreconciled with Lacy, signed up with Rich to
play a summer season of Shakespeare, and then to lead the Covent
Garden company in the fall.

Now that he was back, one of the most pressing things he must
do was to mend his fences with Susannah Cibber and make sure that
the most affecting actress in the land was with him next season at
Covent Garden. His conscience was far from easy regarding her. He
wrote her that he had been disappointed to find her already in the

country when he returned to London, but that he would visit her presently at West Woodhay, carrying with him the ten pairs of Irish linen gloves she had commissioned him to buy for her, and a budget of gossip, including an account of his talk with the Prince of Hesse one evening in Ranelagh Gardens, and the upshot of a prank he was about to play on the aging Mrs. Horton.

The attentions of Garrick's aristocratic friends quickly filled his time, and he was soon writing Susannah that his visit would be much later in the summer and only a flying one. "If you are serious about staying here but a few days I desire you will not come," she replied. "The farmer [Sloper] bids me tell you the same." She wished he would stay a good while and bring horses so that he might ride and his personal servant so that he would be comfortable: "As for your man, you may put him in your pocket if he is the same I remember; a little crumpling won't spoil him." She asked him to leave the gloves in London else she would only have to bring them back to town, begged him not to forget a word of "what the Prince of Hesse said at Ranelagh," and closed with a mock reproof: "I am very glad to find you did not perpetrate your horrid design upon poor Mrs Horton."[34]

Early in September, after sixteen months of correspondence — Susannah's side all persistence, Garrick's all parrying — they met again at Sloper's country mansion. Garrick had come direct from two weeks at the spa at Cheltenham (West Woodhay lay just off the coach road on his way back to London) pleading that he could stop only briefly, so pressing were his theatrical duties in London. He told no one where he was staying — "Newberry" (*sic*) is the only address he put on his letters from West Woodhay — letting it be understood he was writing from some inn on the coach road. He was queasy about visiting this irregular ménage, uneasy about what his polite friends would think of his friendship with a notorious woman, unsure what tone to strike with Sloper, dreading Susannah's reproaches for his uncandid treatment, and fearful of fleshly expectations on her part as a result of the romantic nonsense he had poured out while he was safe across the Irish Sea. Had September not been upon him, and Susannah still not signed at either theater royal, he would probably have avoided calling at West Woodhay altogether.

Some time the past spring Susannah had become aware that Garrick was seeking another partner while temporizing with her on the remote chance that she acquire Drury Lane. From this moment she never mentioned the matter again to Garrick and gave up forever her aspirations toward ownership of a theater. Of her personal feelings she was absolutely silent to Garrick. She regarded recrimination as the shrill weapon of the vulgar part of her sex, unpermissible to a gentlewoman. "Her delicacy never broke into reproach,"[35] Davies said of her fastidious reserve, by which means, he noted admiringly, no matter what the outcome of a struggle, she maintained her moral superiority over any adversary.

Actually, once the question of the patent was dead, her relationship with Garrick changed to her advantage. It was crucial for him to have her this year at Covent Garden if he were to compete with Drury Lane, where Woffington and Clive were under articles. It was he who needed Susannah now, and must come courting her in Berkshire.

There were no buck baskets at West Woodhay. Sloper was manly, open, and welcoming. From Susannah there was not a breath of reproach, no mention of the patent, not a hint of any passionate expectations. She listened to his gossip, admired his successes. The old fashioned mansion at West Woodhay was charming. An avenue approached it, turning and crossing a bridge that spanned one end of the angling pond. Roses climbed in the long windows of the lower rooms, one of which was a library of prints and old books begun by Sloper, Senior, and being added to by the present William.[36] To the south rose the steep bare slopes of the Downs where one could ride in the open for hours. The household was the sort Garrick knew and loved. At night there were games or music or theatricals instigated by himself or Susannah or Margaret Lethieullier, William's younger sister, with Sloper and Smart Lethieullier and old Widow Arne forming the nucleus of the audience. Susannah's mother, pious and stern (young Burney remembered her as a "bigoted Papist"), added a seemly propriety to the irregular household. There was even a wicked-tongued parrot to make the children giggle and old Mrs. Arne frown.

Garrick's "flying" visit stretched and stretched until he had stayed at West Woodhay nearly a month, "never in better spirits or more nonsensical in my life," he wrote his friend Reverend John Hoadly, though he could not muster the courage to mention where he was. In the ménage at West Woodhay, based, it was true, upon an indecency, and yet so decorous, so bourgeois, Garrick was accorded the role he filled on his visits to his old home in Lichfield: favorite son, golden brother, returning hero. How well this agreed with him, how petted he felt, how expanded in spirit (and in flesh) may be judged from his further remark to Hoadly: "I have been lately alarmed with some encroachments of my Belly upon the line of Grace and Beauty. In short I am growing very fat. . . . Unless Shakespeare in ye Winter reduces me to my primitive insignificance."[37]

If Garrick did not wish his genteel correspondents to know where he was, or with what Calypso lingering, Susannah was under no such restraints. On September 25 she was writing her brother ecstatically, "Mr Garrick has been here these three weeks in great good humor and spirits, and in short we are as merry as the day is long." She urged Arne to join them. "Indeed, Tommy, you can scarcely believe how glad I should be to see you, nor can you imagine with what joy I should run out to meet you. I am in charming health and spirits and as full of fun as I can hold. Therefore, if you have a mood to be very agreeably entertained with life, wit and good humor, this is your place!"[38]

There is nothing to suggest that Susannah ever wavered in her fidelity to Sloper. Yet she was certainly exhilarated and infatuated by Garrick, who in many ways might have been a more congenial companion than the silent, humorless, country-loving, self-sufficient Sloper. Urbane, convivial, demonstrative, sympathetic, one of Garrick's outstanding qualities was his capacity to revive the most flagging company, or cheer the most downcast heart. This faculty, which people expected from him offstage as well as on it, was at times an exhausting responsibility.* As a boy he had borne the heavy burden of sustaining his sickly and depressed mother, rallying her every day with his bright spirit. And when he was a grown man it was

* "Garrick never enters a room but he regards himself as the object of general attention, from whom the entertainment of the company is expected." *Early Diary of Fanny Burney* (London, 1889), vol. 2, pp. 159–160.

blithe, robust, uncomplicated, and merry ladies who attracted him, and one of these whom he eventually wed and who made him supremely happy. It is hard to say what might have happened had Garrick seriously laid siege to Susannah Cibber's affections. He never did: the need he sensed in this frail, wistful woman frightened him. Susannah understood the kind of woman Garrick liked and her letters to him are sometimes touching, sometimes painful in their false, determined brightness. Even her rare references to her (by now) serious and chronic stomach disorder were oddly jaunty. She had written him in Dublin, "As I have quite left off wine I can only drink [the health of her friends in Ireland] in small beer, but to make amends I remember them the oftener. Be assured I take large draughts!"[39] What she was glossing over was that she was so thin her worried doctors had put her on a regime of beer between meals to gain flesh.

For nearly a month at West Woodhay Susannah floated upon Garrick's buoyancy and he basked in her appreciation. By the time he left for the city Susannah had agreed to follow him in a few weeks and perform with him at Covent Garden. And although, despite her patient three-year campaign she had failed to achieve her dream of a managerial triumvirate, she had won a portion of that goal. James Quin was to be asked to join the Covent Garden company and Garrick had agreed to divide all capital roles with him, to do joint performances, and even to take second leads from time to time. Susannah would be the first lady at Covent Garden, flanked by the two most renowned players in England.

✒ *15* ✑

I F bringing together Quin and Garrick was an old dream of Susannah's, it was also something for which the public had been chaffing for years. Quin and Garrick themselves had long avoided such a confrontation. They made light of each other's gifts in public, but they felt considerable mutual awe. "If that young fellow is right, the rest of us are wrong,"[1] Quin had muttered after he had gone to see Garrick's *Richard III* in 1741.

Now that they were in the same company they still skirted direct comparison by playing on alternate nights. But this polite, arm's-length arrangement was not the *mano a mano* duel for which their partisans thirsted. And the opportunity to see David and Goliath face to face came at last on November 14, when Covent Garden presented Rowe's *The Fair Penitent*. Garrick played the seducer, Lothario; Cibber was his victim, Calista; and Quin played the noble avenger, Horatio.

The Fair Penitent is a She tragedy, a variation on the theme of man's inhumanity toward woman, which had fascinated the British from tales of Patient Griselda in the Middle Ages to *The Duchess of Malfi* in the seventeenth century. Woman, tried to the limits of her frail powers, was an old theme with new appeal to the tenderhearted eighteenth century. Calista struggles, succumbs, and dies in the end by her own hand, abused by father, lover, and husband, but she goes under with a queer, crazy disdain, and she has one surprisingly militant speech:

> How hard is the condition of our sex,
> Through ev'ry state of life the slaves of men!
> In all the dear, delightful days of youth
> A rigid father dictates to our will,
> And deals out pleasure with a scanty hand.
> To his, the tyrant husband's reign succeeds;
> Proud with opinion of superior reason
> He holds domestic business and devotion
> All we are capable to know, and shuts us,
> Like cloistered idiots, from the world's acquaintance
> And all the joys of freedom. Wherefore are we
> Born with high souls but to assert ourselves,
> Shake off this vile obedience they exact
> And claim an equal empire o'er the world
>
> (act III, scene i).

In the audience of the Garrick-Quin-Cibber *Fair Penitent* was a fourteen-year-old schoolboy, who drank in his first view of these three legendary figures, and still vividly recalled them when he was an old man. Of Cibber: "I have her now in my mind's eye. I behold a slender, graceful form from between the wings of a wide, expanded hoop petticoat, pushed sideways on the stage, rise like an exhalation. . . . Her very frame was fashioned to engage your pity, for it seemed wasted with sorrow and sensibility: The cheek was hollow and the eye was joyless. . . ."[2] Of Quin and Garrick: "Quin presented himself upon the rising of the curtains in a green velvet coat embroidered down the seams, an enormous, full-bottomed periwig, rolled stockings and high heeled, square toed shoes. With very little variation and in a deep, full tone, accompanied by a sawing kind of action which had more of the senate than the stage in it, he rolled out his heroicks with an air of dignified indifference. . . . After long and eager expectation I first beheld little Garrick, then young and light and alive in every muscle . . . come bounding on the stage, pointing at the . . . heavy paced Horatio. Heavens, what a transition! It seemed as if a whole century had been stepped over in . . . a single scene."[3]

In the second act, when Lothario (Garrick), maddened by Horatio's (Quin's) sententious pronouncements upon his character and morals, challenged him to a duel, Quin before replying entered one of his famous "grand pauses," drawing out the silence so long that a Garrick afficionado in the gallery called out, "Well —? Why don't you tell the gentleman whether you will meet him or not?"[4] Both Quin and Garrick changed color at this, but, buffered by Susannah Cibber's sympathetic presence playing between them, got smoothly through the play. Indeed, they sustained the whole season with every sign of amicability. One night when they were playing *Henry IV, Part I,* Falstaff (Quin) was lugging off the bloody corpse of Hotspur (Garrick) on his broad back when he was heard at the edge of the wings inquiring of his lifeless burden, "Well then — Where shall we sup tonight?"[5]

Quin rolled with majestic indolence through the 1746–47 season. At bottom he was aware that the style he exemplified, the grand, measured, musical, declamatory tradition of Betterton and Booth, was now regarded as old-fashioned fustian. At season's end he withdrew to Bath and did not return to London in the fall.

While Garrick was working at Covent Garden, his negotiations for the purchase of the Drury Lane patent continued, and, on April 9, an agreement was signed making Garrick and Lacy joint patentees. Rich's attitude about the loss of Garrick was curious. With Quin, Garrick, Cibber, and Pritchard all at his house he had been enjoying a season more brilliant and profitable than anything in memory. "Plays only are the fashion," Walpole reported to Mann. "At one house the best company that perhaps ever were together."[6] Although Rich was aware of Garrick's desire to be a part of management, aware of his embarrassment at joining Lacy after his denouncements of him only last year, aware that with an offer of a percent of profit arrangement he could secure Garrick's presence indefinitely, he made no move to hold him. Rich had seemed bewildered and even repelled by the extravagant success of his theater during the year. On nights when the crush was particularly great — when, in order to make sure of places, the capacity crowd had been seated and waiting three hours — he would stalk into his theater, poke an eye through the curtain, glare incredulously at the patient mass, and mutter, "What? Are you there? Much good may it do ye."[7] Rich loathed everything about the great stars of the tragic stage: their extortionary salaries, their hauteur, their rivalries, their temperament, their fawning entourages. If public taste had given him any choice he would have done without them and filled his theater with dancing bears, acrobats, jugglers, sword swallowers, pantomimes, ballets, and pageants. He distrusted the fashionable five-act tragedies of inflated sentiments and windy words. Rich was almost inarticulate himself, though whether he suffered from a speech impediment or had invented a perverse and private dialect no one ever decided. He claimed he could not remember names, and democratized his backstage population by calling everyone "muster," from star to stagehand. And if anyone were rash enough to insist upon his own name, Rich's malapropisms seemed not quite innocent. Garrick, small and sinewy, might hear himself addressed as "Muster Griskin" (a griskin is a small, lean pork chop), and the free-spending, spirits-loving Spranger Barry was "Muster Barleymore."[8]

Rich was more than an eccentric impresario. He was a miming genius. He invented endless adventures for the character of Harlequin (imported to Britain from the Italian commedia dell'arte), and in the comic afterpieces, which traditionally followed a serious play, he danced Harlequin's love for Columbine, his enmity with Pantaloon, his tricks, escapes, disguises, resurrections, sufferings, and triumphs. The polite eighteenth-century playgoer did not regard pantomime as a respectable dramatic form but as primitive stage trickery, fit for the amusement of children or the lower classes. Critics and discriminating patrons complained constantly of Rich's desecration of the stage. Yet Rich had one highborn admirer. George II had been thirty before he set foot on British soil and he had a cruel time of it with his subjects' tongue. He habitually nodded off during five-act tragedies, but came to life for the pantomime, under-

*John Rich as
Harlequin, 1753.*

*David Garrick, from
a portrait by Robert
Pine, engraved by
R. Cooper.*

stood every syllable of Rich's body language, and shamelessly laughed and rocked and clapped his hands in the royal box.

Rich's stage name was Lun, his sly protest against the theatrical cult of personality. When he was Lun he was nul: nobody and Everyman. John Rich was a tongue-tied boor, but Lun was a paradigm of lucidity, every movement irradiating meaning so direct that it was suspect to all but naïfs and yokels.

That memorable winter of 1746–47, while Garrick, Quin, and Cibber were lining his coffers, Rich liked to beckon aside his stage crew and musicians and do imitations of these great ones. His favorite was Garrick as mad Lear, and he would fall on his knees, lurching, rolling his eyes, and plucking at imaginary rags and bed straw.[9] The laughter he drew was headier for its wickedness, for Shakespeare was holy writ to the eighteenth century and a parody of the bard's high priest in the act of interpreting the sacred text was nearly as blasphemous as an imitation of the Archbishop of Canterbury reading the morning lesson.

When Garrick removed to Drury Lane as patentee in the fall of 1747, Susannah Cibber and Hannah Pritchard went with him, and the stage at Covent Garden — since Quin remained at Bath — was bereft of major tragic players. After a time Quin's pride healed and he grew restive in retirement. He let Rich know through emissaries that he could be coaxed back. His hints bringing no response, he sent Rich an imperious note: "I am at Bath, Quin." But Rich had his own theater back this year just as he liked it, and, up to his ears in the wordless backstage bustle he loved — the clatter of carpenters pounding up a scaffold for tonight's rope walkers, the scuffle of dancers' feet from a practice room, the lingering stench of brimstone and resin from last night's fire and lightning scene in the pantomime — Rich scrawled back, "Stay and be damned, Rich."[10]

Despite their former mutual accusations, Garrick and Lacy were contented partners, though they never became close friends. Each reigned over the sphere of management that suited him: Garrick over authors, casting, new plays, actors, and directing; Lacy over tickets, publicity, wardrobe, and the payroll of more than a hundred players, singers, ushers, prompters, candle snuffers, scene painters, barbers, dressers, chimney sweeps, constables, charwomen, and bill stickers.

Order, decency, and decorum were the objectives of the new administration. Garrick regarded a play as an organism, not a seriatim opportunity for each player to shine according to his own light. He required actors to stay in character even when they were not speaking, neither winking at their friends, bowing to patrons, nor attracting attention with comical side play (Theophilus Cibber's specialty). He insisted that all parts, even minor ones, be memorized exactly. Drury Lane's veteran character actors who were ready with dozens of roles had grown nonchalant about a playwright's precise lines. Richard Yates, for instance, before Garrick's stricture, was notoriously adept, when he lost the thread, at "assuming a bold front and forging matter of his own."[11]

Backstage dalliance, gaming, and drinking were forbidden by Garrick. And, under Lacy, "the office" (payday), which Fleetwood had met only when insurrection threatened, was observed with churchlike scrupulosity. By and large the company embraced this revolution of manners. An age, not twelve years, seemed to have passed between that backstage where Macklin had killed Hallam over a wig and Garrick and Lacy's genteel workshop. Drury Lane became a model bourgeois business enterprise: there was industry and craft in the shop, pride in the product, a paternal concern for the employees (with characteristic affection, exasperation, and condescension Garrick called the troupe his "family of froward children"[12]), a steely integrity in fiscal matters, and, as seal of heaven's approval of the venture, a profit for the two owners that grew more dazzling every year. Though Susannah Cibber had no part of the government of Drury Lane, its tone was what she had dreamed of in a theater of her own, and her benevolent and civilizing influence was felt everywhere. She took up the causes of minor players and employees so warmly that Garrick called her "one of Milton's faithful angels."[13] The role of intercestrix, family peacemaker, the one tender friend who had Garrick's ear when it was deaf to others suited her. She had no authority but infinite opportunity for the exercise of her persuasive and reconciling gifts. "She was," Garrick mused after her death, "the greatest female plague belonging to my house. I

Susannah Cibber,
after Thomas
Hudson.

could easily parry the artless thrusts, and despise the coarse language
of some of my other heroines; but whatever was Cibber's object . . .
she was sure to carry . . . by the acuteness . . . and steadiness of her
perseverance."[14]

   Garrick vehemently denied that he treated Cibber differently
from his other leading ladies. Yet Mrs. Pritchard, most equanimous
of women, felt the contrary so strongly that she had her husband
write Garrick a letter on the subject.[15] Certainly Cibber received the
highest salary (£315) of any player except Garrick and had the first
benefit night of the season, after his.* A clause in her articles granted
her the right to read all new plays and claim any new female role she
liked. The salary of her personal dresser, Mrs. Cleater, was assumed
by the theater, as was the cost of her stage wardrobe, including lace

---

* The order of benefits is an accurate gauge of the rank of capital players. In 1747–
48 it went: Garrick, Cibber, Pritchard, Clive, Woffington, Barry, Macklin.

and jewels. Garrick once complained to his diary that she cleared over £700 a year free of any expense whatever, "save ye mere garniture of her head,"[16] from which it would appear she was responsible for her own wigs, coiffeuse, and hair ornaments. It was backstage gossip that, unlike anyone else in the company, she enjoyed that rarity, a "clear" benefit: while others received the profits of all tickets sold their night less a standard £60 house charge, in Susannah's case the managers were reputed to return this £60 out of their discretionary fund.[17]

Just how highly Garrick regarded Cibber and how much he was prepared to risk on her account may be gathered from the fact that no sooner was he manager of Drury Lane than he bearded Kitty Clive, snatched from her her favorite cub, the role of Polly Peachum, gave it to Susannah Cibber, and mounted a new production of *The Beggar's Opera* with Clive as Polly's bested rival, Lucy. Theophilus Cibber had been savagely mauled when he attempted this, and easygoing Charles Fleetwood had never dreamed of trying it. But Garrick had a stature and authority like no theatrical figure since Thomas Betterton. He handled Clive as one might control a spitting kitten — holding it by the skin of its neck at arm's length and laughing at it. And she, whose method had always been to attack her adversaries (sometimes literally) with tooth and claw, was tamer under Garrick's rule than ever before and, in the twenty-two years she worked for him, rarely managed to get in a lick.

Alas, this "perfect" *Beggar's Opera*, which Londoners had longed for more than ten years to see, came too late. Fat, perspiring Clive could no longer, at thirty-six, project a slip of a nimble-witted, teenaged minx. And Cibber, though her maidenly figure still suggested softness and youth, had by now in her face that settled look of suffering which, affecting in tragedy, was too dark a quality for sweet, trusting Polly.

When Garrick took over Drury Lane he dedicated his theater to Shakespeare. "Sacred to Shakespeare was this spot designed; to pierce the heart and humanize the mind,"[18] he declared to his audience in a prologue he wrote himself and published in the newspapers. Garrick's devotion was more than a fashionable pose. He regarded him-

David Garrick, by Thomas Gainsborough.

self as Shakespeare's disciple, prophet, and custodian, even his avatar. Diderot slyly called him David Shakespeare. A Gainsborough portrait shows Garrick with his arm around a bust of Shakespeare in a fraternal, proprietary gesture. The disembodied head — its expression quizzical, its hair, visage, and collar all the same exsanguinate gray — suggests a powerful cerebral presence, but one without the least actuating force. Garrick's figure, in contrast, balanced on one foot, ready to move, the face ruddy, confident, carries a sense of exuberant physical and intellectual capability. It is clear that Shakespeare, poor severed head, unable to defend himself against the vandals or neglect of posterity, knows how blessed he is to be in Garrick's hands.

In his campaign to revive Shakespeare, Garrick, in the fall of 1748, put into rehearsal *Romeo and Juliet,* which had never been performed at Drury Lane. He had in Spranger Barry and Susannah Cibber the most heartrending pair of lovers in the world. Garrick had adapted the tragedy himself for, though he despised the impious tamperings of others, his special relationship to Shakespeare often required amending the sacred text so as to make it palatable to his contemporaries.

Garrick's *Romeo and Juliet* ran for twenty-one glorious nights. Cibber seemed to listen to her lover "with a sort of modest ecstasy."[19] And Barry, with his noble figure and his boyish, ardent, tender manner, invariably caused a few ladies to faint away when his voice, which was naturally ringing, sweet, and steady, broke during Romeo's anguished transports over Juliet's bier — a glottal phenomenon popularly called "Barry's burst of Grief."

On the eve of Garrick's *Romeo and Juliet,* the spoiler Theophilus Cibber published a slender volume containing his own adaptation of *Romeo and Juliet,** which he had produced four years before at the Little Theatre in the Haymarket. The little book included a rambling account of his estranged wife's rise to eminence over his own broken form. At the time of her elopement he had been, he said, too emotionally drained to protect his own theatrical interests. And now that he had recovered, he was still too much a gentleman to force her home to him and attach her enormous earnings as was his unquestioned right. His present wretched state, forbidden to work wherever she was engaged and therefore shuttled back and forth between the two theaters royal, was the result of her collusion with both managers in a vicious attempt to starve him and his innocent children. Nobody took Cibber's account of his problems very seriously, and the reminder of his *Romeo and Juliet* could not tarnish the glory of Barry and Susannah Cibber. Theophilus had made a preposterous Romeo; his sister Charlotte, an obscenely insinuating nurse; and poor little Jenny Cibber, his fourteen-year-old daughter, had been such a faint-voiced, brittle, intimidated Juliet that people pitied her too much to judge her. However, the timing of Cibber's nasty little book did remind the public that the credit for rescuing *Romeo and Juliet* from oblivion was not Garrick's. In justice to Theo Cibber, he had been an energetic and imaginative manager whenever he had the

* Both Cibber's and Garrick's tragedies are deeply indebted to Thomas Otway's *Caius Marius* (1680), an early adaptation of Shakespeare's *Romeo and Juliet* in which the Capulets and the Montagues have become feuding Roman patrician families.

opportunity and had been giving the public heavy draughts of Shakespeare while Garrick was still a schoolboy in Lichfield.

In November, Garrick announced that a new tragedy, *Mahomet and Irene*, by Dr. Samuel Johnson, would be performed at the first of the new year. Back in 1737 when Garrick had traveled from Lichfield to London to seek his fortune, another young local man accompanied him. Garrick had been twenty-one, Johnson twenty-eight, but a generation seemed to separate them. Garrick was a quick and merry bachelor, bursting with self-confidence; Johnson was a lumbering, learned, moody man, as irritable as he was kind, and bowed already beneath family responsibilities — he was a married man with a stepdaughter older than Garrick. Johnson had been Garrick's schoolmaster and he regarded his companion as a glib boy with a mediocre mind and a saucy and vulgar gift for mimicry. Of the two, Johnson knew he had incomparably superior intellectual and moral qualities with which to make his mark in the great world. He was carrying in his pocket as they went the manuscript of *Mahomet and Irene,* which he hoped to see brought out by one of the theaters royal. Eleven years later, Garrick, still but one and thirty, was a brilliant London figure, rich and, with his purchase of Drury Lane, growing richer. Johnson, nearly forty, was still unknown, poor, supporting his dependents by translations and anonymous magazine articles; he still had not produced *Irene*.

How much Garrick admired Johnson's tragedy when he undertook it one cannot tell. But he revered its author, was painfully aware of the discrepancy between his own fate and his old master's, and determined to do everything he could to bring Johnson recognition and reward. Garrick lavished unprecedented money and care on the costumes and sets of *Irene*. And he cast it, not, as was customary, with one or two big names at the head of the company, but with his four top performers. *Irene* tells the fate of two sets of lovers: one pair faithful, chaste, and ultimately happy; the other rash, lustful, expedient, and doomed. Spranger Barry played the incontinent tyrant Mahomet, Mrs. Pritchard his weak-willed mistress Irene, and Garrick and Mrs. Cibber the sorely tried but incorruptible Demetrius and Aspasia.

Traditionally, authors of new plays were invited to come to

rehearsals, and Johnson took this privilege literally. He was presently throwing these occasions into confusion by treating them as elocution classes and interrupting the players with corrections of their accents and emphasis. Like Thomas Sheridan and Aaron Hill, he had rigid convictions about the rules of rhetoric. He also had a low opinion of actors, their judgment, intelligence, and taste. In his schoolmasterly way it was his pleasure to prove their inferior mastery of their own trade by testing them with familiar passages from Shakespeare or the Bible. "Say the ninth commandment," he ordered Garrick one day. " 'Thou shalt not bear *false witness,*' " his old student meekly began. "Wrong!" the sage thundered. " 'Thou shalt *not* bear false witness.' "[20] Of all *Irene*'s principals, Susannah Cibber was probably least disturbed by Johnson's interference; she had been trained by a series of strong-willed masters, and she had a way of bending to them, drawing strength from their attention and approval, then alchemizing their instruction whether it had been dross (as in the case of Colley Cibber and Aaron Hill) or gold (as in the case of Handel) by her own expressive genius.

As the rehearsals went on, Johnson took a fierce dislike to Mrs. Pritchard, whom he found a "vulgar idiot."[21] He could have forgiven her had she been a constitutional simpleton, for he was a defender of human weakness, but Pritchard's deliberate state of ignorance, her refusal to exercise her mental faculties, he could not condone. Lady Macbeth was one of her most powerful characters, but Johnson was positive she had never read through that tragedy — nor his *Irene,* for that matter. "It is wonderful how little mind she has," he fumed. "She no more thinks of the play out of which her part is taken than a shoemaker thinks of the skin out of which the piece of leather of which he is making a pair of shoes is cut."[22] Johnson was not the only man of intellect to be astonished by Mrs. Pritchard's vegetable genius. Edward Gibbon once watched her rehearse a furious tragic queen in a practice room, break off in time to don her strumpet's costume for the evening's comedy, and play both of these roles with incomparable ease and zest and sympathy, all the while knowing nothing — and wishing to know nothing — of either plot beyond the thrust of the scenes in which she figured.[23] Of course, the hours she saved by not reading through the hundred dramas in which she played during her long career gave her more time to devote to her husband, her girls and boys, and her dear friend Kitty Clive; and her lack of inquisitiveness about anything beyond her domestic and professional sphere may have accounted for her sublime placidity.

Garrick, presiding over *Irene*'s acrimonious progress toward opening night, grew more and more alarmed. He tactfully suggested to Johnson that, despite its moral beauties and the propriety of its sentiments, *Irene* lacked action. "The fellow wants me to make Mahomet run mad so that he may have an opportunity of tossing his hands and kicking his heels,"[24] Johnson raged to his old friend, the Reverend John Taylor, whom Garrick had called in to mediate between them. Whatever awe the rest of the world felt about Garrick, before whom public, authors, and players all bowed low, Johnson, his old teacher, knew the mediocrity of his mind, his lazy study habits, his slipshod Latin,[25] and felt outraged to be asked to accept aesthetic judgments from such a person.

Irene opened on February 6, and went "tolerably" well for four acts. The strenuous efforts of Garrick, Barry, Pritchard, and Cibber were respectfully noted, but the only spontaneous burst of applause came when the curtain rose upon Garrick's most elaborate set: a rich and seductively lit seraglio, with ingenious vistas of an oriental garden glimpsed beyond its ogee arches. The fifth act required the courtesan Irene, who had exchanged her maidenhead for the sultan's gold, to be garroted on the stage. As Mrs. Pritchard knelt with a length of catgut around her neck, two turbaned mutes behind her ready to draw it tight, and began her last, remorseful speech, the restive audience burst into howls, hisses, and derisive cries of "Murder! Murder!" After several attempts to speak, the unruffleable lady rose to her feet and made her exit, very much alive, followed by her flustered assassins, still holding the loose ends of their cord. Next day there were hasty changes in the last act, and Irene was strangled offstage. But the fifth act of *Irene* continued to be hissed, despite which Garrick insisted that Johnson's tragedy be played for nine extremely tense nights, which was the number required in order that an author receive his maximum payment.

The failure of *Irene* did not destroy, though it further strained, Garrick's and Johnson's friendship. Johnson continued to treat Garrick as a frivolous person whose worldly success and his own relative lack of it were commentaries on the values of their society. And Garrick, who met idolatry wherever he went, yet never once in his life heard a word of unequivocal praise from his old master, sometimes kicked against the smart by doing impromptu imitations of Johnson's tics and mannerisms, or, crueler still, of the affectations of Johnson's bibulous wife Tetty.

Years later, in 1779, when Johnson watched Garrick's coffin lowered beneath the cold stone floor of Westminster Abbey, the tears ran down his face.[26] What he had never been able to forgive Garrick while he lived was not his fame or his wealth but his happy spirit, his capacity to feel joy and to give it back. Felicity seemed to have its source in Garrick. He beamed it indiscriminately upon a whole audience or one blandished dinner partner. Neither moral force nor physical toil accounted for Garrick's power. He was simply graced. Johnson himself, the best of men, was irascible, uncomfortable, jealous, tortured by fears of madness, and perpetually wrestling with malicious and uncharitable impulses. "Garrick was a very good man," he mourned to Boswell after Garrick's death. "The cheerfullest man of his age."[27] But Boswell, who had extravagantly admired Garrick, was unsatisfied with Johnson's tardy public eulogy. He asked him whether describing the death of the British Roscius as an event which had "impoverished the public stock of harmless pleasure"[28] were not a very faint and tame sort of praise. "Nay," Johnson somberly replied. "It is the highest praise. . . . To be able to furnish harmless pleasure . . . is as great a power as a man can possess."[29]

Though Johnson maintained his uneasy relationship with Garrick after *Irene,* he never again had a good word to say for its two leading ladies, whom he held responsible for its failure. He maintained that Pritchard's acting was "mechanical" and "affected" — all the more vehemently because his listeners never failed to dispute him, for every other contemporary critic describes this lady with words like "free," "spontaneous," "spirited," "natural," "easy," and "open." Johnson's sanction against Susannah Cibber was just as severe. He would rather, he said, "sit up to the chin in water for an hour [he hated bathing] than be obliged to listen to the whining, daggle tailed Cibber."[30]

After *Irene*, Garrick invited Johnson to continue visiting back-stage. Johnson refused: "I'll come no more behind your scenes, David; for the silk stockings and white bosoms of your actresses excite my amorous propensities."[31] It is doubtful that this resolute moralist literally feared seduction if he continued to visit the green room, but in a deeper sense he was always disturbed by the seductive nature of the acting profession itself. A player's power to dissemble, persuade, or inflame was irrational, illusory, in a world of suffering souls who could only find true repose "on the stability of truth,"[32] led there not by enthusiasms and novelties but by judgment, reason, balance, and moderation. Johnson recognized the instructive value of drama; he revered Shakespeare, though he would have been just as happy to read him in his study as to watch him on the stage. He spoke of the need for "naturalness" in playing, as did every eighteenth-century critic and every fashionable playgoer. It was the preternaturalness of players that he suspected — their excessiveness, their personal vivid-ness, their potential demagoguery, their particularity.*

There was only one of Garrick's stage ladies with whom Johnson felt comfortable, and she, significantly, had had nothing to do with *Irene*. "Clive, sir," he said, "is a good thing to sit by. She always understands what you say."[33] With her fiery nose and temper, her loud, honest bray, her taste for tippling, "passionate, cross, vulgar, sensible, generous"[34] Kitty Clive was a woman cut from the same bolt of cloth as Johnson's Tetty. Both were frowsy scolds, and neither of them laid any claims to gentility. They painted their faces thickly, not in hopes of passing for beauties but as a flamboyant emblem of their defiance of old age and mortality. People whose defenses were thus transparent, people who were tetchy, people fighting lifelong battles against private demons appealed to Johnson. But a woman like Hannah Pritchard, who mouthed the divine words of Shake-speare but could not take the trouble to understand the context of what she was saying, and in her private person talked only of her new "gownd"[35] or her children's diseases, was beyond his charity. So was Susannah Cibber, whose private life was an extended, unrepentant

---

* "The business of a poet . . . is to examine, not the individual, but the species; to remark general properties and large appearances: he does not number the streaks of the tulip, or describe the different shades . . . of the forest." *Rasselas*, ch. X.

indecency, while her stage persona, with her diction and manner more refined than any duchess, conveyed an absolutely false propriety. Johnson was right in detecting falseness in Susannah Cibber, the same dissimulation that is so distressing in some of her pretty letters to Garrick, where she totally suppresses her real feelings of frustration and injury.

"Daggle tailed Cibber," Johnson called her. He may only have meant that on stage in a pathetic part she drooped like a half-drowned puppy, but he may also have been thinking that, although as an actress she simulated virtue, her personal life was sunk in mire. In marriage as in politics Johnson was a Tory. He himself was a fond and faithful husband, and he advocated virtue in all relationships between the powerful and the weak, beginning with benevolence and responsibility on the part of the king toward his people. A wife as vilely abused as Susannah Cibber certainly must withdraw from her husband and live as a spinster or widow, taking what comfort she could in religion or good works while hoping for the day of her husband's reform. But no villainy on her husband's part could justify a wife's seeking unlawful happiness. Cruelty was no more an excuse for adultery than tyranny could justify revolution or regicide. With man and wife, as with every class and rank in human society, Johnson believed that "order cannot be had but by subordination."[36]

Johnson's brief acquaintance with Susannah Cibber in 1748 and 1749 did not lead to friendship. He felt no inclination to join the men of arts and letters and politics who made up this "sweet syren's" salon and were her lifelong chevaliers. He found nothing heroic about her fortitude against an implacable husband who never stopped plotting her destruction as long as he lived, nothing admirable about her resiliency and recovery from the most lurid scandal of her day. Above all, Johnson found nothing touching about her precarious toehold upon respectability, her confusion of refinement with virtue, her conviction that if she continued to exemplify every sentimental feminine excellence, she might one day awake to find she had been transmogrified into a real lady.

๙ 16 ๖

[Charles Macklin, comparing Barry and Garrick as Romeo]: Barry comes
on to it [the stage beneath Juliet's balcony] as great as any Lord swaggering about his love, and talking so loud that, by God, sir, if we don't
suppose the servants of the Capulet family dead with sleep they must have
come out and tossed the fellow in a blanket. . . . But how does Garrick
act this? He comes creeping in on his toes, whispering his love and
looking about him *just like a thief in the night.* [Macklin's italics]
— WILLIAM COOKE, *Memoirs of Macklin*

DESPITE Garrick's reforms, two of his "froward children"
were not as content as they should have been in the
service of his shrine to Shakespeare. Barry felt himself
underpaid and underappreciated. Susannah Cibber's unhappiness
was more obscure. Garrick lumped their discontent together and laid
it to the adulation they had received as Romeo and Juliet, which had
inflated their notions of their own importance. In Susannah's case, at
least, he was missing the mark.

On March 2, David Mallet, playwright and assistant to the Lord
Chamberlain, called on Susannah in her dressing room. He had come
on behalf of Aaron Hill, who had written a new tragedy, *Meropé,*
and hoped she would accept the title role and use her influence with
Garrick to bring the play out before the end of the current season.
Susannah replied to Mallet that she was exhausted (the Drury Lane
calendar shows that at this point she had played more nights than
Garrick or Barry). She said she hardly knew how she would get
through the arduous two-month benefit season that still lay ahead, in

which she had promised to play nearly every night on behalf of minor players. She told him she had read *Meropé* with delight and would be honored to do the title role, but that if Hill and Garrick required the play to be staged before next fall, they would have to find themselves another heroine.

After Mallet left Susannah he conferred with Garrick, reporting that he came from a disappointing conversation with Cibber about *Meropé*. Garrick laughed and advised Mallet not to take anything the lady said very seriously. Rumors to the contrary, he, not she, was the master of Drury Lane and determined the scheduling of plays. He was resolved to bring out *Meropé* that spring and had no doubts that when Cibber realized this she would come round and accept the title role. What about her health, Mallet asked. The lady, Garrick replied, was suffering a severe attack of temperament, and he was pretty sure he knew the cure. He advised Mallet to tell Hill to write "an ostensible letter" to him, Garrick, expressing his pleasure at the prospect of Mrs. Pritchard's playing his Meropé should Mrs. Cibber find herself too exhausted. Garrick would make certain that Hill's letter fell under Mrs. Cibber's eye, whereupon she would be "so jealous of the other's acquiring new reputation by a capital part" that she would find herself suddenly well enough to rehearse: this was the way to handle "the pretenses of these rival princesses." Mallet immediately wrote Hill and advised him to send Garrick the "ostensible" letter. As Hill's friend, however, he was bound to warn him that he doubted Garrick's strategy would work, for he had seen how pale and haggard Susannah Cibber looked and had no doubts about the genuineness of her fatigue and the firmness of her decision.[1]

Promptly after his interview with Mallet, Garrick posted the rehearsal schedule for *Meropé* and cast all the parts except the title role. When Hill's letter came, Garrick made sure that Susannah read it. She made no move to claim, as was her privilege, the new role. Pale and thin, she continued to play in the benefits of minor players, those crucial occasions when a magical name like her own on the playbill guaranteed a full house and a sum of money that might equal an under player's yearly salary. Meanwhile *Meropé* opened, was acclaimed, and became part of Drury Lane's repertory. Its title role was the very valuable stage property of Hannah Pritchard.

On May 10, Garrick and Cibber acted together for the last time before she was to leave for West Woodhay for the summer. Garrick had gallantly let her choose their vehicle. It was *King Lear*.* She was Cordelia, the silent, misunderstood, and faithful daughter of a king so blindly arrogant that he could not see which of his children really loved him. After the play, Garrick sensed nothing out of the ordinary in Susannah's departure from the theater. How could Garrick have grown so out of touch with her, so closed to her feelings that he never suspected when she bade him goodbye that she intended to leave Drury Lane not for the summer recess but forever?

The answer is that Garrick had fallen in love and wanted to marry. He had no taste for sustaining the old, inconclusive courtship with his leading lady, and he misinterpreted, belittled, or refused altogether to see her unhappiness. It seemed to him absurd and unjust that his honorable happiness be tainted by responsibility for the suffering of a person who had no claim upon him. When he and Susannah had met she was already married, already a ruined woman with whom a serious alliance was out of the question. When, years before, he had playfully suggested a dalliance she herself had firmly set the limits of their relationship: "You say you want sadly to make love to me. Be my lover on the stage, my friend off it." True as it was that there was nothing between them, Garrick was far too sensitive not to know that he owed her dedication to his interests, her intense performances with him, and her acceptance — despite her delicate health — of a killing work load to feelings which were more than professional friendship, feelings which till recently he had been at some pains to nourish and profit by.

That Susannah was as aware as Garrick that she had no right to expect him to remain a bachelor and her courtly lover in no way lessened her suffering at his neglect. Everyone in Garrick's orbit felt the pull of his charm. Johnson stiffened his Christian will against it. But Susannah's melancholy nature leaned toward its warmth like a white sprout toward the sun. In the sentimental canon of feminine

---

* In the 1687 Nahum Tate version, which held the stage into the nineteenth century.

Susannah Cibber, by Peter Van Bleeck. The scene above is from Nahum Tate's adaptation of King Lear, *which exclusively held the boards from 1687 until the nineteenth century. Here, Cordelia and her attendant, Aranthe, are searching for her father, Lear, in the storm. They have been followed onto the heath by two "ruffians" (lurking in the left side of the picture) sent after them by the wicked Edmund, who wishes Cordelia captured so that he may ravish her at his leisure. The solitary figure on the right is Edgar, disguised as mad Tom. Presently he will rescue the ladies from Edmund's henchmen's attack with his staff. He and Cordelia will fall in love, rescue King Lear, marry, and reign happily ever after, for Lear retires from his throne and with his faithful old friends, Gloucester and Kent, spends his last years in meditation. As in the scene from* Venice Preserved *(p. 264), the figure of Susannah Cibber suggests her melting style. She is always touching, or reaching out for, or being supported by some other player.*

behavior to which Susannah adhered, reproach and recrimination were inadmissable responses. If a thousand acts of devotion could not weave a binding mesh of obligation and gratitude around her beloved, a rejected lady had no other course than proud and silent withdrawal.

The girl Garrick loved was Eva Marie Veigel (La Violette), a dancer trained at the Imperial School of Ballet in Vienna. She had come to England in 1746 to perform at the King's Opera House where she created a furor, and attracted — to her peril — the amorous eye of the Prince of Wales. Fortunately, the Earl and Countess of Burlington noticed her at the same time as His Royal Highness, appointed themselves her patrons and chaperones, and took her to live with them at Burlington House. Every night while she pirouetted on the stage the Countess watched her from the wings with a warm cloak to throw over her bare shoulders before she whirled her away in a coach. La Violette fell as enthusiastically in love with Garrick as he with her. The day he declared his honorable intentions she renounced the stage forever, so that he would never again be pained to think of her little legs in their white drawers twinkling and capering before the eyes of a lubricious prince and public.

The Burlingtons, like all guardians of fairy princesses, were dead set against Garrick's suit. They did not want to relinquish Eva Marie to a man of his shady profession, but had determined to find her a title. Only when she grew pale, stopped eating, and at last took to her bed did the Countess's heart melt and she agree to the match. Garrick and La Violette were married on June 22, 1749, with both Their Graces as witnesses. Along with her warm heart, her sensible, happy, and prankish nature so like his own, along with the fortune the Countess of Burlington settled on her, Eva Marie brought Garrick one other gift: their marriage made Garrick a kind of foster son-in-law to an earl.

The young Garricks honeymooned at Chiswick, a fanciful Italianate retreat of Burlington's. In July, Garrick wrote His Grace:

I have lately had ye satisfaction . . . that your Lordship has now some hopes for Mrs Garrick and I being happy together. Your former doubts proceeded from your esteem for her, and from a very

David and Eva Marie Garrick, from a portrait by William Hogarth.

just opinion you had conceived of ye people in my profession. However, if it should be my good fortune to afford your Lordship an exception to ye general rule against us, I shall then gain the height of my wishes; for with such a wife and such friends I can have nothing more to ask or to desire.[2]

His words sound like the obsequies of a sycophant, but Garrick meant every word. He recognized his good fortune and took full responsibility for growing to deserve the happiness that had been given him. Garrick's life is a history of salubrious enterprises, of exuberant and unflagging dedication to them, and of a miraculous strain of good luck. His marriage, long, lusty, and loving, was the wonder of his friends and the despair of gossipmongers who could not believe that this butterfly had really turned into the most uxorious of men.

In the anxious months before his wedding and the rapturously absorbing ones afterward it is no wonder Garrick had little time or energy to devote to Susannah Cibber. He was confounded when, getting back to work in September, he discovered that she had not returned to town and had sent word that she was too ill to play this season. Mrs. Pritchard was a splendid heavy, and Mrs. Clive assured life to any comedy. But who was there to play Desdemona, Ophelia, Cordelia, Constance, Hermione, Juliet, Isabella, Sigismunda, Calista, Imoinda, Eudocia, Monimia, Arpasia, Indiana, Alicia, Belvidera, and Perdita, all those suffering heroines who were the backbone of his program?

So unquestioningly had Garrick counted on Cibber's devotion that he had gone off for his honeymoon making no provision against her loss. It was too late to recruit in Dublin or the provinces, and he ended up raiding Rich's garden, turning the head of beautiful young Sarah Ward and persuading her to defect from Covent Garden to play romantic leads with him and Barry.

On October 9 this alarming notice appeared in the *General Advertizer*: "Mrs Cibber is so extreamly ill at the Bath that her life is despaired of."[3] The paper retracted this the next day, and from now on it is impossible for many months to find any account of Susannah's health or even her whereabouts. That she was genuinely "indisposed" seems clear, for when in the past she had been out of sorts with management she had played in charitable benefits at the rival theater and sung in Handel's oratorio season. This year she did neither, though Handel revived both *Messiah* and *Samson,* music in which her voice had been part of his design and that her contemporaries felt "lost half its meaning without her." A young Italian male alto, Gaetano Guadagui (1725–1792) took her roles. He had never heard Susannah sing but so deeply was her gentle, grieving personality identified with this music that he consulted Charles Burney about her interpretation.[4] Burney had, by this time, escaped his bondage as Arne's apprentice and become a popular teacher, keyboard virtuoso, and attractive social figure. After his break with her brother he remained one of Susannah's closest friends. Burney had an almost idolatrous reverence for her voice and served until her death as her arranger, coach, and accompanist.

These etchings suggest the elaborateness and splendor of eighteenth-century actresses' stage gowns.

Mrs. CIBBER *in the Character of* MONIMIA.

Mrs. WARD *in the Character of* RODOGUNE.

Sometime early in 1750, and probably at Bath, Susannah bore her last child, a son, Charles. Her long seclusion was due at least in part to this pregnancy, for she and Sloper, in a way untypical of most actresses and their protectors, took elaborate pains to avoid public attention to their private situation.

Despite his domestic happiness, the 1749–50 season was a difficult time for Garrick. William Mills, Drury Lane's mainstay character actor, died. Spranger Barry, missing his romantic partner Cibber, was more sullen and mutinous than ever. Hannah Pritchard had a sharp sick spell and was off the boards for a while. And Sarah Ward, whom even her rival, George Anne Bellamy, conceded "had one of the most beautiful faces I ever beheld,"[5] was a disaster. Garrick had been aware of her reputation for insipidity when he hired her, but he had been desperate and he had confidence in his own directorial skill. Mrs. Ward proved unteachable. Barry took such a dislike to her that he refused to act in the same play with her, dashing a number of Garrick's plans, especially for another run of *Romeo and Juliet*. Even Garrick, whose coolness was legendary, visibly lost his temper during a scene with her. They were playing estranged lovers. The action required them to enter from different parts of the stage believing themselves alone; to see each other and start; for the lady to turn away in confusion, and the hero to fall on his knees and deliver such a moving plea for forgiveness that she impulsively turns toward him, gives him her hands, and bids him rise. During the performance, the audience, at first sight of dazzling Sarah Ward, emitted a gasp of admiration. Garrick, meanwhile, fell on his knees and began his heartrending speech. But Mrs. Ward had been so affected by the audience's response to her beauty that everything else flew out of her head and she struck a fashionable pose and began to fiddle imperiously with the buttons on her glove. Garrick finished his speech, held out his arms imploringly, and still she stood, her back to him, preening. The audience's appreciative murmurs changed to snickers, and Garrick, white about the mouth, rose to his feet, strode across the stage, and tweaked her by the sleeve.

All year he had sent solicitous inquiries after Susannah's health, and he assigned his friend Somerset Draper to act as his ambassador, the function Draper had managed so deftly while Garrick was in

Ireland. To every overture she replied that her health was too precarious to discuss returning to the stage.

In the summer Susannah and Sloper went to try the invigorating air at the fashionable spa at Scarborough. The Garricks were also in the north of England, summering with the Burlingtons on their Yorkshire estate. June 22 was the Garricks' first anniversary and to celebrate it the Earl had organized a day-long fête to which the gentry for miles around had been invited. The village church bells pealed intermittently, and there was feasting all day and dancing that night. On this joyous occasion, when he and Eva Marie were on center stage from morning till late, Garrick nevertheless found time to write a long, worried letter to Somerset Draper about theater matters. Yesterday, from some local gentleman who had dined at the Earl's table, Garrick had learned that Quin had been recognized in the neighboring market town of Beverley, where he boarded the coach for Scarborough. "Is not it something odd?" Garrick asked Draper. "Do you understand it?" Quin was the laziest man in the world. He detested the discomfort of travel. He never willingly took any road except the highway between London and Bath, where there were country houses (like Sloper's) where he was pampered and excellent inns whose cellars and tables he had tested over the years. Why on earth was he exposing himself to bad meals and lumpy beds in the wild north of England? "He knows nobody there," wrote Garrick, "was never there before." What Garrick feared was that Quin was paying a courtly visit to Susannah Cibber in Scarborough in order to secure her for Covent Garden next year. In such an event it was more than ever imperative that Garrick find a more competent heroine than Mrs. Ward for Drury Lane. "Since we know that Cibber will not be with us," he told Draper, "how can we patch up our broken fortunes better than with Bellamy?"[6]

Dear, rash George Anne Bellamy, Susannah's successor in Quin's affection, had, the previous spring, exhausted Quin's avuncular fondness when, between the fourth and fifth acts of *The Provoked Wife,* she eloped, still in costume, with a Mr. Metham, who had promised, of course, to marry her later. Ever since Quin had taken George Anne under his wing he had been clucking over her incontinent passion for gambling, jewels, fine clothes, fast horses, and amorous adventure. A man of strong appetites himself, it was not her immorality that distressed him, but her impulsiveness, in which he discerned a potential for self-destruction. Where the stage was concerned, Quin observed the strictest morality: George Anne's elopement *in the middle of a performance* was a mortal sin, whereas all her other indiscretions had been venial. He continued to be her friend in private, but professionally he turned formal and punctilious and he never trusted her again.

As soon as Draper received Garrick's letter from Yorkshire he hurried to consult with Lacy, who was so enthusiastic about hiring Bellamy that he paid a surprise visit to her. Mrs. Cibber, he told her, casually drawing from his pocket a sheaf of unsigned articles and setting it on a table, was signed up at Covent Garden, and she, George Anne, was out in the cold there. Stung by the apparent perfidy of Quin and Rich, George Anne seized a pen and signed the articles, scarcely glancing at them and waiting not so much as an hour to consult her friends or check the truth of what Lacy had told her. Her move, unlike so many of her impetuosities, was not ill fated. Lacy's terms were honorable and generous, and the three years she spent under Garrick's rigorous tutelage made a real actress of her.

Garrick's hunch about Quin's doings in Yorkshire, and Lacy's consequent lie — or at least his premature certainty — to Bellamy proved to be true, and in July it was officially announced that Cibber was engaged at Covent Garden. As soon as Barry heard, "he flew from his articles"[7] at Drury Lane (which had another year to run) and engaged with Rich too. Charles Macklin, Garrick's implacable enemy, was already at Covent Garden. So was Peg Woffington, Garrick's discarded mistress. Once again John Rich found himself the reluctant head of a troupe of brilliant, thin-skinned players. This time all five of his leading actors nursed grievances, some open, some unadmitted, against Garrick.

The company taking battle stations at Covent Garden was the most formidable adversary Garrick had ever faced. The thought of the strength ranged against him exhilarated him, and on July 27 he wrote his co-general a martial letter from Yorkshire:

Dear Lacy — As our season approaches and we are like to have
warm work, you shall have me in council in less than a fortnight.
I have been informed that Barry and Cibber are certainly engaged
with Rich, which neither amazes nor intimidates me: let them do
their worst, we must have the best company, and by a well layed,
regular plan, we shall be able to make them as uneasy with Rich as
Rich will be with them. . . . I am in great spirits and don't care how
soon we are at work. . . . Our company, I think, will pull at the oars
with their heads and hearts. We shall have no false brothers [Barry],
nor intriguing sisters [Cibber]; and then *that* for Goliath [Quin]
and the Philistines! . . .

> Come what, come may,
> My Soul's in arms, and eager for the fray![8]

Part of Garrick's "well layed plan" was a *Romeo and Juliet* at
Drury Lane, for with Cibber and Barry reunited a revival of this
tragedy at Covent Garden was inevitable. Garrick was neither so tall
nor so beautiful as Barry but he was well made and lithe, had a voice
of great range, a mobile face, dark, passionate eyes, and commanding
brows. He was looking forward to offering the public an intelligent
Romeo to compare with a mellifluous one. In Yorkshire, while Eva
Marie and the Countess were out making calls in the pony cart, he
was already studying the role. "I shall soon be ready in Romeo," he
wrote Lacy, "which we may bring out early. . . . If Bellamy agrees
with us she may open with it."[9]

On September 28, 1750, both theaters royal played *Romeo
and Juliet,* each committed to play nothing else till the other capitulated. Both theaters overflowed. People went to one house one night,
the other the next. A third night they bought tickets for both plays
and jostled back and forth, catching, perhaps, the balcony scene at
Covent Garden, Mercutio's death at Drury Lane, and the tomb scene
back at Covent Garden. By the end of a week, everyone had seen
both versions at least once, read interminable comments in the papers, argued the virtues of the rival players, and was sick of *Romeo
and Juliet.* Yet neither Rich nor Garrick showed any signs of giving
up, though money was no longer the issue, only pride, since both

managers were giving away tickets in order not to play to empty houses. The *Daily Advertizer* summed up the public's impatience:

> "Well, what tonight?" says Angry Ned
> As up from bed he rouses.
> "Romeo again!" and shakes his head
> "A pox on both your Houses!"[10]

All at once the matter was resolved when, on October 11, Susannah announced she would play no longer. Garrick continued one more night, and then he too closed with relief, and the regular theatrical season began. For Susannah the experience had been an uneasy balance between gratification and pain. She was relieved to be back on the stage: no matter how fragile her health, she was only free from anxiety when she was in harness. She loved the role of Juliet, and Barry was one of her most sympathetic partners. On the other hand, the absurd public feud that the situation created between herself and Bellamy was a degradation she had gone out of her way to avoid ever since the Polly War. Even worse, these combative *Romeo and Juliet*s marked with a lurid glare her estrangement from Garrick, in whose shelter she had hoped always to work and thrive. Now he was her friend no more, but her exulting adversary. After twelve nights she had had enough.

Garrick had won the endurance contest but not the critical crown. Most people preferred Rich's production. Never a man to scrimp on music and spectacle, Rich had interpolated a whole new scene, "Juliet's Funeral Procession," with music especially composed by Arne. Across the stage, to the tolling of a bell, paced liveried Capulet servants bearing live torches, followed by flower girls strewing blossoms in the path of Juliet's bier, which was borne by more liveried servants and followed by clergy in medieval ecclesiastical finery, the Capulet family, and a throng of Veronese nobles in magnificent mourning. Garrick hastily got together a funeral procession of his own with music by William Boyce, but it was a slapdash effort and never as admired as Rich's.

Harry Woodward at Drury Lane was everyone's favorite Mer-

Harry Woodward pulls off the mask of tragedy and reveals his irresistibly good-humored face. Portrait by Joshua Reynolds.

cutio. Macklin was too old, too savage. Woodward was a handsome dog with something ironic and rakehell about him. He had started his career playing heroes and lovers, but because "the moment he opened his mouth on the stage a certain ludicrous air laid hold of his features and every muscle of his face ranged itself on the side of levity,"[11] he early resigned himself to comedy.

Both Romeos had their admirers: Barry was fervent; Garrick, fiery. One witty lady spoke for many when she said that had she been Juliet and Garrick her Romeo, she would have been happy to let him climb up on her balcony. Had she been Juliet and Barry her Romeo, though, she would have jumped down to him.[12]

As for the Juliets, Bellamy astonished people with her new power. Unlike Sarah Ward she had blossomed under Garrick. In the early scenes, her young, impatient Juliet, reaching with sweet reck-lessness for love — a girl very much like Bellamy herself — touched people more than Cibber's pensive maid, who seemed from her first line to know that she was the heroine in a tragedy. Later in the play Bellamy's love scenes were more delicious than the fleshless raptures of Cibber, who managed to sigh in her lover's arms as if she were kneeling alone on a cold chapel floor in a religious transport. In the last, darkening acts, however, when death becomes the poetic mystery that transmutes earthly passion into an incorruptible ideal, Cibber was a transfigured Juliet. When she kissed her lover's lips to draw out the poison that might bring her immortality, when she plunged the dagger into her heart with her famous shudder[13] that shimmered over her taut little body as it changed from flesh to spirit, there was no one in her dumbstruck audience who would have argued that she had a rival in the world.

In Juliet, Susannah came close to her ideal of the actress as romantic priestess, not public courtesan. Bellamy was luscious but Cibber was sublime. "Her excellence was of a superior kind,"[14] said Tate Wilkinson, the mimic, who could take off anyone, even Garrick, to the life, but admitted he could never catch the magic of Cibber. Indeed, the power of her Juliet so weighted the last part of the play that, moved as people were, some critics felt that it amounted to an aesthetic impropriety. "At Covent Garden I saw *Juliet and Romeo*," frowned a correspondent to the *Gentleman's Magazine*. "At Drury Lane I saw *Romeo and Juliet*."

The previous summer when Garrick wrote Lacy about his stratagems for defeating Covent Garden, he prophesied that the renegades, Barry and Cibber, "would soon be as uneasy with Rich as he with them." He was right. Detesting tragedians and the art of tragedy, Rich always turned over the preparation of serious drama to Quin whenever he was at Covent Garden. Quin was an autocrat and a thorough taskmaster. Unfortunately, he did not these days inspire the veneration he had ten years ago. Macklin, who had been running an acting academy in the new "natural" method, thought Rich should have made *him* his deputy. Barry, who considered himself crown prince in the new aristocracy of natural players — Garrick's heir if not his peer — would not take the mildest suggestion from old-fashioned Quin. He declined to show up at rehearsals Quin posted, but called his own for any scene in which he appeared. Here he settled the cues and business for the whole supporting cast, who, of course, found Barry's directions countermanded by Quin. The demoralization of the under players and stage crew was the most destructive result of the strife between the capital players. Woffington and Macklin were old cronies who stuck together and despised the rest. Barry and Quin agreed on nothing except their contempt for Woffington and their insistence that Cibber, not she, was reigning queen of the company. Their protective and chivalrous attitude enraged Woffington who took out her spite upon Cibber. Woffington regarded her as a prig and a hypocrite who had never fought her own battles but had reached preeminence by wheedling and whining to a succession of powerful men. Whenever she and Susannah were together Peg bragged in vivid and explicit language of her promiscuity, her independence, her contempt for bourgeois morals, and her political radicalism. The more Peg strutted, the more Susannah recoiled. With Woffington in her present incendiary mood the green room at Covent Garden had regressed to the moral tone of a Restoration theater, and Susannah withdrew to hold her court in her dressing room. One night the Duchess of Queensberry swept backstage to find Woffington entertaining a crew of male friends at a table laden with mutton pies, waving a flagon of porter and crying, "Confusion to all order! Let Liberty thrive!" Whether the Duchess was most offended by Peg's appearance — she was still in her outlandish oriental costume after the night's play — by the grossness of the victuals (Her Grace may never have seen a female eating mutton pie and drinking porter), or by the egalitarian tone of Peg's remarks is not clear. At any rate, after standing transfixed for a moment she exclaimed, "Is Hell broke loose?", turned on her heel, and was helped outside to her sedan chair.[15]

Rich took pleasure in the mortifications of all his players, but the ill will between Cibber and Woffington especially tickled him. To his cronies who brought him tales of their latest confrontation he referred to Susannah as his Catherine Hayes and Peg as his Sarah Malcolm, after two vicious murderesses.*

* Hayes was convicted of murdering and dismembering her husband, and burned alive in 1726. Malcolm was hanged in 1733, having been found guilty of murdering and robbing her mistress and two fellow servants.

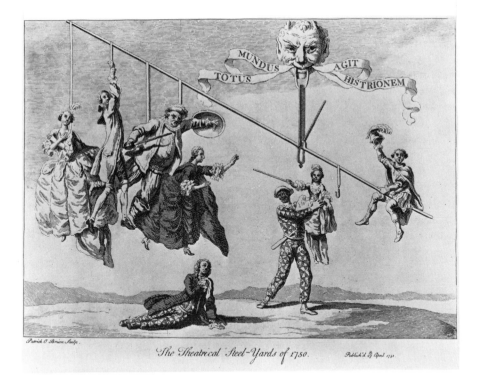

The Theatrical Steel-Yards of 1750.   Publish'd 2 of April 1751.

At Drury Lane, meantime, Garrick was doing well with his small, tight company, plenty of Shakespeare, and a pantomime, "Queen Mab," created by Harry Woodward. A contemporary cartoon called "Theatrical Steelyards" shows a huge scales. On the light side, high in the air, four dejected figures hang from meat hooks: Quin as Falstaff, Barry, Woffington, and Susannah Cibber, holding out her arms in futile supplication to her former ally, little Garrick, who ignores her, sitting victorious and all alone astride the heavy side of the scale, waving his plumed hat from *Richard III*. Two harlequins occupy the ground below the scales. Rich lies on his side, hand on his heart, eyes turned heavenward, apparently expiring. Woodward is triumphantly holding up his doll-like Queen Mab. There is a hook to hang her on if necessary, but Garrick's weight is more than sufficient without his pantomime queen.

During the summer recess of 1751, Rich sent Susannah to France to audition dancers. It was an unusual responsibility for a woman, and people talked about it. Henry Fielding, who loved to burlesque the doings of the London theaters and theater personalities by treating them like rival states and jealous princes, speculated on Susannah's delicate political mission. It was an audacious move on Rich's part, he said, and he approved. For one thing it was a very French thing to do and just what the French deserved, "for they have often succeeded in very deep schemes by sending over their fine women here."[16]

Garrick, summering again in Yorkshire with the Burlingtons, heard rumors of Susannah's trip and wrote Draper: "What is the meaning of her leaving us at this time? Quere — does she not want to get rid of Barry and takes this method of doing it delicately?"[17] As soon as she returned to England Draper called on her, and to his suggestion that she return to Drury Lane she replied that she was perfectly content where she was. But the dissension at Covent Garden was even more serious in the 1751–52 season than the year before, and Quin at last capitulated. He was nearly sixty, perpetually undercut by Barry and Macklin and unsupported by Rich, the one person who might have controlled, if he could not resolve, the discord. Still, Quin was a doughty spirit and might have survived Macklin and Barry. But there were worse blows. The first was the sudden death, in March 1751, of his beloved old pupil and personal patron, Frederick, Prince of Wales, whose passing meant the end of the royal favor Quin had enjoyed for years. Second, he was losing his teeth and could not control the humiliating and senile lisps and hisses that occasionally adulterated his impeccable diction. "By God," he blurted one night in the spring, "I'll whistle Falstaff for no man!"[18] At season's end he retired to Bath, this time for good.

Spranger Barry now became chief player, and Rich's assistant in charge of tragedy. Davies says he "was the easiest man in the world to live with as companion and friend,"[19] but the worst man in the world to work for. Barry was sweet natured, thin-skinned, emotional, generous, trusting, and incurably naïve. The technical aspects of stagecraft, its administrative details and rehearsals, bored him. He had a romantic idea that a scene gained spontaneity if it had a hair-breadth, improvisatory quality. His productions were always under-prepared: lines were unsure, props were in the wrong place. There were cancellations and unannounced substitutions of one player for another. The public grumbled and stayed away. The players were distraught. After each debacle Barry sulked and blamed others for letting him down. He treated everyone magnanimously, and expected in return an ecstasy of personal devotion, which should seek out occasions to express itself by saving him from tight spots. People called him the "Mark Antony of the stage,"[20] not only on account of his classic beauty, the princely splendor in which he lived, the extravagance of his entertainments, and the beautiful women who loved him, but because of his swashbuckling overextension in everything he undertook. In the long run this Antony was no match for the Octavius at Drury Lane.

Susannah Cibber was the one sure rock in Barry's life at this time. The extraordinary demands he made upon his fellow actors were those she was peculiarly able to satisfy. She could follow his mood in a scene, enhance it and dilate upon it, and, if he lost his control or his place, could exquisitely draw him back home. Barry's dependency upon her, and her sympathy for him, was a current so palpable on the stage that it was widely believed that they were lovers. One gentleman wrote a friend after seeing *Romeo and Juliet* that "she and Barry burn with a mutual flame, much to the disturbance of Mr Sloper's quiet."[21]

But even Susannah was not always enough to rescue Barry. One night he, she, and Luke Sparks were playing in *Tamerlane* — as usual scantily prepared — when one of the men forgot his part. Both of them turned to where Susannah stood between them and stared at her blankly. She looked sadly from one to the other and murmured, "Gentlemen, it is not my turn to speak," by which time the drowsing prompter found his wits, supplied the line, and the play went forward.[22]

But there were worse disasters than muffed lines. One night Barry was playing Macbeth and Lacy Ryan was Macduff. Barry was a lyric fencer. It was worth the price of a ticket just to see him leap, thrust, and parry. Characteristically, he had not (as Garrick always did in any scene with swordplay) choreographed every move of the Macbeth-Macduff encounter, but merely roughed in its course, leaving the rest to inspiration. Ryan, unfortunately, was merely mortal.

When he closed with Macbeth and stabbed him, it was a clumsy business; either the buttons of his sleeve or something on his sword handle became entangled in Barry's profuse full-bottomed wig, so that, when he drew back his arm, Ryan drew off the Scottish usurper's hair. "Our hero was left exposed in the last agony of death — bare headed," the *Drury Lane Journal* crowed next day. "Ryan . . . with some confusion contemplated Full Bottom which he held dangling in his hand, but sadly out of curl. At length he adjusted it on the bald pate of the tyrant, who was thus enabled to make his dying speech with proper regularity and decorum."[23] Even when Barry's wig had been restored, the audience could not recover its seriousness and went home laughing.

Barry's humiliation took place on an occasion of significance for Susannah. It was her benefit night, March 17, 1752. Carpenters had enlarged the seating capacity of Covent Garden to accommodate the crush. The pit and boxes had been "laid together" and a kind of amphitheater erected at the back of the stage for several hundred of her admirers in the nobility. For the first time she was attempting Lady Macbeth, a character of enormous prestige, but one of the virago type which she had always found uncongenial. Besides this, the evening's afterpiece was *The Oracle,* a pastoral allegory she had seen while she was in Paris and adapted and translated from St. Foix. Tonight she was to be judged for the first time as a Shakespearean heavy and as a lady of letters, and yet the occasion went down in theatrical annals as the night Barry lost his wig.

The anecdotes about Susannah during her years at Covent Garden all reflect her stoicism, her resourcefulness, and her increasing strain. Tate Wilkinson — a young member of the troupe at this time — describes one night during *Romeo and Juliet* when she discovered that a careless property man had forgotten to place her fatal dagger by her bier. Firmly, she made a fist with her empty hand, a gesture of raising a knife on high. She gazed with fierce absorption at an imaginary blade and plunged it into her breast with her incomparable shudder.[24] The audience cheered; it found nothing more admirable than sangfroid under fire.

Wilkinson also recalls that it was during these years that Susannah's stomach disorder grew so frequent and severe that it became a serious problem for the entire company, which always had to have another play ready in case she had an attack. Peg Woffington regarded Susannah's failing health as a provocation against herself. It was she, after all, who was frequently called back to the theater from an evening of revelry to substitute for a woman who she felt was a sanctimonious malingerer.

Early in 1753, Somerset Draper, for at least the fifth time in as many years, begged Susannah Cibber to consider returning to Drury Lane. She did not agree to do so; on the other hand she did not, as before, dismiss the idea. The public first suspected a rapprochement between Garrick and Cibber when, on February 21, following the premiere of *The Earl of Essex,* she read a charming epilogue expressly written for her on this occasion by Garrick. It was an extraordinary gesture for the master of one theater royal thus to honor a rival production. A month later, Garrick favored her again when he added her *Oracle* to the Drury Lane repertory and gave it an even more lavish production than had Rich. Garrick, usually parsimonious about spectacle, had cast the little fantasy with children in exquisite costumes. They sang and danced before an elaborate background of grottoes, rocks, clouds, and fountains.

The reconciliation of Garrick and Cibber proceeded like the preliminaries of a royal marriage: he all gestures of eager gallantry, she a study in modest hesitation. He was weary of Bellamy, who was a delicious little creature in her carnal way, but no substitute for Cibber. Besides her aesthetic limitations, George Anne was a chronic embarrassment because of her annual habit of swelling maternally (after she had been cast, rehearsed, and advertised in such virginal roles as Cordelia and Juliet) and then taking several weeks off to lie-in (usually just in the thick of the benefit season). George Anne was still styling herself "Miss" Bellamy, though in view of her highly visible fecundity people were beginning to suggest that it was time she took over the more matronly "Mrs.," even though no husband existed.

For the final performance of the year, Covent Garden played *Romeo and Juliet.* It was the last time Barry and Cibber were ever

Portrait by John Zoffany showing Garrick and Cibber as Jaffier and Belvidera in Venice Preserved. *Garrick is all virile impetuosity and dominance as Cibber kneels, one soft hand fending him off, the other sweetly clinging.*

together, for she was on the roster of Drury Lane in the fall. Despite the chaos at Covent Garden, they had been the most poignant stage lovers of their generation.

Susannah stayed with Garrick for the rest of her life. He made sure that he never again lost the most intelligent, most responsive partner he had ever known through neglect of her sensibilities. After Susannah and Garrick were reunited, people liked to compare their effect together with hers and Barry's. It was her physical similarity to Garrick that they remarked. They were both smaller than average, dark and intense. They used every part of their bodies, not broadly but with focus and refinement. Their voices were similar, their features not beautiful but strong and mobile, capable of projecting precise and concentrated emotions across the footlights. Barry on the other hand was as tall as Cibber was slight, as expansive as she was contained, as ingenuous as she was subtle, as courageous as she seemed racked by fearful premonitions. Barry seemed as eager to spend love as she to need solace. Their otherness was their attraction; with Garrick and Cibber it was their likeness. The public thought of Susannah as Garrick's sister. She and Barry could only be thought of as lovers.[25]

To the smoothly functioning company at Drury Lane, to Garrick's authority, so light, so sure, Susannah returned with relief. Garrick treated her with elaborate consideration, but there was no real return to their tender friendship. The letters that survive between them from now till Susannah's death are elaborately courteous. When Garrick had been a bachelor he had entertained Susannah at little suppers in his rooms, along with Fielding, Lord Tyrawley, Macklin, and other players, poets, and noblemen. He still saw all the men from his bachelor days, either at home at Southampton Street or at his club. But the only women who remained in his social circle after his marriage were ladies with whom his wife could converse without compromise, and Susannah was not one of them.

She was at the pinnacle of her reputation. She had an elegant town house at 65 Scotland Yard and a suburban villa at Hammersmith for short retreats when West Woodhay was too far to travel. She had the equipage and wardrobe of a great lady, and an income, independent of Sloper's, of £700 a year. But her position in society had as little substance as the illusory nature of her calling itself. The one aspect of her profession — a share in management — that might have given her real security when her youth was gone, her health had failed, or Sloper left her had been denied her. Both Garrick and Rich had recognized her taste, her tact, her judgment and diplomacy, and had used them for their own advantages, but refused to admit her to real responsibility and power. As for her private life, nothing but the deaths of both Theophilus Cibber and Catherine Sloper before either she or Sloper died could make a respectable woman of her or legitimize her children.

Her father long ago had uprooted her from her tradesman class, nourished her with tutors, music masters, fine clothes, refinements, and seductive promises into a forced, exotic bloom. But he had never acquired enough money to transplant her in the rich soil of a good marriage. Like a seed fallen on ledge she had managed to clutch and clench a sort of picaresque life for herself without a supportive social matrix. She was very much her father's child. The difference between Susannah and old Thomas Arne was that her ambition was far more vaulting than his had been, her spirit more stoic and tenacious, her willingness to cut her losses and retreat temporarily to a safe position much more realistic. The last years of her life were a dogged campaign to accomplish for her children what she was resigned never to achieve for herself — to establish them in bastions of unassailable financial and social security.

The Duchess of Northumberland may do what she pleases. Nobody will say anything to a lady of her high rank. [Dr. Johnson reproves Boswell for questioning the propriety of the Duchess's behavior.]
— BOSWELL, *Life of Johnson*

The Blue Stocking Lady was strongly conservative . . . She had none of the indifference to public opinion of the Great Lady.
— EMILY J. PUTNAM, *The Lady*

"Does Mrs Clive live with her husband? No, ma'am. Does Mrs Cibber live with her husband? No ma'am. So now, ma'am, you see the best women of fashion upon y'earth don't live with their husbands, ma'am." [A stage momma harangues her actress daughter to leave her husband and take up a liaison with a rich protector.]
— TATE WILKINSON, *Memoirs of His Own Life*

ONE stormy Sunday morning in March 1752, the Duchess of Somerset was sitting in her bedroom in Downing Street while Payne, her maid, helped her dress. All at once a violent gale shook the house. There was a crash overhead as one of the chimneys on the roof collapsed, and then bricks hurtled down the flue and clattered out on the hearth. Smoke began to fill the room, and the Duchess and her maid started for the stairs. As they went they could hear "the most dreadful yelling"[1] in the entrance hall. Her Grace's footman had just let in out of the storm a group of hysterical women and children, of whom the Duchess recognized only one, her close neighbor Lady Caroline Petersham. Lady Caroline was young and giddy, unhappily married to a sulky lout, loved balls and pleasure gardens, masquerades, and, above all, the theater, and Horace Walpole thought her "gloriously jolly and handsome."[2] Just now, though, her face was smeared with tears and soot, she was "screaming as if bewitched," and her famous raven locks "hung about her ears." There were four sobbing children with her, five or six blubbering housemaids, and another woman, a stranger to Her Grace, white and silent with terror. At the Petershams' house close by, the damage from that gust had been severe: not one but the whole stack of chimneys had fallen. Fires had started in several broken flues and the women in the house had fled. The Duchess of Somerset dispatched her footman to the Petershams', who presently returned with the good news that the menservants had put out the fires, though the house was in shocking condition. Smoke filled the rooms, soot covered everything. All the chimneys were inoperative so there could not be a particle of warmth, nor any cooking done in the kitchen.

The pious Duchess had planned to spend this sabbath in solitude and meditation, as was her custom since the deaths of her husband and only son. Now she insisted that poor Lady Caroline stay and share her meal, and Lord Petersham too — if the servants who had been sent out to his various haunts to tell him of the disaster had found him by then and brought him home. Meanwhile the housemaids, reassured the Petershams' house was neither ablaze nor likely to fall on their heads, returned to start cleaning up. The four unknown children and the pale woman slipped out with them into the windy street. The Duchess of Somerset had no idea who they were, or what connection they had with the Petersham ménage until later, when Lady Caroline, chattering cozily at the Duchess's table, explained that the woman was Mrs. Cibber and the children juvenile players, and that they had been at her house this Sunday morning to do a dramatic reading of Mrs. Cibber's *Oracle* due for its premiere two days hence at her benefit.[3]

It had no more occurred to Lady Caroline Petersham to introduce her visiting players than her housemaids to her fellow aristocrat, nor to ask her kind hostess to invite these stage people to refresh themselves at her table than to suggest she put extra places round it for the wet and frightened servants. Mrs. Cibber's call on Lady Caroline to interest her in making up a party for her benefit was a business matter analogous to a visit from an upholsterer to discuss redecorating a room, or from a fashionable dressmaker to plan a gown. All sorts of people solicited Lady Caroline's custom, and a great lady like herself (she was a great-granddaughter of Charles II) could be as graciously condescending as she pleased with people of the lower orders. This did not mean drawing them into acquaintance with a person of her own rank.

During the eighteenth century, players were personally responsible for selling all the seats to their benefits. The general public was obliged to go round to the actor's home and buy tickets there. But in the case of the nobility, who subscribed to expensive boxes and sometimes conspicuous and costly chairs on the stage itself, a player waited upon such people at their homes, and with particularly important patrons and a new production, sometimes even solicited their presence with a private preview. If we understand this, some of Susannah's public behavior toward the end of her life seems less incomprehensible, though even in her own day there were radical young critics who took her to task for it. "I was never more astonished in my life," declared an anonymous correspondent to the *Theatrical Review* in 1763, "than at an action of Mrs Cibber's. As that lady sat upon the stage with Hamlet at her feet, in the 3rd act she rose up three several times and made as many courtesies — and those very low ones — to some ladies in the boxes. Pray, good sir, ask her in what part of the play it is said that the Danish Ophelia . . . is acquainted with so many British Ladies?"[4] The ladies before whom Susannah prostrated herself had come expressly to see her, had paid handsomely for their boxes, perhaps as much as £100 for a chair on the stage,[5] and they may well have expected the recipient of such ostentatious favor to acknowledge their presence.

Still, the charge of toadying had never been leveled at Susannah in her early career, and at least some of her contemporaries felt her exercise of an old theatrical custom had grown excessive by the late 1750s. Increasingly, the purpose of her performances seemed to be to elicit signs of love and favor in high places. To ingratiate had always been her need; now it became an obsession. The goal of her last years, when there were no further theatrical honors left to win, was to establish a beachhead for herself and her children in respectable society. But admittance into the company of the aristocracy was as unattainable as the moon. While they were in the theater powerful lords and ladies sat under her spell. But in the Duchess of Somerset's antechamber it never occurred to Lady Caroline Petersham to single Susannah Cibber out from a gaggle of sniffling housemaids.

There was a type of British lady with whom one might have expected Susannah Cibber to have an affinity. The middle-class blue-stockings were known for their learning, their sensibilities, and their artistic and literary accomplishments. Susannah was fastidious of manner, earnest about her art, and mistress of French and Latin; after the production and publication of *The Oracle* she even had credentials as a lady of letters. For *The Oracle* was genuinely success-ful. It was revived year after year at Drury Lane and Covent Garden, and Thomas Sheridan produced it many times during the years he was managing Smock Alley. The only people, in fact, who did not admire *The Oracle* were the bluestockings.

Mrs. Elizabeth Carter, terrifyingly erudite mistress of nine lan-guages* and almost as many musical instruments, went to see it and spotted it at once as an example of a current pernicious ploy by ambitious players to insinuate themselves into the middle class by posing as literary figures. She wrote at once to her friend Miss Talbot and described two examples of this ugly phenomenon: Garrick's comedy, *A Miss in Her Teens,* was "an idle and foolish" business, she said, and the sort of vulgar person who would be taken in by his literary pretensions could be expected to "find Wit, good Sense and Morality in Mrs Cibber's *Oracle.*"[6]

The British aristocracy never felt threatened by the swagger of theater folk. They found it amusing to make pets of these bumptious and charming people who devoted their lives to entertaining them. But the middle class, especially the women, marked and deplored every instance of the tireless and sinister upward struggle of the lower classes. They saw themselves as guardians of both social order and private morality, and these concepts were somewhat blurred in their minds. Whether it was more reprehensible to them that Mrs.

---

* Greek, Hebrew, Latin, Arabic, French, Italian, Spanish, German, and Portu-guese. Mrs. Carter was not a natural linguist, but a dogged one. When she was a child her father, who started her on Latin and Hebrew, begged her to desist, for she had no aptitude and he feared the strain would injure her brain. However, in a lifetime of "incessant application" (D.N.B.) she laid siege to and reduced tongue after resisting tongue — Arabic and Portuguese in old age — and her health proved equal to the stress for she lived till her ninetieth year.

Cibber was living with a man not her husband, or that she had for years been using her poetic sensibility *to earn money* would be hard to say. The bluestockings guarded their amateur standing as closely as their chastity. They pursued their intellectual or aesthetic efforts in order to elevate their leisure time to something higher than gossip and gambling — two pastimes they abhorred. But they were proudly dilettantes, these *hautes bourgeoises* wives and daughters of affluent brewers and colliery owners and politicians, for that was what distinguished them from their *petites bourgeoises* sisters-in-letters, the widows and daughters of impoverished clergymen and schoolmasters, who had to make their livings as governesses, dame school mistresses, and anonymous Grub Street scriveners.

Susannah never belonged to any "set" of women. When she was a child her father frowned on friendship with other tradesmen's daughters lest she pick up an accent or manners unsuited to a future lady of quality. Later, she was sincerely shocked and alienated by the coarseness of singers and actresses, and they were put off by the lady-like airs of one whose private life proved more lurid than most of theirs. Her isolation from so much of her sex made her cling to the women with whom she had even a tenuous family claim. She was devoted to her mother and daughter. But she also maintained friendship with her various sisters-in-law: with Cecilia Arne, abused and abandoned by her brother, and even more surprising, with Theo's sisters, even the disreputable, mad Charlotte Charke. And she was close to Sloper's sister, Margaret Lethieullier, who was not her sister-in-law, but who chose to act the role anyway and defied convention year after year to visit West Woodhay for long stays.

Margaret Lethieullier was one of the only respectable women who ever stayed under the roof at West Woodhay while Sloper and Susannah lived there in sin. It was in this lovely and retired spot, which Margaret's husband, Smart Lethieullier, called "one of the sweetest places in England,"[7] that Susannah was most acutely lonely. She was utterly without companionship except for house guests, since the local gentry never acknowledged her existence. Almost every surviving letter from West Woodhay is a plea that her correspondent come and stay and cheer her. And there were many male visitors, literary, theater, and musical people like Handel, Burney, Quin,

Mason, Mallet, and Thomson, who broke their trips to or from Bath to stay a few days or weeks. Summer after summer, Susannah beseeched Garrick to visit and to bring "sweet Mrs Garrick," but the Garricks stopped at West Woodhay rarely and briefly. Garrick dared not offend Susannah, but he was skittish of encouraging intimacy between her and Eva Marie — a lady received in the finest houses in Britain. Even when he had been a bachelor he had disguised his address when he wrote from West Woodhay. As a married man, he put off Susannah's persistent invitations, promising to come and then pleading last-minute business. After one of these disappointments she wrote him teasingly:

> What is become of all that *fire* of friendship and *seeming* heartiness with which you almost said you would surely come? . . . You have actually starved us, and prevented our having a morsel of venison the whole summer! For Mr Sloper has positively declared he will not write for a buck unless you and sweet Mrs Garrick compensate him by your company for the infinite fatigue he must be at in writing a note to his Royal Highness' keeper. If you have any bowels you will consider all this, and generously send us word to air our beds and stock our larder: if you do not, I thank my stars I have it in my power to be even with you; for not a dimple (I do not mean wrinkle) in my face shall you see till towards next Christmas. As we have not succeeded with trying every soothing means to induce you to make us happy, I would have you reflect upon the consequences of provoking us, and look upon this letter as the prelude to many things more terrible!
>
> As we are not in the least angry with good Mrs Garrick (who, I am sure always does what you would have her) we beg our best respects and compliments to her. As for you, though you do not deserve it, I think, before I conclude, I shall just give you a hint that upon your ordering your horses immediately and appearing before me *here*, with all due submission, it is possible I may be prevailed upon to make it up with you; for I feel myself very much disposed to be, most sincerely,

> Your truly Affectionate friend
> And most obedient humble servant,
> S. Cibber.[8]

Susannah wrote this only five months before she died. There is
no hint in its saucy, rap-of-the-fan imperiousness (the only tone in
which she ever allowed herself to reprove Garrick) of her despondency, of her ominously accelerating loss of weight, of the worsening
of her tremor of the head and hands, of her dread that she could
never withstand the coach trip to London, much less play again, or of
her hunger to see Garrick, whose radiant vitality always revived her.

During the more than twenty years that Susannah spent part of
each year in Berkshire, the neighbors, who never recognized her
presence, were nonetheless keenly aware of her. West Woodhay was
only a few miles from Sandleford Priory, the country estate of Mrs.
Elizabeth Montagu, "Queen of the Blue Stockings." Back in 1744
Mrs. Montagu had written her sister the delectable news that with
old Mr. Sloper barely cold in his grave, young Mr. Sloper was doing
over the old mansion "entirely in white satin" for his actress. One
July afternoon a few years later, Mrs. Montagu took it into her head
to entertain her house guests, Anne Donnellan and Père Courayer,
the fashionable, ecumenical curé, by driving them over to West
Woodhay to see Mr. Sloper's quaint house and gardens. She had been
assured that Sloper was absent on his election duties, which meant
that Mrs. Cibber would not be there either, for she never passed a
night in her lover's house unless he was there. As Mrs. Montagu's
coach turned into the avenue of elms that led along the pond to
Sloper's house, its occupants noticed a solitary figure on horseback far
ahead. "I took it into my head it might be Mr Sloper," Mrs. Montagu wrote next day to her friend the Duchess of Portland; but by
the time they reached the front steps of the house the rider had
disappeared beyond the brick wall of the stable yard. The three
visitors from Sandleford sat uneasily in their coach. To retreat would
be undignified: the Montagu equipage had certainly been recognized. Still, if that horseman had been Sloper and if Mrs. Cibber
were within, the Sandleford party had put themselves in a position
where social exchange with this woman might prove unavoidable;
worse still, Mrs. Montagu would appear to have sought it.

While they sat there, the front door opened and the housekeeper came down the steps toward them. She was accustomed to
showing off the place when her master was away. The old house, its

classic chapel hard by, the vista of the Downs rising from the foot of the south lawn, and Sloper's fine library made the place a local treasure.[9]

"She asked if I would walk in," Mrs. Montagu continued to the Duchess, to which Mrs. Montagu replied that she "would be glad to 'if *Mr Cibber* was not at home.' The housekeeper looked aghast, as if she had spoiled a custard or broke a jelly glass. I colored, Mrs Donnellan twittered, Dr Courayer sputtered half French, half English." Mrs. Donnellan's fit of giggles proved so intractable that the Sandleford visitors had to remain seated for "near a quarter of an hour before we got out of the coach, and after so long a pause I walked into the house greatly abashed."[10] After Mrs. Montagu had described her scare about coming face to face with the infamous Mrs. Cibber she lost interest in West Woodhay and had nothing, alas, to tell the Duchess about its interior or whether she had spied a swatch of white satin anyplace.

Of Cibber's three great contemporaries, Clive, Pritchard, and Woffington, only Hannah Pritchard was ever received in genteel society. As an ingenue, she had made a sensible marriage to William Pritchard, who "invented" ingenious effects for pantomimes and later became treasurer at Drury Lane. She was an exemplary wife and a devoted mother. Her nature was calm and kindly, her manner self-effacing, her conversation discreet, her taste in clothes understated. She made no claim to wit. She did not aspire to a salon. She merely practiced her art so admirably that middle-class and upper-class ladies began to vie with one another to be her particular patroness. First, they dropped in to compliment her in her dressing room, then they called at her house in Great Queen Street. Here they found such quiet propriety and elegance that they saw it would be perfectly safe to invite her to their homes. Mrs. Pritchard's dignity and contentment with her lot set any lady's mind at rest. Since she nursed no ambitions to climb they rewarded her by holding out their arms and drawing her up — at least partway up — to their level. Even Horace Walpole asked her to dine, and having done so spent the day in apprehension. That evening he scrutinized her clothes, her table manners, the timbre and volume of her laugh, and the subject matter of her discourse, and next day wrote his friend George Montagu that somewhat to his surprise he had found absolutely *nothing to criticize*.[11]

At the wedding and coronation of George III in 1761, Mrs. Pritchard was appointed dresser to the young Queen. This did not mean she served as lady's maid and laced up Her Majesty's stays or drew on her stockings, but (since actresses were fashion leaders and knew all about styles and fabrics and cosmetics and wigs) that she acted as a consultant and coordinator for Queen Charlotte's costumes during the weeks of celebration. For these same court festivities Susannah Cibber was dresser to the Marchioness of Kildare, for which the Marquis gave her an honorarium of five pounds.[12] The Marchioness was a beauty and a great lady in her own right: like Lady Caroline Petersham she was one of Charles II's great-grandchildren. She was married to Ireland's first and richest peer; still, the honor of overseeing her court gowns was not to be mentioned in the same breath as dressing the Queen. Only Mrs. Pritchard combined the spotless private virtue and public esteem for such a post.

Hannah Pritchard's best friend, Kitty Clive, never reached Pritchard's social triumphs, but her friendships were much less constricted than Susannah Cibber's. Susannah had a circle of protective champions; Kitty could defend herself — her world was sharply divided into friends and foes. In 1733 she impulsively married a young barrister, George Clive. They parted at once. Something happened on the honeymoon — neither of them would ever discuss their brief marriage — which so repelled her that she never ventured into another sexual relationship. Her love affair with the public contained all the rapture and despair, all the jealousy and triumph over rivals that her passionate nature required. Despite Kitty's celibacy she was too raucous, too frank, for gentlewomen to be really comfortable in her presence. They acknowledged her genius and her virtue, but most of her excursions into society were in the company of men. She was the only actress Johnson could abide. "Clive, sir," he had said, "is a good thing to sit by. She always understands what you say." And she said of him, "I like to sit by Dr Johnson. He always entertains me."[13] She found nothing offensive in his calling her a "thing," however "good," no insult in being regarded as a commodity, an institution. She did not care a fig to be a lady, but she was ready to draw blood to defend her position as Britain's first comedienne. Just as Pritchard's diffidence reassured English ladies, so Clive comfortably fitted Johnson's notion of an actress in "the Grand Subordination of Things": vulgar, honest, painted, good company, industrious, and incapable of "cant." She knew her place and she liked it.

Horace Walpole gave Clive a cottage on his Twickenham estate, whose little gate opened into his private garden. It was such an absurd little box of a house that of course he dubbed it "Cliveden" after the Prince of Wales' grandiose pile in Buckinghamshire. When she retired from the stage she went there to live. No longer expected to make everyone in London laugh, she found there a peaceful pasture, where she was required only to be resident jester to her landlord, to enliven Walpole's supper parties, play cards with him when he was bored, and supply him material for amusing anecdotes for his letters. What had been said a generation earlier of Colley Cibber's relationship with the mighty was true of Kitty now: "He could be noisy or silent, saucy or well bred, obscene or modest, the joker or the jest, the pleasure or the contempt of the company, just as he found they required it."[14] To be given a place at the tables of the mighty in the capacity of a buffoon was impossible for Susannah Cibber. She did not view herself as a figure of fun. She was as dogged a Tory and as orthodox and conservative in her views as Peg Woffington, her third great rival, was a flamboyant rebel.

Very early in her life Woffington realized that her birth and childhood placed her forever beyond social redemption. Her father had been an Irish bricklayer, her mother a washerwoman. A vividly beautiful child, she had grown up in the streets of Dublin hawking salad greens. She was desperately poor and unprotected; there was not much she had not seen or experienced. When she was about twelve she joined a traveling company of juvenile players and took on the whole support of her family. In the world she lived in and managed to survive, weak, trusting women went under and strong men prevailed. She accepted this, adopting the standards of the oppressor and despising his weeping victim. Her contempt for her own sex — particularly its genteel members — was vehement and unrelenting. She played by the harsh rules of the military bloods and rakes who had debauched her as a girl. She gambled, made love, and caroused, took her pleasures and her knocks without a whimper, and lived and died a fascinating, brittle, and isolated figure.

Whatever her denouncements of the conventions and the silly sex who lived by them, with the first real money Peg earned she took her younger sister Mary ("Polly") out of her mother's hovel and off the streets of Dublin and sent her to school, first in Ireland, then England, and then in France, with the best-bred young girls in the realm. Five or six years later Polly returned to her, a "finished lady," mistress of needlepoint, a Parisian accent, and the art of vivacious conversation. Peg bought a villa in Teddington so that Polly could meet "county" families, and married her to the impecunious second son of Lord Cholmondely. From that moment on, the greatest joy in Peg's life was underwriting the Cholmondely household and equipage, and hearing of the social triumphs of the Honorable Mary Cholmondely.

During the two years she lay dying of a long, wasting disease, Peg was devotedly nursed by a Colonel Caesar, who had loved her at a distance for years and now neglected his offices and his estate to care for her. When her will was read she had left everything to the popular hostess Mrs. Cholmondely. There was no mention of — not a silver spoon nor a ring for — faithful and depleted Colonel Caesar.

Woffington's forte on the stage was the cold, brilliant, diamond-witted lady of high Restoration comedy. Both in her art and in her molding of her sister's character she created dazzling and devastating examples of a type she could never be.

Eighteenth-century society was stratified but porous. A person could burst up dramatically through many layers — cheap little "Polly" Fenton really *did* become the Duchess of Bolton after the randy old Duke snatched her off the stage — or fall through to the bottom, like so many of the overreaching Arnes. Susannah Cibber's personal position was every bit as compromised as Peg Woffington's and yet, as had been the case with the Honorable Mrs. Cholmondely, it was not unreasonable to believe that she and Sloper could greatly advance their two children. Susannah was the highest paid actress at Drury Lane. Sloper was a man of fortune and power. Fox had appointed him Deputy Cofferer to the Royal Household and Pay Master General of His Majesty's Forces in Gibraltar,[15] positions comfortably out of the public eye, but within the inner circle of patronage and influence. Hundreds of army officers, people in trade, and civil servants prospered or languished according to Sloper's pleasure.

In 1757 Sloper enrolled his little natural son, Charles, aged eight, as a boarder at Westminster School, where he was registered as Master Cibber.[16] If the lad showed an aptitude for books he was to go on to university. If, like his older half brothers, Robert and William Charles, he was no scholar, his father would buy him a commission in a good regiment. The army was Sloper's chief sphere of influence and he was already doing well by his oldest boy.* What little Charles might have become his parents would never know. He died in April of his first year away at school, "in his boarding house in Dean's Yard, Westminster."[17] He was not quite nine, the third of Susannah's four children to die. No explanation remains of his illness or accident, and the only suggestion of his mother's grief survives in a terse note in the diary of Drury Lane's prompter, Richard Cross. April was benefit time, and among his reports about attendance and receipts Cross scrawled on the twenty-fifth, "Mrs Cibber's son dy'd two days ago and she never came to play for Holland, Mrs Yates or me, ye olde Game at this season."[18]

After Charles's death, Susannah, Sloper, and Molly withdrew to West Woodhay. Their isolated little family was diminished by two this sad spring, for Susannah's mother had also died. Sloper's and Susannah's dreams now centered around eighteen-year-old Molly.

---

* In 1744 when Robert turned fifteen, Sloper had procured him an ensignship in Morduant's Eighteenth Foot. In 1752 he transacted a brilliant marriage between Robert and Jane Willes, daughter and heiress of his friend Sir John Willes, wealthy Lord Chief Justice of the Court of Common Pleas. By 1755, only twenty-six, Robert was a major in the Tenth Dragoons. He was a colonel in General Bland's First Dragoons four years later. In 1760 at Lord George Sackville's court-martial for cowardice under fire at the battle of Minden, Colonel Sloper was the unshakable chief witness for the prosecution. Sackville was convicted and disgraced and young Sloper endeared himself to Sackville's powerful enemies, George II, Lord Morduant, and the Marquis of Granby. William Sloper lived long enough to see his firstborn made a general and Sir Robert Sloper, K.C.B., Governor of Madras and Commander in Chief of all His Majesty's forces in India, a post from which he was recalled for incompetence a scant year later, and replaced by Lord Cornwallis. Sir Robert's history suggests a mediocre man advanced beyond his abilities by the indefatigable efforts of his father, and by the good offices of his father's friends who owed political favors. Historical Manuscripts Commission, Duke of Rutland, vol. 3, pp. 289, 357, 388.

She must be married, and married well, to secure her future and ex-
punge the stain of illegitimacy. Old Thomas Arne had failed to
make his only daughter a lady, but Susannah was determined to
accomplish this for her last child. More than a generation seems to
have elapsed between the coarse figure of old Arne, the undertaker,
and his civilized and subtle daughter. She was not only more sophis-
ticated in her methods, but infinitely more humane. Her own marriage had been arranged because of its immediate advantages for her
and her family, and with little thought of her distaste for her husband or of his dangerous character. Although she and Sloper were
determined that Molly wed a gentleman, he need not have a fortune:
she would be rich enough for both. But he must be a man she loved
and who, even if he did not love her, would not abuse her.

Molly had drawbacks as a marital prospect. She was plain, her
complexion coarsened by pox scars. She was a bastard. Connection
with her could bring no luster to her husband, whose name and
position must be substantial enough to absorb hers. On the other
hand she was sole heir to a rich mother and the favorite child of a
powerful father who would feel, not only at the time of her dower
settlement but all his life, a sense of gratitude to a son-in-law who
made his treasure happy. And Molly had a very endearing nature.
She had been tenderly raised, never far from her mother's and
grandmother's side. Her slim body and soft ways were like her mother's. Her voice had the same melodious and melancholy ring.[19] They
had been so much together that she was like a sweet, blurred replica
of her brilliant parent. Though she had had hardly any acquaintance
with people her own age, she had considerable poise with older men
because she was a favorite of her mother's salon. Garrick, who loved
children and never had any, made so much of her when she visited
backstage that people were forever whispering he was really her
father.[20] This amiable girl, cherished by her parents and reared as it
were by a dozen fond uncles, was not apt to break the hearts of young
blades at a ball; but a prudent man should be able to see that her
loving and filial heart and her fortune were elements that would go
far to ensure a happy union.

The problem was to find opportunities to expose her. Her
mother's London salon of elderly bachelors and respectable married

men was not a fertile ground. Like Susannah, Molly was not admitted to the homes of decent people. Sometimes she accompanied her parents to masquerades[21] or evenings at Ranelagh, but these crushes of brilliant personages were not congenial places for her homely virtues to shine. For the part of the year she lived at West Woodhay she was, like her mother, a nonperson to their neighbors and dependent on the company her mother could entice from London.

The most promising, most relaxed, and natural atmosphere for Molly to meet young men was at a spa. Here was a world reassuringly structured and infinitely various. For the family invalid — often the excuse for going — there were the curative course of waters and hours of consultation with the celebrated local physicians. For restless husbands and grown sons there were horse races, cockfighting, and gaming. For young people there was dancing in the evening and strolls and picnics and excursions to beauty spots during the day. For every age there were musicales, theatricals, incessant clothes-changing and promenading, ritual tea drinking in the public rooms, and the pleasure of watching one another and of being seen. Garrick had cured himself of Peg Woffington by flitting from spa to spa and dancing all night — light-headed from the purgative waters he was drinking — with dozens of marriageable daughters on display.

Sloper and Susannah had always visited spas for Susannah's health, but when Molly reached her late teens they began to spend a long part of the year at two: Bath every spring and fall, Scarborough in August. At Scarborough they invariably stayed at Dr. (later Sir) Noah Thomas's establishment. Thomas had a brilliant practice and he specialized in digestive disorders. One August when he was seventeen, a sickly young country squire, Joseph Cradock (1742–1826), was packed off by his guardians to reside a few weeks with Dr. Thomas to "strengthen" his stomach. Because Cradock was so young, and because his dead father had been a patient and friend of the doctor's, Thomas took the lad under his wing and put him to eat at his own table. To young Cradock's inexpressible delight he discovered that his companions at the head table were none other than His Royal Highness, Edward Augustus, the Duke of York; the military hero the Marquis of Granby and his frail wife; Laurence Sterne; and William Sloper, with Mrs. Cibber and their daughter. Young

Susannah Arne Cibber, by W. Hoare.

Cradock did not take much notice of Molly, who was three years his senior, but he lost his heart to her mother. In the mornings Susannah was taking Dr. Thomas's cure, which included sea bathing. In the afternoons she sat for a portrait in the character of the Fair Penitent, while young Cradock watched and worshiped. So blissful was the young squire that he delayed his return to his rustic seat and ignored the inquiries of his guardians. When they finally discovered the company their ward was keeping they thought it much too heady for his youth and inexperience and hastily recalled him.[22]

There was nothing like the atmosphere of a spa — half holiday, half hospital — to lower social barriers. At Dr. Thomas's table, licensed by their bad digestions, a dissipated young Prince of the Blood, a military hero with "Gout of the Stomach," a literary man of the cloth, a wide-eyed young squire, and a notorious actress could all sit down together. But even at Scarborough there were vigilant representatives of the middle class to make sure the proprieties were not mocked. Cradock remembered all his life Mrs. Cibber's humiliation by a bishop's lady. Mrs. Tabitha Terrick, an heiress married to the Bishop of Peterborough, was, on account of her wealth and her husband's position, conceded to be the ex officio social arbitress of Scarborough. "On a Sunday Evening," Cradock wrote, "at the great Tea Drinking in the [public] Rooms, Mrs Terrick, who presided, addressed the company on the impropriety of Mrs Cibber being admitted to the table. This made an immediate uproar. Some were for the Bishop's lady, but more for the well-behaved actress. However, I think Mrs Cibber offered to retire."[23] Of course she did. Appeasement was always her way. But one setback did not defeat this resilient campaigner, whose efforts to be admitted at least to the antechambers of respectable society were less for her own sake than as part of her plan to see her last child safely married and established.

A public humiliation even more painful than the one at Scarborough lay in store a year later at Bath. This one is described with relish by Mrs. Patrick Delany, second wife of that pious Dean who, years before, as a newly bereaved widower, had heard Susannah sing *Messiah* and cried aloud that for this gift of comfort to her listeners her sins must be forgiven her. Tenderhearted clergymen might find it in their hearts to forgive a woman like Susannah; never their

wives. For Mrs. Delany and Mrs. Tabitha Terrick, Susannah's trans-
gression against marriage cast her beyond Christian compassion.
"Oct. 28, 1760," wrote Mary Delany:

> There was a great Tea-Drinking in the Rooms, and a Bustle that
> startled me! Mr Sloper, who is here with Madam Cibber and a
> daughter by her, has been much offended that his daughter was
> not taken out to dance. She was the first night, and a sensible, clever
> woman whose daughter was taken out after, *refused* to let her dance;
> this put a stop to Miss Cibber's being asked again, and on Sunday
> Night in the midst of the Rooms, Mr Sloper collared poor Collet,*
> abusing him, and asking if he had been the occasion of the affront
> put upon his daughter. Collet said it was, "By Mr Nash's direction."
> The poor wretch [octogenarian Nash] was now wheeled into the
> rooms: Sloper had some discussion with him, and so the matter
> ended.[24]

So it ended for Mrs. Delany, but not for gentle Molly, her tirelessly
propitiating mother, nor her helplessly raging father. Molly was already twenty-one, a late age to be a spinster.

Nearly all the struggle of Susannah's last years lay in the social
area. At Drury Lane she reigned serene, "in quiet possession of all
the best parts." There were, to be sure, a few skirmishes with management over what part of her enormous salary should be docked
during seasons when, because of her frail health, she made only a
handful of appearances. That Garrick and Lacy put up with her at
all is an indication of her prestige and drawing power, for she was
surely more trouble than any other performer. The theatrical season
opened in September and ended in May, but Susannah rarely returned to town from Bath till December, and always left directly
after the April benefits. Her health was so uncertain that whenever
she was scheduled to perform Garrick had to have another play
ready, its cast on call at a moment s notice. Susannah's stomach disorder had a way of coming on without warning, and an understudy
was not the answer. Her roles were sacrosanct to her admirers, and
they would not tolerate another woman's attempting them.

* Master of Ceremonies at Bath, and successor to the by now decrepit Beau Nash.

Whenever Susannah found herself out of accord with management she turned her case over to some powerful third person whose good opinion Garrick also valued. Dr. Edward Barry, the Dublin physician who had met Susannah and Garrick the summer they were in Dublin, had warmly corresponded with both of them over the years. In 1759 he took up Susannah's cause from across the sea, and we still have Garrick's exasperated letter to him explaining management's position:

> You say, Sir, that Mrs Cibber attended the whole season. Had she done that we would not have had a single word with her. Mrs Cibber attended only a third of her business last year, and indeed her merit and sallary [sic] are so great that it can not surely be thought unreasonable that a small portion of the latter be given up for losing so great a proportion of the former. . . . Mrs Cibber herself acknowledges that she *greatly disappointed* us last winter, and had our Success wholly depended upon *her*, we must have been bankrupt. . . . I am surprised a little that she should urge an attendance upon Rehearsals as a sufficient Plea for her Sallary; the Managers must support their large Property not by Rehearsals but by her Appearance in Public, and had she constantly attended every Rehearsal . . . and not acted one night, She certainly could not have been entitled to a farthing of her Agreement. . . .[25]

Garrick had a heavy chore controlling and cajoling his large theatrical family of "froward children." Among his actresses only Hannah Pritchard was a model of sweet reasonableness and dependability. The active love lives of Miss Bellamy and Miss Haughton often confounded his scheduling. Both these young ladies tended to wax big-bellied at the height of the season, disqualifying themselves for ingenue roles, and giving birth sometimes within a few hours before or after a performance.

Kitty Clive, who had forsworn men, never missed a performance to lie-in. Still, the trigger of her temper was perpetually cocked, and if she felt that she had been upstaged during a performance, or that the orchestra had not accompanied her sensitively enough during a ballad, she was apt to seek physical revenge backstage.[26] When she came off the stage in a swinging mood Garrick was the only authority she recognized, and in their thirty years' association she never lifted a hand against him. Often, though, she flailed him with pen and paper. Her furious letters were written in a surprisingly neat, heavily inked hand, and full of original spelling. She declared she would not stand on "cerimony," but accused him to his face of "culumity."[27]

"You gave Mrs Cibber £600 for playing 60 nights, and £300 to me for playing 180," she raged to him once.[28] And there is no denying that Garrick valued Susannah's rare appearances at five times the rate of anyone else's. When he wrote Kitty Clive he addressed her, man-to-man, as "Dear Clive,"[29] or as "My Pivy,"[30] like a younger sister or lovable family retainer. He did not trouble with elegant phrases or gallantries. "How can you be so ridiculous and still so cross?"[31] he opened one letter, and closed another, "Ever thine, my dainty Kate,"[32] to tease her about her resemblance to Shakespeare's shrew and remind her he was confident of keeping her tamed. "I solely conquered Clive myself," he remarked to Walpole. "Cibber could persuade me out of anything."[33] He was a little in awe of Susannah. His letters to her, politic, convoluted, drafted over and over, are different from his easy, sovereign tone with most of his actresses. "Dear Madam," he began to her in 1760. "I should not have given Mr Sloper the trouble of a letter, had I imagined that you were well enough to receive or write letters — the subject of mine might have ruffled you in your condition, and therefore in regard to you I left it to Mr Sloper to judge how to act in it. I beg to know how you find yourself today; if you feel your disorder going off and you think you may be able to play Mrs Lovemore I will not give the part to Mrs Yates, but if you are doubtful —"[34] and so on. He was as relieved as she to turn over their occasional disagreements to a third party for resolution, as if he were unsure of the outcome should he and she come to grips with it face to face. He was dealing with a woman with suasive powers almost as formidable as his own. He and she had come close to being lovers, even nearer to being business partners. There had been a time when he had feared he could only escape her nets by slipping away over the sea and equivocating with her through mediators. "I could easily parry the artless blows and coarse language of some of my other heroines," he said after her death. "But whatever was Cibber's object, whether it was a new gown or a new part, she always got her way."[35] In trivial matters of clothes and perquisites she may have prevailed, probably because Garrick could never rid himself of the sense that he had once used her shabbily. But in the important things, which she had wanted from him and which would have changed their lives, she had always lost, and they both knew it.

For the most part during her last years she played those tragic roles that were regarded as sacred to her: Juliet, Ophelia, Desdemona, Cordelia, Perdita, Zara, Calista, Alicia, Indiana, Sigismunda, Belvidera, Elvira. But, just as Kitty Clive burned to be taken seriously and to play passionate, romantic parts opposite Garrick, so Susannah had an unaccountable wish to succeed in comedy. "This actress," Davies says, ". . . by nature formed for tragic representation, was uncommonly desirous of acting characters of gaiety and humour, to which she was an absolute stranger: she had no idea of comedy."[36] In 1754 she decided to do Constantia in Garrick's revival of Beaumont and Fletcher's bawdy *The Chances*. The first-night audience was too respectful of her to hiss, but it was glum and restive. The newspapers were scathing, and Susannah turned the part over to saucy Miss Haughton, whom Garrick had wanted in the first place. Bad reviews were very rare for Susannah. In general the press commented upon her performances in the same unctuous and reverent style with which they described His Majesty's gracious behavior at a levee, or the Bishop of London's latest sermon. Here is the *London Chronicle* swooning over Susannah's Lady Essex: "In the Scene where her conjugal Affection rises to a kind of Phrenzy for the Loss of her Husband, such Wildness, such Despair, such a tender Indignation takes Possession of her that her Powers of Voice become astonishing from the Strength they acquire and the Melody that accompanies them in that furious Elevation."[37]

The decade from the mid-fifties to the mid-sixties was characterized by obstreperous audiences and nervous managers. In Dublin in 1754, when Thomas Sheridan was managing Smock Alley, he refused to stop the play one night so that the audience's favorite player might repeat a fiery speech they admired. The shouting public pulled up their benches, dashed them against the floor, and shouldered the jagged pieces. Then they tore the lighted sconces out of the walls, and, armed with staves and brands, climbed onto the stage while the players fled before them. Backstage, the rabble ransacked the scene and property rooms and, piling everything they could move in the middle of the stage, lit an enormous bonfire. Smock Alley was gutted and Sheridan ruined.[38]

News of his fate persuaded his brother managers in London that, when an audience's mood turned ugly, the sacrifice of principle was preferable to conflagration. Garrick and Lacy at Drury Lane, and Rich and his son-in-law, John Beard, at Covent Garden handled the mob with what sometimes seems to us slavish deference. Even so there were riots at both theaters, usually when management tried to raise the price of tickets. Between these eruptions there was always an undercurrent of potential violence. People were pushed off the teaming galleries into the pit below, and there was chronic danger of being struck by a hurled object. The *Public Advertizer* of February 15, 1755, carried this notice from Drury Lane: "If any person will discover who it was that flung a hard piece of cheese of near a half pound's worth from one of the galleries last Tuesday Night and greatly hurt a young lady, he shall receive Ten Guineas from Mr Pritchard, The Treasurer of the Theatre."[39]

Drury Lane, David Garrick himself, and even his fine town house on Southampton Street all barely survived the mob's rage that year. The summer before, he had engaged a company of European dancers to perform a fanciful afterpiece called *The Chinese Festival*. The costumes had been made and the dancers had crossed the channel when hostilities broke out between Britain and France; and when this elaborate chinoiserie opened on November 8 it was greeted with catcalls and fruit from the pit, who found it an insult to their patriotism and manhood to watch these effeminate, Papist "Frenchmen" leaping about their English stage. It did no good for Garrick to announce that of the sixty members of the ballet corps, only nine were French. Forty were Garrick's own English dancers, the others a sprinkling of Italian, German, and French. Their leader, Jean Georges Noverre, was no more French or Catholic than he was effeminate, being a muscular Swiss Protestant and an intensely uxorious man at that. The costumes and salaries of *The Chinese*

Festival had cost Garrick £2,000, and the grievance of the public was so absurd that he was determined to ride out the storm. Yet every night the audience grew more violent. Mirrors and chandeliers were smashed. There were threats to burn down the theater. Not only was the ballet interrupted by howls and flying objects and shouts of "No French Dancers," but the main piece was stopped over and over, and Garrick himself became the rabble's target. And presently the affair took on sinister aspects of class war, because Garrick's friends among people of fashion warmly espoused the dance, looked with contempt at the mindless uproar in the pit and gallery, and vowed to educate their low taste by force if necessary. Fashionable young bloods took to coming to the theater armed and looking for trouble, so that there were scuffles, fistfights, or stabbings at every performance. In vain did practical Lacy, who usually gave Garrick a free hand in dealing with the public, look up from his account books and beg his fellow manager to terminate the "French" dance while they still had a theater.

Remembering the destruction of Sheridan's Smock Alley a year before, Garrick drilled his stage crew and male players into a smart theatrical militia. At the first sign of a rush over the footlights, the curtain was to be rung down and some beloved figure like Susannah Cibber was to step before it and cajole the horde as long as possible. Meanwhile, every man had his task and station. Some were to open up the stage trapdoors and the cover of the great fire reservoir beneath the stage, so as to drown anyone who rushed across unheeding. Other strong arms would meanwhile be carrying the most valuable properties, costumes, and papers across the back alley into a strong storage building. In precisely three minutes every able-bodied man in the company, armed with swords and halberds, could be in his assigned place lining the stage wings.

While these martial preparations were perfected in secret, the public face of Drury Lane was as pacific as Garrick could make it. London's favorite and least controversial plays were put on, with emphasis on pathetic tragedies. It was a canon of sentimental doctrine that no man newly washed with tears was capable of lifting his hands in violence, and since "when Mrs Cibber [performs] the most brutal and unfeeling never refuse the true applause of tears,"[40] Garrick offered her famous heartbreakers — *The Orphan, Romeo and*

Juliet, and *The Earl of Essex* — to tranquilize his audience before the nightly ordeal of *The Chinese Festival*. But even Susannah's lachrymal genius could not subdue the brute in the pit. All November Richard Cross made his brief, mordant notes: "8 Nov . . . a great deal of hissing and clapping and some cries of 'No French Dancers!' . . . 12 Nov . . . a great deal of hissing — but the Boxes being on our side some swords were drawn and several turned out of the Pit and Galleries. . . . Nov 13. More noise against the Dancers. . . . Nov 15. Great noise . . . amazing noise, no pelting, except one Apple; ye Pit to ye Boxes cried, 'Now draw your swords!' which makes us think the Riot was occasioned by the Box . . . turning some out of the Pit and Gallery before. Some benches were pulled up." On November 18 Garrick and Cibber got through *The Earl of Essex* with innumerable interruptions and the greatest difficulty. "And then," Cross wrote,

> the Rout was on. Ye Boxes drove many out of the Pit, and broken heads were plenty on both sides. The Dance began — was stopped, and so on again and again. While this was doing, numbers were assembled in the Passage of the Pit . . . but were repulsed by our Scenemen — Heavy blows on both sides. Justice Fielding and Welch came with Constables and a Guard. . . . After ye battle in ye Passages numbers went and broke Garrick's windows in Southampton Street — part of ye Guard went to protect it. Garrick was obliged to give up the Dancers — [41]

Carpenters working through that night and all next day made the theater operational by the next evening. But the riot had been too much for Susannah. Not till December 13 did Cross report that she had returned to Drury Lane to do Indiana in *The Conscious Lovers,* having "been ill ever since ye Riot."[42]

It was a paradox of Susannah's deteriorating health that she retained the illusion of youth much longer than her robust contemporaries. Pritchard had grown so enormous by the 1750s that, even laced beneath and swathed outside in gauzy scarves, it was impossible to disguise her girth or think of her as a young or romantic figure. She had always been a rangy woman, taller than Garrick, but when she grew fat, too, they made such a risible pair that the audience

John Zoffany's portrait of Garrick and Pritchard as Macbeth and Lady Macbeth. Even if one supposes that Zoffany did his best to flatter and diminish Pritchard's figure to harmonize with Garrick's, it is clear that she outweighed him, was several inches taller, and that their passionate moments together teetered on the edge of the ludicrous.

could not help tittering at serious moments. Garrick, always sensitive about his size, began to avoid these situations. Playing comedy with Clive was another matter, for if the audience chose to snicker at the contrast between Garrick's neat, springy, well-preserved figure and Clive's hammy arms and quivering nest of chins, there was no injury thereby to his amour propre.

Meanwhile, year after year, Garrick and Cibber, with their lissome, fine-boned bodies, produced a wonderful effect together. Like some long and happily married couple, the more they played together, the more they looked alike and the more attuned to one another they grew. "Mr Garrick is not handsome," Dr. Hill said, "nor did the most enthusiastic admirer of Mrs Cibber ever call her a beauty, but both have features large, strong, and formed for marking the passions; each has the eye piercing in the greatest degree."[43] Garrick preferred to play with her than any other actress, and she refused another partner. They seemed born to affect each other — he to assert, she to assent. Up to the very last, one of them would suddenly move the other to tears in the middle of a scene.

Without stage makeup and close to, Susannah looked her age, worn and ill. One winter morning in 1762, the playwright William Whitehead walked into Garrick's drawing room in Southampton Street, where Garrick, Mrs. Cibber, Mrs. Clive, Mr. Palmer, and Mr. O'Brien were reading through Whitehead's new sentimental comedy, *The School for Lovers*. In the cold grey light Mrs. Cibber, in a dark dress, her hair pulled back, spectacles on her nose, was reciting the tender words of his seventeen-year-old heroine, Celia. Garrick introduced the playwright, and Whitehead complimented the company. Since the play was new, he said, and the characters as yet unborn, they could still be shaped; this was the time for any of the players to tell him if there were changes which might make a role sit more comfortably. Without any harm to the plot, for instance, he could advance Celia's age to twenty-five or so. No one spoke. Garrick began to talk animatedly to somebody. Mrs. Cibber looked up mildly at Whitehead over her spectacles and said that, speaking for herself, she was happy with Celia exactly as she was, and begged him not to trouble himself to change a word. Celia was played as seventeen, and *The School for Lovers* much applauded. Above all, people admired Mrs. Cibber's Celia. There was always something soft, suspended, and expectant about her stage presence. "It was impossible to view her figure and not think her young, or look in her face and not consider her handsome."[44]

Though she lived before the romantic period, she was an early example of the idea of the artist as sufferer, a person with special insights into the emotions because of his own intense experiences. No one would have dreamed of trying to account for Garrick's understanding of Lear's madness, Richard's malice, or Othello's jealousy in terms of the circumstances of his life. But people always saw in Cibber's shriek of anguish at little Prince Arthur's death in *King John* the reflection of her grief at her son's death, in her pitiful protestations as Desdemona something of what she must have undergone from her cruel husband, in her transfigured Juliet an echo of her "amorous situation" with Sloper and proof that "her heart was more formed for love"[45] than ordinary mortals'.

In 1763 a young man visiting London wrote his brother, "I am . . . charmed with Mrs Cibber . . . her merit exceeds anything I can say . . . what is amazing — though she is about the age of 60,* she can very well do the parts of a girl. . . . Nobody here could take her place were she to die."[46] Were she to die? It was clear she was dying. Besides her emaciation she had developed a rhythmic wobble of the head, and her voice often flagged. Even her detractors no longer muttered about her malingering and Garrick's favoritism. Part of the pathos of her rare appearances was their evident physical cost and the public's tearful realization that each might be her last. Her attacks had grown so severe that her physicians had several times given her up, and newspapers, eager to be first with the news, had actually announced her death. While other great ladies of the stage swelled and stiffened into matrons, Susannah grew more insubstantial, not growing old but flickering out. To her public she lost none of her poetry as she waned. More than ever, "Cibber, sir, seemed to *need* your tears, from the delicacy of her frame."

---

* In his enthusiasm, Dalziel gives her eleven years. She had just turned forty-nine.

❧ 18 ❧

Iɴ December of his eightieth year Colley Cibber suffered a sick
spell so severe that no one expected him to recover, least of all
his only son. For a few weeks Theo's creditors stopped yapping
at his heels while they waited respectfully for his rich old father to
die. But life was too delicious for Colley to relinquish, and he enjoyed spending his fortune too much to want to leave any more of it
than necessary to his heirs. From his sickbed on Christmas day he
wrote his friend Samuel Richardson: "Though Death has been
cooling his Heels at my Door these three Weeks, I have not had time
to see him. The daily Conversation of my Friends has kept me so
agreeably alive that I have not passed my Time better in a great
While."[1] Seven more years must pass before he would admit his cold
and patient visitor. At six o'clock one morning in 1757 Cibber's man-
servant heard him stir and went into his room. They chatted. Colley
was in fine spirits, anticipating calls that day from a number of distinguished gentlemen and lovely ladies. He said he thought he would
doze again till nine. At that hour his servant returned with his mas-

ter's chocolate on a silver tray. Cibber lay dead just as his man had left him, his head undisturbed on his smooth linen pillow.[2]

He had made sure his son would not benefit significantly from his death, and left him £50. Poor destitute Charlotte, his youngest child, whom he loathed even more than her brother, he cut off with £5. But £1,000 went to each of Theo's girls, Jenny and Betty. There was no time for Theo to prize loose his daughters' fortunes: he did not survive his parent a year, but died a death as full of horror and confusion as Colley's had been insouciant.

Ever since the two trials, Theo had been harassing his wife with legal suits, threats of others, and defamatory letters to the press. But as Susannah's star rose, his own set, and his claims became so absurd and his person so repudiated that his well-wishers begged him to stop exhausting his energy in plots, his small means in lawyers' fees. In 1751 Benjamin Victor wrote to Theo from Dublin to enquire about his "present state of health and warfare — I wish I could say welfare."[3] He begged Theo to abandon his siege. Susannah was the public's darling, he pointed out. They would not tolerate seeing her driven off the stage and unable to entertain them. The more Theo hounded her, the more his spite would rebound against himself.

Victor's good-humored advice made no impression. To the last day of his life Theo clung to the belief that he could bring his wife to her knees, force her to acknowledge him her lawful master, and then graciously raise her up to go back to work bringing home her enormous earnings to him. Although Susannah remained Theo's ultimate target, his more immediate enemy as the years passed was Garrick. Here was a man indecently happy and rich, reigning over Theo's stolen birthright, the kingdom of Drury Lane, with Theo's wife beside him as Queen Consort. To all practical purposes, Garrick supplanted Sloper as his rival. He poured out an unquenchable torrent of pamphlets, epistles, public lectures and dissertations, which accused Garrick of stealing the patent of Drury Lane while Theo was too broken by his wife's perfidy to defend it. He accused Garrick of arrogance, parsimony, fawning on the mighty while forgetting old friends, crushing the talents of young rivals, and debauching Shakespeare. There was enough truth in Cibber's accusations to make them sting, despite which Garrick showed him extraordinary tolerance and magnanimity. Once, in 1753, while Cibber was languishing in the King's Bench, Garrick interceded for his release long enough for Theo to rehearse and perform Dr. Wolf in *The Non Juror* at a benefit for himself. Drury Lane overflowed for the occasion and Theo earned £220,[4] an amount which did not make him solvent but set him free and allowed him to work again.

It was Theo's contention that Garrick and Susannah were joined in a satanic alliance to prevent his earning a living and to starve him and his children. Garrick's motive was fear and envy; Susannah's, female malevolence. It was true that ever since Susannah had returned from exile she had stipulated that she would not work in any theater where her husband was in the company, but for the first few years after her return to London Theo had no difficulty finding work at whichever of the theaters royal Susannah was not engaged. There were plenty of playgoers who never felt comfortable clasped in the soft tentacles of sentimental drama, and who would rather pay their money to see Theo strut and leer, plot and blaspheme, than listen to the interminable scruples and sufferings of a sentimental heroine. The ingenious knave is a timeless comic type, and Theo's effrontery could always make people laugh. It was not Garrick's envy or Susannah's spite, but his own genius for troublemaking that eventually so antagonized his fellow players and enraged his employers that it destroyed his career.

When Theo returned from his summer holidays in 1755, he found that John Rich had vowed he would never hire him again at Covent Garden. Drury Lane was barred to him because Susannah was there. Within two weeks he had gathered a company of unemployed players and opened a season at the Little Haymarket. When the Lord Chamberlain, the Duke of Grafton, protested that Cibber had no license, he explained that this was not a theatrical company but an academy for aspiring players. The plays were public rehearsals designed to give the fledgling students experience and assurance. And they were free. Any sums that the Lord Chamberlain's agents may have seen being collected at the door were donations to sustain this "nursery for young performers."[5] The names of some of Theo's drama students were odd. They included some persons who called themselves Mrs. Midnight, Mrs. Quelch, Mrs. Sweetlips, and Mr.

Pleasevery, and sound more like classmates of Doll Tearsheet or Diana Trapes than blushing ingenues.

The Lord Chamberlain was not convinced of the altruism of Theo's enterprise and ordered the Little Haymarket shut. Theo never doubted that this was Garrick's doing, and he spent all fall composing a long diatribe against him, which he advertised he would deliver, for a charge, at the lecture room of the Robin Hood Tavern and at the Piazza Coffee House: "Mr Cibber will deliver a Dissertation on Theatrical Subjects: a sly Tyrant . . . Authors discouraged . . . Actors starved . . . Shakespeare lacerated . . . Shakespeare's works [degraded] by mincing, mangling, mutilating, momacking and castrating his Plays into Farces, Drolls, and Mock Operas."[6]

Theo Cibber was not the only person who found Garrick's proprietary attitude toward Shakespeare unwarranted, and his alterations of the plays sacrilegious. But Theo was too disreputable a figure to lead a serious attack against the great actor-manager. Though Theo was obsessed by Garrick and Susannah, they were only faintly aware of him. In his voluminous private correspondence Garrick rarely mentions Theo, and never seriously or at length, and Susannah, once she was free of him, never could be provoked into responding in any way to his continual public attacks.

By the summer of 1756 Theo had despaired of finding a livelihood in the London theater and, as was his habit, he took the world into his confidence to explain: "To the Public:" he wrote,

> Oppressed and overpowered as I am by the wicked Influence of some present, avaricious, theatrical Tyrants, I have taken . . . every decent and proper Step to obtain a License to get my Bread by my Profession in my native Country. . . . Neither Reason, Humanity, or Justice have yet been able to prevail . . . against the surprising Influence of certain all-powerful Patentees. . . . Therefore I am determined to go into Trade.

He proposed to become a snuff merchant and would shortly "open a Snuff Warehouse, where will be sold a most excellent CEPHALIC SNUFF."[7]

The snuff venture failed. Theo tried again to open an unlicensed theater called "Cibber's Histrionic Academy on the Bowling Green." This one was in Richmond, a little removed from the Lord Chamberlain's nose, but His Grace sniffed it out and closed it. The winter after Colley died and turned him off with £50, Theo began writing queer, desperate letters to the highest peers in the land, men like the Dukes of Dorset and New Castle. He even petitioned the King. He explained that he was the only son of Colley Cibber, Poet Laureate, dramatist, former patentee of Drury Lane, man of letters, friend of the great, and he begged them to intercede with the Lord Chamberlain to grant him a patent to run a legitimate theater. No one answered. Theo's plight was so hopeless that people pitied him but dared not help. It would have been like reaching out a hand to a mad dog, already half dead from stoning, who would, with his last breath, make sure to bite his benefactor.

Providentially, in the fall of 1758 Theo heard from Benjamin Victor in Dublin, asking him to come to Smock Alley for the season. Victor and Thomas Sheridan were joint managers there, and were trying to pull together a competent company to rival a new theater, Crow Street, led by Spranger Barry and Henry Woodward. The Smock Alley regulars were very weak, and Victor had written Garrick for ideas about reinforcements.[8] Garrick had suggested that Cibber was available and unemployed. Victor needed a strong comedian and crowd-catcher, and he flattered himself that he had always gotten along with the man, however bitter his partner Sheridan's experience had been with the matter of Cato's cloak.

As soon as Theo read Victor's letter he packed his trunks. He owned very little after these years of evictions and pawnings. All he had were the tools of his trade: some costumes and false noses, his beards and wigs (greasy ones and kinky ones), his wide-topped, rolled boots for the part of Pistol, the urine vial with the false bottom that leaked and dribbled so comically when he played Abel Drugger in *The Alchemist*, and his papers, scripts with his parts marked, manuscripts of plays he was writing or doctoring, scraps and fragments from his unfinished "Lives of the Actors and Actresses of Great Britain" and "Lives of the Poets." His luggage was not very elegant. Some of his papers he crammed into an old fiddle case he had picked up backstage somewhere.

In the middle of October he started for Chester to take passage for Ireland. He was accompanied by a Mrs. Pockeridge,[9] a shadowy lady whose husband was still alive, and who had apparently been sharing Theo's wretched life for several years. It was a party of five London stage people, plus a wife or mistress or two, that convened in Chester to embark for the engagement at Smock Alley. Victor had managed to recruit Maddox, the famous Sadler's Wells wire dancer and acrobatic pantomimist, who would be a serious match for Woodward's Harlequin, and there were three other Sadler's Wells acrobats, including "a genius, the man who played on the 12 bells fastened to his head, hands and feet."[10]

To embark from Chester in the eighteenth century really meant to sail from one of the towns nearer the mouth of the River Dee. Chester harbor was perpetually silting in, and the dredging projects which had been going on for centuries never managed to keep the channel deep. At Parkgate, then, eight miles west of the city, the *Dublin Trader* lay at anchor, taking on passengers and goods. The players who jostled aboard her with their bulky theatrical gear were the least distinguished of her passengers. Already at his ease in his private cabin was the Earl of Drogheda with his third son, The Honorable and Reverend Edward, chaplain for the House of Commons. Most of the other nearly seventy souls aboard were wealthy linen and wool merchants from Dublin, returning en masse from the annual October Chester Fair, bringing home with them £150,000 sterling, £70,000 in specie, and unsold bolts of cloth worth £80,000 more.

At noon on October 27, Captain White gave orders to weigh anchor, and Maddox and the other acrobats turned away from the rail where they had been watching for the last of their party. This important person was the stage carpenter from Sadler's Wells, whom Victor had engaged for £20, plus his passage, to uncrate, reassemble, and fit to the Smock Alley stage the intricate pantomime set he had bought from Sadler's Wells for £100, "Story, Musick, Scenes, and Machinery, all compleat."[11] The set itself, packed in crates, had already started by barge down the Thames to proceed along the south coast of England and up the coast of Wales to Ireland. The carpenter, having seen the crates properly numbered and stowed, was to have met his mates from Sadler's Wells in Chester and accompanied them to Dublin to await the shipment. He did not reach Parkgate till three in the afternoon, and when he came to the water's edge, the *Dublin Trader* was still glimmering in sight. Cursing his luck he went to find a room and wait for another packet.

It was still daylight when the *Dublin Trader*, tacking back and forth over the shallow estuary of the River Dee, struck a sand bar and held fast. There was nothing to do but wait for the rising tide to set her afloat. But three of the Irish merchants declined to stay. During their brief hours aboard, Messrs. Crump, Holland, and McDonnell had been so unnerved by the seamanship of the crew, by the terrible groaning and rending of timbers when the ship went aground, and by the quantity of water that had come hissing through a hundred cracks, that they abandoned ship there and then, wading ashore over the treacherous sands and making it back to Chester with only the wet clothes on their backs, leaving their goods and fortunes to reach Dublin without them. While they dried themselves before the inn's fire and arranged for horses to take them to Holyhead — from which the passage to Ireland was only half as far as from Chester — they reported that the *Dublin Trader* was not only unsound, "fresh painted over rotten timbers," but wickedly overloaded and under-staffed, the entire crew consisting of "three hands and a boy besides the master."[12]

Meanwhile, as night fell and the flood tide set her free, the *Dublin Trader* righted herself and sailed out into the Irish Sea. She carried the Earl and his godly son, some sixty merchants and their fortunes, four supple acrobats, and Theophilus Cibber and his Mrs. Pockeridge to their turbulent deaths. A wild gale blew out of the south that night, driving the barge carrying Victor's pantomime scenery so quickly before it up St. George's Channel that she completed a month's voyage in four days.[13] But of the *Dublin Trader* nothing was heard. For a week there were rumors that she had been driven north and lay safe in Douglas Harbor on the Isle of Man. In the second week of November some of the Earl of Drogheda's men outfitted barges to probe the rocky shores of counties Downe and Antrim, and Luce and Wigtown bays on the Scottish coast. What they found near the Mull of Galloway left no doubt of the fate of the *Dublin Trader* and all aboard. The God-fearing Scots in that region who made a good living from wrecks never reported finding any of the £200,000 aboard her, or a single bolt of wool or linen, but they dutifully turned over to the authorities several mildewed trunks filled with stage costumes, as well as other heathen theatrical paraphernalia, including a fiddle case "directed to Mr Cibber in Dublin."[14]

When the evidence of his father's and younger brother's fate was laid before the new Earl of Drogheda, he knew how closely it concerned the management at Smock Alley and graciously asked Victor to come and view it. On a table in the Drogheda business offices in Dublin Victor saw an old, battered fiddle case, "filled with papers of no worth belonging to Cibber, and a part in a play with his name wrote on it. The sight of them afflicted me. It was I that persuaded him into that fatal engagement. Poor Cibber! He had long felt the blasts of adversity! His life was tempestuous; his fate to end it in a storm!"[15]

The sinking of the *Dublin Trader* meant the foundering of Smock Alley, too. Victor and Sheridan had lost not only their crowd-catcher, Cibber, but Maddox, their ingenious Harlequin. The pantomime set was safe in Dublin and so was the tardy stage carpenter. But Maddox and the other acrobats were at the bottom of the sea with the pantomime's plot and stage business and all its tricks and dances in their heads.

Victor's sense of loss and his honest pity were the closest things to mourning Theo received. Mrs. Pockeridge, who would have grieved for him, was gone. His daughters breathed easy for the first time in their lives. Never again would their father shoulder his way into their kind aunt's house and, having ignored them for years, insist they come live with him in his shabby rooms and go into rehearsals for some benefit for themselves, the proceeds of which were instantly applied to Theo's debts. They were safe from him now, and so were the little fortunes their grandfather had left them so that they might find husbands. For Susannah, Theo's death meant the lifting of a twenty-year siege. At last she was undisputed mistress of her own property, and should she die, it would go without question to Molly, who would otherwise have faced a legal battle with Theophilus.

The average Londoner was amused by Theo's death. The laughter he generated had always been cruel and this last act was the best joke of his life. Born in a gale, living in the eye of a private hurricane that lashed and leveled everyone in his orbit, he had died in a howling storm. Goldsmith wrote a lugubrious mock elegy for the occasion, called "Serious Reflections on the Life and Death of the late Mr T . . . C . . . , by the Ordinary of New Gate Prison." Theo had been a young man,* went the piece, born of creditable parents who had given him such a thorough classical education that he could both read and write before he was sixteen. The author concluded by praying that T . . . C . . .'s sad death by drowning might be a lesson in humility to those smug persons who had long believed "that a man so bad was born to be hanged."[16]

---

* A week shy of fifty-five.

Mr Powell, Holland, and Mrs Yates scream at each other like screech owls, and hollow their parts without any feeling or sense. Mrs Cibber is gone. . . . In short, the whole is terrible.
— *Letters of Lady Sarah Lennox*, March 8, 1766

BEFORE he blew out to sea, Theophilus Cibber had howled like an unlaid ghost round the chinks in the Georgian theatrical establishment. Inside, Garrick basked before the hearth of public admiration, with his "children," Cibber, Pritchard, Clive, Havard, Holland, Yates, and the others, gathered round to share the warmth. Garrick was apotheosized in odes and allegorical portraits, and little salt glaze figurines of him and Susannah Cibber shone from many a provincial china cabinet whose owners had never been to London.

And yet, beginning about 1759, Londoners began to desert the Drury Lane veterans. Though they loved them they were satiated with them and bored by a repertory they knew by heart. Meanwhile, Rich, aware that he could never match Garrick in the area of pure drama, leaned on music and spectacle. Ballets, operas, oratorios, pantomimes, acrobats, fat ladies, and fire-eaters mingled with traditional plays at Covent Garden. Garrick's admirers called Covent Garden a circus and a bear garden, and wrote letters to the papers

Thomas Arne,
from a portrait by
R. Dunkarton,
engraved by
W. Humphrey.

Thomas Arne as a
Young Man, at-
tributed to John
Zoffany (published
in Musical Times,
1900). Compare it
with the Hudson
portrait of Susan-
nah (frontispiece).
Brother and sister
strongly resemble
each other, but
her long, heavy-
lidded gaze seems
as benign as his
seems sly. The
Dunkarton por-
trait on the right
suggests what
twenty more years
of envy and dissi-
pation would do to
this intelligent
young face.

demanding that the Lord Chamberlain suppress its antics. Rich, silent man, did not defend himself, but continued to spin his web of color and scene and music and eloquent gesture, and to pocket his profits.

As Covent Garden grew more successful, Garrick grew more intransigent, showing traces of the pedantry that had blighted Thomas Sheridan's career, who despised the vulgar portion of his audience and saw his theater as a school for teaching the lower orders better manners and more refined taste. Penurious about stage decoration, Garrick was altogether tone deaf when it came to music. As Davies put it, "a taste for music, or even a tolerable ear for a song was not among Mr Garrick's endowments."[1] Not only had he a low opinion of music and musicians in general, but he particularly abhorred his resident composer and director, Thomas Arne, who violated every one of Garrick's principles of decency. Arne was a rapacious exploiter of women, and consumed by a cold, depersonalized lechery. "He could not pass any woman on the street without concupiscence,"[2] wrote Burney, who always held his own wife's arm firmly when she accompanied him to or from his work at Drury Lane, lest Arne, seeing her unattended, attempt, and all with no sign of recognition, to pull her into a closet or alley. One of the few souls who never stopped defending Arne and advancing his interests was his sister. Susannah served as mediator between her brother and Garrick, since the latter's aversion was so intense he could only deal with Arne through another or by letter.

After Arne had abandoned Cecilia in Dublin where they had gone on tour in 1755,[3] he returned to England in the company of his most promising pupil, Charlotte Brent (1735–1802). Two years later, when he was satisfied her voice was ready, he approached Garrick, through Susannah, to hear her and consider hiring her as a major attraction. Garrick said he had all the singers and all the music he wanted at Drury Lane. Susannah pressed him. Would he at least hear Miss Brent? Garrick consented. When the audition was over he told Susannah to inform her brother that Miss Brent would not do. She was ugly, coarse, and awkward. But had he not admired her voice? Susannah asked. As to that, Garrick replied, Miss Brent ought to seek a living in opera, concert halls, or pleasure gardens, where "sing song," Garrick's phrase for all vocal music,[4] was everything. In a theater the entire presence of a performer was important: voice, figure, grace, expression. In spite of Garrick's rejection, Susannah and Garrick's other musical friends continued to plead for Charlotte Brent, for when she opened her mouth her limitations were forgotten. She had a sumptuous voice of great range, color, and nuance. "Though she owed a great deal to nature," Dibdin said, "she owed a great deal to Arne, without whose careful hand her singing might perhaps have been too luxuriant."[5] Garrick was unmoved: Miss Brent repelled him, and he would not work with her.*

Arne left Drury Lane and took his protégée directly to Covent Garden, where Rich hired them both, put Charlotte into a revival of *The Beggar's Opera,* engaged Arne to compose and arrange other stage music, and commissioned him to write an Italian opera for Brent and his son-in-law, the tenor Beard. When London heard Charlotte Brent sing Polly in October 1759, it was as if they had never heard Gay's opera before. Lavinia Fenton, Kitty Clive. and Susannah Cibber had been famous Pollys on the strength of their winsome personalities and sweet voices. Charlotte Brent could not act, did not charm, and was wide of Gay's purpose when she sang the simple street ballads with dazzling ornamentation and cadenzas. Yet the glorious authority of her voice silenced objection. "Her variety was incessant," Dibdin said. "Her power was resistless."[6] Garrick's temple to Shakespeare was deserted, while London ran to hear the young woman he had discarded. Rich cleared £5,000 from his *Beggar's Opera,* while Drury Lane, one gala night when both Cibber and Garrick were playing, took in exactly 3 pounds, 8 shillings, and 6 pence.[7]

Those years while Garrick watched the public worship false gods at Covent Garden were also a time of savage theatrical rioting. Whatever their precipitating cause, at bottom, riots in the theaters were a symptom of the larger social unrest which culminated in

---

* Poor Brent, living before the age of recorded sound, is remembered today mainly through anecdotes about her physical repulsiveness. Among her other burdens she suffered from halitosis. When someone asked the player-wit Samuel Foote what he thought of her version of a new song, he replied that he found the words pretty, but could hardly "relish the air." William Cooke, *Memoirs of Samuel Foote, Esq.*, 3 vols. (London, 1805), vol. 2, p. 80.

On February 24, 1763, opening night of Arne's Italian opera
Artaxerxes, *a riot was sparked off by Covent Garden management's refusal to follow custom and admit people for half price
after the third act. The theater was very nearly destroyed.*

*In the center of the stage, wearing a turban, stands John
Beard, popular tenor, son-in-law of John Rich, and co-manager
of Covent Garden. On one side of him, Arne's protégée, Charlotte Brent, is fanning herself and seems ready to faint. On
the other side, arms spread placatingly to the audience, stands
the opera's composer, lean and hungry Thomas Arne.*

revolution in France and America. In Britain the lid was never
sealed down as tightly upon the people's grievances as it was in
France. There were many small opportunities — often absurd — for
the mob to boil over, and these occasions were treated in general by
British authority with extraordinary and even foolhardy license and
lack of panic. "It was this refusal to believe in the . . . seriously ill
intentions of [the restless lower classes] which saved the English
aristocracy," said T. H. White. "They refused to have the sense to
realize that they were in danger, and the Mob, for lack of being
taken seriously, remained comic."[8] The threat to life and property
affected Covent Garden just as seriously as Drury Lane. In fact, the

most famous and destructive riot in British theatrical history took place in 1763 at Covent Garden at a performance of Arne's *Artaxerxes,* the Italian opera Rich had commissioned. Garrick found the mob more personally upsetting than his brother manager. His theater was an extension of himself. His belief in the drama's almost sacred civic importance had transformed old Drury Lane from a hangout for drunks and bawds, where the upper classes came to prowl for low adventures, into a chaste meeting place for all classes and both sexes. Here every citizen could feel pleasure without vice, the exhilaration of heroic deeds, the salutary release of tears, and could celebrate the glory of the English tongue. The materialization in his pit of that hundred-eyed monster, reeking of gin and trying to climb over his footlights armed with jagged staves, was more than a threat to Garrick's property. It was a glimpse into hell, a repudiation of his conviction that the anarchic, bestial side of human nature could be mollified by laughter and morally redeemed by the example of the noble and the beautiful.

At the end of the 1762–63 season he decided to lay down his duties at Drury Lane and give Londoners a holiday from him, and himself a respite from them, while he tried the restorative effects of Europe's famous spas, beauties, and antiquities. When he wrote Susannah in August he explained his decision entirely in terms of his health: "I have been advised by several Physicians, at ye Head of which I reckon Dr Barry,* to give myself a Winter's Respite; I have dearly earned it."9 Two weeks later he and Eva Marie left London bound for Dover and Boulogne. The *London Chronicle* printed a fanciful account of their departure:

> Yesterday departed this Kingdom, to the inexpressible Grief of Drury Lane, David Garrick, Esq.; Poet, Painter and Philosopher; Musician, Manager and Mimic; Critic, Censor and Composer, and Professor of Tragedy, Comedy and Farce. . . . His Chariot was attended out of Town by innumerable Sons of the Buskin and a prodigious Train of Danglers on the Sock — Mr Holland in the Character of Tragedy was drest in a deep suit of Mourning, and poor Mrs Cibber had her hair all dishevel'd, representing a Picture

---

* Their old friend from Dublin, now practicing in London.

of the greatest Distress — A universal silence for a long time reigned thro' the cavalcade, which Mrs Clive at last broke by an exclamation of G–d's Bl—d! and a rivulet of tears.[10]

Actually, Susannah's grief at Garrick's departure was not so abandoned as the *London Chronicle*'s fantasy suggests. She was at West Woodhay when he left, and there she stayed until she and Molly and Sloper went to Bath for the winter, so frail and emaciated that she was relieved to have a season's reprieve. She was far too depleted to muster the energy to develop with young Charles Holland or William Powell, who were dividing the capital parts at Drury Lane, the intense rapport she shared with Garrick.

From Paris, from Naples, from Venice, and from Rome, Garrick wrote his friends of his social triumphs and of the beauties of nature and old ruins. But he never forgot his theater and his "children" there. "News! News!" he begged his correspondents. "No news from Cibber? What of Yates?"[11] And, "How do Holland and Powell agree? Jealous? Clive, I suppose, more fussucky than ever?"[12]

He was indignant to learn that Susannah had not come back to work after he left, but was wintering in Bath. "Mrs Cibber, I find, is still prudent," he wrote young George Colman, his deputy manager, "and will run no risques of reputation to support poor Old Drury, to whom she has many, many obligations."[13] His own health and Eva Marie's figured prominently and saltily in his letters. But Susannah's chronic delicacy had always made him impatient. He was not one of those who called her a malingerer, but he did suspect that her trouble was brought on by nerves and melancholy. Whenever he faced the subject of her health in a letter to her, he assumed a kind of avuncular heartiness. "I am sorry to hear you are so thin," he had written her just before he left England, "but congratulate you at ye same time upon ye return of your Spirits, for be assured that your flesh will not be long after them — laugh and be fat all ye world over."[14]

The Garricks were gone a year and a half and returned to England in the spring of 1765. Garrick let Colman finish off the season. He was not sure how many of his old responsibilities he wanted to pick up. Perhaps he would act but sell his share of the patent. Perhaps he would resume the management of Drury Lane and leave the exhaustion of playing to Holland and Powell. Then again he might give up the theater entirely and retire to his villa at Hampton. He was rich enough to play the role of country gentleman for the rest of his days, writing his memoirs, weeding through his correspondence, entertaining his old friends from the British aristocracy and literati and his new friends from Europe, and improving his grounds with more grottoes and ruins and temples to Shakespeare.

But he could not get the theater out of his mind. What he really wanted was to be ordered back by a royal command, which would vanquish his reluctance and assuage his amour propre. All this required negotiations, beginning with a letter to his friend at court, Richard Berenger, Gentleman of the Horse, which was intended to reach the attention of Nicholas Ramus, Senior Page of the Backstairs, in charge of the King's entertainment. It read, ". . . You know I had some time ago labour'd so much that I was obliged to retire from the fatigues of the theatre. . . . I had determined to give up Acting. . . . This, sir, was my Resolution, which can only be broke through by a Command; which my Duty, my Pride, my Inclination and my Gratitude will always make me obey."[15]

While Garrick was angling for a royal command he was engaged in equally sensitive negotiations with Susannah Cibber. She must be with him when he returned to the stage, but since his public position was that his acting days were over, he must persuade her back while making no commitments himself until the King's move. In August he wrote her at West Woodhay to hope she was well and planning to perform in the fall. The company sorely needed her. As for himself, he said, he was torn between a sense of duty toward his old mates, and his selfish inclination to rest and look after himself and let the rudderless troupe find its own way. What he most regretted about retirement, he added playfully, was that it would mean that all their years of lovemaking were over.

She replied:

I have friendship enough for you to wish to know particulars with regard to your health, which you were lazy enough never to mention, yet could cruelly knock me down with hinting all our amours

The interior of the theatre royal at Drury Lane in 1775.

While they wait for their tea, the Garricks relax before Shake-speare's Temple at their villa at Hampton. The Temple, like all the improvements of Garrick's country property, was built with profits from Drury Lane. The dogs are family pets, the little boy may be a nephew. Childless, Garrick was paternally fond of his own and his wife's nieces and nephews, and indeed of all children. Painting by John Zoffany.

were at an end, and if I had any thought of playing the fool again it should be by myself. This is so unpleasing a situation that I believe, like yourself, I shall take care of number one, and leave them a clear stage and all the favour they can get; for my health is at present so indifferent, and my inducements to join them so demolished with your barbarous resolution, that I must wait for a fresh recruit of strength and spirits before I can venture upon so formidable an undertaking as attempting to prop others when I am in danger of tumbling down myself.[16]

Susannah's letter made it clear that no appeal to vanity or to her sense of duty to Old Drury would bring her back to London. To persuade her, he was going to have to court her, visit her in Berkshire as she so persistently begged him, be more candid about his own intentions, and above all, let her know how much he esteemed and needed her. The letter he now wrote so pleased her that she responded in a tone of exhilaration we have not seen since the letter she dashed off to her brother years ago when Garrick, still a bachelor, was visiting her for the first time at West Woodhay.

Dear Sir,

If I had followed my inclinations, I should have immediately returned you thanks for your most agreeable and kind letter, as I was then overflowing with gratitude for the most flattering commendations I ever had in my life. But as they unfortunately had the usual effect of all undeserved praises, (that is, as they made me for some time as conceited as the d—l,) I thought it best to reserve my acknowledgments till I was able to express myself like a reasonable creature.

You cannot imagine how much we are obliged to you and sweet Mrs Garrick, for your kind intentions of looking upon us at Woodhay. To be sure, this is not the right season of the year to show the lions. But let things make what appearance they will without doors, I believe I may say without vanity, true wit and humour reign within. . . . Our common way of passing our time is in lively jokes, smart repartees, etc. We have it at our finger's ends, and are not only witty ourselves, but, as Falstaff says, are the cause of wit in others. My very parrot is the wonder of the time!; equally excellent in the sock or buskin, and when you come, shall cut a joke and tip you a tragedy stiffle that will make your very foretop stand on end. As I hoped to be saved! I have taught him to speak tragedy. . . .

And now, Sir, let me tell you, I should be excessively shocked at your intention of quitting the stage, if I did not hope that the judgment, taste, and authority of that great Personage you hint at, would put it out of your power to keep such a barbarous resolution! . . . Be as ill natured as you please, but depend upon it, there are those who will never suffer such *talent* as *yours* to be long hid, and my comfort is, they will force you to shine whether you like it or not. . . .

I am sensible how much better you can employ your time than in reading and answering my nonsense. But when you are kicking your heels at the fire, and have nothing else to do, to remember your friends is not ill-timed, amongst whom no one is more warmly and sincerely so than,

Dear Sir, your ever affectionate and obedient servant,

S. CIBBER

Mr Sloper and my daughter's best compliments wait on Mrs Garrick and you.

P.S. I hope you remember that I have lost poor little Swivel-eye that was blind, and also that you promised me a dog that could see. If Biddzy* has any children, I should be infinitely obliged to Mrs Garrick and you if you would be so good to spare me one.[17]

Chilly fall weather or not, the Garricks did visit West Woodhay, and Garrick came away with Susannah's promise that she would follow him to London as soon as she was strong enough. His rare visits to Sloper's country seat were never ones Garrick bragged about. He mentioned this one not at all in his letters and therefore we have no idea of his reaction to Susannah's appearance. Charles Burney, though, who came to visit her at about the same time as the Garricks, saw at once that she was dying. Like Garrick he had been abroad and had not seen her for some time. He brought with him to West

* The Garricks, who were childless, always kept dogs, of whom they were very fond.

Woodhay the score of his new comic opera, *The Cunning Man*. Susannah was captivated by the part of Phoebe and told Burney she wanted to play it that winter. During the weeks of his visit they rehearsed it together every day. On Burney's part these hours were an act of love, for he saw she would never sing again on any stage: "her voice, however sweet and touching, was too much in decay, as well as her constitution."[18]

Nothing in Garrick's behavior after he left West Woodhay suggests that he had any doubts about her return to Drury Lane as his female twin, reflecting moon to his refulgent sun. His need for her, his optimistic nature, his twenty years' experience that he could always rally her, seem to have blinded him to the fact that she had slipped beyond his invigorative power. Yet he was aware that she required more than his usual hearty exhortations to support her resolve to come to town, for during October and November he instigated a more intense and affectionate correspondence than they had shared in years. In these busy weeks, as he was picking up the reins of his theatrical empire, rehearsing for the command performance (Benedick in *Much Ado About Nothing*) with which His Majesty had at last obliged him, he still managed to write her long and frequent letters. Something was warning him not to let go.

Garrick's command performance on November 14 was all he could have wished: a vast, emotional crowd, the King and Queen in their box, and a tumultuous ovation after the curtain. He wrote Susannah at once about his triumph. She replied that he had been "the subject of my thoughts and discourse the whole day" of the performance, and that at six o'clock, curtain time,

I obeyed your commands and had for you all the feelings of a sincere friend. As your imaginary apprehensions are now all over, give me leave to congratulate you upon the infinite pleasure you have given and received, for there is not the least doubt of these being the assured consequence of your appearance again in public. I always highly honored and loved his Majesty for his sweet disposition and many amiable qualities, but am now charmed to find he has added so noble a one to those he already possessed, as openly to profess himself the admirer and patron of merit.

She said she longed to hear Garrick's prologue, and here she could not resist a little cadenza of erudition: "I have taken it into my head that you have planned it upon Horace's First Epistle to Maecenas, as it is so strikingly applicable and fine for your purpose."[19] Garrick copied out his prologue for her and enclosed it in his next. She wrote him to express her admiration for it, and to promise that she would keep the copy sacred.

The single subject of the correspondence between Susannah and Garrick that fall was his triumph and her admiration. She said nothing of her own life, and very little about her health. When she did mention it, it was in disparaging and apologetic terms. "I sometimes fear I shall not be able to venture the fatigues of the stage till toward Christmas," she wrote him wistfully in October. "But I am a queer, uncertain animal and a week or ten days often make an amazing alteration in me."[20] She referred to her illness as "nerves," the term she knew would most reassure Garrick, bearing out his own opinion of the root of her disorder. "I still hold my resolution of being in town on the 30th, though my nerves are plaguey ones," she wrote on November 15, and later, "I have been ill these two or three days past, but I hope I am getting better. This cold, damp weather plays the vengeance with my delicacy . . . and I wish with Lady Townshend that my nerves were made of cart ropes."[21]

True to her word she left West Woodhay on November 29, lay that night at Reading, and reached her town house in Scotland Yard next day at dinner time. As soon as Garrick learned of her arrival he called on her and they agreed to do *Venice Preserved* as their first vehicle. He was confident enough of her health when he left her house to send a puff to the press saying, "Mrs Cibber is come to town and so well recovered as to be able to appear in Belvidera the latter end of the week."[22]

But the King had a better idea. Though it had taken many weeks and many hints from Garrick's friends at court before His Majesty perceived that it was his duty to be Garrick's particular patron this season, now that he understood what was required of him he was doggedly enthusiastic. As soon as he learned that Mrs. Cibber was in town, he had word sent to Drury Lane that he would be in the theater Thursday next to honor her and Garrick together, and he wanted to see a comedy. (*Venice Preserved* always put George III to sleep.) What the King meant by a comedy was the kind of play Shakespeare, Ben Jonson, and the Restoration wits had written about frustrated lovers, mistaken identities, intrigues, clowns, and cuckolds. It was a genre totally antithetical to Susannah's nature, and the King's request reduced her choice and Garrick's to one play, *The Provoked Wife.*

Vanbrugh's play concerns a lovely, high-spirited young woman, wretchedly married to Sir John Brute, who not only neglects, but loathes and even physically assaults her. Meanwhile she is being tenderly wooed by Constant, a perfect lover, discreet, eloquent, patient, and faithful, and although she has not yet become his mistress, the idea of doing so is gaining more and more appeal. Even in the considerably cut and tidied version which Garrick and Cibber played, the statement remains: if a husband makes his wife unhappy she has a right to find comfort with a man who will cherish her.

That *The Provoked Wife* was played at all in the eighteenth century is surprising, for of all the Restoration comedies it was the most difficult to reconcile with sentimental drama, where the suffering of women at the hands of men had only two admissable resolutions: in tragedy, death; in comedy, a last minute convulsion of remorse on the part of the oppressor. But Lady Brute is neither ready to die nor in the least reconciled to her life as a battered wife. "What did I vow?" she asks herself, remembering her marriage promises but yearning for Constant. "I think I swore to be true to my husband. And he promised to be kind to me. But he hasn't kept his word. Why, then, I'm absolved from mine!"[23]

Susannah Cibber's passionate fondness for Lady Brute surprised her contemporaries, since she specialized in long-suffering ladies. Of course, in the years immediately after her elopement with Sloper, her private situation lent poignancy to the role. But long after Theo had become a hollow threat, and she and Sloper an established, if irregular, couple, she continued to play Lady Brute with special animation. Like her own, Lady Brute's was a world where husbands are varlets and lovers are saviors, faithful till death.

On Thursday, December 5, she and Garrick played Sir John and Lady Brute before Their Majesties. An old friend of hers, Benjamin

By His MAJESTY's Company,
At the Theatre Royal in *Drury-Lane*,
This present *FRIDAY*, the 13th of *December*, 1765
Will be presented a COMEDY, call'd

The PROVOK'D WIFE.

Sir *JOHN BRUTE*
By Mr. GARRICK,
Constant by Mr. HAVARD,
Heartfree by Mr. PALMER,
Col. *Bully* (with a Song) Mr. Vernon,
Lord *Rake* by Mr. ACKMAN,
Razor by Mr. YATES,
Lady *Fanciful* by Mrs. ABINGTON,
Mademoiselle by Mrs. CROSS,
Belinda by Mrs. PALMER,
Lady *Brute* by Mrs. CIBBER.
TO WHICH WILL BE ADDED,

The MUSICAL LADY.

Mask by Mr. KING,
Old Mask by Mr. YATES,
Freeman by Mr. PACKER,
Lady *Scrape* Mrs. BENNET,   *Laundress* Mrs. BRADHAW,
The *Musical Lady* by Miss POPE.
To conclude with a COUNTRY DANCE.
†‡† *Ladies are desired to send their Servants by Three o'Clock to keep*
Places, to prevent Mistakes.
Places for the Boxes to be had of Mr. JOHNSTON, at the Stage-Door.
** *No Money to be received at the Stage-Door, nor any Money returned*
after the Curtain is drawn up.   *Vivant Rex & Regina.*

To-morrow, (the 4th *Day*) The PLAIN DEALER;
With (*Not acted This Season*) The FAIRY TALE.

A playbill for The Provoked Wife *printed before Mrs. Cibber collapsed*
after the play on December 5. The performance on December 13 never
took place.

Scotland Yard, around 1800. Susannah Cibber's last town house
was in this quiet court, and here she died.

Victor, was watching in the wings. He had returned to England after his Dublin disasters, and taken the post of treasurer at Drury Lane when William Pritchard died. He had known Susannah since she was a shy young singer in her teens. Tonight, her voice flagged and grew inaudible. Her tremor, which resembled a perpetual, mournful shaking of her head from side to side, obliterated the expressive intention of her movements. Victor wrote, "it was the last, and, I am sorry to say, the worst performance of her life."[24] She was helped to her house after the play and never left it again.

Meanwhile, in Bath, James Quin was dying. He had been gouty and obese and dyspeptic for years, but now a "mortification" had set into his hand.[25] As his pain intensified, this proud old prince of the stage began to dread lest he be unable to stay in character, to maintain the stately phlegm which had been his hallmark for half a century. He murmured that "he wished the last tragic scene was over, though he hoped he should be able to go through it with becoming dignity."[26] Quin's last curtain was rung down on January 14, 1766.

Susannah survived her old cavalier by two weeks. She died on

January 30, aged fifty-one. When they brought Garrick word he exclaimed, "then half of Tragedy is dead!" So closely had she incorporated him that he could not think of her passing as the loss of an
ally, but as an amputation. He ordered Drury Lane closed that night.
More surprisingly, Covent Garden was dark, too. It was an unprecedented honor for a player, for performances were customarily canceled only for deaths of royalty or military heroes, and no such
observations had marked the recent passings of James Quin, John
Rich, or Colley Cibber.

On Monday night, February 3, Susannah's body was interred by
torchlight in the North Cloister of Westminster Abbey in the presence of Sloper, Molly, and a crowd of politicians, literati, and stage
people. Though she was buried in a bastion of Anglican respectability, all that week a note fluttered on the door of the Portuguese
embassy chapel asking those who passed by to pray for the soul of
Susannah Maria Cibber.

The physicians who had helped her so little in her lifetime came into
their own after her death. Following the autopsy they issued several
learned if conflicting reports. One stated that she had been carried
off by "a bilious colick," another that she had suffered "a rupture of
one of the linings of the stomach," a third, that her illness stemmed
from "worms of the stomach." This last seems unlikely — parasites
were common in those days, and might have compounded the problems of a debilitated person, but they were rarely a primary cause of
death and could scarcely account for Susannah's severe attacks for
twenty years. Even the phrase, "worms of the stomach," may play
tricks on us. The discovery of bacteria as a cause of disease was nearly
a century away, but doctors had long believed that illness was carried
on night winds or the vapors from graves or sewers. They thought
that the process of decay spontaneously generated invisible animal-
culi, called worms, which swirled in these noxious airs, ready to
penetrate the human body at any of its openings. Therefore, any
organ or part of the body which was inflamed or mortifying was said
to be afflicted with worms.[27] A person with abscessed teeth suffered
from "worms of the gums," and the Scots to this day call toothache
"the worm," just as we still call the common skin fungus "ring-

worm." Susannah's physicians' phrases may have been descriptive not of parasites but of the morbid condition of her stomach.

Susannah's daughter never believed any of the doctors' explanations of her mother's malady. She maintained that Susannah, constitutionally delicate, had been fatally weakened by Sir Noah Thomas's sea bathing treatments at Scarborough, to which she had always submitted with great terror and suffering, and which, the last summer of her life, gave her such chills and convulsions that she was days recovering from each immersion.[28]

We will never diagnose Susannah's chronic stomach disorder from her doctors' statements, or her own euphemistic letters which never give us anything so vulgar as a symptom. But whether she suffered from gall-bladder disease, ulcers, or colitis, it seems certain she was never a malingerer as her detractors insisted. Far from using illness as an excuse to avoid performing, she drove herself to perform when she was too ill to attempt it. And yet her disease may well have had its origin in her personality, which was perfectionistic, stoical, impenetrably amiable, fearful of anger in others and incapable of displaying it herself, accommodating and ingratiating, as if forever warding off attack.

After Susannah's death, William Sloper resigned his office as Commissioner for Trade and Plantations for the American Colonies,[29] and retired with Molly to West Woodhay. In August 1767, Molly was married there in the church her grandfather had built. Her older half brother, William Charles, was witness to the ceremony.[30] She was twenty-eight, sole heiress to her mother's fortune. Her husband was the Reverend James Burton, Esquire, of Crux Easton, Hampshire, a well-born young man with land in Hampshire and Wiltshire. Like the Garricks, the Burtons were to be childless, and devoted to one another.

Sloper's neighbor, Lord Craven, gave Burton a living on his estate at Benham, only a few miles from West Woodhay. Lady Craven, youngest daughter of the Earl of Berkeley, was another of Charles II's high spirited and imperious descendants. Next to her love affairs she devoted her energies to her theatricals, in most of which she played the leading role. She was delighted to add the daughter of the legendary Susannah Cibber to her household circle.

Mrs. Burton's speaking voice was indistinguishable from her mother's. She dressed exquisitely, wearing her mother's diamonds, and she had her mother's figure and manners. That, unlike her mother, she was plain and had no aspiration to leading roles in the Benham theatricals may have added to Lady Craven's fondness for her.

Molly's life was everything her mother had dreamed for her. Marriage to a well-born clergyman had effectively expunged the bar sinister of her birth. Her manners, her musical accomplishments, her wealth and taste made her an ornament in any company. And her romantic birth and precocious girlhood, tutored and petted by the literary and musical and dramatic giants of the last generation, added an exotic but perfectly harmless aura. Peg Woffington had created a Restoration comedy heroine of her younger sister. Susannah Cibber, who did not live to see it, achieved something of the same triumph in her daughter: a Georgian bourgeois lady, domestic, accomplished, devoted to her husband and to charitable works. Like her mother, Molly was delicate, and she died in 1786, at forty-six. Her inconsolable husband survived her by twenty-six years, never remarried, and was buried in the same grave with her in the chapel of their manor at Holt.

Burton's will scrupulously distinguished between the two sources of his wealth. To his nephews and their issue he left his own inherited lands and holdings. But Molly's fortune he distributed in a highly personal manner as a memorial to her. First, he remembered the women who had been her special friends or nursed her during her long, last illness.

I give and bequeath to Lady Marsh, the widow of Sir Charles Marsh, of Reading, Berks., Knight, the sum of three hundred pounds of lawful British money as a Pledge of the Friendship and Esteem I had for her in my life, at the same time bearing in mind her extreme, friendly attention to my late, dear Wife during a very long illness. . . . I give and bequeath to Miss Amelia Goddard . . . all my Capital or Share in the Stock or Fund called the three per cent consolidated Bank Annuities transferrable at the Bank of England, together with the Interest and Dividends due thereon at the time of my decease. I also give and bequeath to the same Amelia Goddard

the Sum of Five hundred Pounds of lawful English money . . .
likewise . . . all my late Dear Wife's Rings, Diamonds and Trinkets
of every sort and kind, together with four Silver Salt Cellars, one
pair of Silver Candlesticks, one Silver Candlestick for a wax light,
one Dozen of Silver handled Knives and Forks, one Dozen of large
Silver Spoons, Two Gravy Spoons, and the smallest silver Cruet
Stand, the large Mahogany Drawers with the top which stands in
my Breakfast room, two little Tent Beds with Check Furniture, my
late dear Wife's enamelled Watch which I constantly wear.[31]

These friends of his wife remembered, Burton distributed over
£2,000 to a dozen needy women, old and young, widows, spinsters,
and young girls without dowries. Forty-six years after her death, the
fortune of Susannah Cibber, disreputable Papist actress, was scattered
by a tenderhearted Anglican clergyman who had never known her,
but in a way that would have pleased her: first, to reward those who
had been kind to her child, and next, to relieve the helplessness of
twelve women who certainly never suspected the real origin of their
blessing.

William Sloper survived his daughter by three years, vigorous to
the end. Lady Craven always remembered him.

I had a neighbor in Berkshire [she wrote in her memoirs], who was
nearly 90 years of age, Mr Sloper, who . . . passed his life in retirement after the death of the celebrated actress, Mrs Cibber, to whom
he had been for many years attached. . . . This old gentleman was
quite of the vieille cour in his manners and exterior. He was extremely fond of reading since he had withdrawn himself from
London and the world. . . . He took such a fancy to me that he
would come and stay at Benham two or three days together. . . .
I considered him an old book full of information and entertainment, and of anecdotes of nearly a century past. He thought nothing
of walking four miles to Benham and back again within the twenty
four hours.[32]

Lady Craven attributed Sloper's visits to his infatuation with
her. In a sense she was right. Only a few miles from the solitude of
his library at West Woodhay this charming woman ruled over a

bustling theater. The house guests at Benham ranged from stage-struck noblemen and ladies, nervously memorizing lines in the corners of rooms, to musicians and players and scene painters hired down from London for a production. Lady Craven's two favorite roles had been Susannah's, too: Zara and Lady Brute. Sitting quietly at rehearsals Sloper could hear the old lines again. At meals he could talk to young players to whom the name Susannah Cibber was magical, and the history of his love and constancy a legend.

After he died at West Woodhay in 1789, his sons found a private will written in his own hand. Like his own father's, it was brief and direct, leaving everything to Sir Robert and William Charles, whom he also named executors. His fortune he had already settled on them to help them raise their families in comfort, so there was little to do but divide the land, his household effects, his farm equipment and carriages. The manor house, which he called "The Belvidere," and its fourteen hundred acres went to Sir Robert. The spacious parsonage and some land in Wiltshire went to William Charles. The old man wrote that he thought there would be no debts to worry them since "I always pay my bills as soon as I can get them in."

There was only one piece of unfinished business he would have to leave to their trouble:

> My Request is that in less than a fortnight after my death the following old Horses may be killed, and that Wm. Hamblin, my present Bailiff may shoot them and to have the Flesh and Skins for himself. The Names of the Horses to be shot: Captain, an old Bay Horse, long tail, Pedlar, an old Bay Horse, long tail, Poppet, a black Horse, short docked, Crop, a crop't eared Mr Beckford gave me. The first three mentioned I have had a number of years and their work is done. I promised Mr Beckford when he pressed me to take his old horse I would order him to be shot when I died.[33]

After William Sloper's death, Sir Robert — back from India under a cloud — moved into West Woodhay. He and Lady Sloper were joined by Sir Robert's mother, Catherine Sloper, who had been living for the last half century in her South Audley Street house in London. Now that they were ensconced at West Woodhay, William

Sloper's ancient widow and daughter-in-law destroyed every letter, picture, every memento, every piece of evidence of the thirty-year incumbency of Susannah Cibber. Catherine Sloper died in 1797 at the age of ninety. Sixty years after her husband had left her, his grave was opened at her request and her body placed beside his in the family church.

There is aptness and some irony in the last resting places of the four chief actors in the Sloper-Cibber drama. The atoms of Theophilus Cibber belong to the wind and waves. William Sloper sleeps within the bosom of the land he loved, but his dust mingles with that of the woman he had left forever for another. And Susannah Cibber's mortal remains rest in an alien church, near the door of the North Cloister of Westminster Abbey, under a pile of dusty workmen's scaffolding. Her life was a sustained and eloquent supplication for acceptance in the British establishment. Yet she lies, not like Garrick or Congreve or Dryden or Mrs. Oldfield, theater's royalty, within the Abbey itself, but in an anteroom of fame, within the sound of ceremony, neither remembered nor utterly forgotten, not really a private person nor quite a public figure.

Epilogue

We found king cups in the Belvidere Wood, that sinister place of box
and yew, still holding memories of Sloper misdeeds.
— MARY H. McCLINTOCK, *Portrait of a House*

FOR several years before the American Revolution, Benjamin
Franklin lived in London as agent for the colonies. Among
his English friends was William Shipley, Bishop of St.
Asaph. This able, outspoken man had been slated to be Archbishop
of Canterbury until his radical views about religious dissenters and
the American colonies antagonized George III, who passed him over
and kept him out of harm's way in his remote Welsh diocese. In
1771, Bishop Shipley invited Franklin to spend a part of August with
him at his summer place in Twyford. Franklin gladly came. He
loved the good bishop, his wife and five lively daughters. The Shipley
girls could never hear enough of his boyhood and travels in faraway
America. Partly at their instigation and for their pleasure, he began
to write his autobiography in the mornings at Twyford, before the
family gathered in the garden for lunch.

When he drove back to London Franklin had under his wing
the youngest Shipley, eleven-year-old Kitty, who was returning, reluctantly, to school. As soon as he had set her safely down and
reached his house he wrote her mother:

Dear Madam, this is just to let you know that we arrived safe and well in Marlborough Street about six, where I delivered up my charge.

The above seems too short for a letter, so I will lengthen it by a little account of our journey. The first stage we were rather pensive. I tried several Topics of Conversation, but none of them would hold. But after Breakfast we began to recover Spirits and had a good deal of Chat. Will you hear some of it? We talked of her brother and she wished he were married. And don't you wish your sisters married too? Yes, all but Emily; I would not have her married. Why? Because I can't spare her, I can't part with her. The rest may marry as soon as they please, so they do but get good husbands. We then took upon us to consider . . . what sort of husbands would be fittest for every one of them. We began with Georgiana. She thought a country gentleman that loved traveling and would take her with him. . . . I added, that had a good estate and was a Member of Parliament. . . . This she agreed to; so we set him down for Georgiana and went on to Betsy. Betsy, says I, seems of a mild, sweet Temper, and if we should give her a Country Squire and he should happen to be of a rough, passionate Turn, and be angry now and then, it might break her Heart. Oh, none of them must be so, for then they would not be good Husbands. . . . Then suppose we give her a good, honest, sensible City Merchant, who will love her dearly and is very rich? I don't know but that may do. We proceeded to Emily, her dear Emily. I was afraid we should hardly find anything good enough for Emily, but at last . . . we agreed that, as Emily was very handsome we might expect an Earl for her. . . . We went on to Anna Maria. She, says Kitty, should have a rich man that has a large family and a great many things to take care of; for she is very good at managing, helps my Mama very much, can look over Bills and order all sorts of Family Business. Very well, what do you think of giving her a Duke? Oh no! I'll have the Duke for Emily. You may give the Earl to Anna Maria if you please: but Emily shall have the Duke.[1]

Kitty's dear Emily did not marry a duke or even an earl. Three years after Franklin's and Kitty's journey, Emily Shipley married William Charles Sloper, and when the American war was over and the Shipleys and Franklin could resume their affectionate correspondence, Kitty wrote him in Philadelphia that Emily "had done much better for herself than if she had married the Duke we allotted to her on our journey."[2] Like his father and grandfather, this third William Sloper went into politics, and served as M.P. from St. Albans, Hampshire, in the sixteenth Parliament.[3] He was an ardent Whig like his forebears: his grandfather had been a Walpole man, his father a protégé of Fox, and this William Sloper attached himself to the interests of his wife's noble relations, the powerful Spencer family.

The wealth and influence of the Slopers waned after the generation of Sir Robert and William Charles. The latter had but one child, a daughter, while Sir Robert was cursed with too many offspring. Besides his children by Jane (Willes) he had a younger, illegitimate family whom he conscientiously educated at Cambridge and Oxford and set up in the world with church livings and army commissions. It was probably this large, expensive family that tempted him into dishonesty in India. After he had replaced Sloper in Madras, Lord Cornwallis wrote: "Having a number of hungry dependents was the Rock that Sloper split upon, who, I sincerely believe, came out with very upright intentions."[4]

The Sloper and Shipley families maintained their habit of intermarrying and their close connections. In June 1829, John Sloper, the present squire of West Woodhay, invited his cousin, the Reverend Augustus Hare (son of Georgiana Shipley, for whose husband Franklin and Kitty had once proposed a travel-loving country squire, M.P.) to spend his honeymoon at West Woodhay. John Sloper, Sir Robert's grandson, was a bachelor of thirty, a sportsman and farmer. His half uncle, George Stokes Sloper, one of Sir Robert's natural sons, was rector at West Woodhay, absent most of the time and at odds with his nephew. One of the reasons John was so anxious to have his cousin Augustus come stay all summer was to take over West Woodhay's pastoral chores.

The bride, Maria Hare, loved West Woodhay from the moment she saw it; and her letters home described the old house in detail:

> It is the perfection of an old manor — the house very large, which in this hot weather is very agreeable. . . . The drawing room where

I now write is a capital room, very well furnished, with three windows down to the ground opening on a long lawn running up to the hills, with trees on each side — roses clustering in at the windows, and all looking so retired I should almost say lonely. Then there is a very nice dining room and sitting room for Augustus, besides a great hall and small library; and upstairs my room is magnificent, and there is a large tapestried chamber with family pictures. I don't know how we are to come down to rectory accommodations afterwards.[5]

Before the Hares had been two days at West Woodhay, Mary Lea, Maria's lady's maid, told her mistress that the servants said the house had been the scene of scandal back in the days of Mr. John Sloper's great-grandfather and was haunted by guilty spirits. The bride was amused by this gossip, never aware of any malevolent emanations, and sensed nothing about the old house but a dreaming benignity. Catherine Sloper and Lady Sloper had done their work well. Maria Hare never heard the name Susannah Cibber while she was at West Woodhay.

Mrs. Hare was very moved by the natural beauty around her. She could not comprehend how Mr. Sloper could live in the midst of such loveliness and walk with his head down, kicking the grass, or squinting up at the clouds for signs of rain. Her husband explained that they had come to West Woodhay at haying time, a period of great anxiety for farmers. Nonetheless, Maria was determined to enlarge this cousin's perceptions. On June 30 there was such a splendid sunset that she insisted Sloper leave his supper to attend to it. "It was a glowing sea of fire with the streams issuing out of it," she wrote home, "and the splendid battlements of clouds piled one above another closing it in. Even Mr Sloper was obliged to stand still and admire it, in spite of the ominous appearance for the hay." Mr. Sloper had reason to be apprehensive. Next day, "the heavens seemed inclined to pour out their utmost fury upon us,"[6] Maria reported, and a great deal of hay was spoiled.

The old books at West Woodhay delighted Maria. "Do you know the pleasure of hunting about in a library full of old volumes and old editions of books, all mixed in strange confusion?" she wrote.

"We found yesterday an old *Pilgrim's Progress* with queer cuts and engravings."[7] Though the Hares did not know it, they had come upon what was left of William Sloper's library, solace of his old age after Susannah and Molly were gone, now sadly disordered after generations of unbookish descendants.

Augustus Hare was horrified to discover that hardly any of the West Woodhay villagers had been confirmed; what was worse, they did not seem to know what they were missing. " 'Do you know who Jesus Christ is?' " he asked a white haired man. " 'Why, please you, your honor, I canna rightly say,' " was the reply.[8] The summer at his cousin's seat in Berkshire was like a season of missionary work in Africa. During his stay, Augustus succeeded in bringing twenty-seven rustics to Christ.*

One morning in September, Sloper told Maria that he had invited forty people to West Woodhay next day for a Bow Meeting. A little later he and his hunting dogs departed for the Downs. As was often the case he did not return that night. Next morning the Hares began nervously making preparations for the guests.

Augustus and I laid our heads together to arrange the dinner, measure the table and set in some sort of order the profusion of game which filled the larder . . . some of the party arrived while I was writing out the bill of fare. It was awkward having to receive people I never saw in my life; however, Mr Sloper returned and about 1:00 thirty six people were assembled. The day was fine and fair. The lawn, mown smooth, with the meadows and hill beyond, was just made for such a purpose. . . . Luncheon was laid at two o'clock and the shooters came on by turns. Six ladies and about 14 Gentlemen shot. Of the former, a surly looking girl who had the good wishes of none of the party, carried everything before her, and succeeded in winning the prize. . . . I had little to do but look on,

* Some heathen core must still have persisted in their natures, though, for the very next year, November 1830, the Hares were shocked to learn that the West Woodhay peasants were among the most violent participants in the machine riots that broke out in Wiltshire and Berkshire. Fearing that the new agricultural machines would destroy their livelihoods, farmer laborers broke threshers in the fields, set fires to ricks and barns, and, at West Woodhay, ransacked the lovely Sloper mansion (Hare, *Memorials of a Quiet Life* (London, 1873), vol. 1, p. 353; Ditchfield and Page (eds.), *The Victorian History of Berkshire* (London, 1906–1927), vol. 4).

and every now and then Augustus and I escaped to rest ourselves and moralize on the wearisomeness of pleasure. . . .

It was half past seven before we got to dinner in the hall. Really, considering all things, it was wonderfully well arranged and very little confusion. After dinner there were speeches and toasts and the presenting of the prize. . . . I stole out to supervise the lighting of the ball room. The Saloon upstairs was capital for this purpose. . . . About 10:00 we began dancing, and I found myself dancing away with all the gaiety — I was going to say of fifteen, but no, at fifteen I never danced with half the spirit. . . . You cannot imagine in what demand I was as a partner. You may guess how thoroughly Augustus was bored! It was nearly three o'clock before we went to supper, and four before . . . we went to bed. . . . Everybody seemed pleased. The supper was very pretty, and there was much marvel how Mr Sloper could have managed it so well. . . . It was rather amusing likening the different people to those one knows; they are exactly the sort of class described in *Emma*.[9]

Although Maria was very happy at West Woodhay, she never lost her condescension toward Augustus's country cousin and his neighbors. What a pity she did not know that in that very saloon where the fiddles had squealed and these robust provincials had leaped and clapped beneath the old Sloper portraits, Handel had played the harpsichord; Arne and his sad Cecilia, good Charles Burney, and Susannah Cibber had sung Palestrina madrigals; and Garrick had convulsed an audience of Sloper's Whig colleagues with imitations of some of their number who were not present.

Still it cannot be denied that a quality of uncouthness had crept into the Slopers of West Woodhay. If the Reverend George Sloper had let Christianity die out among his flock, one of his successors attempted to enforce church attendance by rounding up his parishioners with a shotgun. And the story goes that his cousin, the squire who had given him the living, sat in the front row of the church interrupting the sermon with a stream of blasphemy whenever he did not care for its thrust.[10] Without their connections with the great world, without political power and money from patronage, the Slopers grew poor, cantankerous, and insular. In 1880 Gerard Sloper sold West Woodhay to William Cole and went to live, it was said, in Paris.

The Coles came from yeoman stock in Norfolk. They were newly rich London importers and bankers. Alfred Cole, who owned West Woodhay from 1912 to 1921, was governor of the Bank of England. Like the first Sloper when he bought the place from the impoverished Rudyerd family, the Coles brought an infusion of bourgeois money and energy to West Woodhay. But whereas the first William Sloper had revered his seventeenth-century house, old even then, and faithfully preserved it, spending his fortune on his model village, his school and church and almshouse, William Cole immediately hired a fashionable architect, razed Sloper's severe Georgian church because it was too near the manor house and spoiled his view, and, using the existing house as the east facade, erected a Victorian Gothic castle — three more rectangles, west, north, and south — with a courtyard in the middle. Fortunately he did not change the old house substantially, merely raising the roof to a sharper pitch to accord with the additions, and frosting it with gables, cupolas, and crenellated chimneys. Writing in 1948, Mary McClintock, one of the Cole grandchildren, apologized thus for her grandfather's taste: "he had built something ugly in accordance with the taste of the day; yet in destroying some of the beauty he had given the place a quality it had not possessed for nearly two hundred years — the quality of wholesome goodness."[11]

The Coles liked to think that they had bought West Woodhay to rescue it from the Slopers. "Such a curiously unattractive lot, the Sloper men," mused this Cole granddaughter, "jealous, foul mouthed, wild and unbalanced. But what about their women folk? Not a word had come down to us about any of them."[12] Although the Coles occupied West Woodhay during the heyday of private genealogical investigations, they never explored the Slopers' history. What they heard from local gossip, and what they wanted to believe about their predecessors, was enough. The Sloper squires were transformed into Heathcliffs and Rochesters: "We heard of the wicked Mr Sloper who shut up his wife for years in one of the bed rooms,"[13]

West Woodhay, 1972.

said Mrs. McClintock, while he caroused below with his London actress.

Alas for the Coles, hungry as they were for evidence that their grand house had a proud or at least a romantic past, not to know that between 1743 and 1766 it had been a favorite stopping-off place on the road between London and Bath for wits, men of letters, statesmen, musicians, and players — though not for their wives.

One June day in 1965 when I was in London doing research for this book, I decided to drive down to Berkshire and look for West Woodhay. The last thing I had read about the place was that Alfred Cole had lent it as a Red Cross hospital in the First World War. I did not know if the house still stood or, if it did, whether it was a private residence or an institution.

Turning south off the A4 I kept an eye out, whenever there was a glimpse between the hedges, for the steep, ornamental roofs of

William Cole's monument to "wholesome goodness." Then, across a pond, I saw a seventeenth-century manor house of mellow brick with a classical stone portico. Was it possible that West Woodhay had an identical twin, unspoiled? I drove through the gates and down the avenue and stopped on the gravel below the steps. There was no one in sight. I thought of Mrs. Montagu, two hundred and twenty years ago, on just such a summer's day, sitting abashed in this same spot (or its double) and wishing herself away. Just then a little car came along the avenue and stopped near mine. A woman got out. So did I. I was looking for a place called West Woodhay, I said. This was West Woodhay, she answered, and she was the housekeeper here. She would just run inside and see if Mr. or Mrs. Henderson were about. A moment later an elegantly dressed man came down the steps. "I am Woodhead the butler, madam," he told me. Mr. Henderson was not at home, but Mrs. Henderson was. I said I had driven down from London to find the house where a family named Sloper had lived. This was the place, he said. He had a book that told all about them. If I would walk round the side of the house, I would come on the ruins of the old Sloper church and could see their graves, while he went to find Mrs. Henderson and fetch his book.

In a moment I was standing on the stone floor of the little church of St. Lawrence, chinked with myrtle and Saint-John's-wort, looking down at the gravestones of the first William Sloper and his Rebecca, of the second William and his Catherine, of Sir Robert and Jane, and of their oldest son, Robert Orby, and his Georgiana Clementina. Beyond me, wide grass fell away to the foot of the bare Downs. In the distance there were horses grazing.

I walked round the corner of the house and looked along the south side. No suggestion of a Victorian castle there, no sign in the landscaped grounds that there ever had been. Mrs. Henderson, a quick, light figure, was coming across the gravel. She apologized for keeping me waiting. She had been in the stable with an ailing horse. She said that Woodhead had explained that I was interested in the Sloper family. She was afraid she could be very little help. History was not her interest, really. Woodhead knew much more about the house than she did. He had a book, she understood, that told everything.

The house looked exactly like its eighteenth-century description, I said, and that astonished me, for I had read that it had been wrapped in a Victorian shell. Mrs. Henderson laughed. Indeed it had been, when her husband inherited it. The Coles had sold the place in 1921 to her husband's grandfather, W. H. Henderson, who left it to her husband, passing over his son because, as she put it, "my husband's father was a little bit naughty." When the young Hendersons acquired West Woodhay in 1949 it had been variously used in both wars as a hospital, a school for evacuated children, and a convalescent home. It had stood empty for long periods, and been scarred, vandalized, and neglected. Even if it had been in the best of repair, she said, it was enormous — twenty-six bedrooms and ten sitting rooms. She and her husband had wanted to tear it down and put up a small, convenient place, but they could not get permission to do so from the National Trust. What they were allowed to do was tear down the Victorian pile and restore the original house.

She asked me if I would like to come inside and wished I had let her know I was coming; she would have been happy to ask me to lunch. I apologized for appearing without the least warning, but explained that I had had no idea whether the house was still standing, much less who its owners were. We went into the dark, paneled hall, with its carved staircase. Was my book about the Sloper family? she asked. No: about Susannah Cibber, an actress who had been the mistress of one of them and lived here for over twenty years. Mrs. Henderson confessed she had never heard of her. But the local people and the servants all assured her the house was haunted. If my Mrs. Cibber were the ghost she must be a very benevolent one, for Mrs. Henderson and her family had been very happy in the house. We went into the large room that faced south toward the Downs. This was the room Maria Hare had loved, where she had written her letters on soft June afternoons like this one. The Coles had made it their formal dining room, but now it was a sitting room again, furnished with easy chairs and sofas, wide tables with magazines, flowers, and photographs of children and horses.

Despite Mrs. Henderson's graciousness, I was sure her heart was not in my talk about the past, but in the stable with her sick horse. I thought to myself that William Sloper would have approved of this lady, and indeed of everything about his home, two hundred years after his death. Though I was longing to go upstairs and see the saloon and the bedroom where Susannah had slept, I said I must be starting back to London.

Mrs. Henderson left me in the hall with Woodhead. He pressed his book into my hand. It was Mary McClintock's *Portrait of a House,* a memoir of her girlhood at West Woodhay. The book was to prove invaluable in tracing the history of the house, and suggesting the connection between the Augustus Hares and the Slopers, which I probably would never otherwise have discovered.

As we stood together on the porch, Mr. Woodhead pointed across the lawn. In the midst of the woods over there, he said, was the ruin of a pleasure pavilion called the Belvidere. One of the Slopers had built it for an actress. Nothing was left of it now but parts of its brick floor, slippery with moss, and a deep, mysterious pool. There was a secret, underground tunnel leading from this house to the Belvidere — though no one could find the entrance these days — and along it this old Sloper used to run at night to his mistress's embraces. The suppressed story of William Sloper and Susannah Cibber had retreated another step, it seemed, from Brontësque Gothic tale to this more recent burrowing into the forest. Even William Sloper's name for his mansion, Belvidere, had fled with the lovers, a name so apt for this house where I stood, with its limitless prospect of sky and hills, so preposterous for a midnight trysting place in the heart of the woods.

To have become a sort of local tutelary spirit of the land he had loved seemed an appropriate apotheosis for William Sloper, but wood nymph was a curious role for Susannah, city child, daughter of a Covent Garden tradesman, whose years at West Woodhay were only in part a respite, and more often an exile, from her London world.

Only the most unlikely shreds of her were left, a woman the least particulars of whose life had once been as avidly discussed by her countrymen as the British queen's: a name on old playbills, a grave in an unfrequented corner of the cloister at Westminster Abbey, a shadowy incarnation as a forest enchantress, and some music of Handel from which the magic of her voice may still be guessed.

With Mr. Woodhead's book on the car seat beside me, I started back to London and the task of gathering these scattered fragments and reconstituting a life.

Notes

CHAPTER 1

1. Abel Boyer, *History of the Reign of Queen Anne, Digested into Annals*, 11 vols. (London, 1703–1713), vol. 9, p. 189.
2. Richmond P. Bond, *Queen Anne's American Kings* (Oxford: Clarendon Press, 1952), pp. 2–3.
3. Richard Steele, *Tatler*, no. 171.
4. John Oldmixon, *History of England during the Reign of William and Mary, Queen Anne, and George I* (London, 1735), p. 452.
5. *Journals of the House of Commons*, George II, vol. 21 (1728), pp. 274–283.
6. *Representations of Cruelties at Marshalsea Prison, 1729* (British Museum prints and drawings), print no. 1837.
7. Richard Davey, *A History of Mourning* (London, 1889), p. 109.
8. Ibid., pp. 177–179.
9. Notes of Charles Burney for his *History of Music*, Osborn Collection, Yale University Library, box 36, item 2.

CHAPTER 2

1. Charles Burney, *A General History of Music*, 2 vols. (New York: Harcourt, Brace & Co., 1935), vol. 2, p. 1001.
2. Frederick J. Crowest, *Musicians' Wit, Humour, and Anecdote* (London: Walter Scott Publishing Co. Ltd., 1902), pp. 18–19.
3. Ibid.
4. Notes of Charles Burney for his *History of Music*, Osborn Collection, Yale University Library.
5. Ibid.
6. Ibid.
7. John Perceval Egmont (later first Earl of Egmont), Diary, British Historical Manuscripts Commission, London.
8. Burney, *General History of Music*, vol. 2, p. 1002.
9. William H. Cummings, *Dr. Arne and "Rule, Britannia"* (London: Novello & Co., 1912), preface.

CHAPTER 3

1. *Annual Register*, 1766; *London Magazine*, 1766.
2. "See and Seem Blind: or a critical Dissertation on The Public Diversions," in a letter from Lord B. to A—— H——, Esq., 1732, in Otto Erich Deutsch, *Handel, a Documentary Biography* (London: Black; New York: W. W. Norton, 1955), pp. 300–301.
3. Ibid.

4. *London Morning Advertizer*, October 7, 1743.
5. *Spectator* 18.
6. James Boaden, *Memoirs of Mrs. Siddons*, 2 vols. (London, 1827), vol. 1, p. 80.
7. Aaron Hill, *Works*, 4 vols. (London, 1754), vol. 1, pp. 174–175, December 5, 1732.
8. Charles Burney, *A General History of Music*, 2 vols. (New York: Harcourt, Brace & Co., 1935), vol. 2, p. 899.

CHAPTER 4

1. Colley Cibber, *An Apology for the Life of Colley Cibber* (London, 1740), p. 488.
2. Abel Boyer, *History of the Reign of Queen Anne, Digested into Annals*, 11 vols. (London, 1703–1713), vol. 2, p. 167.
3. Richard Hindry Barker, *Mr. Cibber of Drury Lane* (New York: Columbia University Press, 1939), p. 19. *Weekly Journal*, or *Saturday's Post*, March 1, 1718.
4. Charlotte Charke, *A Narrative of the Life of Mrs. Charlotte Charke* (London, 1755), p. 22.
5. George Anne Bellamy, *An Apology for the Life of George Anne Bellamy*, 6 vols. (London, 1785), vol. 6, p. 76.
6. Laetitia Pilkington, *Memoirs* (Dublin, 1748), pp. 168–169.
7. Aaron Hill, *The Prompter*, ed. William Appleton and Kalman Burnim (New York: Blom, 1966), November 19, 1734, pp. 7–8.
8. Thomas Davies, *Dramatic Miscellanies*, 3 vols. (London, 1785), vol. 1, p. 294.
9. *Common Sense*, June 11, 1737, attributed to Lord Chesterfield.
10. October 5, 1732.
11. January 27, 1733.
12. *Daily Post*, May 29, 1733.
13. Benjamin Victor, *A History of the Theatres of London and Dublin*, 3 vols. (London, 1761–1771), vol. 1, p. 14.
14. Tate Wilkinson, *Memoirs of His Own Life* (Yorkshire, 1790), vol. 3, p. 42.
15. *An Apology for the Life of Mr T . . . C . . . , Comedian* (London, 1740), ch. 8.

CHAPTER 5

1. *The Theatric Squabble*, Folger Library Broadside, 1733.
2. English Term Reports, King's Bench, Barnardison 2.
3. William W. Cooke, *Memoirs of Charles Macklin, Comedian* (London, 1804), p. 80.
4. Benjamin Victor, *A History of the Theatres of London and Dublin*, 3 vols. (London, 1761–1771), vol. 1, p. 34.
5. Ibid., p. 30.
6. Susannah Cibber and Anne Arne vs. T. Cibber, 1741, British Public Records Office, C. 11, bundle 1572, no. 15.

CHAPTER 6

1. Francis Truelove [pseud.], *The Comforts of Matrimony; exemplified in the memorable Case and Tryal, lately brought by Theo—s C—r, against W— S—, Esq., for criminal Conversation with the plaintiff's wife* (London, 1739), pp. 10–11.
2. *Life of James Quin* (London, 1766), p. 50.
3. Thomas Davies, *Memoirs of the Life of David Garrick*, 2 vols. (Boston, 1818), vol. 1, p. 38.
4. Ibid.
5. Ibid., p. 39.
6. William W. Appleton, *Charles Macklin, An Actor's Life* (Cambridge, Mass.: Harvard University Press, 1960), pp. 34–35.
7. J. T. Kirkman, *Memoirs of the Life of Charles Macklin, Esq.* (London, 1799), p. 141.
8. Ibid., p. 191.
9. Ibid., p. 192.
10. Ibid., p. 202.
11. Appleton, *Charles Macklin*, p. 33.
12. *London Daily Post and General Advertizer*, July 4, 1735.
13. *An Apology for the Life of Mr T . . . C . . . , Comedian* (London, 1740).
14. *Tryal of a Cause for Criminal Conversation* (London, 1739), pp. 8–9.
15. Aaron Hill, "Essay on Acting," in *Works*, 4 vols. (London, 1754), vol. 4, pp. 339–396, and *The Prompter*, December 26, 1735.
16. Abraham Rees, *Cyclopaedia*, 1st American ed., 41 vols. (Philadelphia, 1810–1824), Susannah Cibber article.

CHAPTER 7

1. Susannah Cibber and Anne Arne vs. T. Cibber, 1741, British Public Records Office, C. 11.
2. *The London Stage, 1660–1800*, William Van Lennep, Emmett L. Avery, Arthur H. Scouten, George W. Stone, Jr., and Charles B. Hogan (eds.), 11 vols., 5 pts. (Carbondale, Ill.: Southern Illinois University Press, 1968), vol. 1, pt. 3, p. 546.
3. Francis Truelove [pseud.], *The Comforts of Matrimony; exemplified in the memorable Case and Tryal, lately brought by Theo—s, C—r, against W— S—, Esq., for criminal Conversation with the plaintiff's wife* (London, 1739), pp. 12–13.
4. *Grub Street Journal*, December 30, 1736.
5. *Comforts of Matrimony*, p. 15.
6. *London Stage*, vol. 2, pt. 3, p. 626.
7. Thomas Davies, *Dramatic Miscellanies*, 3 vols. (London, 1785), vol. 1, p. 36.
8. Susannah Cibber and Anne Arne vs. T. Cibber.
9. Letter of David Mallet to Aaron Hill, February 3, 1738, 39 letters from David Mallet to Aaron Hill, 1731–1750, Harvard University Theatre Collection, Cambridge, Mass.
10. Theophilus Cibber, *Four Original Letters, viz. Two from a Husband to a Gentleman, and Two from a Husband to a Wife* (London, 1739), letter 4.
11. *Comforts of Matrimony*, p. 13.

12. Benjamin Victor, *Original Letters, Dramatic Pieces, and Poems*, 3 vols. (London, 1776), letter 8.
13. Ibid.
14. *Tryal of a Cause for Criminal Conversation* (London, 1739), p. 26.

CHAPTER 8

1. *Grub Street Journal*, June 16, 1737.
2. Diary of Benjamin Griffin (and others) for Lincoln's Inn Fields Theatre (1715–1721), Little Theatre in the Haymarket (1733–1734), and Drury Lane Theatre (1721–1738 and 1742), September 11, 1737. Egerton 2320, British Museum, London.
3. Ibid., September 17, 1737.
4. *The London Stage, 1660–1800*, William Van Lennep, Emmett L. Avery, Arthur H. Scouten, George W. Stone, Jr., and Charles B. Hogan (eds.), 11 vols., 5 pts. (Carbondale, Ill.: Southern Illinois University Press, 1968), vol. 4, pt. 3, p. 682.
5. *Tryal of a Cause for Criminal Conversation* (London, 1739), p. 26.
6. Ibid., pp. 28–29.
7. Susannah Cibber and Anne Arne vs. T. Cibber, 1741, British Public Records Office, C. 11.
8. Diary of Benjamin Griffin, September 11, 1737.
9. *Tryal of a Cause*, p. 25.
10. Ibid., p. 16.
11. Ibid., p. 14.
12. Ibid., p. 27.
13. Ibid., pp. 13–14.
14. Theophilus Cibber, Letter to S. A. C., in notebook called *Autographs, Musical and Dramatic*, Harvard University Theatre Collection, Cambridge, Mass. This letter is not in Theophilus Cibber's hand, but in a fluent, rapid, crimpy manner, filling up entirely a large piece of twice-folded paper, on all four sides. On the outer corner in the same hand is the following:
"Sloper Esq.
vs. Cibber
          Copy of letter sent
          by Mr Cibber to Mrs Cibber."
It is apparently a copy by a law scrivener of the original letter which Sloper put in the hands of his attorneys at the time of the trial as evidence of Theo's collusion in the love affair.
15. *Tryal of a Cause*, pp. 27–28.
16. Ibid., p. 28.
17. Ibid.
18. Ibid.

CHAPTER 9

1. In 1730, Lady Abergavenny's husband collected £10,000 from a Mr. Lydal, partner in one of her "Gallantrys." Robert Halsband, *Complete Letters of Mary Wortley Montagu*, 3 vols. (Oxford: Clarendon Press, 1965–1967). vol. 2, p. 295n.

2. Sir William S. Holdsworth, *A History of English Law*, 14 vols. (London: Methuen, 1956), vol. 8, pp. 429–430.
3. The others were Lord Perceval, James Oglethorpe, and Thomas Coram.
4. *Tryal of a Cause for Criminal Conversation* (London, 1739), p. 19.
5. Ibid.
6. Ibid.
7. Ibid., pp. 19–20.
8. Ibid., p. 20.
9. Ibid., p. 21.
10. Ibid., pp. 21–22.
11. Diary of Benjamin Griffin (and others) for Lincoln's Inn Fields Theatre (1715–1721), Little Theatre in the Haymarket (1733–1734), and Drury Lane Theatre (1721–1738 and 1742), Egerton 2320, British Museum, London.
12. "Beneath this stone lie the remains of Janey Cibber, the famous actress; her friends mourn her death. Nay, rather rejoice, for she is not dead but changed. Both as maiden and wife, with her lovely face and admirable figure, her virtue was proven and she clung to her faith. In her most sweet memory, Theophilus Cibber, her husband and sad survivor, has placed this [monument]. Born 1705 — Passed away 1732."

CHAPTER 10

1. John Lord Campbell, *The Lives of the Chief Justices of England, from the Norman Conquest till the Death of Lord Mansfield*, 2 vols. (London, 1849), vol. 2, pp. 215–232.
2. *Tryal of a Cause for Criminal Conversation* (London, 1739), p. 3.
3. Ibid., pp. 8–9.
4. Ibid., pp. 9–11.
5. Ibid., pp. 11–14.
6. Ibid., pp. 14–15.
7. Ibid., p. 18.
8. Ibid., p. 30.
9. Ibid., pp. 26–27.
10. Ibid., pp. 3–6.
11. Ibid., pp. 22–24.
12. Ibid., p. 25.
13. Campbell, *Lives of the Chief Justices*, vol. 2, p. 308.
14. Ibid., pp. 342–343.
15. Ibid., p. 343.

CHAPTER 11

1. J. Cartwright (ed.), *The Wentworth Papers, 1705–1739* (London, 1883), Lord Wentworth to Lord Strafford, January 4, 1739.
2. Ibid., January 6, 1739.

3. Mathews and Hutton, *Actors and Actresses*, Quin scrapbook, Harvard University Theatre Collection, Cambridge, Mass.

4. *The London Stage, 1660–1800*, William Van Lennep, Emmett L. Avery, Arthur H. Scouten, George W. Stone, Jr., and Charles B. Hogan (eds.), 11 vols., 5 pts. (Carbondale, Ill.: Southern Illinois University Press, 1968), vol. 2, pt. 3, p. 780.

5. "A Short Account of the Trial for detaining The Plaintiff's Wife," *An Account of the Life of that Celebrated Actress, Mrs. Susannah Maria Cibber, with Interesting and Amusing Anecdotes: Also The Two Remarkable and Romantic Trials between Theophilus Cibber and William Sloper* (London, 1887), p. 55.

6. Ibid.

7. Copy of a bill from the Burney Notebooks, British Museum, b. 1, vol. 4, undated, no name of newspaper, Folger Shakespeare Library, Washington, D.C.

8. "A Short Account," p. 52.

9. Ibid., p. 54.

10. Ibid., p 55.

11. Ibid., pp. 49–50.

12. Robert Halsband (ed.), *The Complete Letters of Lady Mary Wortley Montagu*, 3 vols. (Oxford: Clarendon Press, 1965–1967), vol. 2, p. 182.

CHAPTER 12

1. William W. Appleton, *Charles Macklin, An Actor's Life* (Cambridge, Mass.: Harvard University Press, 1960), p. 45.

2. Otto Erich Deutsch, *Handel, a Documentary Biography* (London: Black; New York: W. W. Norton, 1955), pp. 515–517.

3. *Pue's Occurrences* and *Faulkner's Journal*, December 1–5.

4. Robert Hitchcock, *A View of the Irish Stage*, 2 vols. (Dublin, 1788), vol. 1, p. 115.

5. Charles Burney, *An Account of the Musical Performances . . . in Commemoration of Handel* (London, 1785), p. 26n.

6. Deutsch, *Handel*, p. 530.

7. Swift once remarked to Lady Carteret: "I know nothing of music, Madam. I would not give a farthing for all the music in the universe. For my own part I would rather say my prayers without it." Patrick Delany, *Observations upon Lord Orrery's Remarks on Dr Jonathan Swift* (London, 1754), p. 192.

8. Paul Henry Lang, *George Frideric Handel* (New York: W. W. Norton, 1966), p. 340.

9. Jens Peter Larsen, *Handel's "Messiah": Origins* (Copenhagen: E. Munksgaard, 1957), p. 141.

10. Ibid., p. 240.

11. Ibid., pp. 221–222.

12. *Faulkner's*, April 13, 1742.

13. Ibid., April 17, 1742.

14. Ibid., December 5–8, 1741.

15. Ibid., April 20, 1742.

16. The story of Dr. Delany's outburst is attributed to young Thomas Sheridan, who sat next to him, but I cannot find it in his surviving work. The earliest reference to it is in Thomas Davies, *Memoirs of the Life of David Garrick* (London, 1780), vol. 2, p. 110, and it is widely quoted after this in most accounts of the history of *Messiah's* performances. Davies attributes it to "a certain Bishop," and he may be confusing Chancellor (later Dean) Delany with Dr. Edward Synge, Bishop of Elphin, who was

at the first performance of *Messiah* and recorded his ecstatic impressions. See Deutsch, *Handel*, pp. 554–555.

17. Chancery Proceedings, C. 11, bundle 1572, no. 15, British Public Records Office, London.
18. Orrery Papers (Letters from Ireland, 1753–1754), Lord Orrery to Riley Towers, Esq., Dublin, January 13, 1750, Harvard University Library, Cambridge, Mass.
19. Thomas Sheridan, *British Education* (London, 1756), p. 417.
20. David Little and George Kahrl (eds.), *The Letters of David Garrick*, 3 vols. (Cambridge, Mass.: Harvard University Press, Belknap Press, 1963), letter 237, vol. 1, p. 313.
21. Burney, *Commemoration of Handel*, p. 35.
22. Little and Kahrl, *Letters of Garrick*, letter 24, vol. 1, p. 40.
23. *Dublin News Letter*, August 21–24.
24. Little and Kahrl, *Letters of Garrick*, letter 25, vol. 1, pp. 40–41.
25. Davies, *Life of Garrick*, vol. 1, p. 68.

CHAPTER 13

1. *An Account of the Life of that Celebrated Actress, Mrs. Susannah Maria Cibber, with Interesting and Amusing Anecdotes: Also The Two Remarkable and Romantic Trials between Theophilus Cibber and William Sloper* (London: Reader, 1887), p. 11.
2. *A Clear Stage and no Favour, or Tragedy and Comedy at War, occasioned by the Emulation of the two Theatrick Heroes, David and Goliath* (pamphlet, 1742).
3. *Daily Advertizer*, January 17, 1743.
4. Wills, Somerset House, London.
5. Otto Erich Deutsch, *Handel, a Documentary Biography* (London: Black; New York: W. W. Norton, 1955), p. 608.
6. Abraham Rees, *Cyclopaedia*, 1st American ed., 41 vols. (Philadelphia, 1810–1824), vol. 8, Susannah Cibber article.
7. Mrs. Paget Toynbee (ed.), *Letters of Horace Walpole* (Oxford: Clarendon Press, 1903–1905), vol. 1, pp. 327–328, February 24, 1743.
8. Just how scrupulous Patrick Delany was in his choice of public entertainment may be judged from the fact that in 1744, no longer a mourning widower but a radiant bridegroom, having just wed the agreeable and well-connected Mary Granville Pendarves, he refused to go with her to see Handel's *Semele* because the subject — an extramarital love affair of Jove's — was too profane for a clergyman. Lady Lhanover (ed.), *Autobiography and Correspondence of Mary Granville Delany* (London, 1867), vol. 2, pp. 266–267, February 21, 1744.
9. Deutsch, *Handel*, pp. 563–565.
10. Ibid., p. 565.
11. Emily Climenson (ed.), *Elizabeth Montagu*, vol. 2, p. 243.
12. *The Buskin and the Sock*, Letters between T. Sheridan and T. Cibber (Dublin, 1743), pp. 35–36.
13. Ibid., p. 5.
14. Ibid., p. 29.
15. Ibid., p. 46.
16. Ibid., p. 45.
17. *34 Queries to be answered by the Manager of Drury Lane Theatre* (pamphlet, 1743),

quoted in *The London Stage, 1660–1800*, William Van Lennep, Emmett L. Avery, Arthur H. Scouten, George W. Stone, Jr., and Charles B. Hogan (eds.), 11 vols., 5 pts. (Carbondale, Ill.: Southern Illinois University Press, 1968), vol. 1, pt. 3, p. xcv.

18. *Mr Macklin's Reply to Mr Garrick's Answer, to which is prefixed all the Papers which have publickly appeared in Regard to this important Dispute* (London, 1743), p. 12.

19. Deutsch, *Handel*, p. 591.

20. George Anne Bellamy, *An Apology for the Life of George Anne Bellamy*, 6 vols. (London: J. Bell, 1785), vol. 1, p. 139.

21. Ibid., p. 59.

22. *London Stage*, vol. 2, pt. 3, pp. 1124–1129.

23. Charles Dibdin, *Professional Life of Mr Dibdin* (London, 1803).

24. William W. Cooke, *Memoirs of Charles Macklin, Comedian* (London, 1804), pp. 88–89.

25. Benjamin Victor, *A History of the Theatres of London and Dublin*, 3 vols. (London, 1761–1771), vol. 1, p. 34.

26. Thomas Davies, *Dramatic Miscellanies*, 3 vols. (London, 1785), vol. 1, p. 37.

27. James Boaden, *Memoirs of Mrs Siddons*, 2 vols. (London, 1827), vol. 2, p. 59.

28. Thomas Davies, *Memoirs of the Life of David Garrick*, 2 vols. (Boston, 1818), vol. 1, pp. 68–69.

29. Theophilus Cibber, *"Romeo and Juliet," revised and altered from Shakespeare by Mr Theophilus Cibber, to which is added a Serio-Comic Apology . . . interspersed with Memoirs and Anecdotes . . .* (London, 1748), pp. 93–94.

30. John Downes, *Roscius Anglicanus, London, 1708, with additions by the late T. Davies* (London, 1789), p. 58.

CHAPTER 14

1. The Forster Collection of Garrick's Correspondence, Victoria and Albert Museum, London; James Boaden (ed.), *The Private Correspondence of David Garrick, with the most celebrated persons of his time*, 2 vols. (London, 1831–1832), vol. 1, p. 33.

2. Notes of Charles Burney for his *History of Music*, Osborn Collection, Yale University Library, New Haven, Conn.; Madame D'Arblay (Fanny Burney), *Memoirs of Dr Burney, by his daughter, Madame D'Arblay*, 2 vols. (London, 1832), vol. 1, p. 14. Madame D'Arblay called Mrs. Cibber's Sunday evenings "a constellation of wits, poets, actors, authors, and men of letters."

3. Review of *The Fair Penitent*, March 8–10.

4. William W. Cooke, *Memoirs of Charles Macklin, Comedian* (London, 1805), pp. 120–121.

5. David Little and George Kahrl (eds.), *The Letters of David Garrick*, 3 vols. (Cambridge, Mass.: Harvard University Press, Belknap Press, 1963), letter 31, vol. 1, p. 49.

6. Forster Collection; Boaden, *Correspondence of Garrick*, vol. 1, p. 34.

7. Ibid., p. 35.

8. Ibid., p. 34.

9. Little and Kahrl, *Letters of Garrick*, letter 36, vol. 1, p. 63.

10. Forster Collection; Boaden, *Correspondence of Garrick*, vol. 1, p. 39.

11. Notes of Burney; Charles Burney, A letter to Sir Joseph Banks, 1806, Egerton 3009, British Museum, London.

12. Benjamin Victor, *Original Letters, Dramatic Pieces, and Poems*, 3 vols. (London, 1776), vol. 1, p. 118.

13. Little and Kahrl, *Letters of Garrick*, letter 37, vol. 1, p. 65.
14. Ibid., letter 35, p. 58.
15. Carola Oman, *David Garrick* (London: Hodder & Stoughton, 1958), p. 82.
16. Little and Kahrl, *Letters of Garrick*, letter 32, vol. 1, pp. 50–51.
17. Ibid., letter 37, pp. 64–65.
18. Forster Collection; Boaden, *Correspondence of Garrick*, vol. 1, pp. 37–38.
19. Little and Kahrl, *Letters of Garrick*, letter 38, vol. 1, pp. 66–67.
20. Forster Collection; Boaden, *Correspondence of Garrick*, vol. 1, p. 36.
21. Ibid., pp. 38–39.
22. Little and Kahrl, *Letters of Garrick*, letter 41, vol. 1, p. 71.
23. Forster Collection; Boaden, *Correspondence of Garrick*, vol. 1, p. 36.
24. Victor, *Original Letters*, vol. 1, p. 203.
25. Forster Collection; Boaden, *Correspondence of Garrick*, vol. 1, pp. 47–48.
26. Little and Kahrl, *Letters of Garrick*, letter 41, vol. 1, pp. 71–72.
27. Forster Collection; Boaden, *Correspondence of Garrick*, vol. 1, pp. 48–50.
28. Little and Kahrl, *Letters of Garrick*, letter 42, vol. 1, p. 74.
29. Forster Collection; Boaden, *Correspondence of Garrick*, vol. 1, p. 40.
30. Little and Kahrl, *Letters of Garrick*, letter 41, vol. 1, p. 72.
31. Forster Collection; Boaden, *Correspondence of Garrick*, vol. 1, pp. 39–40.
32. Ibid.
33. Charlotte Charke, *A Narrative of the Life of Mrs Charlotte Charke* (London, 1755), pp. 102–103. An undated letter from Colley Cibber to Charlotte in the Enthoven Collection at the Victoria and Albert Musuem reads: "Madam, The strange career which you have run for some years (a career not always unmarked by evil) debars my offering you that succor which otherwise would naturally have been extended to you as my daughter. I must refuse, therefore with this advice — try Theophilus. Yours in Sorrow, Colley Cibber."
34. Forster Collection; Boaden, *Correspondence of Garrick*, vol. 1, pp. 43–44.
35. Thomas Davies, *Memoirs of the Life of David Garrick*, 2 vols. (Boston, 1818), vol. 1, pp. 100–101.
36. Augustus Hare, *Memorials of a Quiet Life*, 2 vols. (London, 1873), vol. 1, pp. 247–279; Mary Howard McClintock, *Portrait of a House* (London: Carroll & Nicholson, 1948); and The Correspondence of Smart Lethieullier and C. Lyttleton, LLD, Dean of Exeter, 1743–1760, Stowe MS. 752, British Museum, London.
37. Little and Kahrl, *Letters of Garrick*, letter 49, vol. 1, p. 86.
38. September 25, 1746. Theater Collection, The New York Public Library at Lincoln Center. Astor, Lenox, and Tilden Foundations.
39. Forster Collection; Boaden, *Correspondence of Garrick*, vol. 1, p. 39.

CHAPTER 15

1. Thomas Davies, *Memoirs of the Life of David Garrick*, 2 vols. (Boston, 1818), vol. 1, p. 46.
2. Richard Cumberland, "Theatrical Retrospections," in Mathews and Hutton, *Actors and Actresses*, Quin scrapbook, Harvard University Theatre Collection, Cambridge, Mass.
3. Richard Cumberland, *Memoirs, by Himself* (London, 1807), vol. 1, pp. 80–81.
4. Davies, *Life of Garrick*, vol. 1, p. 82.
5. Carola Oman, *David Garrick* (London: Hodder & Stoughton, 1958), p. 94.

6. *The London Stage, 1660–1800*, William Van Lennep, Emmett L. Avery, Arthur H. Scouten, George W. Stone, Jr., and Charles B. Hogan (eds.), 11 vols., 5 pts. (Carbondale, Ill.: Southern Illinois University Press, 1968), vol. 2, pt. 3, p. 1269.
7. Davies, *Life of Garrick*, vol. 1, p. 86.
8. Percy Fitzgerald, *Life of David Garrick* (London, 1899), p. 139.
9. Davies, *Life of Garrick*, vol. 1, p. 86.
10. *Life of James Quin* (London, 1766), p. 45.
11. Davies, *Life of Garrick*, vol. 1, p. 90.
12. David Little and George Kahrl (eds.), *The Letters of David Garrick*, 3 vols. (Cambridge, Mass.: Harvard University Press, Belknap Press, 1963), letter 299, vol. 1, p. 370.
13. John Bernard, *Retrospections of the Stage*, 2 vols. (London: Colburn, 1830), vol. 1, p. 204.
14. David Baker, *Biographia Dramatica*, 2 vols. (London, 1782), vol. 1, p. 85.
15. Little and Kahrl, *Letters of Garrick*, letter 51, vol. 1, pp. 88–90.
16. G. W. Stone, Jr. (ed.), *The Journal of David Garrick, 1763* (New York: Modern Language Association of America, 1939), p. 8.
17. *Tit for Tat, the first [and second] Season of Mr G. . . . . k's Management*, by John Powel, deputy treasurer of Drury Lane (1747–48), Harvard University Theatre Collection, Cambridge, Mass.
18. New Occasional Prologue, September 21, 1750.
19. Dr. John Doran, *Their Majesties' Servants: Annals of the English Stage*, 3 vols. (London, 1888), vol. 2, pp. 122–123.
20. James Boswell, *Life of Johnson*, R. W. Chapman (ed.) (New York: Oxford University Press, 1970), p. 122.
21. Ibid., p. 1252.
22. Ibid., p. 616.
23. Edward Gibbon, *Journal* (New York: W. W. Norton, 1929), p. 186.
24. Boswell, *Life of Johnson*, p. 140. In the early negotiations about *Mahomet and Irene*, Johnson probably assumed that Garrick would take the title role. Actually, he gave it to Barry.
25. Ibid., pp. 636–637.
26. Cumberland, in Mathews and Hutton, *Actors and Actresses*, vol. 2, p. 210.
27. Boswell, *Life of Johnson*, p. 1021.
28. Ibid., pp. 58, 1021.
29. Ibid., p. 1021.
30. James Boswell, *Private Papers*, Marshall Waingrow (ed.), 2 vols. (New York: McGraw-Hill, 1950 and on), vol. 2, p. 181.
31. Boswell, *Life of Johnson*, p. 143.
32. Walter Raleigh, *Johnson on Shakespeare* (London, 1908), p. 11.
33. Boswell, *Life of Johnson*, p. 1070.
34. Tate Wilkinson, *Memoirs of His Own Life*, 4 vols. (Yorkshire, 1790), vol. 3, p. 42.
35. Boswell, *Life of Johnson*, p. 1252.
36. Ibid., p. 1018.

CHAPTER 16

1. 39 letters from David Mallet to Aaron Hill, 1731–1750, Harvard University Theatre Collection, Cambridge, Mass.
2. David Little and George Kahrl (eds.), *The Letters of David Garrick*, 3 vols. (Cam-

bridge, Mass.: Harvard University Press, Belknap Press, 1963), letter 57, vol. 1, p. 96.

3. *The London Stage, 1660–1800*, William Van Lennep, Emmett L. Avery, Arthur H. Scouten, George W. Stone, Jr., and Charles B. Hogan (eds.), 11 vols., 5 pts. (Carbondale, Ill.: Southern Illinois University Press, 1968), pt. 4, vol. 1, p. 141.

4. Otto Erich Deutsch, *Handel, a Documentary Biography* (New York: W. W. Norton, 1955), p. 685.

5. George Anne Bellamy, *An Apology for the Life of George Anne Bellamy*, 6 vols. (London: J. Bell, 1785), vol. 1, pp. 198–199.

6. Little and Kahrl, *Letters of Garrick*, letter 89, vol. 1, pp. 146–147.

7. *London Stage*, pt. 4, vol. 1, p. 205.

8. Little and Kahrl, *Letters of Garrick*, letter 93, vol. 1, pp. 152–153.

9. Ibid., p. 152.

10. *London Stage*, pt. 4, vol. 1, p. 211.

11. Thomas Davies, *Memoirs of the Life of David Garrick*, 2 vols. (Boston, 1818), vol. 1, p. 191.

12. Kalman Burnim, *David Garrick, Director* (Pittsburgh: University of Pittsburgh Press, 1961), pp. 131–132.

13. *Gentleman's Magazine*, October 1750, vol. 20, p. 438.

14. Tate Wilkinson, *Memoirs of His Own Life*, 4 vols. (Yorkshire, 1790), vol. 4, p. 164.

15. Bellamy, *Apology*, vol. 2, pp. 50–51.

16. Henry Fielding, *Covent Garden Journal*, ed. G. E. Jensen (New Haven: Yale University Press, 1915), vol. 2, no. 71, p. 137.

17. Little and Kahrl, *Letters of Garrick*, vol. 1, letter 108, p. 172.

18. *Life of James Quin* (London, 1766), p. 80.

19. Davies, *Life of Garrick*, vol. 2, p. 179.

20. Ibid.

21. Thomas Bowlby to Phillip Gell, October 11, 1750, British Historical Manuscripts Commission Ninth Report, British Museum, London.

22. Wilkinson, *Memoirs*, vol. 4, p. 169.

23. *London Stage*, pt. 4, vol. 1, pp. 300–301.

24. Tate Wilkinson, *Original Anecdotes* (London, [ca. 1805]), p. 18.

25. Davies, *Life of Garrick*, vol. 1, pp. 68–69.

CHAPTER 17

1. Helen Hughes, *The Gentle Hertford* (New York: Macmillan, 1940), p. 405.

2. Wilmarth S. Lewis (ed.), *Horace Walpole's Correspondence*, 39 vols. (New Haven: Yale ed., 1937–1974), vol. 9, p. 109.

3. Hughes, *The Gentle Hertford*, p. 405.

4. The *Volunteer Manager*, April 24.

5. George Anne Bellamy, *An Apology for the Life of George Anne Bellamy*, 6 vols. (London: J. Bell, 1785), vol. 3, p. 2.

6. *A Series of Letters between Mrs Elizabeth Carter and Mrs Catherine Talbot, 1741–1770* (London, 1809), May 9, 1752, pp. 77–78.

7. The Correspondence of Smart Lethieullier and C. Lyttleton, LLD, Dean of Exeter, 1743–1770, Stowe MS. 752, British Museum, London.

8. The Correspondence of David Garrick, S. A. C. to D. Garrick, August 20, 1765, Forster Collection, Victoria and Albert Museum, London.

9. Augustus Hare, *Memorials of a Quiet Life*, 2 vols. (London: Strahan, 1873), vol. 1, p. 253; and Lethieullier, Stowe 752.
10. Emily Climenson (ed.), *Elizabeth Montagu, the queen of the Blue Stockings, her correspondence from 1720–1761*, 2 vols. (London: John Murray, 1906), vol. 1, p. 242.
11. Lewis, *Horace Walpole's Correspondence*, vol. 9, pp. 70–73.
12. Brian Fitzgerald (ed.), *Correspondence of Emily, Duchess of Leinster*, 3 vols. (Dublin: Irish Manuscripts Commission, 1949), vol. 1, p. 117.
13. James Boswell, *Life of Johnson*, R. W. Chapman (ed.) (New York: Oxford University Press, 1970), p. 1070.
14. *The Laureat, or The Right Side of Colley Cibber* (London, 1740), p. 106.
15. Horace Walpole, *Memoirs of George II*, 3 vols. (London, 1847), vol. 2, p. 44.
16. Alan Stenning and George Barker, *The Record of Old Westminsters; a Biographical List*, 2 vols. (London: Chiswick Press, 1928), vol. 1, p. 186.
17. *Public Advertizer*, April 19, 1758.
18. The Hopkins-Cross Journals and Play Lists (1747–1776), Folger Shakespeare Library, Washington, D.C.
19. Joseph Cradock, *Literary and Miscellaneous Memoirs*, 4 vols. (London, 1826), vol. 4, p. 100.
20. Carola Oman, *David Garrick* (London: Hodder & Stoughton, 1958), Lord Rochford's letter, pp. 266–267.
21. Letter of S. A. C. from Scotland Yard to D. Garrick, June 4, no year, Folger Shakespeare Library, Washington, D.C.
22. Cradock, *Memoirs*, vol. 1, pp. 5–9.
23. Ibid., vol. 2, p. 100.
24. Lady Lhanover (ed.). *Autobiography and Correspondence of Mary Granville Delany* (London, 1867), pp. 606–607.
25. David Little and George Kahrl (eds.), *The Letters of David Garrick*, 3 vols. (Cambridge, Mass.: Harvard University Press, Belknap Press, 1963), letter 237, vol. 1, p. 313.
26. Roger Lonsdale, *Dr. Charles Burney* (Oxford: Clarendon Press, 1965), pp. 17–18. "One night Mrs Clive having undertaken a song in which she was imperfect — as she was out of time as well as out of tune — calls out aloud to the band, 'Why don't the fellows mind what they're about!' At the end of the act, Arne [the orchestra leader] went upstairs in the name of the whole band to remonstrate against her insolence, where the only satisfaction he obtained was a slap in the face. In return, he literally turned her over his knee and gave her such a manual flagellation as she probably had not received since she quitted the nursery. But as proof that she made a good defense he came back without his wig, all over blood from her scratches."
27. Letter of Catherine Clive to David Garrick, ms. W.B.492, Folger Shakespeare Library, Washington, D.C.
28. James Boaden (ed.), *The Private Correspondence of David Garrick, with the most celebrated persons of his time*, 2 vols. (London, 1831–1832), vol. 1, p. 204.
29. Little and Kahrl, *Letters of Garrick*, letter 488, vol. 2, pp. 596–597.
30. Ibid., letter 855, vol. 3, pp. 950–951.
31. Ibid., letter 488, vol. 2, pp. 596–597.
32. Ibid., letter 1244, vol. 3, p. 1277.
33. Margaret Barton, *Garrick* (London: Faber & Faber, 1948), p. 279.
34. Little and Kahrl, *Letters of Garrick*, letter 247, vol. 1, p. 321.
35. David Baker, *Biographia Dramatica*, 2 vols. (London, 1782), vol. 1, p. 85.
36. Thomas Davies, *Memoirs of the Life of David Garrick*, 2 vols. (Boston, 1818), vol. 1, p. 141.
37. The *London Chronicle*, 1757.

38. Letters of Dr. Edward Barry and George Faulkner to Lord Orrery, March 1754, Orrery Papers (Letters from Ireland, 1753–54), vol. 2, pp. 123–125, Harvard University Library, Cambridge, Mass.

39. *The London Stage, 1660–1800*, William Van Lennep, Emmett L. Avery, Arthur H. Scouten, George W. Stone, Jr., and Charles B. Hogan (eds.), 11 vols., 5 pts. (Carbondale, Ill.: Southern Illinois University Press, 1968), pt. 4, vol. 1, pp. 468–469.

40. Ibid., pp. CLXXXVI–CLXXXVII.

41. Hopkins-Cross Journals.

42. Ibid.

43. Dr. John Hill, *The Actor* (London, 1750), p. 148.

44. Baker, *Biographia Dramatica*, vol. 1, p. 84.

45. Hill, *The Actor*, p. 198.

46. Edward A. Langhans, ms. notes for the *Dictionary of Actors*.

CHAPTER 18

1. Anna Barbauld (ed.), *Correspondence of Samuel Richardson*, 6 vols. (London, 1804), vol. 2, pp. 174–175.

2. Benjamin Victor, *A History of the Theatres of London and Dublin*, 3 vols. (London, 1761–1771), vol. 2, p. 52.

3. Benjamin Victor, *Original Letters, Dramatic Pieces, and Poems*, 3 vols. (London, 1776), vol. 1, p. 201.

4. *The London Stage, 1660–1800*, William Van Lennep, Emmett L. Avery, Arthur H. Scouten, George W. Stone, Jr., and Charles B. Hogan (eds.), 11 vols., 5 pts. (Carbondale, Ill.: Southern Illinois University Press, 1968), pt. 4, vol. 1, p. 350.

5. Theophilus Cibber, *An Epistle to David Garrick, to which are prefixed some occasional verse, petitions, etc.* (London, 1755), p. 24.

6. *Gazeteer* and *London Daily Advertiser*, February 18, 1756.

7. Ibid., July 1, 1756.

8. Victor, *Original Letters*, vol. 1, p. 288.

9. Dictionary of National Biography.

10. Victor, *A History of the Theatres*, vol. 1, p. 251.

11. Ibid., p. 240.

12. *Daily Advertiser*, November 28, 1758 (dated Dublin, Nov. 18th).

13. Victor, *A History of the Theatres*, vol. 1, p. 252.

14. *London Chronicle*, dated Dublin, November 14, 1758.

15. Victor, *A History of the Theatres*, vol. 1, pp. 250–251.

16. Arthur Friedman (ed.), "The Bee," *Collected Works of Oliver Goldsmith*, 5 vols. (Oxford: Clarendon Press, 1966), vol. 3, pp. 267–268; and *Weekly Magazine*, vol. 3, pp. 46–48.

CHAPTER 19

1. Thomas Davies, *Memoirs of the Life of David Garrick*, 2 vols. (Boston, 1818), vol. 2, p. 55.

2. Roger Lonsdale, *Dr. Charles Burney* (Oxford: Clarendon Press, 1965), p. 14.

3. For a glimpse of Mrs. Arne's struggles in Ireland, see Lady Lhanover (ed.), *Autobiography and Correspondence of Mary Granville Delany*, 3 vols. (London, 1867), vol. 3.

4. Charles Dibdin, *Professional Life of Mr Dibdin*, 4 vols. (London, 1803), vol. 1, pp. 28–29.

5. Charles Dibdin, *History of the Stage*, 5 vols. (London, 1800), vol. 5, p. 369.

6. Ibid.

7. Davies, *Life of Garrick*, vol. 2, p. 55.

8. T[erence] H[anbury] White, *The Age of Scandal* (Harmondsworth: Penguin, 1964), p. 116.

9. David Little and George Kahrl (eds.), *The Letters of David Garrick*, 3 vols. (Cambridge, Mass.: Harvard University Press, Belknap Press, 1963), letter 315, vol. 1, p. 385.

10. Ibid., letter 315, p. 386n.

11. Ibid., letter 331, pp. 414–416.

12. Ibid., letter 337, vol. 2, pp. 422–424.

13. Ibid., letter 321, vol. 1, pp. 395–398.

14. Ibid., letter 315, p. 385.

15. Ibid., letter 373, vol. 2, pp. 476–477.

16. The Correspondence of David Garrick, Forster Collection, Victoria and Albert Museum, London; James E. Boaden (ed.), *The Private Correspondence of David Garrick, with the most celebrated persons of his time*, 2 vols. (London, 1831–1832), vol. 1, p. 197.

17. Ibid., vol. 1, pp. 200–201.

18. Charles Burney Notebooks, folder 4, Berg Collection, New York Public Library, New York City.

19. Forster Collection; Boaden, *Correspondence of Garrick*, vol. 1, pp. 207–208.

20. Ibid., p. 201.

21. Ibid., p. 208. Lady Townshend (1708–1788) was the wife of Charles, third Viscount Townshend, a woman of mordant wit. During the 1750s and 1760s she suffered considerable family stress, including the deaths of several children, her own poor health, the elopement of a daughter, and the prolonged and nervewracking absence of several sons in foreign wars. Horace Walpole was shocked at her apparent lack of feeling during this period, for she never gave up her social appearances, and her famous wit bit more sharply than ever. Her private letters reveal that she was not as impervious to pain as her public self suggested. I can find no source for Mrs. Cibber's remark about Lady Townshend's wishing she had "nerves like cart ropes." However, it is interesting that Susannah should have chosen this stoic, brittle lady as her model of feminine behavior. See Errol Sherson's *The Lively Lady Townshend* (London: Heinemann, 1926).

22. *The London Stage, 1660–1800*, William Van Lennep, Emmett L. Avery, Arthur H. Scouten, George W. Stone, Jr., and Charles B. Hogan (eds.), 11 vols., 5 pts. (Carbondale, Ill.: Southern Illinois University Press, 1968), vol. 2, pt. 4, p. 1140.

23. Act I, scene 1.

24. Benjamin Victor, *Original Letters, Dramatic Pieces, and Poems*, 3 vols. (London, 1776), vol. 3, pp. 84–85.

25. *Daily Advertizer*, January 6, 1766.

26. *Life of James Quin* (London, 1766), pp. 111–112.

27. Lester King, *The Road to Medical Enlightenment* (New York: American Elsevier, 1970), pp. 152–153.

28. Joseph Cradock, *Literary and Miscellaneous Memoirs*, 4 vols. (London, 1826), vol. 4, p. 102.

29. Beverley McAner, "An American in Paris," *Pennsylvania Magazine* (1940), p. 188.

30. William Phillimore, *Berkshire Parish Registers: Marriages* (London, 1908).
31. Wills, Somerset House, London.
32. A. M. Broadley and Lewis Melville (eds.), *The Beautiful Lady Craven, the Memoirs of Elizabeth, Baroness Craven, afterwards Margravine of Anspach and Beyreuth (1750–1828)*, 2 vols. (London, 1914), vol. 2, p. 145.
33. Wills, Somerset House, London.

EPILOGUE

1. James M. Stifler, *My Dear Girl: The Correspondence of Benjamin Franklin with Polly Stevenson, Georgiana and Catherine Shipley* (New York: George Doran, 1927), pp. 214–217.
2. Ibid., p. 260.
3. Sir Lewis Namier and John Brooke, "House of Commons," vol. 3, *The History of Parliament*, 3 vols. (London: Oxford University Press, 1964), pp. 445–446.
4. *Duke of Rutland*, vol. 3, British Historical Manuscripts Commission, London.
5. Augustus Hare, *Memorials of a Quiet Life*, 2 vols. (London: Strahan, 1873), vol. 1, pp. 247–248.
6. Ibid., p. 258.
7. Ibid., p 253.
8. Ibid., p. 272.
9. Ibid., pp. 277–279.
10. Mary Howard McClintock, *Portrait of a House* (London: Carroll & Nicholson, 1948), p. 39.
11. Ibid., p. 35.
12. Ibid., pp. 95–96.
13. Ibid., p. 39.

Selected Bibliography

PUBLISHED WORKS

An Account of the Life of that Celebrated Actress, Mrs. Susannah Maria Cibber, with Interesting and Amusing Anecdotes: Also The Two Remarkable and Romantic Trials between Theophilus Cibber and William Sloper. London, 1887.

Angelo, Henry. *Reminiscences of, with memoirs of his late father and friends, [including] . . . the most celebrated characters that have flourished in the past 80 years.* London, 1828–1830.

The Annual Register (periodical). London, 1766 and on.

An Apology for the Life of Mr. T . . . C . . . , Comedian. London, 1740.

Appleton, William W. *Charles Macklin, An Actor's Life.* Cambridge, Mass.: Harvard University Press, 1960.

Baker, David. *A Companion to the Playhouse, or Biographia Dramatica.* 2 vols. London, 1782.

Barbauld, Anna (ed.). *Correspondence of Samuel Richardson.* 6 vols. London, 1804.

Barker, Richard Hindry. *Mr. Cibber of Drury Lane.* New York: Columbia University Press, 1939.

Barton, Margaret. *Garrick.* London: Faber & Faber, 1948.

Bate, Walter Jackson. *The Achievement of Samuel Johnson.* New York: Oxford University Press, 1955.

Beatson, Robert. *A Chronological Register of both Houses of British Parliament, 1708–1807.* London, 1807.

Bellamy, George Anne. *An Apology for the Life of George Anne Bellamy.* 6 vols. London, 1785.

Bernard, John. *Retrospections of the Stage.* 2 vols. London, 1830.

Boaden, James. *Memoirs of Mrs. Siddons.* 2 vols. London, 1827

———— (ed.). *The Private Correspondence of David Garrick, with the most celebrated persons of his time.* 2 vols. London, 1831–1832.

Bond, Richmond P. *Queen Anne's American Kings.* Oxford: Clarendon Press, 1952.

Boswell, James. *Life of Johnson.* Edited by R. W. Chapman. Oxford: Oxford University Press, 1970.

————. *Life of Johnson.* Edited by J. W. Croker. London, 1860.

————. *Journal of a Tour of the Hebrides.* Edited by Frederick A. Pottle and Charles H. Bennett. New York: Literary Guild, 1936.

————. *Private Papers.* Edited by Frederick A. Pottle et al. (Yale edition). 2 vols. New York: McGraw-Hill, 1950 and on.

Boyer, Abel. *History of the Reign of Queen Anne, Digested into Annals.* 11 vols. London, 1703–1713.

British Army Lists.

British Historical Manuscripts Commission Reports.

Broadley, A. M., and Melville, Lewis (eds.). *The Beautiful Lady Craven, the Memoirs of Elizabeth, Baroness Craven, afterwards Margravine of Anspach and Beyreuth (1750–1828).* 2 vols. London: John Lane, 1914.

Burney, Charles. *An Account of the Musical Performances . . . in Commemoration of Handel.* London, 1785.

————. *A General History of Music* 2 vols. London: G. T. Foulis; New York: Harcourt, Brace & Co., 1935.

Burnim, Kalman. *David Garrick, Director.* Pittsburgh: University of Pittsburgh Press, 1961.

Campbell, John Lord. *The Lives of the Chief Justices of England, from the Norman Conquest till the Death of Lord Mansfield.* 2 vols. London, 1849.

Cannon, Garland (ed.). *The Letters of Sir William Jones.* 2 vols. Oxford: Clarendon Press, 1970.

Carlyle, Alexander. *Autobiography.* Boston, 1861.

Cartwright, J. (ed.). *The Wentworth Papers, 1705–1739.* London, 1883.

Charke, Charlotte. *A Narrative of the Life of Mrs. Charlotte Charke.* London, 1755.

Chetwood, W. R. *The British Theatre.* Dublin, 1750.

Churchill, C. *The Rosciad.* London, 1761.

Cibber, Colley. *An Apology for the Life of Colley Cibber.* London, 1740.

Cibber, Susannah Maria. *The Oracle, As it is acted at the Theatre Royal in Covent Garden.* London, 1752.

Cibber, Theophilus. *Dissertations on Theatrical Subjects as They have several Times been delivered to The Public.* London, 1756.

———. *An Epistle to David Garrick, to which are prefixed some occasional Verse, Petitions, etc.* London, 1755.

———. *Four Original Letters, viz. Two from a Husband to a Gentleman, and Two from a Husband to a Wife.* London, 1739.

———. *The Lives and Characters of the most eminent Actors and Actresses of Great Britain and Ireland, from Shakespeare To The Present Time.* Dublin, 1753.

———. *Lives of the Poets of Great Britain and Ireland.* London, 1753.

———. *"Romeo and Juliet," revised and altered from Shakespeare by Mr Theophilus Cibber, to which is added a Serio-Comic Apology . . . interspersed with Memoirs and Anecdotes. . . .* London, 1748

Cibber, Theophilus, and Sheridan, Thomas. *The Buskin and the Sock.* Dublin, 1743.

A Clear Stage and no Favour, or Tragedy and Comedy at War, occasioned by the Emulation of the two Theatrick Heroes, David and Goliath (pamphlet). 1742.

Climenson, Emily (ed.). *Elizabeth Montagu, the queen of the Blue Stockings, her correspondence from 1720–1761.* 2 vols. London: John Murray, 1906.

Coke, Mary. *Letters and Journals of Lady Mary Coke.* Edinburgh, 1892.

Cooke, William. *Memoirs of Samuel Foote, Esq.* 3 vols. London, 1805.

———. *Memoirs of Charles Macklin, Comedian.* London, 1804.

Cork and Orrery, Countess of (ed.). *The Orrery Papers.* London: Duckworth & Co., 1903.

Cradock, Joseph. *Literary and Miscellaneous Memoirs.* 4 vols. London, 1826.

Crowest, Frederick J. *Musicians' Wit, Humour and Anecdote.* London: Walter Scott Publishing Co., 1902.

Cumberland, Richard. *Memoirs, by Himself.* London, 1807.

Cummings, William H. *Dr. Arne and "Rule, Britannia."* London: Novello & Co., 1912.

D'Arblay, Madame [Fanny Burney]. *Memoirs of Dr. Burney, by his daughter, Madame D'Arblay.* 3 vols. London, 1832.

Davey, Richard. *A History of Mourning.* London, 1889.

Davies, Thomas. *Dramatic Miscellanies.* 3 vols. London, 1785.

———. *Memoirs of the Life of David Garrick.* 2 vols. Boston, 1818.

Dean, Winton. *Handel's Dramatic Oratorios and Masques.* London: Oxford University Press, 1950.

Delany, Patrick. *Observations upon Lord Orrery's Remarks on Jonathan Swift.* London, 1754.

Deutsch, Otto Erich. *Handel, a Documentary Biography.* London: Black; New York: W. W. Norton, 1955.

Dibdin, Charles. *History of the Stage.* 5 vols. London, 1800.

———. *Professional Life of Mr Dibdin.* 4 vols. London, 1803.

Ditchfield, P. H., and Page, William (eds.). *The Victorian History of Berkshire.* 4 vols. London, 1906–1927.

Doran, Dr. John. *Their Majesties' Servants: Annals of the English Stage.* 3 vols. London, 1888.

Downes, John. *Roscius Anglicanus, London, 1708, with additions by the late T. Davies.* London, 1789.

Fitzgerald, Brian (ed.). *Correspondence of Emily, Duchess of Leinster.* 3 vols. Dublin: Irish Manuscripts Commission, 1949.

Fitzgerald, Percy. *Life of David Garrick.* London, 1899.

Foster, Joseph. *Alumni Oxonienses.* Liechtenstein: Kraus Reprint Ltd., 1968.

Friedman, Arthur (ed.). *Collected Works of Oliver Goldsmith.* 5 vols. Oxford: Clarendon Press, 1966.

Funeral Discipline, by Paul Meagre, once Mourner in Chief to The Funeral Undertaker, Strip Corps. London, 1701.

Genest, John. *Some Account of the English Stage, 1600–1830.* London, 1830.

Gentleman, Francis. *The Dramatic Censor.* London, 1770.

Gibbon, Edward. *Journal, 1763.* New York: W. W. Norton, 1929.

Greenhill, Thomas. *The Art of Embalming.* London, 1705.

Grove, Joseph. *The Lives of all the Earls and Dukes of Devonshire.* London, 1764.

Halsband, Robert (ed.). *The Complete Letters of Lady Mary Wortley Montagu.* 3 vols. Oxford: Clarendon Press, 1965–1967.

Hare, Augustus. *Memorials of a Quiet Life.* 2 vols. London, 1873.

Henslowe, Cecilia Maria Bartholemon. "A preface from the Oratorio of *Japta in Masfa* by the late F. H. Bartholemon." London, 1827.

Highfill, P. H.; Burnim, Kalman; and Langhans, E. A. *A Biographical Dictionary of Actors, Actresses, Musicians, Dancers, and Other Stage Personnel in London 1660–1800.* Carbondale, Ill.: Southern Illinois University Press, 1973 and on.

Hill, Aaron. *Works.* 4 vols. London, 1754.

———. *The Prompter.* Edited by William Appleton and Kalman Burnim. New York: Blom, 1966.

Hill, Dr. John. *The Actor.* London, 1750.

Hitchcock, Robert. *A View of the Irish Stage.* 2 vols. Dublin, 1788.

Holdsworth, Sir William S. *A History of English Law.* 14 vols. London: Methuen & Co., Ltd., 1956.

Hughes, Helen. *The Gentle Hertford.* New York: Macmillan, 1940.

Ilchester, Countess of (ed.). *The Life and Letters of Lady Sarah Lennox.* London: John Murray, 1902.

Jensen, G. E. (ed.). *Covent Garden Journal,* by Henry Fielding. New Haven: Yale University Press, 1915.

Johnson, Samuel. *The Life of Richard Savage.* Menston: Scolar Press, 1971.

Journals of the House of Commons, George II. Vol. 21 (1728).

Kemble, John Phillip. *Kemble's Irish Stage, 1730–1751.* N.p., n.d.

King, Lester. *The Road to Medical Enlightenment.* New York: American Elsevier, 1970.

Kirkman, J. T. *Memoirs of the Life of Charles Macklin, Esq.* London, 1799.

Lang, Paul Henry. *George Frideric Handel.* New York: W. W. Norton, 1966.

Langley, Hubert. *Doctor Arne.* Cambridge: Cambridge University Press, 1938.

Lap Dog, The. London, 1753.

Larsen, Jens Peter. *Handel's "Messiah": Origins.* Copenhagen: E. Munksgaard, 1957.

Laureat, or The Right Side of Colley Cibber, The. London, 1740.

Lecky, William E. H. *A History of England in the Eighteenth Century.* 8 vols. London, 1878–1890.

Lewis, Wilmarth S. (ed.). *Horace Walpole's Correspondence.* 39 vols. New Haven: Yale Edition, 1937–1974.

Lhanover, Lady (ed.). *Autobiography and Correspondence of Mary Granville Delany.* 3 vols. London, 1867.

Life of James Quin. London, 1766.

Little, David, and Kahrl, George (eds.). *The Letters of David Garrick*. 3 vols. Cambridge, Mass.: Harvard University Press, Belknap Press, 1963.

Lodge's Peerage and Baronetage.

London Stage, 1660–1800, The. Edited by William Van Lennep, Emmett L. Avery, Arthur H. Scouten, George W. Stone, Jr., and Charles B. Hogan. 11 vols., 5 pts. Carbondale, Ill.: Southern Illinois University Press, 1968.

Lonsdale, Roger. *Dr. Charles Burney*. Oxford: Clarendon Press, 1965.

Lun Jr., Mr [pseud.; Henry Woodward?]. *The Beggar's Pantomine, or the Contending Columbines*. London, 1736.

McAner, Beverley. "An American in Paris." *Pennsylvania Magazine* (1940), p. 188.

McClintock, Mary Howard. *Portrait of a House*. London: Carroll & Nicholson, Ltd., 1948.

Manning, James A. *Memoirs of Sir Benjamin Rudyerd, Knt.* London, 1841.

Mawhood, William. *Diary*. Catholic Record Society, vol. 50. 1956.

Mr Macklin's Reply to Mr Garrick's Answer, to which is prefixed all the Papers which have publickly appeared in Regard to this important Dispute. London, 1743.

Munk, William. *Rolls of the Royal College of Physicians*. London, 1878.

Musgrave's Obituaries, 1773–1800. 6 vols. London: Harleian Society, 1899–1901.

Namier, Sir Lewis, and Brooke, John. *The History of Parliament*. 3 vols. London: Oxford University Press, 1964.

Newton, Douglas. *Catholic London*. London: Robert Hale, 1950.

Nichols, John. *Biographical and Literary Anecdotes of William Bowyer*. London, 1782.

Notes and Queries. London: Oxford University Press, 1849 to present.

Oldmixon, John. *History of England during the Reign of William and Mary, Queen Anne and George I*. London, 1735.

Oman, Carola. *David Garrick*. London: Hodder & Stoughton, Ltd., 1958.

Pevsner, Nicholas. *The Buildings of England*. Berkshire vol. Harmondsworth: Penguin, 1966.

Phillimore, William. *Berkshire Parish Registers: Marriages*. London, 1908.

Pilkington, John Carteret. *The Real Story*. London, 1760.

Pilkington, Mrs. Laetitia. *Memoirs*. Dublin, 1748.

Plumb, J. H. *England in the Eighteenth Century*. Harmondsworth: Penguin, 1950.

Putnam, Emily James. *The Lady*. New York: Sturgis & Walton, 1910.

Quennell, Peter. *Samuel Johnson, His Friends and Enemies*. New York: American Heritage Press, 1973.

Raleigh, Walter. *Johnson on Shakespeare*. London: H. Froude, 1908.

Rees, Abraham. *Cyclopaedia*. First American Edition, 41 vols. Philadelphia, 1810–1824.

Representations of Cruelties at Marshalsea Prison, 1729. British Museum Print No. 1837.

Series of Letters between Mrs Elizabeth Carter, and Mrs Catherine Talbot, 1741–1770, A. London, 1809.

Shaw, Watkins. *Companion to "Messiah."* London: Novello & Co., 1965.

Sheldon, Esther. *Thomas Sheridan of Smock Alley*. Princeton: Princeton University Press, 1967.

Sheridan, Thomas. *British Education*. London, 1756.

Smith, William C. *Concerning Handel*. London: Cassell & Co., Ltd., 1948.

Steele, Richard. *The Funeral, or Grief a la Mode*. London, 1702.

———. *Tatler*, no. 171.

Stenning, Alan, and Barker, George. *The Record of Old Westminsters: A Biographical List*. 2 vols. London: Chiswick Press, 1928.

Stifler, James N. *My Dear Girl: The Correspondence of Benjamin Franklin with Polly Stevenson, Georgiana and Catherine Shipley*. New York: George Doran Co., 1927.

Stone, G. W., Jr. *The Journal of David Garrick, 1763*. New York: MLA, 1939.

Summerson, John. *Georgian London*. London: Pelican, Penguin Books, Ltd., 1962.

Taylor, John. *Records of My Life*. London, 1832.

Theatric Squabble, The. Folger Library Broadside, 1733.

Truelove, Francis [pseud.]. *The Comforts of Matrimony; exemplified in the memorable Case and Tryal, lately brought by Theo—s C—r, against W— S—, Esq., for criminal Conversation with the plaintiff's wife.* London, 1739.

Tryal of a Cause for Criminal Conversation, between Theophilus Cibber, Gent., Plaintiff, and William Sloper, Esq., Defendant, The. London, 1739.

Vanbrugh, Sir John. *The Provoked Wife.* London, 1765.

Venn, J. A. *Alumni Cantabrigienses.* Cambridge: Cambridge University Press, 1953.

Victor, Benjamin. *A History of the Theatres of London and Dublin.* 3 vols. London, 1761–1771.

———. *Original Letters, Dramatic Pieces and Poems.* 3 vols. London. 1776.

Walpole, Horace. *Letters.* Edited by Mrs. Paget Toynbee. 16 vols. Oxford: Clarendon Press, 1903–1905.

———. *Memoirs of George II.* 3 vols. London, 1847.

Webb, Sidney and Beatrice. *English Local Government,* vol. 4: *Prisons.* London: Longmans, Green & Co., 1922.

White, T[erence] H[ansbury]. *The Age of Scandal.* Harmondsworth: Penguin, 1964.

Wilkinson, Tate. *Annals of the Two Theatres Royal.* London, [ca. 1805].

———. *Memoirs of His Own Life.* Yorkshire, 1790.

———. *Original Anecdotes.* London, [ca. 1805].

Willcox, William B. (ed.). *The Papers of Benjamin Franklin.* Vol. 18 (1771). New Haven: Yale University Press, 1974.

Young, Sidney. *Annals of the Barber-Surgeons.* London, 1890.

MANUSCRIPTS

British Museum, Add. MS 25390 and 25391: *Notitia Dramatica,* Isaac Reed.

British Museum, Add. MS 33488: Diary of Productions at Little Theatre in the Haymarket (1733–1734).

British Museum, Egerton 2320: Diary of Benjamin Griffin (and others) for Lincoln's Inn Fields Theatre (1715–1721), Little Theatre in the Haymarket (1733–1734), and Drury Lane Theatre (1721–1738 and 1742).

British Museum, Egerton 3009: Burney, Charles. A letter to Sir Joseph Banks, 1806.

British Museum, Stowe MS. 752: The Correspondence of Smart Lethieullier and C. Lyttleton, LLD, Dean of Exeter, 1743–1760.

British Historical Manuscripts Commission: Egmont, John Perceval, later 1st Earl of. *Diary.*

Folger Shakespeare Library: *The Hopkins-Cross Journals and Play Lists* (1747–1776).

Folger Shakespeare Library: Winston ms.

Harvard University Library: Folland, Harold F. "Theophilus Cibber, An Essay in Biography." Bowdoin Prize Essay, 1929.

Harvard University Library: Orrery Papers (Letters from Ireland, 1753–1754).

Harvard University Theatre Collection: Cibber, Theophilus. Letter to S. A. C. In notebook called *Autographs, Musical and Dramatic.*

Harvard University Theatre Collection: 39 letters from David Mallet to Aaron Hill, 1731–1750.

Harvard University Theatre Collection: Mathews and Hutton. *Actors and Actresses.* Scrapbooks.

Harvard University Theatre Collection: *Tit for Tat, the first [and second] Season of*

Mr G . . . . . k's Management, by John Powel, deputy treasurer of Drury Lane (1747–1748).

Harvard University Theatre Collection: *Theatrical Duplicity,* Joseph Reed.

Langhans, Edward A., ms: Letter from Archibald Dalziel to his brother, April 7, 1763. From Langhans's notes for the *Dictionary of British Actors.*

New York Public Library, Berg Collection: Charles Burney Notebooks.

New York Public Library at Lincoln Center: Letter of Susannah Cibber, September 25, 1746.

Public Records, Item C. 11, London, January 18, 1741: Susannah Arne Cibber and Anne Arne, her mother, Joint Complainants against Theophilus Cibber.

Somerset House, London: Wills of James Burton, Esquire, 1812; Catherine Hunter Sloper, 1797; William Sloper, Esquire, 1789; Susannah Maria Arne Cibber, 1766.

Victoria and Albert Museum, London: The Forster Collection of Garrick's Correspondence.

Yale University Library, Osborn Collection: Notes of Charles Burney for his *History of Music.*

Illustration Credits

Unless noted below, the illustrations are from The Harvard Theatre Collection.

Frontis-   Courtesy of the National Portrait Gallery, London.
piece,
page 5:

Page 4:   Prints Division, The New York Public Library;
               Astor, Lenox, and Tilden Foundations.

Pages 8, 37:   By permission of the Trustees of the British Mu-
               seum.

Page 15:   By permission of the Houghton Library, Harvard
               University.

Page 72,   The Garrick Club, London.
right:

Page 148:   The Governing Body of Christ Church, Oxford.

Page 205:   By permission of the Library, Victoria & Albert
               Museum.

Page 246:   From the Collection of Mr. and Mrs. Paul Mellon.

Page 281:   From a private collection in Scotland.

Page 310,   By kind permission of the Earl of Durham.
left:

Page 331:   Photograph by Mary Pendleton.

Index